W9-AVQ-547

Praise for Michael Clarkson

"Michael Clarkson's perspectives on fear and the
use of emotions intrigues us."
—*Dr. Benjamin Spock*

"I find Clarkson's research fascinating. There is
a lot of insecurity in achievers, but they overcome their
fears where others do not."
—*Ted Turner*

"Michael Clarkson got to the next millennium before the
rest of us did. His theories on psychology and how to
concentrate under intense pressure are ahead of his time."
—*The Amazing Kreskin*

"Michael Clarkson's work and theories are truly superb."
—*Dr. Edward M. Hallowell, Professor of Psychiatry,
Harvard Medical School, and best-selling author*

"Clearly, Michael Clarkson's work is more realistic while mine is
more idealistic, but I think both perspectives are needed. I admire
his clear-sightedness and guts in telling it like it is."
—*Dr. Mihaly Csikszentmihalyi, Professor of Psychology,
Claremont University, and best-selling author*

Quick
Fixes

for EVERYDAY
FEARS

A Practical Handbook to Overcoming
100 Stomach-Churning Fears

Michael Clarkson

UPPER DARBY
FREE PUBLIC LIBRARY

Marlowe & Company
New York

To my wife, Jennifer Clarkson (nee Vanderklei), who has been anything but a quick fix for me. Her love, dedication and humor, as well as her perseverance through life's pain and her celebration of its pleasures, have provided me and all of our family with inspiration and comfort. And to my granddaughter Skye, with the hope and expectation that her generation will learn to deal more productively with fear.

QUICK FIXES FOR EVERYDAY FEARS
A Practical Handbook to Overcoming 100 Stomach-Churning Fears

Copyright © 2004 Michael Clarkson

Published by
Marlowe & Company
An Imprint of Avalon Publishing Group Incorporated
245 West 17th Street • 11ᵗʰ Floor
New York, NY 10011

All rights reserved. No part of this book may be reproduced in whole or in part without written permission from the publisher, except by reviewers who may quote brief excerpts in connection with a review in a newspaper, magazine, or electronic publication; nor may any part of this book be reproduced, stored in a retrieval system, or transmitted in any form or by any means electronic, mechanical, photocopying, recording, or other, without written permission from the publisher.

Library of Congress Cataloging-in-Publication Data is available.

ISBN 1-56924-429-4

9 8 7 6 5 4 3 2 1

Designed by Jack Steiner
Electronic formatting by Jean Lightfoot Peters

Printed and bound in Canada
Distributed by Publishers Group West

CONTENTS

PART *1: An Introduction to Fear*
    What Fear Is   2
    Where Our Fears Come From   10
    Coping with Fear   15
    How This Book Is Organized   22
    The Awareness Quiz   24

PART *2: General Fears*
    Fear of the Unknown   28
    Fear of Not Having Control   30
    Fear of Change   32
    Fear of Taking Chances   34
    Fear of Responsibility   36
    Fear of Confrontation or Conflict   38
    Fear of Not Being Loved   40
    Fear of Intimacy or Love   42
    Superstition or Fear of the Supernatural   44
    Fear of Religion   46
    Fear of Destiny   48

PART *3: Physical Fears*
    Fear of Flying   52
    Fear of Terrorism   54
    Fear of Being Mugged   56
    Fear of Getting Involved in an Emergency   58
    Fear of Blood (and Blood Injury)   60
    Fear of Death   62
    Fear of Illness or Pain   64
    Fear of Doctors or Dentists   66
    Fear of Aging   68
    Sexual Fears   70
    Fear of Enclosed Spaces   72
    Fear of Heights   74
    Fear of Falling   76
    Fear of Travel   78
    Fear of Driving   80
    Fear of Dogs and Animals   82

764172

Fear of Snakes and Spiders 84
Fear of Water and Swimming 86
Fear of Loud Noises 88
Fear of Weather 90

PART *4: Fears of the Ego*
Fear of Embarrassment 94
Fear of Failure 96
Fear of Making Mistakes 98
Fear of Success or Happiness 100
Fear of Criticism 102
Fear of Rejection 104
Fear of Getting a Compliment 106
Fear of What Others Think 108
Fear of Invasion of Territory or Privacy 110
Fear of Losing Status 112
Fear of Oneself 114
Fear of Showing Emotions 116
Fear of Having a Photo Taken 118
Fear of Choking in Sports 120

PART *5: Fears at Home*
Fear and Stress in Children 124
Fear for Your Children's Safety 126
Fear of Your Children Leaving Home 128
Fear of Becoming a Parent 130
Fears for Your Marriage/Partnership 132
Fear of Family Get-Togethers 134
Fear of a Break-in 136
Fear of Delivering Bad News 138
Fear of Disorder or Untidiness 140
Fear of Solicitors and Telemarketers 142
Worry at Night and Sleeplessness 144
Fear of Being Alone 146
Fear of the Dark 148

PART 6: *Fears in Social Settings*

Fear of People   152
Fear of Panic Attacks in Public   154
Fear of Public Speaking   156
Fear of Crowds   158
Fear of Strangers   160
Fear of Other Races   162
Fear of Singing or Dancing   164
Fear of Dating   166
Fear of the Opposite Sex   168
Fear of Commitment   170
Fear of Ending a Romantic Relationship   172
Fear of Homosexuality   174

PART 7: *Fears at School*

Fear of School   178
Fear of the First Day of School   180
Fear of Appearing Stupid   182
Fear of Exams   184
Fear of Teachers   186
Fear of What Friends Think   188
Fear of Cliques   190
Fear of Your Appearance   192
Fear of Bullies   194
Fear of Not Having or Getting a Job   196

PART 8: *Fears at Work*

Stress at Work   200
Financial Fears   204
Fear of a Job Interview   206
Fear of Downsizing   208
Fear of Retirement   210
Fear of Technology   212
Fear of Asking for a Raise or Promotion   214
Dealing with Deadline Pressure   216
Fear of the Boss   218
Fear of Quitting   220
Fear of Firing an Employee   222
Fear of Harassment   224
Fear of Competition   226

PART 9: *Serious Worries and Ways to Relax*
      Serious Worries   230
      How to Relax   232
      How to Cope with Pressure   234
      How to Deal with Stress   235
      How to Deal with Anger   237
      When Nothing Works   239
      When You Don't Fear Enough   240
      Other Phobias   242

Acknowledgments   243
Index   245

PART 1

An Introduction to Fear

What Fear Is

If you are like me, you have a number of fears and worries. I like to think of myself as relatively well adjusted, and yet I don't like going to the doctor or the dentist—to the point of occasionally avoiding visits. Sometimes I worry about what people think of my work, or even of me as a person. I still worry about my children even though they are now adults. Other times, I can't sleep at night because my mind is filled with images of things that might happen, or of things that didn't work out the way I wanted them to.

As I interview people for my books on fear management and travel as a professional speaker, I'm finding that people of all ages and backgrounds are also feeling fear. In addition to our personal fears, global problems also worry us: conflicts in the Middle East, threats of terrorism and an uncertain economy, and health concerns such as AIDS, SARS and the West Nile virus.

And yet, as I research the fascinating subject of fear, I'm realizing that it's quite all right to be afraid and to worry. Without fear, we would not be motivated to excel at work or in relationships, and we would not watch out for cars as we crossed the street. Without worry, we would not plan effectively to meet challenges at work and at school. Indeed, without fear, we would not feel the satisfaction or the adrenaline buzz of overcoming a challenge. And as nations, we would not rally to meet global problems.

Fear is our survival instinct, our number one primal emotion, even more primal than love, which I consider more of a long-term spiritual resource. Ever since our species appeared on earth, fear has helped us overcome tremendous challenges posed by the environment, by predators and by fire. But, alas, as we have evolved from cave people into more complex thinkers, fear has taken some strange twists and turns. Sadly, it has taken on forms that are often counterproductive. We have developed more fears than we ever had—fear of failure, fear of loss of control, fear of change and, particularly, fear of what others think about us. We view far too many things and situations as threats.

As a relatively new species, we do not deal particularly well with our fears. Under pressure or in emergency situations, most people perform worse than they normally would. Worry is even more of a nuisance—one study at the University of Wisconsin showed that only 8 percent of worries are legitimate; the other worries are a waste of time, energy and resources. As individuals, we allow phobias—exaggerated fears of specific things or situations—to cause ongoing disruptions in our lives. The American Psychiatric Association estimates that 10 to 13 percent of the population suffers from a phobia. The number of people who suffer from specific fears that are not quite phobias is much higher. In too many cases, fears hold people back from going for their dreams or living a fulfilling life. "Fear defeats more people than any other one thing in the world," wrote Ralph Waldo Emerson.

We deal poorly with fear for a number of reasons. For one, we are still hardwired like our cave ancestors, but society protects us too much from fearful situations, preventing us from getting used to our feelings of anxiety and learning how to deal with them. Furthermore, for most of our species' time on the planet, our average life span was 18 years. Little wonder that we're still having trouble getting used to growing into our 50s and 60s and beyond—and the emotional wisdom that this experience can bring.

Sometimes we are not fully aware of what our fears are, or what is causing our anxiety. We just know that something is wrong. In this book, we will try to identify your fears and give you ways you can deal with them. In some cases, we will even suggest ways for you to use them to your advantage. This book is primarily about everyday worries and phobias. Although it is entitled *Quick Fixes for Everyday Fears*, there are no quick fixes for some of the more serious phobias. You might have to see a doctor or therapist for those, or perhaps take medication (see "When Nothing Works" in Part 9).

There are basically three types of fear:

- **Worry**—a medium- to long-term fear, mostly about things that might happen or that have occurred in the past
- **Specific phobia**—fear about certain things or circumstances, such as fear of flying. A specific fear is considered a phobia if it becomes irrational and prevents us from doing things such as getting on a plane
- **Emergency fear**—a sudden threat that sets off our nervous system, such as a mugger or a deadline at work

To deal with these fears, nature has provided us with what I call the *fear defense system*. It is complex, with components that are psychological, emotional and physical. The first stage of fear is psychological—we interpret the world around us and identify what we believe are threats. Let's say we decide that the threat is downsizing at work. Then the second stage kicks in, the emotional response—whether to react with fear, anger, grief or another emotion. Let's say you respond with fear; you are afraid that you will be laid off, and that would spell financial trouble for you and your family. The third and physical stage releases what I call *fear energy*, a rush of powerful hormones, such as adrenaline, dopamine, endorphins and cortisol, which are dispatched from your brain throughout your body to give you added energy, strength and focus to deal with the threat. The fear defense system also gives you an inner emotional drive, a long-range determination to meet the threat.

Your fear defense system has two basic parts: the *emergency fear system* (which some people refer to as the sympathetic nervous system), which deals with sudden emergencies, and the *worry system*, which deals with long-term threats. These two branches of the fear defense system are related psychologically, emotionally and physically, and yet they sometimes call upon different hormones, or fear energy, to do their work—for example, the emergency fear system heavily relies on adrenaline, while the worry system has cortisol as one of its main fuels. Specific fears and phobias tap into the powers of the worry system.

Worry, emergency fear, and specific fears and phobias often interact with one another. Worry over a job interview can set off your emergency fear system, which can make you start to tremble or sweat. And a phobia can trigger symptoms of the two other types of fear.

This book focuses on specific fears and phobias, although worry and emergency fear often come into play. Let's take a closer look at all three fears.

Worry

Worry is perhaps our greatest resource, yet it can also lead to our greatest failures. Worry occurs when we think intensely about things that have happened to us or to those around us, or when we ponder what may transpire in the future. Even without global concerns such as terrorism and the economy, people find lots of things to fret about—an upcoming event in their lives, their job, their family situation or their relationships. Worry can lead to anxiety, tension, stress, nail biting, sleeplessness, illness, poor performance and the scuttling of a person's confidence or dreams. Some people fear thinking too much (phronemophobia). And yet there is a brilliant benefit to worry: "healthy" worriers become motivated, energized and even excited, and they plan efficiently. They are the ones who get the job done. Effective worry manifests itself in terms of planning and taking action against a genuine threat or challenge.

Where does worry come from? Unbelievably, the average person has 66,000 thoughts per day, two-thirds of them negative. The University of Wisconsin research shows that of the things people worry about, 40 percent are about things that never occur, 30 percent are about things from the past, 12 percent are needless concerns about health, 10 percent are petty and miscellaneous cares, and only 8 percent are legitimate concerns. In other words, most worry is wasted, even counterproductive, energy. We are equipped to deal quite effectively with the legitimate 8 percent because the worry system employs an elaborate network of hormones and resources to help us improve our planning and boost our energy to carry out tasks.

Effective worry can increase achievement. In researching the 500 most influential people in history, in science, business, sports, politics and other fields, I found that the majority of them came from a dysfunctional, or at least a challenged, home environment, but they learned to harness their insecurities to meet challenges on their way to the top. Less than 5 percent of the 500 came from what would be considered a well-adjusted, two-parent family. (Of course, most people from dysfunctional homes live unproductive lives, but that is the subject for another book.)

A close relative of worry is anxiety—often described as ambiguous worry, an uneasy free-floating feeling, sometimes accompanied by tension. Anxiety is from a Latin word meaning "worried about the unknown." It can be triggered by an upcoming event, by a buildup of stress or pressure, or by a person's fear of a certain situation. Sometimes it appears as a type of messenger, indicating unresolved conflicts or issues. People may not even know what is causing their anxiousness, but it can affect their ability to act or deal with everyday occurrences. In severe cases, they may feel dizzy, out of breath, sweaty or numb. They may even have heart palpitations or fear they are having a heart attack or going crazy. Anxiety can sometimes be produced by pain, such as what we experience when we have a migraine headache.

Anxiety is a common feeling affecting almost everyone to some degree. Each year, doctors write billions of prescriptions worldwide for anti-anxiety treatments! Psychologists believe there is more anxiety these days because people have not had time to react to the faster pace of society, especially to technological changes. Some people are genetically prone to anxiety; others are anxious because of traumatic events, insecure childhoods or uncertain present circumstances. Anxiety disorders are the leading mental health problem among American women and second only to alcohol and drug abuse among men. About 10 percent of Americans (up to 30 million people) suffer from panic attacks, phobias and other anxiety disorders.

Specific Phobia

A phobia is a worry that is out of control. "Phobia" was originally a Greek word, and thus words connected with it are usually Greek, such as claustrophobia (the fear of being in a tight space). Most psychologists believe there are three types of phobias:

- **Situational phobia** (fear of snakes, airplanes, heights, etc.)
- **Social phobia** (fear of looking inadequate in others' eyes or becoming embarrassed, such as in public speaking)
- **Agoraphobia** (fear of being away from a safe place, usually home, or panicking in public)

A specific fear is considered a phobia if it is out of proportion to the danger, if you become preoccupied with it, or if it interferes with your life. Phobias are often fueled by the imagination and a tendency to expect the worst. If you constantly avoid a situation, such as a medical checkup, because of your fear, then you have a phobia.

But you may have specific fears without them reaching the phobic stage. If you are squeamish about blood and still have blood work done occasionally at the hospital, you have a specific fear. If you always avoid it, you have a full-fledged phobia (hemophobia). If you are afraid of drowning and yet continue to swim, you have a fear of water. If you avoid the water, then you have a phobia (hydrophobia). Either way, you may want to do something to lessen your specific fears and your phobias, and that's where this book comes in. Don't overreact, though; most people with specific fears or phobias are otherwise healthy psychologically.

It's common for people to have phobias in areas in which they have little control, such as flying, or in areas of unpredictability, such as thunderstorms. Many phobias are complex and interrelated. For example, you may think you have a fear of being a passenger in a car because of the potential of physical harm, but looking deeper, you may also fear loss of control (to the driver) or what the driver thinks of you because you are relinquishing that control. Some fears mask deeper fears; for instance, a person who cringes at the thought of retirement may actually be afraid that death lies around the corner.

Where do phobias come from? They may be genetic (phobics tend to have at least one phobic parent), they may have their source in a traumatic experience, or they may have been taught by parents or learned from watching friends or even extreme cases in the media. Fears of specific things, such as animals or crowds, tend to run in families. Phobias are often more intense when a person is depressed.

Neuroscientist Joseph LeDoux believes that only recently in human history has fear taken such pathological forms as phobias, obsessive-compulsive behavior, panic disorders, anxiety, mental illness and post-traumatic stress disorder. All the more reason to study and understand fear better.

Emergency Fear

We all feel the symptoms of emergency fear—up to 40 times a day. It comes in a wide variety of forms, including tension, anxiety, distress and, on the good side, an increase in strength, speed and concentration. Some people feel and even invoke this fear energy more than others; they are considered to be "adrenaline sensitive" because of their chemical hardwiring.

Your emergency fear system activates automatically to help you deal with sudden threats in a variety of circumstances—when you are startled by a stranger who suddenly appears around the corner, for example, or when you are under the pressure of a deadline at work. In a split second, your mind and body go through a whole series of changes to deal with the threat: your heart pumps out more blood, your pain threshold increases, and powerful hormones such as adrenaline and endorphins are released to give you added power and focus. There are various levels of change, depending on the severity of the threat, or what you think of the threat. Some bodily systems can shut down as blood is sent from the fingers and the abdomen to the larger muscles, leaving you trembling, with a sinking feeling in your gut. At its peak, this response is known as *fight or flight*, which sometimes leads to near miracles as people produce feats of strength to overcome life-threatening situations.

The emergency fear system is as old as man and was intended to help us survive against harsh living conditions, predators and warring tribes. Some people have been able to adapt its powers to work, business and school, but these days it is largely outdated and counterproductive because we do not have nearly as many physical challenges as we once had. Although we have evolved into thinking creatures, our outmoded fear system continues to kick in when we perceive a social, academic or professional threat; it even springs into gear when we feel a need to defend our pride or ego. This fear energy often causes tension, distress and illness and can make us freeze under pressure.

It is easy to confuse emergency fear with *pressure* or *stress*. They are connected with fear, but they have separate qualities as well. Our emergency fear system activates when we face pressure, demands or threats. It can either inspire us to meet the threats or make us feel distressed if we feel they are too much to handle. Under pressure, people can perform better or worse than they do without pressure, but most perform worse.

There are two types of pressure: external and internal. External or *physical* pressures are things like your workload, a strict boss or demands to pay the bills or to score high marks in school. *Internal pressures* are self expectations or goals, or expectations that we feel other people have for us. Without a certain amount of pressure or challenge, life would be boring. We meet pressure through our fear reaction, and this reaction can cause good stress (eustress) or bad stress (distress); in other words, extra energy or debilitating tension. We all react differently to pressure. Our reactions depend on our genes, upbringing and experiences.

A Word About Stress

Stress is the outcome of our fear response. It stems from the extra fear energy, the hormones and focusing powers that are sent by our emergency fear system to help us deal with threats. We are hardwired to meet any type of threat with a physical response, just as we were thousands of years ago. When we are able to channel the fear energy productively, we experience what has been termed eustress, but when fear energy becomes too much for us to handle and is counterproductive, we experience distress.

For most people, stress means distress, because that is often the unfortunate outcome of our reaction to things. When people are distressed, they feel overly nervous, anxious, irritable, confused, tired and, often, unmotivated. Distress affects many of the body's systems—nervous, cardiovascular, endocrine and immune. It can even lower resistance to colds. There are two types of stress: *acute stress* is reaction to sudden demands, while *chronic stress* accumulates over time, often from a variety of pressures. Generally, the most stressful events are serious life changes, such as divorce or the death of a loved one.

Fear's Rowdy Cousin: Anger

We don't often think of anger as being related to fear, but it is. When we are fearful of certain things, we often get angry—when our son or daughter is misbehaving, when someone moves into our territory at work, or when we believe a teacher is unfair to us at school. This isn't *fear*, just annoyance, you say? But a deeper look may reveal that we get angry at our children because we are afraid of losing control of them, afraid of the coworker because she may knock us down in the office pecking order, and afraid of the teacher because he might fail us in a subject.

Whenever we want to take action against a threat, we get angry. Anger is fear's roughhouse cousin. It is the built-in enforcer that helps us meet our threats. Take the "d" out of danger and you have anger. It prepares us to fight, or at least to fake a fight, by releasing potent hormones like dopamine and testosterone from our emergency fear system. Like fear, anger can be productive or debilitating. It can force us out of the "freeze" mode to take action or to solve problems, but if it is unfocused, it can send us out of control.

We're all familiar with different types of anger. Anger can take the form of a violent burst of energy toward an attacker, a slow burn toward someone who has wronged us, or frustrated rage at a computer we can't control. It can seem like such a negative emotion that it suddenly makes us feel like a different person. In a sense, we *are* a different person, as our emergency fear system kicks in to make us stronger and more alert. People who always seem angry or on the verge of anger may have a hair-trigger chemistry or come from a competitive or embattled home environment. Angry people are often sick, with high blood pressure and a weakened immune system. If you keep pumping out the hormone cortisol, it can weaken your cardiovascular system. Angry people tend to overreact to things and to smoke, drink and overeat. Anger can wreck their lives by ruining their friendships and slashing their life spans.

A lot of anger is based on pride. People in business and sports who feel threatened often use anger as an achievement tool. Basketball star Michael Jordan would get angry when he felt opponents disrespected him, but he was able to channel this energy into his game. In researching the 50 top athletic performances of all time, I found that fear and anger were factors in most cases. Like humans, most animals get angry to protect their lives or their territory. If we didn't become angry from time to time, there would be no such thing as justice, but out-of-control anger can lead to great injustice.

Where Our Fears Come From

We have established that we have many fears and that some are actually good for us. But where do they come from? How on earth did some of us develop a fear of computers or a fear of saying no to our children? Why are we so frightened of public speaking or what others think of us? This is a complex subject and, although there has been much research, some of the findings remain unscientific, even fuzzy. After researching this subject since 1988 and interviewing many experts and phobics, I believe that our fears have four major roots, some of which can interact with one another. Let's take a look.

Our Primitive Genes

We all have worries and specific fears that were embedded in our ancestors millions of years ago, such as fear of the dark, fear of strangers (potential predators), fear of being alone (and thus losing the protection of others) and fear of death. These instinctual reactions to threats help to keep our species alive. They keep us cautious in the face of unknown circumstances. Without them, we'd always be walking in front of cars, putting our hands on hot stoves, hanging out in dark alleys and jumping into questionable relationships. Some experts call these *prepared fears*. They are visible in some people's fear of snakes and animals, which were threats to early humans' survival. Our predisposed fear of such creatures may be dormant, but it can be awakened by a single encounter. Once the fear is out in the open, it is difficult to suppress in some people, but not impossible.

Family Genetics

Many specific fears—such as fear of blood, fear of going to the dentist, or fear of heights—are passed along for generations through family genes. The genetic strain of some of these fears is stronger in some relatives than it is in others; one brother might fear heights while another happily goes skydiving or roller-coaster riding. (This is the case with my two sons.) Sometimes, specific fears skip a generation, for example, from grandmother to granddaughter.

Conditioning

Some experts call this *behaviorism*. You learned to be afraid of something because you saw (usually in childhood) how other people reacted to it. In other words, fear can be contagious. Or perhaps your parents told you to be fearful of something in order to protect you, although their worries might have been misguided. This phenomenon is a major root of racism: people who show fear or hatred toward other groups teach these feelings to their children and grandchildren. Of course, behavioral conditioning can also be good for us if it teaches us to avoid genuine dangers.

Trauma

People often learn to fear things that have hurt or shaken them in the past. The most striking example is post-traumatic stress disorder, in which soldiers and accident victims become fearful of certain situations linked to past traumas (they may even feel that they are reliving those traumas). A woman who was badly hurt in a car crash might recoil years later in a minor accident, or she might be too scared to drive. Tennis player Monica Seles became less aggressive and efficient after she was stabbed by a fan. Traumatic events may leave more than just psychological wounds: they may even change a person's brain chemistry. We often see the effects of trauma in animals; a pet may become fearful of going to the veterinarian's office after having a serious operation. Trauma is not *always* a bad thing; it can also discourage people from returning to dangerous activities when they are not skilled enough to handle them.

How many of the above four roots of fear contribute to the fears you have? It's difficult to say, since we are all unique and complex beings. It's possible that a combination of the roots is at play. For instance, I have what is classified as a blood (and blood injury) fear that borders on a phobia. If I give blood, I feel faint. I also feel anxious or sweaty when I see a gory movie, even though I know it is all fake. How did I get this way? For starters, my fear probably has a *primitive* base. Some experts believe that nature programmed us to pass out at the sight of a lot of blood so that in our panic we would not cause ourselves physical harm and more loss of blood (in my case, this is an exaggerated fear because I'm not physically threatened by a simple blood test). *Family genetics* may also come into play because several of my relatives also have a fear of medics and blood. In addition, I might have *learned* this behavior of avoiding medics because I saw that some of my relatives avoided them. I believe that a *traumatic event* was also a contributing factor: at age five, after living without my father for a year, we moved from England to Canada, where I developed blood poisoning in both of my legs and had some painful visits to the doctor.

In short, our twenty-first century fears come from a combination of things in our ancestral and our personal past. This combination, in itself, is changing our evolution of fear. In fact, fear is probably more complex now than it has ever been. In primitive times, our fears were more fierce but less numerous and more visible—we feared fire, predators, enemy tribes and a harsh environment. We have overcome many of these threats over time, thanks to our consciousness, cooperation with one another, planning and powers of adaptation.

As our brains evolved and our society became faster paced, our fears changed along with our needs. We are now in a transition stage between animals and a species of the future. We're sophisticated creatures, caught between the age of body and the age of brain, between cave and computer, with needs and fears tied to both. Many of our physical needs are now ensured by our government's safety nets, and yet we have more fears than ever: fear of technology, fear of keeping up with the neighbors, fear of downsizing and fear of saying no to our many responsibilities. This book covers a long list of more than 100 fears, but there could have been many more.

Many new fears stem from our ability to know what is happening around the globe. Our communications technologies alert us to such potential threats as recession, downsizing, weather disasters and crime trends. Some of these threats are legitimate, but many people exaggerate them and worry needlessly, especially if they watch a lot of TV news or tabloid reporting.

Because so many of our modern threats are social and professional in nature, we have adapted our fear defenses to help us "survive" in these areas. In our competitive, status-oriented society, it is vital that we be successful in our workplace or our school. Many of our needs and threats revolve around ego and self-esteem. A survey in the late 1990s revealed that more people were afraid of public speaking (and thus of making fools of themselves) than of death. That's what you call fearing for your ego!

A Word About Defense Mechanisms

These are psychological and/or emotional devices we put up to protect our pride or ego against perceived threats. These defenses and patterns of behavior are often developed unconsciously in childhood, and we are often unaware that we are using them. For example, if a father constantly tells a child she is inadequate, the child may feel threatened and anxious. To protect her psyche, she may develop a strong defense mechanism by always denying that she is inadequate. Once it is developed, this defense mechanism can become an automatic reaction, which can be repeated for the rest of her life in a variety of situations, not just those involving her father. When the child grows up, she may view constructive criticism from her spouse as a threat and react to it by putting up walls of denial. This mechanism can cause people to see too many things as threats, thus preventing them from growing and from learning the truth about themselves and the world.

Defense mechanisms can nevertheless be productive. They are evoked all the time by successful business people and athletes, whose mindsets are challenged and threatened as youngsters. My research shows that most of the people at the top of every profession come from unusually challenged backgrounds. They often develop a defensive mode of "I'll show you," and they use it in productive ways as they go through life.

Everyone Reacts Differently

We all react differently to pressure and to fearful situations, depending on our genes, our upbringing, our age, our experiences and even on our mood on a particular day or in a particular situation. Some people freeze while giving a speech while others are the life of the party.

"Our fear systems are all unique and they react depending on our nervous hardwiring, our self-esteem, our upbringing and our view of the world," says Karen Matthews, a professor of psychology at the University of Pittsburgh. "Some people are more sensitive than others and are so-called hot reactors, responding up to 30 times a day (to situations)."

Our hardwiring is crucial to the way we respond to situations. Some people are more highly strung or sensitive to dopamine and other aggressive hormones, while others have less access to endorphins and therefore tend to be less humorous. We are all born with a so-called worry gene; in some people it is shorter than it is with others and pumps out less of the soothing hormone serotonin. Furthermore, some people are born with a livelier left side of the brain, predisposing them to be generally more energetic and optimistic.

Environmental factors are also important. If you had a loving but not overprotective childhood, you may have a less fearful outlook on life. If you constantly get rejected, you may become fearful of criticism and taking chances, which may in turn result in low self-esteem, a common trait in anxious people. If you experienced a major trauma, you will likely be afraid of things associated with the trauma.

Gender sometimes makes a difference in peoples' reactions to threats. Through a combination of factors, men tend to be less fearful of physical situations and women tend to deal with social challenges better, although this is not always the case, especially in these times of changing gender roles. Age can also be a factor: as people accumulate more experiences that make them feel threatened, they may become more cautious. Adults often get more nervous during exams than children, but experiences in business and sports can give them confidence in such pressure situations.

Coping with Fear

Don't let the word "fear" scare you. There is good news because this book is more about solutions than problems. We can adapt to our fears, and we can even train some of them to work for us. In fact, we already have. Long ago, we overcame a fear that almost all other species have not been able to cope with—the fear of fire—and now we harness fire to our advantage by using it to heat our homes and fuel our rockets.

We can adapt to our new fears in similarly constructive ways. As a society, we are better aware of fears and phobias than we used to be, which puts us in a good position to deal with them effectively. We will probably never conquer all of our fears and worries. If we did, we would not survive as a species. The purpose of this book is to help you identify what fears you should act upon, which ones you should cope with and which ones you can use to your advantage.

We all cope with fear in different ways, depending on our personality, the type of fear and the circumstances. A remedy for one person may be poison for another. We can often deal with fear by simply relaxing, breathing deeply and putting things in perspective. That prevents our emergency fear system from kicking in beyond levels we can control, and it keeps our adrenaline output within reasonable bounds.

However, the world's most successful people often like to remain hyper and to use fear and its byproduct *eustress* as a performance tool—especially emergency fear. They learn not only to cope with their fears, but sometimes they redirect them over both the short and long term. For instance, basketball great Michael Jordan admitted at the peak of his career that he was afraid of looking inferior, so he sometimes got himself worked up and focused his hormonal energy and launched himself into "the zone."

There are even times when *distress* can be used productively. When we feel stressed out by situations at work or at home, we can focus this adrenaline and cortisol into whatever it is we are doing, or we can use it for the social good by volunteering for community organizations, churches or hospitals. (Of course, most people allow their emergency fear system to act as a sort of friendly fire to turn against them, but we can learn how to perform better under pressure through use of focusing techniques.)

In my own life, I have been able to get many of my fears and some specific fears and phobias under control through greater awareness and visualization, and by gradually facing my fears and gaining experience in pressure situations. For most of my life, I've been afraid of the water, but at age 49 I finally taught myself to swim. I've also learned to use some of my fears to my advantage. For example, when I was in my early 20s, I was so shy about my freelance writing that I was too scared to go into the office to pick up my weekly paycheck. But now I worry so much less about social embarrassment that I've become a professional speaker. I have been in "the zone" approximately 40 times in my journalism and amateur athletic careers. Much of my success has come from education—in researching fear since 1988, I have learned the techniques of psychologists, psychiatrists and average people who have learned to cope with their worries. In this book, I am passing them on to you.

As we continue to research, there is hope—even excitement—that the new facets of fear that we are discovering will help us deal with this powerful emotion more effectively. Let's take a look at ways of coping with worry, with specific fears and phobias, and with emergency fear.

Coping with Worry

Strategies:

- Identify if you are in a state of worry. Are your muscles tense? Is your mind racing? Are your teeth clenched? Are you feeling depressed?
- Schedule a time each day to do your worrying (no more than 20 minutes). Write down all that you are worrying about and what type of "threat" caused it. Identify the worries that really affect you and the ones you have some control over. Take action on those.
- Balance your worry. People who *always* worry never get anything done. People who *never* worry never get anything done. The trick is to worry about things we can have some influence over.
- If you determine that your worry is unhealthy and unproductive, try to defuse it by changing your thinking pattern. Or use deep breathing, meditation, music or humor.
- If worry is justified, redirect it into planning or action to meet the challenge. Don't let worry be an excuse for inaction, as it often is.
- Practice the serenity prayer: Grant me the serenity to accept the things I cannot change, the courage to change the things I can and the wisdom to know the difference.
- Focus on the solution, not the problem.
- If worries persist, make them 3-D by writing them down, putting them on a tape recorder and playing them back to yourself or sharing them with other people. This gives you a better perspective on worry and underscores that we all worry and we are all in this life together.
- Think and talk positively. Optimists are less likely than the

average person to have an accident or become ill. Avoid negative people; they can create a pity party.
- Bring balance and harmony to your life physically, professionally, socially and spiritually to reduce pressure and stress.

References:

What You Can Change and What You Can't by Martin E. Seligman, Pocket Books, 1993

Worry by Edward M. Hallowell, Ballantine, 1997

Dealing with Specific Fears and Phobias

There are no treatments that offer a 100 percent cure for specific fears and phobias, but some produce encouraging results. At the least, we can make our fears more rational and manageable. The following are some ways that specific fears and phobias are treated (you will see many references to them throughout this book). Some of these methods can be used without professional assistance, perhaps with help from family or friends. Others may be more effective with the guidance of a therapist or a support group.

Strategies:
- Become more aware of your fears. Identify whether you are afraid of something if it is affecting your life, and then be willing to admit it to yourself so you can do something about it.
- Face your fears. By exposing ourselves to what we fear, we tend to become less afraid of it. Usually this is done over a period of time, such as gradually getting used to fear of heights by slowly stepping to the edge of a balcony. Therapists call this behavior therapy.
- Use visualization techniques. Many people can simulate and desensitize their fear by imagining themselves going through a fearful situation step by step. If they are afraid of going to the dentist, they picture driving to the dentist's office, sitting in the waiting room and going through a dental procedure to a successful conclusion. There are even some virtual reality programs available in which sufferers are hooked up to a sophisticated computer experience for a realistic type of imagery.

- Make yourself less vulnerable by developing your resources. If you find you are shy, develop your people skills to boost your confidence. If you are self-conscious or arrogant, develop your spirituality through meditation, religion or volunteering.
- Get professional help. The most effective way to treat a phobia is to seek the help of a doctor, counselor or psychologist. Therapists may use one or more of the methods discussed in this section, or they may use group therapy or drugs such as the antidepressant Paxil, which helps to manage social phobias.
- Consider cognitive therapy and reprogramming. If your fears have developed from low self-esteem, you may have to assess your attitudes, needs and beliefs—and you may have to change them.

Unfortunately, less than 10 percent of people with phobias ever seek help for their problem; instead, they look the other way and hobble through their lives in denial, while avoiding the thing they are afraid of. Often, they are worried about their overreaction to their fears and are afraid that facing up to them will bring shame, feelings of inadequacy and other negative social consequences.

Thankfully, you do not have to be one of these people. As we proceed in this book to the various fears, you can use one or more of the above strategies to help you confront your fears.

References:

The Anxiety and Phobia Workbook by Edmund J. Bourne, New Harbinger, 1995

Facing Fears by Ada P. Kahn and Ronald M. Doctor, Checkmark, 2000

Phobias: Fighting the Fear by Helen Saul, HarperCollins, 2001.

The Phobia List, www.phobialist.com

Phobias Cured
4838 Delridge Way SW, Suite A
Seattle, WA 98106
(206) 721-8751
keith@phobiascured.com

Coping with Your Emergency Fear System

Strategies:

- Be aware that your emergency fear system has kicked in. With some people, it is subconscious and they are so intent on what they are doing, such as working on a job, that they don't notice they are tense or hyped up. You must also identify what caused your system to kick in: was it because of the natural pressures of a job or were you just defending your pride? Don't send your hormones on unnecessary journeys.
- You have two choices of how to deal with this fear energy: defuse it or lose it. You can calm down or you can redirect the energy into whatever you are doing at work, home or school.
- In most instances, you will simply need to defuse the fear energy and calm down. You can use traditional methods like slow, deep breathing, which adds oxygen and the soothing hormone serotonin to your system and also takes your mind off what was making you tense for a few moments, allowing you to get back into a rhythm. Humor, music and thoughts of loved ones can also relax you.
- Exercise. When you get too aroused, your body is asking for a physical response, so why not give it one through productive exercise, which also helps you become more healthy? If you don't have time for sports, 50 jumping jacks can do the trick. Also, rocking in a chair can alleviate stress buildup.
- Another way to calm down is to change your environment for a few minutes. At work, go outside and take a walk, or simply sit back in your chair and envision being on a beach somewhere. Your emotional chemistry can change by thought alone.
- There are situations in which you can *use* the extra energy and powers of fear, such as in physical jobs, sports and deadline work. Channel the fear energy directly into what you are doing, but trust your skills under this new pressure and don't allow the energy to distract you. Think of this technique as a two-stage process in which you go from fear to a dispassionate response.
- If you have problems channeling fear energy directly into your task, you may need a bridge between the fear and the dispassionate response, perhaps another emotion, such as anger, joy

or excitement. If the fear is making you too tense or hyper, think briefly of something that makes you angry or excited, then plug yourself into the dispassionate task. This changes your hormonal chemistry from too much adrenaline into more aggressive hormones such as dopamine and noradrenaline—and then your energy is mobilized and you can channel it into your work. But you must practice this formula until it becomes a type of flow from *fear* to *passion* to *dispassion*.

- The best way to keep your fear energy at a manageable level is to keep your pressures at manageable levels before you enter a situation. You do this by upgrading your skills, staying in good health and maintaining a positive frame of mind.
- If you are feeling too much distress, consider the possibility that pressures upon you may be too great at work or at home, or that you may be allowing your emergency fear system to be activated too often. You may be seeing too many things as threats. If so, try to put things into proper perspective.

Reference:

Intelligent Fear by Michael Clarkson, Key Porter, 2002

How This Book Is Organized

The following pages discuss more than 100 of the most common fears and phobias. Be aware that just because you have the symptoms does not necessarily mean that you have a full-blown phobia. You might just have a specific fear, which is not as serious. However, without treatment, it could develop into a phobia.

Here's how each section is organized, with fear of terrorism as an example.

fear of terrorism

Xenophobia (*fear of foreigners*) In this spot, each fear is given its phobic name, if it has one. If it does not, a phobic name closest to the one we are describing is used. For example, there is no phobic name for fear of terrorism, so the fear of foreigners (*xenophobia*) is used.

Quote: Each fear has a quote near the top. It could be a general quote about the fear or how to deal with it. "*People should be concerned, but I don't think that should keep you from seeing the world. You have to go on with life.*"—Barbara Ruth of Texas, visiting New York in 2003 during a heightened terrorism alert

Characteristics: This section examines the symptoms or feelings a person experiences in relation to a specific fear. For the fear of terrorism, here is a sample:

> In these times of terrorism alerts, many people report a general feeling of anxiety and lack of control; others feel angry about an unseen enemy and what that enemy might do. Some describe a feeling of insecurity and a loss of trust in others.

Background: This section examines why you feel afraid of a situation, and perhaps where the fear comes from. A sample from the fear of terrorism:

> Although North Americans had not experienced a strong fear of terrorism until September 11, 2001, and the subsequent war in Iraq, fear of an unknown attacker is a deep, primitive fear, closely tied to the fear of the unknown and fear of other races.

Strategies: This section contains strategies for coping with the fear. Examples:

- Don't become preoccupied with a threat that may never come. Remain active and keep up your normal routine. You should not allow fear of terrorism to wreck your way of life.
- Discussing your thoughts and feelings about terrorism from time to time is helpful, as long as you don't engage in inflammatory discussions that lead to more tension or to hatred.
- Keep up with news developments, but don't watch so much television news that the terrorism threat grows in your mind and becomes a constant preoccupation. Some people believe that becoming newshounds reduces their uncertainty about the world, but it usually creates more anxiety.

A mantra to tell yourself: "Life goes on." A mantra is a word or phrase that you can repeat to calm yourself or to gain confidence in a fearful situation. I have made a suggestion of a mantra for each fear, but you may want to come up with your own.

Quotable: In some chapters, there will be an additional quote on the subject.

References: The information about each fear is taken from a number of sources, such as author interviews with experts in the field, books, magazines and websites. One or two of them will be mentioned.
Why Terrorism Works by Alan M. Dershowitz, Yale University Press, 2002

See: fear of flying, fear of travel, fear of the unknown, fear of not having control, fear of death, fear for your children's safety, fear of other races, fear of strangers, fear of crowds

This is a section for cross-referencing the fear. If you have a fear of terrorism, it could be related to a fear of flying or a fear of other races of people.

Other boxes: There may be small boxes with various titles, such as "the facts are with you" (statistics showing that your chances of getting hurt in an airplane are extremely slim) and "author's two cents" (personal anecdotes).

The Awareness Quiz

Becoming aware of your fears is a big part of dealing with them. How many fears do you have? Do you really know? Have you really thought them through? It's human nature to feel uncomfortable about your fears. Many people don't even like thinking about them, and that is partly why these fears are never dealt with properly.

Take a moment to make a list of the things that make you feel uncomfortable, even fearful. With each thing, mark whether it makes you a little uncomfortable or afraid to the point of avoiding situations. Then decide if you need to do something about these fears (for example, if you have a fear of snakes and live in the city, it might not be a pressing concern). In addition, ask yourself if you are dealing with your fears as you mature and gain experience, or if you are getting more fearful about some things. If you aren't too afraid of what others think (or even if you are!), pass your answers around and encourage feedback. Indeed, encourage others to answer questions about their own fears. You might find that we all have worries and are looking for reassurance.

I've prepared the following quiz to help you assess your fears, worries and phobias. Don't fret; there's no rating system that would classify you as anywhere from emotionally healthy to nervous to certifiable. Simply examine your answers and put them into perspective. Are your fears affecting your life? In some instances, are you actually using your fears to your advantage?

In the space provided below, list some of the fears discussed in this book that affect you. Decide whether you are somewhat afraid of them or very afraid of them, if you are less afraid of them or more afraid of them than you used to be, and if you think you need to do something about these fears. You may want to comment on why you are afraid and what you could do about it, if anything. As an example, I'm including one of my own fears:

Situation: fear of strangers
Somewhat nervous: yes
Afraid to the point of avoidance: no
Less or more fearful than before: less fearful
Comments: As I've grown older, especially with my journalism experience of interviewing strangers, I've lost much of my fear.

Situation:

_____dork, image things_____

Somewhat nervous:

_____extremely_____

Afraid to the point of avoidance:

_____yes_____

Less or more fearful than before:

_____about same_____

Comments:

_____usually late at night, image she's shut_____

_____coming out and [attacking] me_____

_____

Situation:

_____

Somewhat nervous:

_____

Afraid to the point of avoidance:

_____

Less or more fearful than before:

_____

Comments:

_____

_____

_____

2

General
Fears

Fear of the Unknown

| xenophobia (fear of foreigners) | *The future is called "perhaps" and the important thing is not to allow that to scare you.* —TENNESSEE WILLIAMS |

Characteristics: Fear of the unknown can produce anxiety or insecurity in people, or cause them to avoid upcoming events or new relationships, jobs or projects. It can make people freeze, keeping them in old jobs they dislike or relationships that are unhealthy. And it can make them overreact to unfamiliar threats such as bioterrorism and the West Nile virus. On the other hand, fear of the unknown can keep people alert and inspire them to prepare for challenges, and to be careful when they are in unfamiliar surroundings.

Background: This is one of our most basic instincts, a first cousin to the fear of not being in control. It is a fear of the future. It was very useful in primitive times because people had less knowledge of what threats lay in other regions and so they had to be cautious and plan carefully for excursions. Fear of the unknown remains part of our basic genetic makeup. Today, of course, we are much more in tune with our world and what's to be expected. Our evolving brain is constantly analyzing, trying to predict the future and solve any problems it may bring. There are not as many things waiting in the dark, although many people remain puzzled, even fearful, of where we came from in this vast universe and what our place is in it. The need to understand such things is hardwired into us.

On a daily basis, fear of the unknown remains stressful and debilitating for many people, especially those who need to control things and have assurance about the outcome of their jobs and relationships. On the positive side, it can motivate them to prepare for legitimate challenges and add some spice and mystery to life.

Strategies:

- It sounds simple, but taking the time to research can eliminate many things you don't know about a project, an event, a health concern publicized in the media or a relationship. When you are prepared, doubt retreats and confidence grows. In short, expect the best, prepare for the worst.

- During a stressful job with many unknowns, you should prepare ahead of time, but once the job begins, try to stay in the present and focus on the process of what you are doing.
- Remember, if everything was known, we wouldn't continue probing. We might become so self-satisfied that we'd fizzle away as a species. If explorers and scientists had not surmounted their fear of the unknown, we'd still be all cooped up on one or two continents and terrified of fire.
- Many unknown fears and worries turn out to be exaggerated, such as the AIDS "epidemic" in North America. Think back to something you fretted over that never came to pass, or brought you much less discomfort than you anticipated—a trip to the dentist or a confrontation with a relative, for example.
- "Expect the unexpected" is a healthy mindset as long as you don't spend all day expecting to be successful 100 percent of the time and in control of every detail.
- Accept that there will be things in the future that you may feel deeply concerned and even helpless about. But remember that if there are no unknowns in your life, you likely aren't taking any chances. For example, you may be afraid to ask someone you've met on a date because of the "unknown" risk that they might reject you.
- If you fear the future too much, you may not be living enough in the present. If you constantly think about eternity, you will miss one of the precious moments that make up eternity—and that moment is now.

A MANTRA TO TELL YOURSELF: *"Give it what it's worth."*

Reference:
Embracing Fear by Thom Rutledge, Harper San Francisco, 2002. He writes: "When we fear the unknown, two kinds of reassurance are available—when we reach out to someone we trust to have confidence in us . . . and the acceptance that there are no guarantees in new, unexplored territory."

See: This fear underlies many fears and phobias in this book, including the fear of not having control, fear of change and fear of taking chances.

Fear of Not Having Control

asthenophobia (fear of weakness)

Whenever I fear lack of control, I force myself to go into those situations—getting into a plane or driving in heavy traffic. It empowers me to know that I have hired these vehicles to get me from one place to another. —PSYCHOLOGY STUDENT LISA LINDEMAN

Characteristics: This is a worry that things and circumstances will be out of a person's sphere of influence. It causes some people to get involved in everything, trying like a movie director or drill sergeant to control people and the outcome of events. It causes others to get frustrated and give up control. People who feel powerless at work often become inefficient and distressed.

Background: It's quite normal to seek control over one's destinies, large and small, but some people try to control everything—often in good faith—and they succeed as long as others allow it. Seeking ultimate control may be rooted in self-centeredness, but it can also show that a person cares enough to make an effort. In other cases, people who believe they have no influence may blame the outcome of events on fate.

This fear manifests itself in a wide variety of areas—from people being afraid of flying or being a passenger in a car to parents' confrontation with relatives or teachers over their children. Often it stems from a lack of sufficient trust in others. People who seek too much control may come from an overprotected or underprotected environment. A parent may try to do too much for a child, and that is also an attempt to control everything.

Strategies:

- Step back and evaluate the amount of control you should have in relation to your abilities, the task and other people. For example, a teenager could seek primary control of the family dog if he has time to walk it and if others don't want that chore. But that should not give the teen the right to keep the dog in his room all the time.
- Some things are completely out of your control—tomorrow's weather, the way your father-in-law thinks and the way your

favorite professional sports team performs. Learn to accept these things. Having an overload of control and responsibility can make you anxious and give you an unrealistic perspective on things.

- The above having been said, you probably have more control over many things in your life than you believe, starting with your own health, which you can improve by eating, exercising and sleeping properly. If you feel powerless at work, perhaps you haven't tested your authority or are not willing to put in the effort or take the necessary risks. Perhaps you are afraid of being laughed at or being seen as incompetent. Take a position of power or leadership, perhaps in a group or committee. Use positive self-talk: "I have power. I have influence and I am going to exert it in a reasonable manner." If you rarely seek control in your life, perhaps you are afraid of responsibility.

- Learn to take satisfaction from cooperation and teamwork. Sharing and delegating and empowering others can be productive and can make you less anxious and less selfish.

- Let go once in a while. Showing responsibility and leadership is great, but once in a while, sit back, take a deep breath and remember that life will march on, even if you don't make all the decisions. Hard to imagine, isn't it?

  A MANTRA TO TELL YOURSELF: *"Grant me the serenity to accept the things I cannot change, the courage to change the things I can and the wisdom to know the difference."*

Reference:

Stop Obsessing! How to Overcome Your Obsessions and Compulsions by Edna B. Foa and Reid Wilson, Bantam, 2001

See: Many or most of the specific fears and phobias in this book are related to the fear of not having control, including fear of the unknown, fear of change, fear of taking chances, fear of flying, fear of responsibility, fear of embarrassment and fear of panic attacks in public.

Fear of Change

tropophobia (fear of moving or making changes)	*Perhaps it is change without our consent that makes us cling to jobs we don't like, relationships that have grown stale or habits that don't make us happy, but are at least familiar.* — MANAGEMENT AUTHOR AND EDUCATOR JANE GREENE
asthenophobia (fear of weakness)	

Characteristics: This is the fear of trying new things or creating new habits. Because change often brings unrest, people may live in the same region all their lives or stay in the same job, surrounding themselves with safe or sentimental things, or they may refuse to consider new ways of thinking or behaving. Children may feel lonely or resentful after being forced to leave friends or group activities.

Background: If you don't think that humans have always been creatures of habit, check the anecdotes and observations in old books, including the Bible and other religious texts. The speed of social change has greatly accelerated, yet progress was relatively slow prior to that. As a group, we tend to latch onto familiar things in culture, religion and society like a security blanket. Throughout history, the majority of people have been cautious; it's the leaders and risk takers who drag us onto new ground.

In these often unsettling times, we have perhaps more need for familar things, structure and security than ever before, and change can be seen as a threat to those facets of our lives. Adults who fear taking chances may come from sheltered homes or may have been discouraged from branching out on their own or making their own decisions. Those who fear change tend to have repetitive patterns in their lives.

Strategies:
- Try to establish what your fear of change represents. It could really be fear of the unknown, fear of failure, fear of taking chances or fear of what others think. If you are afraid of taking risks in your career, it could actually be the uncertainty of the work environment that scares you, or fear of responsibility (more work and leadership), or fear of being judged or not measuring up.

- If it ain't broke, don't fix it. If you are truly satisfied with your life, your job and your family, don't look for ways to disrupt them. But spend some time examining this issue. Structure can be a good thing at work or in a task, but once in a while you might need variety to keep from getting bored.
- In today's world of uncertain jobs and an influx of new cultures, it's vital that we be flexible and ready to change our thinking patterns, and even our beliefs, if we are to succeed. And it *is* possible to change ourselves, even in midlife.
- Look upon a needed change as shedding a skin and coming out of it with new vitality and ideas. As author Lucinda Bassett says, "How many times have you heard someone say, 'Well, that's just the way I am... it's the mold you're fixed in.' There are many exciting things to try—new foods, dances, clothes, new countries to explore, friends to meet. You can be reborn at any time."
- Perhaps you should fear *never changing* because that could make you rigid, narrow-minded and dull.
- To change a bad habit, take small steps; research shows that people who try to lose weight or quit smoking too quickly often get discouraged when success doesn't happen overnight.
- Make sure that when you go through a change, you seek out opportunities to grow. In most people's lives, some type of change is inevitable, but growth is optional. You grow when you adapt to change and learn from the old ways.
- Keep doing what you're doing and you'll keep getting what you're getting. If you are okay with that, then there is not as much need for change.

A MANTRA TO TELL YOURSELF: *"What if I don't change?"*

Reference:

From Panic to Power by Lucinda Bassett, Quill, 2001

See: fear of the unknown, fear of not having control, fear of taking chances, fear of aging, fear of travel, fear of losing status, fear of your children leaving home, fear of becoming a parent, fear and stress in children, fear of disorder or untidiness, fear of ending a romantic relationship, fear of school, fear of downsizing, fear of retirement, fear of technology, fear of quitting

Fear of Taking Chances

ideophobia (fear of ideas)	*Ships in a harbor are safe, but that's not what ships are built for.* —WRITER JOHN SHEDD

Characteristics: This has similar symptoms to the fear of change—having a safe, conservative attitude and perhaps a reluctance to make decisions or try new things. It can hold people back in business, personal finances and relationships, and affect things like choosing a partner, a school or a profession.

Background: Although the human race has shown signs of creativity and risk taking, in many ways we are a conservative lot; change has come slowly over the course of thousands of years. "Taking a new step, uttering a new word, is what people fear most," said Dostoyevsky. It is natural for people to want to stay in a secure comfort zone, but without risk taking, there is little chance for growth.

If you are afraid of taking chances, you might be from a sheltered family or you may have had a controlling parent. But, of course, sometimes it's actually dangerous to take chances; if you agree to a business gamble with your family's security on the line, or if you risk large sums on the stock market or on horses, you may be acting foolishly.

Strategies:

- Before you take a chance, assess the risk of a situation. If you jump into every opportunity that comes along, you might become a reckless driver, an unfaithful spouse or an irresponsible employee.
- As in the fear of change and many other generalized fears, try to establish what exactly scares you about taking a chance. Is it fear of the unknown, fear of failure, fear of criticism or fear of what others think?
- Once in a while, try something fresh—a different strategy for a project, a meal you've never tried or even an alternative way to get to work or to school. If you have to, make a note on your calendar that you will try something new. Without risk, there

would be no inventions and no new friends. McDonald's Corp. founder Ray Kroc once said, "When there is no risk, there can be no pride in achievement and consequently no happiness."

- Don't believe that fate is entirely out of your control. Believe in opportunity and learn to recognize when it comes along. Many people can't or won't recognize opportunities, or they may complain of being powerless or not having enough luck or talent to venture into a new area. Don't keep saying that things *happen* to you. Consider *making* things happen.
- At work, be ready to take reasonable initiative. My wife, Jennifer, was advised not to take phone calls in her first six weeks as an account executive at the National Speakers Bureau, but when her boss stepped out of the office, she took the chance at a call and the risk led to the biggest sale by an account "rookie." This sparked Jennifer's confidence en route to a record first month of sales.
- If you lack confidence, especially in a new area, find a mentor who has expertise and confidence in that area. Pick that person's brain. It will flatter them and bolster you.
- Learn to become more resilient if your risk taking happens to fail once in a while. You'll feel more comfortable taking chances if you bounce back from the misses and you'll gain courage for the next "opportunity."
- Join the small percentage of people in the world who make the real changes because they're not afraid to go out on a limb or be vulnerable. Don't have inscribed on your epitaph: "Could have. Would have. Should have."

A MANTRA TO TELL YOURSELF: *"It's time for a little adventure."*

Reference:

Facing Fears by Ada P. Kahn and Ronald M. Doctor, Checkmark, 2000

See: fear of the unknown, fear of not having control, fear of failure, fear of criticism, fear of what others think, fear of change, sexual fears, fear of becoming a parent, fear of dating, fear of quitting

Fear of Responsibility

hypegiaphobia (fear of responsibility)

As our culture increasingly glorifies the carefree pleasures of youth, many people grow despondent when the reality of adult responsibility pulls them farther away from their youthful hopes and expectations. —FRANK PITTMAN, AUTHOR OF *GROW UP! HOW TAKING RESPONSIBILITY CAN MAKE YOU A HAPPY ADULT*

Characteristics: This is anxiousness or reluctance to assume responsibility or leadership in family life, work, school or relationships. It is often seen in young people as they are growing up. It can even prevent people from having children.

Background: There is an old saying that there are many more sheep than shepherds. Some people are afraid of the increased workload, commitment and complexities that responsibility brings. For many, it is natural to want to hold onto their carefree youth, but many people carry that attitude into midlife.

Many people never identify what it is about responsibility that frightens them. Sometimes, this fear is genetic, but often it has to do with the environment a person comes from, or an environment the person is presently living or working in.

Strategies:

- Assess how much responsibility you have in your life. How often do you make decisions? Do people look to you for leadership or just for a good time? Do you want more responsibility but are afraid of it or feel you can't handle it?
- Try to identify the aspect of responsibility that makes you uneasy—is it really fear of dealing with others and their issues, fear of added workload, or fear of criticism because of a decision you will make?
- Look around—other people have responsibility and, if they do not allow it to overburden them, they may enjoy it. Talk to them about it and try to apply their strategies to your situation.

- Learn to realize the satisfaction and growth that comes from something other than yourself and your own needs. "Responsibility is the thing people dread most of all," says author Frank Crane. "Yet it is the only thing in the world that develops us, gives us manhood or womanhood fiber."
- With responsibility, setting goals, and making decisions for yourself and others comes an adrenaline rush! You feel part of a team, and you feel a sense of accomplishment when you have input, whether it is for a work project, a Boy Scout troop or a Neighborhood Watch program.
- With a leadership role, you'll meet more people, find new opportunities and gather confidence. But you may want to take small steps at first; don't suddenly run for president. As you go along, explore responsibility but keep your workload in perspective.
- Develop people skills. Everybody has them, but perhaps they are dormant or unrealized. Maybe you even have leadership qualities. The world needs more good leaders. But, of course, not everyone is a leader. Perhaps you are an individual who works better alone.
- If you are a teenager, growing up isn't as bad as it seems. Life really isn't over at 20 or 30. You can still act like a kid during play.

A MANTRA TO TELL YOURSELF: *"Get in the game."*

QUOTABLE: *"A chief is a man who assumes responsibility. He does not say, 'My men were beaten.' He says, 'I was beaten.'"* —Antoine de Saint-Exupéry

Reference:

Free Yourself from Fear by Valerie Austin, Thorsons, 1998

See: fear of the unknown, fear of failure, fear of criticism, fear of taking chances, fear of the opposite sex, fear of commitment, fear of becoming a parent

Fear of Confrontation or Conflict

testophobia (fear of being tested)

You can stand up for yourself, expressing the way you truly feel. You are considerate of other people's feelings. You do not attack or blame, nor do you become meek and withdrawn.
—CLINICAL PSYCHOLOGIST ALLEN ELKIN

Characteristics: People are often reluctant to confront someone or to bring a situation to a head. Some people will either avoid a problem or intervene without careful preparation, just to get it over with. Most people get nervous prior to conflict, but some freeze and cannot express themselves properly.

Background: Most of us deal poorly with confrontation and conflict because we don't allow ourselves to experience them fully. We are uncomfortable with the emotions and issues, and so we remove ourselves as fast as possible without resolving the situations or expanding our abilities to deal with them. Confrontation and conflict resolution are usually distressing, especially when they involve serious issues. Emotions can rise and there may be the threat of becoming physical. At work, some conflicts will resolve themselves and produce healthy competition or change. Others hurt cooperation.

Many people avoid conflict for fear of losing friends, others because they are very sensitive to emotional situations. Women are generally less likely to confront than men. People from large families tend to learn about confrontation early in life. Resolving things productively can be liberating, can build confidence and can also prevent problems from festering. How you handle adversity at work can have more impact on your career than how you handle the good times. Those who overcome conflict and adversity rise to the top of their organization.

Strategies:
- In approaching conflict, you must be brave but also clear-minded and cautious. Be certain that the issue you want to confront someone about is legitimate. Write it down and look at it the next day to see if it holds up.

- Prepare yourself with the facts before you confront or try to resolve a conflict. This will give structure and power to your meeting. In addition, prepare yourself emotionally by imagining in advance what might happen. In your mind, take yourself through all of the steps. You should even imagine a negative response, and see yourself reacting well. Try to imagine the emotions that may arise. This is called visualization or imagery.
- Try to confront the person face-to-face; the phone or a letter or e-mail should be secondary options because these have less impact.
- If you are squeamish, force yourself to show up. You'll find that once you are face-to-face with the person, the words will come. If they don't, take deep breaths. Remain calm, but be mentally tough and stand up for yourself.
- When confrontational or emotional issues come up at work, talk them through and allow each person time to express thoughts and feelings. Have a group session to air grievances.
- Remember that confrontation can be healthy. Although constant arguing can be harmful to a marriage, research shows that couples who never argue are 35 percent more likely to divorce, in part because they won't deal with their frustrations and therefore let them build up.

A MANTRA TO TELL YOURSELF: *"Take the bull by the horns."*

References:

The 100 Simple Secrets of Great Relationships by David Niven, Harper San Francisco, 2003

What Every Supervisor Should Know by David Engler and Lester R. Bittle, McGraw-Hill, 1992

See: fear of competition, fear of not being loved, fear of taking chances, fear of oneself, fear of showing emotions, fear of asking for a raise or promotion, fear of the boss, fear of firing an employee, fear of choking in sports, fears for your marriage/partnership

Fear of Not Being Loved

anuptaphobia (fear of staying single)

The one thing we can never get enough of is love. And the one thing we never give enough of is love. —HENRY MILLER

Characteristics: People may avoid contact with others for fear of rejection or not being accepted, or they may seek to fill an emotional hole with constant work or substance abuse. This fear can result in possessiveness, depression or cynicism. It can also lead people to put up defensive walls to protect themselves. But a person who makes an effort to be loved may inspire the feelings and affections of others.

Background: Our need to be loved—socially, spiritually and physically—is as strong as our needs for food, drink and oxygen. It keeps us together as a species and prevents us from becoming hermits. But love is a very complex emotion and spiritual resource. It takes many forms—sexual attraction, love of family and self, love of work and spiritual love. Love can be composed of trust, respect, acceptance, strong affection, tenderness and devotion. Some people may seek affection in one area of their life (their job) to compensate for lack of it in another (at home). If people's needs for affection and attention are too great, they may have come from a loveless home. But this fear can also be genetic and run in families.

Strategies:

- Examine your motives for seeking people's attention and love. They may be very natural and healthy, but they may be misplaced or out of proportion. Consider the words of business consultant and author Brian Tracy: "Much of what we do in life we do either to get love or to compensate for the lack of love."
- Don't try too hard to get people's attention or affection. If you throw yourself at them, people may recoil. "In our desperate rush to become intimate, we may tell too much too soon," says relationship psychologist Harriet Lerner. "Sharing vulnerability is one way we feel close to each other, but sharing indiscriminately or prematurely has the opposite effect."

- If you don't get the reaction you require from a person, don't take it personally; they may react the same way to others. Some people may not be able to love you because they don't know how to love themselves. Learn to give love yourself. As the old song goes, "You got to give love to get love."
- If people close to you don't give you enough affection, open up the communication lines and talk with them about it. Tell them that their affection is important to you, a way of showing that they care about you. If you continue to get a lack of love at home, seek gratification through volunteering or through work, or perhaps seek deeper spirituality through meditation, by becoming a mentor to others or by joining a volunteer organization or a church. By giving your love to others, you receive it in return.
- Learn to balance your life and your needs. Love is important, but so are career, school, play and peace of mind.
- If you come from a loveless home, don't overcompensate by expecting too much attention from your spouse, children, friends or coworkers. Deep emotional issues may require the attention of a therapist.
- Learn to love yourself and not rely so much on others. It's not the end of the world if everybody doesn't like you. If everybody loved you, you would have far too much responsibility and pressure. Take the advice of actress Drew Barrymore: "I want people to love me, but it's not going to hurt me if they don't."

A MANTRA TO TELL YOURSELF: *"Love myself first."*

References:

Centering and the Art of Intimacy by Gary Hendricks, Fireside, 1993

The Dance of Connection by Harriet Lerner, HarperCollins, 2001

See: fear of intimacy or love, fear of rejection, fear of criticism, fears for your marriage/partnership, sexual fears, fear of being alone

Fear of Intimacy or Love

philophobia (fear of being in love)

aphenphosmphobia (fear of being touched)

What we want most in life is love. What we're most afraid of is love. Sad but true.
—PSYCHOLOGIST PAMELA L. CHUBBUCK

Characteristics: This is an inability or refusal to love or to share yourself, particularly your deepest thoughts and feelings, with others. It may prevent close relationships, social or romantic. Some people fear being kissed or touched or having their work or interests closely examined. If you find it easier to have relationships with nature or pets or to watch television, you may have this fear.

Background: Many people are reluctant to love or to be intimate for a number of reasons. Love is a very complex emotion (see fear of not being loved). Although humans are social beings, we may feel that we are unlovable to others, defective or unworthy, perhaps from our childhood experiences or from a feeling of being abandoned or rejected. This fear may also be genetic, and it can skip a generation or two in a family tree. Sufferers may not be aware that they are afraid of being loved or touched. This fear is beneficial when it keeps people from falling in love or jumping into relationships too easily.

Strategies:

- Be aware that, generally, love is good for your health. It activates the parasympathetic nervous system, which reduces stress and activates soothing hormones such as endorphins and serotonin. It is also good for your social life and spiritual well-being.
- Try to understand your own needs better. Establish a good relationship with yourself by being emotionally honest and intimate with yourself before you try to become intimate with others. Explore your inner feelings, especially those you have about yourself. You may have many false beliefs and attitudes about yourself that were drummed into you as a child. They may be painful or subconscious, so you may have to force

yourself to write them down, say them aloud and root them out.

- If this fear is severely affecting your life and relationships, consider seeing a therapist or counselor. You might have serious issues from your childhood. Counselor and author Robert Burney writes about such cases, "We were traumatized as children and the defenses we adapted to protect us caused us to traumatize ourselves as adults. We have experienced getting our hearts broken, our hopes and dreams shattered...[and] feel[ing] rejected over and over again."

- It's possible that you feel safe when you're in a comfort zone in which you don't reach out to others. But are you happy? Is this situation healthy? Do you have enough confidantes?

- Show your emotions once in a while. Laugh, cry or rejoice with others. Rather than revealing weakness, this vulnerability can actually make you appear stronger to others. If you feel a sense of shame about intimacy, reduce it by listing the good things you have to offer to others.

- You are worthy of having close relationships with others. Seek them out and don't shrink at the first sign of criticism or rejection. Yes, getting burned can be a painful experience. If it happens, join the club, because all of us have been emotionally rejected at one time or another. Learn something from it, especially about yourself, then move on with your life.

- Consider that besides a fear of intimacy, you may also fear relationships with others because they often require commitment and hard work.

A MANTRA TO TELL YOURSELF: *"Open up a little."*

Reference:

Codependence: The Dance of Wounded Souls by Robert Burney, Joy to You and Me Enterprises, 1995

See: fear of not being loved, fear of showing emotions, fear of invasion of territory or privacy, fear of the opposite sex, fear of commitment, sexual fears, fear of failure, fear of what others think, fear of criticism

Superstition or Fear of the Supernatural

wiccaphobia (fear of witchcraft) phasmophobia (fear of ghosts)	*Virtually all superstition is created by primitive limbic reasoning. Most cultures—most individuals—are a mixture of primitive reasoning and sophisticated reasoning.* —Rush W. Dozier, author of *Fear Itself*

Characteristics: Some people believe that rituals or symbols will bring good luck or stave off evil. They will knock on wood, avoid black cats, visit psychics or move to condos without a 13th floor. Some people believe in jinxes; they think that by talking about the possible outcome of an event, they will alter it.

Background: Our ancestors explained the mysteries of life and the universe through myth. Many ancient beliefs have been passed down through ritual and tradition, in part because of our enduring need to understand the world and our place in it. As well, there are many things we still do not understand and thus fear. For those things, we often put up defenses that we imagine will protect us from the unknown, such as good-luck charms. People who believe in the paranormal tend to be more willing than skeptics to see patterns or relationships between events; there is some evidence that they also have higher levels of the hormone dopamine in the brain. Many religions and cultures have superstitious components. Some people still fear a hex or curse placed upon them.

Strategies:
- In the big picture, we must understand that many superstitions are harmless, even funny, but they are less so if you waste a lot of time and effort humoring them. They can even be hazardous if you trip while constantly trying to avoid cracks in the pavement, which some people consider bad luck.
- Think superstitions through: what unseen power will stave off disaster or failure if you suddenly wave a rabbit's foot in front of it? And how powerful would that dark force be if it backed away from such a trinket?

- We are all seeking patterns and structure in our lives. Establishing a rigid schedule prior to a high-pressure event can give you structure and confidence. For example, superstitious baseball star Wade Boggs would eat chicken before every game to ensure his success. But what happens to your psyche if something occurs to change that routine—if chicken is not available?
- If you think you are jinxed, you are. If you think you aren't, you aren't. Your mindset can become a self-fulfilling prophecy as you either "give in" to unseen forces ("I can't win, so what's the use of trying?") or try harder because you believe you have some control over your fate.
- If you are constantly worried about fate, superstition or the supernatural, examine the amount of control you have, or don't have, in your life. It's possible that, in feeling you are powerless, forces beyond your control are dominating you. If you fear bad luck, you could miss opportunities and be gullible.
- It is hard to disprove the supernatural. But for many years, magician James (The Amazing) Randi has offered $1 million to anyone showing evidence of the paranormal or supernatural. No one has been able to collect. He says, "Those who allow themselves to be taken in by psychics and supernaturalists are not stupid; they are naïve, trusting and perhaps careless." And perhaps they have been conditioned by their superstitious parents.
- Have fun with superstition; make a game of it at a party.

A MANTRA TO TELL YOURSELF: *"You only have bad luck if you think you do."*
QUOTABLE: *"Fear is the main source of superstition."*
—*Bertrand Russell*

References:

The Encyclopedia of Superstition, edited by Christina Hole, Metro, 2002

The James Randi Educational Foundation, www.randi.org

See: fear of the unknown, fear of not having control, fear of religion, fear of destiny, fear of the dark, fear and stress in children

Fear of Religion

theophobia (fear of gods or religion)

peccatophobia (fear of sinning)

Religion is a great force, but you must get a man through his own religion, not yours. —GEORGE BERNARD SHAW

Characteristics: Distrust, fear or loathing of "other people's" religion is common throughout the world. A person may feel tense in the presence of someone from a particular faith. In extreme instances, religions and cultures may come into conflict. Lesser symptoms are a person feeling discomfort from being lectured, talked down to or converted. There may also be a fear of becoming regimented.

Background: We all have an "us vs. them" gene from primitive times that makes us distrustful, even fearful, of people who are different from us, and that fear can be directed toward other cultures and religions. This instinct once kept us vigilant against potentially harmful tribes from other regions. As we've become civilized, we've tamed this instinct significantly and become more tolerant, although it is still strong in many parts of the world. In moderate forms, it prevents strangers from walking all over us. People who fear the heavy influence of outside forces such as a god are more likely to develop anxieties than other people.

Fear of religion is actually often fear of people from other *regions* because, throughout the world, religion tends to be geographic—predominantly Christian in the West, Hindu and Buddhist in the East, Muslim in the Middle East, and so on.

There are 22 religions in the world with more than 150,000 adherents, from Christianity (2 billion) to Islam (1.3 billion) to Scientology (600,000).

Strategies:

- Educate yourself. It wasn't until the horrific events of September 11, 2001, that many North Americans became aware that some extreme elements in the Muslim community were targeting Western culture. In fact, until then, there was little understanding of Islam in the West. Imagine how others might view your beliefs if they knew nothing of your background.

- Be tolerant of others who have beliefs that don't correspond with your own. A tolerant society may be a more advanced society.
- Visit a temple or church from a religion you know little about. Many religions won't try to convert you to their way of thinking. If a religious person does try to convert you through fear of damnation, you might want to consider if you want to join a religion that uses such fear tactics.
- Don't dismiss the value of religion. Many, if not most, religions have a strong upside in charity work, compassion, a sense of values and community involvement. They give people structure and peace of mind in an often stressful world. As well, they can keep some cruel people in line.
- Don't feel inferior or left out if you are one of the 850 million atheists in the world; you may believe in evolution, you may be a humanist, or you may be spiritual without adhering to a traditional religion. In North America, there is freedom of religion, and perhaps there should also be freedom *from* religion.
- Keep an open mind. Beliefs *can* change. Try to remain open-minded about the "facts" of religion and where humans came from, even to the point of considering a change of belief. And don't be swayed by popular opinion. Remember that, until fairly recently, most of the people on earth *believed* that it was flat. More recently, many people *believed* that women were second-class citizens. As we became enlightened and gathered the facts, we realized that neither of these beliefs was well-founded.

A MANTRA TO TELL YOURSELF: *"My beliefs are important."*

Reference:

The World's Religions: Our Great Wisdom Traditions by Huston Smith, Harper San Francisco, 1992

See: fear of the unknown, superstition or fear of the supernatural, fear of death, fear of other races, fear of strangers, fear of terrorism, fear of destiny

Fear of Destiny

Zeusophobia (fear of fate)

> *The word "fate" is the refuge of every self-confessed failure.* —ANDREW SOUTAR

Characteristics: This fear includes feelings of cynicism and powerlessness as well as a sense that everything is meant to be, and thus has been preplanned, perhaps as part of God's will. It can also involve the belief that others get more breaks than you do. Many people who fear destiny are attracted to astrology, psychics and religion. Some people get the feeling that something terrible is going to happen to them even if they have no reason to think so.

Background: This fear is as old as history and is related to early humans' inability to explain or conceptualize their place in the universe. They felt they had little control over their future, which they thought must be influenced by the stars, the weather or the gods. Even today, many people feel that they have little control over their lives, and some hold destiny or fate responsible for their condition. As Andrew Soutar said, it's an easy excuse for failure.

Throughout history, most people have been followers; only a small percentage have been true leaders who make key decisions. Some followers, through either lack of talent, effort, opportunity or healthy thinking, believe their future is largely out of their hands. People who believe in the heavy influence of outside forces in their lives are more likely to develop anxieties.

Strategies:

- You probably have more influence over your "destiny" than you think. You might believe that promotions at work are given out not through anything you can do, but through office politics. Even if this belief is partly right, you can still improve your chances by good performance. Don't fall into what psychologist Martin Seligman calls "learned helplessness," in which people believe they will not make a difference, so they do not try.
- Work hard at the things you have some control over and increase your skills in those areas. Once you assert some control, you will develop confidence and more control.

- Don't give up too easily, and don't use excuses or blame invisible outside forces for your failures. That's an easy way to absolve yourself of personal responsibility.
- Don't believe too much in luck. Remember, bad breaks happen to everybody. It's how you react to them that separates winners from those who don't get ahead. Remember the words of self-help guru Dale Carnegie: "When fate hands you a lemon, make lemonade."
- Make a self-fulfilling prophecy work for you. Believe that destiny is on your side or that there are ways for you to force your will on the future. The night before the final round of the 1999 Ryder Cup, U.S. captain Ben Crenshaw told his players that destiny was with them. They went out and played their best golf and came from behind to defeat the Europeans.
- Consider that if everything is predestined, then we are just going through the motions. Just get up in the morning and go to work, take few risks, don't allow your voice to be heard and don't seek new acquaintances or experiences. If you accept that, then perhaps destiny *is* out of your hands.

A MANTRA TO TELL YOURSELF: *"I have a say in my destiny."*

Listen up:

"Que sera, sera. Whatever will be, will be." A catchy old tune. But don't be so quick to swallow the lyrics. Maybe you've been conditioned by other such mindsets and aren't aware of it. Do your part, and then whatever will be, will be.

Reference:

The Anxiety and Phobia Workbook by Edmund J. Bourne, New Harbinger, 1995

See: fear of not having control, superstition or fear of the supernatural, fear of religion, fear of death

3

Physical Fears

Fear of Flying

aviaphobia (fear of flying)

My husband was my motivation to fly. I made up my mind I wasn't going to let my fears of flying, my nervousness about driving, control me anymore. —NEW YORK FITNESS EXPERT MANDY LADERER, WHO HAD AVOIDED FLYING FOR 15 YEARS

Characteristics: Sufferers experience apprehension, tension and a variety of other symptoms of anxiety. They may avoid flying for fear of crashing, being the victim of terrorism, feeling turbulence or allowing someone else to control their destiny. Some may also fear embarrassment if they start to sweat or become tense or nauseous in front of other passengers. They may drink alcohol during the flight.

Background: This fear is costly to the airline industry and to corporations, whose executives must fly to get from city to city quickly. Even before the tragedy of 9/11, a poll showed that 44 percent of Americans reported some fear of flying and 52 percent had lost confidence in airline safety. Now those numbers are higher. Overachievers and perfectionists tend to be the most nervous passengers because of their need for control; they tend to have had parents who demanded perfection. Twice as many women as men suffer from this condition. Most fearful fliers never seek help.

Strategies:
- Always remember that the facts are with you. Plane crashes are extremely rare; in the United States, the chances of dying in a plane crash are 500,000 to one for frequent flyers. Flying is the safest mode of travel, far safer than driving. (When plane crashes do occur, they are always reported in the media and often have fatalities.) You think rationally in other areas of your life—you can do that here.
- Admit your anxieties and talk to others about them. You will find that many people have at least some anxiety about flying. If you are honest enough to identify yourself as a nervous flier, tell the flight attendants. They have dealt with many others like you and will reassure you.

- Don't try to suppress all of your worries in one flight. Slowly desensitize yourself and your fears will decrease as you gradually see how safe it is.
- Feel confident about the pilot and crew. They are professionals. When you're driving on the road, most people are amateurs at the wheel.
- Prior to and during the flight, use relaxation exercises and visualize going through all the steps to a successful conclusion.
- If possible, fly with someone you trust.
- Get a massage before you fly; some airports have massage services. Avoid caffeine or alcohol before or during a flight.
- If you control your emotions, your catastrophic thinking will ease. In the words of psychologist R. Reid Wilson: "People who come to me for therapy come to realize it's not about the plane, it's they who are the anxiety-producing machines." Use deep breathing and meditation strategies. Take a relaxation tape or CD with you.
- Pay close attention to safety demonstrations and read the pamphlet in front of your seat. Notice that the attendants describe safety precautions "in the *unlikely* event of an accident." Stay occupied during the flight by reading or working (I get some of my best thinking done on planes, perhaps because of the high altitude), or get up and talk to other passengers.
- Don't become preoccupied with what happened on September 11, 2001. Airport and airplane security have improved since then.
- Check to see if your city has a fear-of-flying class organized by AAir Born.

A MANTRA TO TELL YOURSELF: *"I'm in good hands."*

References:

Flying Without Fear by Dr. Duane Brown, New Harbinger, 1996
The Fear of Flying Clinic, www.fofc.com

Many airlines offer programs. See also the U.S. Federal Aviation Administration website at www.faa.gov

See: fear of not having control, fear of travel, fear of death, fear of the unknown, fear of heights, fear of terrorism, fear of panic attacks in public, fear of destiny, fear of driving

Fear of Terrorism

xenophobia (fear of foreigners)

People should be concerned, but I don't think that should keep you from seeing the world. You have to go on with life.

—Barbara Ruth of Texas, visiting New York in 2003 during a heightened terrorism alert

Characteristics: In these times of terrorism alerts, many people report a general feeling of anxiety and lack of control; others feel angry about an unseen enemy and what that enemy might do. Some describe a feeling of insecurity and a loss of trust in others. These sentiments may keep people from traveling. Since the 9/11 attacks, many people have reduced their flying and bought emergency supplies for home. At the same time, the 9/11 attacks have increased feelings of patriotism and sparked more teamwork, spirituality and blood giving. Some people say the awareness of terrorism actually makes them feel more alive and more appreciative of what they have to lose.

Background: Although North Americans had not experienced a strong fear of terrorism until 9/11 and the subsequent war in Iraq, fear of an unknown attacker is a deep, primitive fear, closely tied to the fear of the unknown and fear of other races. Fear of terrorism has been a fact of life in the Middle East and other regions for a long time. Although people in those areas remain alert, many report becoming desensitized to the threats and going on with their daily lives. Historically, most Americans eventually return to their normal routine after national crises. Immediately after 9/11, many residents of New York turned to psychiatric and antidepression medication, but a few weeks later, prescription levels returned to normal.

Strategies:
- Don't become preoccupied with a threat that may never come. Remain active and keep up your normal routine. You should not allow fear of terrorism to wreck your way of life.
- Discussing your thoughts and feelings about terrorism from time to time is helpful, as long as you don't engage in inflammatory discussions that lead to more tension or to hatred.
- Keep up with news developments, but don't watch so much

television that the terrorism threat becomes a constant preoccupation. Some people believe that becoming newshounds reduces their uncertainty, but it usually creates more anxiety.

- Come up with a safety plan in your home and neighborhood and rehearse it with family. It will give you some sense of control.
- Don't scapegoat or judge an entire race of people, religion or culture because some of its members are terrorists—some members of *your* race and culture may be terrorists as well.
- It takes time to get over traumas like 9/11 and the Iraq war, and it can be difficult to go on if one feels under threat. If you remain anxious after an extended period, see a counselor.
- Without becoming paranoid, report suspicious activity or vehicles in your neighborhood to police. Join a Neighborhood Watch group and share your ideas with others.
- Reassess your priorities. Do those little hassles at work or your grumpy neighbor seem so relevant in light of these bigger issues?
- Be sure to talk to your children about terrorism. Assure them that, although everything in the world is not always good or fair, their world remains stable and they have your unconditional love. Encourage your kids to go about their normal routines.
- Here's what you might need as a safety kit for a potential emergency: bottled water, a three- to five-day supply of nonperishable food, a first-aid kit, a battery-powered radio, a flashlight, duct tape, a utility knife, a small fire extinguisher, toilet paper, soap, clothes and bedding.

A MANTRA TO TELL YOURSELF: *"Life goes on."*

References:

A Faceless Enemy by Glenn E. Schweitzer, Perseus, 2002

Why Terrorism Works by Alan M. Dershowitz, Yale University Press, 2002

American Red Cross, www.redcross.org

U.S. Federal Emergency Management Agency, www.fema.gov

See: fear of flying, fear of travel, fear of the unknown, fear of not having control, fear of death, fear for the safety of your children, fear of other races, fear of strangers, fear of crowds

Fear of Being Mugged

harpaxophobia (fear of robbers or being robbed)

I have three words of advice for victims— breathe, breathe, breathe. —EMERGENCY EXPERT DEBBIE GARDNER

Characteristics: Apprehension or caution about going out, especially alone and in certain areas, affects many people. They may fear being robbed, beaten up or humiliated, and they may carry their good clothes in a bag to be inconspicuous. This condition particularly affects the elderly and people who feel helpless; it can even keep them housebound. Some people get anxious just watching violent movies.

Background: Since our distant past, people (especially the weak) have always been wary of enemies and predators. We are all programmed with an emergency fear system to help us against physical threats. At its peak, this system creates what is known as the fight-or-flight response, giving us enhanced strength, speed and concentration. In primitive times, the hair would stand up on a frightened person's body, making them appear bigger and more powerful to an enemy (this phenomenon still exists to a small extent, which is why the hair stands up on the back of your neck when you're frightened). But since we are generally not used to such physical arousal these days, many people freeze when confronted with a mugger. Men tend to have this fear less than women because they are conditioned through sports and roughhousing to be more confident physically.

Strategies:

- Be sensible about where you go, especially at night, but don't let your fear become so exaggerated or dominant that it affects your life and schedule.
- Don't walk with valuables, flashy jewelry or laptop computers at night. But do carry identification. If you have a headset on, you might not be able to hear things around you. Keep your hands out of your pockets and free.
- Take a self-defense course. Such courses are especially valuable for women, who are generally not as strong as men and not used to the feelings of confrontation and arousal from contact

sports. Many self-defense courses are noncompetitive and feature such components as relaxation and meditation. They will give you confidence on the street.

- Walk confidently with your head up, as though you know where you're going. If you walk a lot at night, carry a whistle or a shrill alarm.
- If you think you are being followed, cross the road or go to a place with a lot of people.
- If you are attacked, the first thing you must do is control yourself. Assess the situation and keep your mind active. If you feel yourself freezing, hyperventilating or panicking, force yourself to breathe deeply from your stomach.
- Don't try to be a hero. Get away if you can. Most people are not trained in defending themselves, whereas the assailant has the advantage of surprise and is probably street-tough. Run fast, pumping your knees high.
- If the thug has a weapon, give him what he wants. Your possessions simply aren't worth it. They can be replaced, but your spleen cannot.
- Screaming or shouting often works by scaring the attacker and releasing you from the freeze mode. If the incident lasts for a while, you might want to change tactics from running to fighting to talking your way out of it.
- If you have no alternative but to fight, inflict pain on the attacker—kick his groin, gouge his eyes or stomp on his foot. Use your head to pop him under his jaw, or use your fingernails or teeth. Fight dirty.
- If you have had a traumatic mugging, put it into perspective: you are just a normal person who experienced an abnormal situation. It doesn't mean it will happen again.

A MANTRA TO TELL YOURSELF: *"Breathe!"*

Reference:

Survive Institute, www.surviveinstitute.com

See: fear of death, fear of illness or pain, fear of strangers, fear of getting involved in an emergency, fear of travel, fear of dogs and animals, fear of the dark, fear of being alone, fear of confrontation or conflict

Fear of Getting Involved in an Emergency

dystychiphobia (fear of accidents)	*Heroes are a window into the soul of a culture.* —PSYCHOLOGIST FRANK FARLEY

Characteristics: If you are afraid of stopping to help someone involved in a mugging, a fire or a car crash, you're not alone. Most people flinch or at least hesitate in such emergencies. Some people leave the scene or freeze in their tracks. Others will not travel in certain areas or at certain times of the day because of this fear. Some people avoid emergencies for fear of fainting or because they don't like the sight of blood.

Background: Sadly, research suggests that most people don't help during an emergency on the street for fear of getting hurt, of later having to go to court or of a lawsuit. Research also shows that in emergencies, it is most often men who come forward to help, perhaps because of social conditioning and because men are more used to feelings of arousal through physical action and sports. As our society gets more insular and less personal, chances are that fewer people will help during emergencies. And yet when teamwork is involved, such as during the tragedies of war and terrorism, people have shown courage and empathy and many heroes have been born.

Strategies:
- Take a first-aid course to give you confidence. If you have such training, calmly tell people so at the scene of an emergency.
- Assess the situation and make sure someone notifies authorities immediately.
- Look at the victim. If you were in such a pickle, would you want people to walk away from you?
- If you start to panic, freeze or lose confidence, go up to a victim and touch him or her. Often this will defuse your fears. Or think of a loved one to motivate you, or even use humor. And remember to breathe deeply.
- Focus on what needs to be done and put your anxiousness and

fear energy into that. If you have trouble focusing, briefly get angry at yourself or others. This activates aggressive hormones such as dopamine and testosterone in your nervous system. Before he rescued three unconscious people from a burning car in Fredonia, New York, Robert Nobel got angry with his friends who refused to get involved because they were worried about a lawsuit if the rescue backfired. His anger sent him into a zone in which his powers were increased.

- If you have panicked in the past, don't consider yourself a coward—even tough people falter from time to time and choke in pressure situations.
- If you decide to take action, remember that your power and certain aspects of your focus will improve as your fight-or-flight system kicks in. As heart rate rises, strength and desire are boosted, but complex motor skills decrease. If you are really pumped, you may experience altered perceptions such as tunnel vision or tunnel hearing, in which you don't notice important things on the periphery.
- If you need to perform a task that requires fine motor skills (such as using car keys), make a fist and release it quickly several times. This ensures that blood will stay in your hands; otherwise the fight-or-flight system will send it to the big muscles of your arms and legs to prepare you to fight or run away.

A MANTRA TO TELL YOURSELF: *"Somebody needs me."*

References:

The American Red Cross First Aid and Safety Handbook by Kathleen Handal and Elizabeth Dole, Little, Brown, 1992

Intelligent Fear by Michael Clarkson, Key Porter, 2002

Carnegie Hero Fund Commission, www.carnegiehero.org

See: fear of blood (and blood injury), fear of not having control, fear of illness or pain, fear of making mistakes, fear of taking responsibility, fear of confrontation or conflict, fear of being mugged, fear of death

Fear of Blood (and Blood Injury)

| hemophobia (fear of blood) | *Children cry oftener from seeing their blood than from the pain occasioned by falls or blows.* —BENJAMIN RUSH, AN 18TH-CENTURY AMERICAN PHYSICIAN |

Characteristics: At just the thought of seeing blood, a person may feel faint, anxious or nauseous and experience rapid breathing. Sufferers of all ages are particularly susceptible to this fear in hospitals, in doctors' or dentists' offices, while getting injections or giving blood, or at the scene of car crashes and accidents. Some people feel faint just from medical odors. Some women avoid becoming pregnant because they fear medical situations and blood. Ironically, few people who suffer from this fear actually feel threatened with injury or blood loss.

Background: Up to 5 percent of the population has this fear. Women are more susceptible than men. People feel faint at the sight of blood because they get a sudden drop in heart rate and blood pressure; this is called a vasovagal reaction. There are two unproven theories as to why nature makes some people pass out: so the victim will not do anything that may cause further blood loss, or so a person seems lifeless to an attacking predator. This fear tends to be genetic and runs in families, although it can be sparked by a traumatic event. It often starts in childhood.

Strategies:

- This can be a serious fear if you let it prevent you or your loved ones from getting regular medical treatment and checkups. That creates a much bigger problem for you, and something you should genuinely be afraid of.
- If you have this fear, admit it aloud. Denial only drives it deeper into your subconscious and prevents you from coping with it. People won't laugh at you; they have their own phobias to worry about.
- Talk to your doctor or dentist about your fear; they have many other patients who suffer from it, and they are experienced in helping you. They certainly won't laugh at you.

- Talk about it with people you trust, particularly if they have this fear. You can even start your own little support group: Fainters Anonymous (FA).
- Come to realize that, while loss of your own blood would be a problem, the sight of someone else's blood causes you no physical harm.
- Toughen up. Desensitize yourself by watching gory television shows and movies, if only for a few seconds or minutes at a time.
- The next time someone is losing blood in your presence, reach out to help, even if you only put on a Band-Aid. When you focus on that process, you won't notice the blood as much. When I was a police reporter, I rarely noticed the trauma at accident sites because I was so focused on getting the story or the photographs. Distracting yourself from a gory site can also work.
- If you do feel faint, sit down and put your head between your legs. This has helped me many times and I have never fainted.

A MANTRA TO TELL YOURSELF: *"It can't hurt me."*

Author's Two Cents:

I have coped better with my blood phobia since I volunteered to be a "victim" in a staged automobile wreck for a television news show. It was a little traumatic, but I was glad I forced myself to do it. When I saw myself in the rearview mirror, made up with artificial blood, I managed a ghoulish smile.

Reference:

Facing Fears: The Sourcebook for Phobias, Fears, and Anxieties by Ada P. Kahn and Ronald M. Doctor, Checkmark, 2000

See: fear of doctors or dentists, fear of getting involved in an emergency, fear of embarrassment, fear of death, fear of panic attacks in public

Fear of Death

thanatophobia (fear of death)	*Fear not death, for the sooner we die, the longer shall we be immortal.* —BENJAMIN FRANKLIN

Characteristics: When surveys are conducted of people's greatest fears, death is always near or at the top of the list. People feel anxious in situations that may result in death, illness or physical harm; they can get uneasy simply by thinking or talking about those situations. Some people avoid hospitals, travel, funerals, the elderly and risk-taking ventures. Others, especially the ill or elderly, can become preoccupied with death.

Background: Everyone has some fear of mortality, and a healthy dose of this keeps us alert to danger. Fortunately, the major defense systems of humans are set up to ward off death. In Western society, life expectancy has risen in recent times, although there is still a high rate of deaths attributed to heart and anxiety problems. In some ways, dying has become more mysterious because seriously ill people are kept in hospitals. Death is the ultimate unknown, and fear of it is particularly intense in teenagers.

We may also fear leaving behind loved ones who rely on us. Many people are uncomfortable talking about death or making a will, and this discomfort can make death more foreboding. At the same time, death is highlighted in the media and the arts. Many people who have faced death lose some of their fear of it. Singer Gordon Lightfoot said in 2003, after recovering from a serious illness: "In the past I had a fear of death. I feel much better about accepting death now."

Strategies:
- The best antidote for the fear of death is to live. We will all die one day; it's how we live that is important. Soak in the details of daily life—the robin's warble, the crimson sunset, the thrill of holding a child. Say, "I will enjoy life." Don't deny death; it should be included in your overall view of life. Say aloud, "One day I will die. It is inevitable, but there is much to experience, enjoy and accomplish in the meantime."

- If you can't imagine a world without you, join the club. Being alive is all that we know. But you can live beyond your flesh by leaving part of you behind in your family and friends, in your work and deeds, and in your kindness.
- Deepen your spirituality with family, friends or religion. Delve into who you are and what you want to achieve, for yourself and others.
- You will die once; don't die a hundred times by constantly thinking about it. Prepare for that day, however, with a will and instructions about your funeral. Review these with your family.
- If someone you know is dying, rather than wallowing in pity, do something for them and share time with them. Help them focus on everyday life.
- If you are terminally ill, remain positive, but briefly visualize the eventual process of dying. "Write down what you would do if you only had six months to live," writes Judy Tatelbaum in *The Courage to Grieve*. "This exercise allows us to contemplate what is important."
- If children have an intense fear of death, it could be that they fear being left alone. Reassure them that they will be safe and that no harmful forces are lurking around the corner.
- Lighten up. Remember what comedian W.C. Fields wanted on his headstone: "All things considered, I'd rather be in Philadelphia." As author/speaker Allen Klein says, "Joking about death, or anything else that oppresses us, makes it less frightening."

A MANTRA TO TELL YOURSELF: *"I'm alive."*

References:

Lessons from the Dying by Rodney Smith, Wisdom Publications, 1998

Video: *Overcoming the Fear of Death* by Deepak Chopra

See: fear of the unknown, fear of illness or pain, fear of being mugged, fear of travel, fear of religion, fears for your children, fear of aging, fear of retirement, fear of delivering bad news, fear of flying, fear of terrorism, fear of heights, fear of water and swimming, fear of doctors or dentists, serious worries

Fear of Illness or Pain

algophobia (fear of painful situations such as visits to doctors and dentists)

There are major differences between being concerned about health and suffering from hypochondria. —DAVID S. GOLDMAN, CLINICAL ASSISTANT PROFESSOR OF PSYCHIATRY AT NEW YORK UNIVERSITY SCHOOL OF MEDICINE

hypochondria (intense and unwarranted fear of illness or a preoccupation with health issues)

Characteristics: This condition involves worry or anxiety over symptoms of illness and pain or the potential that they might occur. Many people avoid physicians, hospitals, funerals and the elderly (or, conversely, they visit the doctor more than they should). A person might be preoccupied with illness and talk about it all the time or watch television shows about emergencies or health issues. Many elderly people fear illness because they believe they would be a burden to others. Hypochondriacs may be preoccupied with bodily functions.

Background: Everyone worries about their health from time. That's good if it motivates us to eat well and exercise often. Exaggerated concern about a variety of illnesses (hypochondria) affects men and women in equal numbers. About 25 percent of all patients seen in health clinics and doctors' offices have this condition. It usually begins between the ages of 20 and 30. Hypochondria costs the U.S. health care system about $30 billion annually. Hypochondriacs have medical costs up to 14 times greater than the average person. Poet Alfred Lord Tennyson was thought to be a hypochondriac.

Strategies:

- You can alleviate many of your fears through education and prevention. Have regular checkups and talk to your doctor about your concerns. If you get anxious about your health, you might get short-term relief through deep breathing, meditation and other relaxation techniques.
- Establish whether you have normal health concerns or hypochondria, which has three symptoms: a morbid fear of

disease; preoccupation or obsession with bodily symptoms and functions; and a firm conviction of having a disease, despite medical assurance and test results to the contrary.

- Hypochondria can be difficult to treat, but results have improved in recent times because of new medications, behavioral techniques, greater awareness of the problem, group therapy and changes in doctor-patient relationships. A diagnostic assessment may be required, including reviewing the medical history of the patient and conducting physical and mental examinations. If you know someone who is a hypochondriac, be empathetic and understand that their symptoms seem real to them.

- If you are worried about upcoming surgery, ask a lot of questions and develop a rapport with your doctor, nurses and surgeon. Visit the hospital ahead of time and get a walk-through of the procedure.

- If you have a serious illness, understand that medical science and procedures have never been more effective. Seek out family and friends for emotional support and perhaps for physical needs (such as getting a ride to a clinic).

- If you are afraid that illness or pain will affect your career, learn new ways to do your work, or find other work to do.

- If someone close to you has an illness, allow yourself to feel concern and pain, but don't allow the person to feel guilty about your concern.

- Avoid television shows about illness, and don't allow your fears to become exaggerated through media hype.

A MANTRA TO TELL YOURSELF: *"Deal with reality."*

References:

Hypochondria: Woeful Imaginings by S. Baur, University of California Press, 1998

Phantom Illness by C. Cantor, Houghton Mifflin, 1996

See: fear of death, fear of the unknown, fear of not having control, fear of aging, fear of doctors or dentists, fear of retirement, fear of blood (and blood injury), fear of embarrassment, serious worries

Fear of Doctors or Dentists

iatrophobia (fear of going to the doctor)

dentophobia (fear of dentists)

Showing up is 80 percent of life.
—WOODY ALLEN

Characteristics: Who doesn't have at least some anxiety over visits to physicians, clinics, dentists or hospitals? Sufferers may worry about needles, viruses, pain, blood, medical procedures or bad news. People may avoid their physician even for routine checkups. Others worry their fear will cause them to blush, to feel embarrassed or even to faint. People who have had a painful experience with a physician or dentist may be reluctant to return.

Background: Anxiety about doctors and dentists has been common throughout history. It can be uncomfortable to have another person poking at you with instruments or diagnosing a little wart or withdrawing your blood. Most people are at least somewhat afraid of pain and of hearing bad news. Much of this fear is left over from times when visits to physicians were more painful because medical science was crude. It is when we avoid doctors and dentists that this fear becomes a phobia. In addition, some people fear that physicians are not qualified to treat them or may cheat them. Research suggests that men are half as likely as women to use health services for prevention purposes, but twice as likely to use emergency services. About twice as many people fear dentists as doctors. Blood phobias tend to run in families. This fear is also produced in people who have had a traumatic experience earlier in life.

Strategies:

- Understand that your anxiety is probably more of a problem than whatever you are going to the physician about. Most of the time, your ailment will be minor and can be handled with medication or relatively painless procedures. Medical procedures have come a long way; in particular, visits to dental offices are far less of a big deal than they used to be. With modern drills and anesthetics, it's rare that dentists hit a nerve.
- It should be repeated over and over that the best medicine is

preventive; get regular checkups and put the upcoming dates on your calendar. Encourage other members of your family to do the same.

- If you are apprehensive about making an appointment, sit down alone and make a firm decision that you will go, then book the appointment that day. Coming to grips with the decision will relieve much of the pressure and fear. Avoid making appointments during a stressful time at work or at home.
- Consult friends and family to find a physician who is not only competent, but understands patients' anxieties. Develop a relationship with a physician you trust.
- Prior to a visit, visualize yourself driving to the physician's office, sitting down in the office and going through the procedure with a successful outcome.
- Talk to others in the waiting room. Laugh at this fear and share it with others and with the doctor. Make cynical remarks about the outdated magazines in the waiting room.
- During a procedure, you may want to have a mild sedative or use "guided imagery," imagining a pleasant experience like sunning on a beach.
- If you are afraid of needles, try to relax, perhaps by progressively tensing muscles in your feet, legs, buttocks, abdomen, arms and shoulders as you wait for the injection, then releasing the muscles.
- Be wary of physicians who readily write prescriptions for you without much examination or consultation.

A MANTRA TO TELL YOURSELF: *"It's good for me."*

References:

Dr. Keith Livingston (phobia expert), (206) 721-8751

Dr. Eric Spielder (Philadelphia dentist), Dr.Spielder@aol.com

See: fear of blood (and blood injury), fear of not having control, fear of the unknown, fear of illness or pain, fear of death, fear of embarrassment, fear of delivering bad news, fear of panic attacks in public

Fear of Aging

gerascophobia (fear of aging)

gerontophobia (fear and hatred of the old)

How old would you be if you didn't know how old you was? —SATCHEL PAIGE, WHO PLAYED MAJOR LEAGUE BASEBALL AT AGE 55

Characteristics: For a variety of reasons, a person may worry about reaching 20, 30, 50 or 65. This fear may be linked with concerns about friends and family, health, appearance, retirement or death. The elderly may worry more after their friends die or become ill, or they may worry about getting Alzheimer's, diabetes or heart attacks (anginophobia), having surgery or becoming a burden to others. Some women fear menopause. Other common concerns of aging are loneliness, poverty, falling and being injured while alone, loss of responsibility for one's life, being attacked, memory loss and sexual inadequacy.

Background: This is a primitive fear that remains strong today, but it is being reduced—people are living longer and are able to enjoy their golden years. Genetically, the human species is not programmed to live as long as we do—for most of our history, the average life expectancy was just 18 years! It is a fact that, after age 30, things start going downhill physically, but the good news is that we are born with 10 times more physical capacity than we actually need.

Intense fear of aging can lead to anxiety and hasten the aging process through the release of aggressive hormones. This fear is good when it forces us to take care of ourselves or, when we are younger, to take on responsibility. In some societies, the elderly are more respected than they are in others. Some studies show that memory loss among the elderly is not widespread.

Strategies:

- As you grow older, discover what millions of people have found—that each age has its benefits. People tend to be most energetic and physically fit in their youth, but they mature in their 40s and they can live very active lives in their 50s and beyond, when they often feel more free after seeing their children leave home. Age brings experience and wisdom.

- Don't get caught up in our society's obsession with youth. Don't listen to the often negative portrayals of various age groups, particularly the elderly, in the media. People are able to work longer and live more vital lives into their 70s and 80s than ever before. And when you turn 30, your social life need not be kaput.
- The most significant predictors of healthy old age are low blood pressure, low serum glucose levels, a good diet, not being overweight and not smoking while young. After age 50, the best diet is low fat with plenty of fruits, vegetables and protein, along with increased calcium and vitamins D and B_{12}. Another predictor of good health is a positive attitude and a zest for life. "No one grows old by living, only by losing interest in living," said novelist Marie Beynon Ray.
- Be sure to get regular physical checkups and exercise in every stage of life. "An ounce of prevention is worth a pound of cure" still rings true. To avoid undue strain, try swimming and cross-country skiing instead of running and tennis.
- If you have problems with memory loss, leave yourself written reminders and lists of things that have to be done.
- If you have physical problems and drive, don't be embarrassed to get a handicap sticker. And welcome the chance to get retested or to refresh yourself with a safe-driving course.
- Remain optimistic as long as you have something to do—like being a friend, a volunteer, a grandparent, a gardener or a reader of books. But understand that others around you may be more pessimistic.
- Enjoy your freedom of speech. As you get older, you can humor people less and feel more comfortable speaking the truth.

A MANTRA TO TELL YOURSELF: *"I'm getting wiser."*

Reference:

Centenarians: The Bonus Years by Lynn Adler, Health, 1995

See: fear of retirement, fear of death, fear of the unknown, fear of not having control, fear of change, fear of being alone, fear of not being loved, fear of illness or pain, fear of falling, fear of driving, fear of losing status

Sexual Fears

erotophobia (fear of sex)	*Don't worry about what others are doing. As long as you are both satisfied and happy, you are normal … our sex drive continually evolves as our life changes. The dynamics of our life and our relationship all affect the ebb and flow of our sexual desire and arousal.*
hypoactive sexual desire (having little desire for sex)	
primeisodophobia (fear of losing one's virginity)	—SEX AND MARRIAGE COUNSELOR RAJAN BHONSLE

Characteristics: Sexual anxieties are common. Some men worry about lack of arousal or poor performance, while some women worry about being frigid or not receiving intimacy, and some even worry that their vaginas are too tight. Some people worry that they have too much sex drive. Many parents worry that their children will get involved in sexual situations too early or with the wrong partner. Some young women mistakenly fear menstruation; they may believe that release of their blood is unnatural (it isn't) or feel shame about it.

Background: Almost everyone has some anxiety about the sensitive subject of sex, and most people experience arousal problems at least occasionally. For others, problems are more serious and could even be linked to deviancy. About 25 percent of Americans sometimes experience little or no sexual desire.

Modern humans have always had fears, guilt and self-consciousness about sex (we are the only animal to have sex in private). Although sex talk and awareness has become more common in the past 20 years, we still don't like to talk about sexual problems. And North American society can be quite judgmental, if not downright Victorian. In the big picture, it's good to be cautious about sexual issues. If we had no sexual fears at all, casual intercourse, unplanned pregnancy and sexually transmitted diseases would be rampant.

Strategies:
- Keep in shape. Get a physical checkup; sexual dysfunction can be the early warning of potential medical problems, or a sign that you need to adjust the medication you are taking.

- Educate yourself. Although our society still has much to learn about sex, there is more good information now than ever before. Some fears, particularly about homosexuality and masturbation, are conditioned through culture and religion and are not necessarily based on facts.
- Be responsible in your sexual decisions—especially with regard to when, at what age and with whom to have sex. Pay attention to the consequences your acts may have on others. Always practice safe sex.
- If you are having problems, examine your relationships and emotional well-being. Emotional factors—such as relationship problems, lack of trust, past trauma and guilt—can affect your sexual life.
- In a society flooded with sexual images, don't compare yourself to models or sell yourself short.
- Mix things up once in a while and ask the other person what they want in bed. Visualize what you want to happen and perhaps talk it over with your partner.
- Focus on what your partner is doing to you. If you always close your eyes, you might lose some of the experience and intimacy. Talk about the experience afterwards; find out what worked and what didn't.
- Try to understand the opposite sex. Men and women tend to have different needs in sex, men for action and women for intimacy. If you find that to be the case, try to reverse roles once in a while.
- If problems persist, see your doctor or perhaps a sex therapist. Some drugs can help.

A MANTRA TO TELL YOURSELF: *"Safe and healthy."*

References:

Resurrecting Sex by David Schnarch, HarperCollins, 2002

Sexual Marriage, www.sexualmarriage.com

Talk Sex with Sue Johanson, www.talksexwithsue.com

See: fear of not being loved, fear of intimacy or love, fear of homosexuality, fear of the opposite sex, fear of dating, fear of embarrassment, fear for your children's safety, fear of religion, fears for your marriage/partnership, serious worries, fear of what friends think, fear of harassment

Fear of Enclosed Spaces

claustrophobia (includes fear of being in closets, elevators and crowds)

stenophobia (fear of narrow places, escalators, tunnels)

It is a curious fact that many people who are afraid of small, enclosed spaces are also frightened by being in large open spaces. —PSYCHOLOGIST STANLEY RACHMAN

Characteristics: If you feel anxious or have a fast heartbeat in a crowded space, you may suffer from this specific fear or phobia. Some people panic or feel like they are going to suffocate, and this is sometimes related to their stepped-up breathing patterns. Sufferers tend to avoid elevators and small offices for fear of getting trapped or becoming embarrassed about their reaction. This fear is common in patients who undergo an MRI scan in a narrow chamber. Some people imagine themselves being buried in sand.

Background: Claustrophobia—almost everyone is familiar with this term. It is perhaps the most common of the *exaggerated* fears, affecting about one in 10 people. About 2 percent of people have a severe case. A 2002 survey revealed the No. 1 fear of men was being buried alive and the No. 2 fear of women was being tied up. Psychologists believe that claustrophobia may be innate, and further developed through a bad experience. One in three cases begins in childhood. It's related to the primitive fear of lurking predators who trapped their prey in a confined area. Claustrophobics often have social phobias. Some experts believe this fear can be traced back to fear of Stone Age humans' fear of being suffocated in a cave.

Strategies:

- Prepare for potential stressful situations in hotels or office buildings by checking in advance the size of the rooms and the availability of stairs.
- Slowly desensitize yourself by going into confined spaces. Start with ones that are not too small, such as large closets, then gradually seek out smaller ones, such as crawl spaces. Have someone there with you.

- Don't allow this kind of fear to trap you. You cannot suffocate in an elevator, and the galvanized steel cables will not snap. Although your fear feels very real, it is unreasonable.
- If you feel enclosed in a theater or an arena, sit in the aisle. However, if you are more afraid of what people think of you squatting in the aisle, then get back in your seat (some fears are worse than others!).
- On escalators, proceed slowly but surely while holding the railing. You may want to have someone go in front of you. Remember, there are very few accidents involving escalators or elevators. Safety standards are high. Your chances of an accidental fall will increase, however, if you feel overly nervous.
- In all situations of feeling enclosed, keep a sense of perspective about your exaggerated fear; try to use deep-breathing techniques and humor. Hey, you could make the Guinness Book of World Records as the first person to die from claustrophobia!
- Bring your fear out into the open and write or talk about it. Edgar Allen Poe dealt with his claustrophobia by writing horror stories such as "The Black Cat" and "The Premature Burial." If you voice your worries into a tape recorder, hearing your own voice talk about them can help you put things in perspective.

A MANTRA TO TELL YOURSELF: *"Snug in a womb."*

Reference:

Facing Fears by Ada P. Kahn and Ronald M. Doctor, Checkmark, 2000

See: fear of panic attacks in public, fear of embarrassment, fear of crowds, fear of not having control, fear of driving, fear of the dark, fear of crowds, fear of dogs and animals

Fear of Heights

acrophobia (fear of high places) *catapedaphobia* (fear of jumping from high or low places)	*Don't get me started on intuitive. You know what's intuitive? Fear of heights. Everything else we call intuitive, such as walking or using a pencil, took years of practice.* —DONALD NORMAN, *RISKS DIGEST*

Characteristics: Sufferers of this condition may feel discomfort, intense fear, vertigo (dizziness) or panic while standing atop high buildings, elevated highways or hills, or while skiing or on amusement rides. Some people may feel drawn to jump. Those who fear heights may have nightmares about falling, but they may not be afraid of flying or living in glassed-in apartment buildings. Babies may begin to respect heights after they start to crawl.

Background: This is a common fear, especially in mild forms. If we didn't have it, we'd be hurtling off rooftops and escarpments. It is probably a leftover from the days when primates started walking on two legs and left the plains for the Great Rift Valley and needed an inner protective device to keep them from going off cliffs. Most animals do not fear heights.

People with problems of coordination, balance or the inner ear may have this fear. It is sometimes related to the fear of falling (basophobia), the fear of looking up (anablepophobia) and the fear of high objects (batophobia). People with the latter fear may avoid ladders and ask others to get things from high shelves.

Strategies:

- Exposure therapy often works; people can be gradually exposed to heights while in a relatively relaxed state. For example, they can look out of a window from the third floor until they feel relaxed, then repeat the experience on higher floors (but perhaps not all in the same day).
- Give yourself control. In a program called LearningMethods, sufferers are taken to a hill where they slowly walk toward the edge, always giving themselves the chance to go back but reminding themselves that they control their decision. They are

told to let their feelings of anxiety come out and to stay near the edge for some time. Gradually, they relax.

- If you have little need to be in tall buildings or on top of hills, you may want to ignore this fear. But, of course, you can try to control it to give yourself satisfaction or to open up your world. Looking down from on high can even be exciting!

- There is no shame in going to a therapist. Wendy Black had an embarrassing fear of climbing a slide at the playground with her children. "I was freezing and couldn't move my feet," she said. "It affected my self-esteem." With help from psychologist Martin Antony of St. Joseph's Hospital in Hamilton, Ontario, Black began climbing small ladders until she was able to join her kids on the slide. Eventually, she was even able to go up Toronto's CN Tower, the world's tallest free-standing structure.

- Lean on your friends. Hironobu Yasuda of Japan was afraid to go up the Eiffel Tower, but was encouraged by his friends to try skydiving. "I couldn't have jumped out of a plane without my wonderful friends," he said. "There was a whole new world and the beautiful sky; I had never seen such a beautiful world!"

- Safety in childhood can reduce such fears. The Navajo Indians, who were carried on their mother's back in a cradle in infancy, were often hired as fearless construction workers on high-rises.

- If your children have no fear of heights, they may be prone to injury and falls. They may have *hypophobia* (lack of fear) and an underactive nervous system.

A MANTRA TO TELL YOURSELF: *"Slow, but safe."*

Reference:

The Anxiety and Phobia Workbook by Edmund J. Bourne, New Harbinger, 1995

See: fear of falling, fear of death, fear of not having control, fear of illness or pain, fear of embarrassment, fear of flying

Fear of Falling

basophobia (fear of falling)	*A major problem confining older people to their homes isn't falling itself, but fear of falling.* —JONATHAN HOWLAND, PROFESSOR
climacophobia (fear of falling down stairs)	OF SOCIAL AND BEHAVIORAL SCIENCES AT BOSTON UNIVERSITY

Characteristics: This is cautiousness or lack of confidence with walking, running or bicycling, especially among children, the elderly or the injured. People may avoid long walks, escalators, crowds or winter weather and become housebound. Some athletes may be cautious because of this condition. Elderly people often fear that constant falling will motivate others to institutionalize them.

Background: This fear may be partly physical and partly psychological, involving a potential loss of control or embarrassment. Even for a healthy person, tripping or falling is embarrassing. Falling can be caused by an illness, problems of balance, the inner ear or coordination, or overcompensating to deal with potential dizzy spells. The good news is that this fear makes us more cautious during the times we are physically vulnerable. At least one-third of people over 65 fall every year.

Strategies:

- If you feel you are cautious because of a physical problem, check with your physician. You may be afraid because of a condition you aren't consciously aware of, such as an issue with medication or an equilibrium problem. If you are undergoing therapy, check with your therapist to see if you need a brace, a walker, a cane or a wheelchair. Don't be embarrassed to get a handicap sticker for your vehicle.
- Develop confidence as you go along. You might have more control than you think; human balance is a wonderful resource if you trust it.
- If you have a history of falling but are in relatively good health, check out martial arts centers; they can teach you methods to break your fall that limit injury.

- If you are recovering from a sports injury, the best thing to do is get right back in the saddle to regain your confidence. Everyone falls occasionally; it's all about how you react to it.
- Note that when children fall on the playground while with their friends, they often bounce up laughing, even if they are bleeding. But when their parents are around, they often stay down crying. This fact can teach us not to tumble too easily into self-pity.
- A regular exercise routine, especially in a group, can raise your physical and mental confidence.
- Walk with a buddy. It will give you more confidence and a support system in case you do fall.
- For the elderly, try to keep active, especially after periods of immobilization. By moving around less, you will lose conditioning in muscles and balance, and that may increase your risk of falling. If you are a senior, you should install handrails on stairs, review all medications, increase lighting in your home, get routine checkups and wear sturdy shoes.

A MANTRA TO TELL YOURSELF: *"Slow, but sure."*

References:

The Complete Idiot's Guide to Conquering Fear and Anxiety by Sharon Heller, Alpha, 1999

Professor Jonathan Howland, jhowl@bu.edu

Subtle Fact:

A study revealed that people aged 63 to 90 who wear bifocals are twice as likely to fall as those wearing single-vision glasses. The bifocals decrease their ability to discern potential dangers on the ground when walking or climbing stairs.

See: fear of heights, fear of embarrassment, fear of illness or pain, fear of not having control, fear of aging, fear of flying

Fear of Travel

hodophobia (fear of
road travel)

The world is a book, and those who do not travel read only one page.
—St. Augustine

Characteristics: This is an uneasiness about leaving your area. Some people rarely stray from one place. Others are fearful of traveling in a car or on public transit or in a boat, or of crashing or being the victim of a terrorist attack. Some people don't like going on vacations because they are afraid of people or crowds.

Background: Most people have always had some anxiety about travel, which takes them away from the safety, friendly faces and routine of their home. Having a safety or comfort zone is natural. However, travel is educational and those who do little of it risk being narrow-minded and may stereotype people they've never met. They end up relying on rumors and media reports for their notions about life outside their little world. Following the tragedy of September 11, 2001, tourism suffered and flying became less popular.

Strategies:

- Try to identify what is behind your fear of travel—is it a physical or health fear, apprehension about strangers, fear of change or a general lack of confidence? Once you have identified it, you can work on improving those specific areas in your life.
- Research your trips well through travel agencies, the Internet, chambers of commerce, magazines and videos. Keep a list of important phone numbers, hotels and addresses in a small book. Leave your itinerary with others. Travel only with essentials, especially for air flight. And carry medical information and two forms of identification.
- Don't let finalizing all the details drive you crazy. There will always be one little thing you'll miss. As long as the big plans are taken care of, the small details don't matter so much.
- Don't stick to a rigid schedule; if you miss one stop, your strict plans could all fall apart. Leave some room for spontaneity.
- If you don't like crowds or heavy traffic, go on vacation after Labor Day, when you'll find less congestion and fewer tourists.

- Be wary of media reports about the dangers of big cities; the media tend to focus on the sensational. When I started extensive travel in the mid-1990s, I was surprised to find that most U.S. cities are safe as long as one avoids certain neighborhoods. At the same time, don't go out of your way to look like a target; when in a strange place, don't display jewelry or wealth or bring attention to yourself.
- Travel gives you a great chance to broaden your view of the world while seeing other cultures. People who never travel can be closed-minded and have distorted views. Allow yourself to try something new that you've seen in your travels, such as a way of dancing or a new dish.
- To gain some control in a new city, rent a car. Toronto writer Craig Daniels has anxiety about traveling, but partly overcomes it by driving, even in cities like Los Angeles and New York.
- Despite the fear of terrorism, most travel is safe and airports are more secure now than they were prior to 9/11. Accept that long lineups and security checks are there for your safety. Rather than whine about them, relax by taking deep breaths.

A MANTRA TO TELL YOURSELF: *"I'm competent enough to travel."*

References:

Frommer's Fly Safe, Fly Smart by Sasha Sagan, John Wiley and Sons, 2002

Traveler Beware by Kevin Coffey, Corporate Travel Safety, 1999

www.travel.com

> ### The Facts Are With You:
> Despite worries over terrorism, more than 600,000 people board planes each day in the United States.

See: fear of the unknown, fear of flying, fear of driving, fear of strangers, fear of people, fear of terrorism, fear of change, fear of weather, fear of panic attacks in public

Fear of Driving

amaxophobia (fear of riding in a car)

dystychiphobia (fear of accidents)

Being a friendly driver is contagious.
—LEON JAMES AND DIANE NAHL, IN THEIR BOOK *ROAD RAGE AND AGGRESSIVE DRIVING*

Characteristics: Driving or riding in a vehicle makes some people nervous or angry. Others get tense and grip the steering wheel so tightly, it's referred to as the "white knuckle" response. People may fear losing control of the vehicle, getting hurt in a crash, getting annoyed by traffic jams, or being on the receiving end of road rage from other drivers. Some fear criticism from backseat drivers.

Background: Hurtling along in a 2,000-pound vehicle can make anybody hesitant. There may be more emotions on the roads than ever before because of the increase in the number of vehicles and drivers, a variety of driving styles, more cell-phone use by drivers and the high levels of stress in our society. Driving is not exactly natural to humans—it's about as far away from the cave as you can get! Some people, feeling their territory has been invaded by another driver, act out behind the wheel because they feel anonymous in the confines of their vehicle. Others fear driving because they have physical or coordination problems. Because of the risk of accidents, a healthy respect for driving is good for everyone.

Strategies:

- Driving is safe if you have the proper mental, emotional and physical perspective. Before you start your ignition, put your mind in neutral and remind yourself that you just want to get from point A to point B safely and in a reasonable time.
- But don't be *too* relaxed. You want an arousal level just slightly above neutral for driving, to keep you alert to potential problems. If you are apathetic, your reaction time will decrease.
- Treat your car as your home away from home. You spend a lot of time in it. Make it quality time.
- If you worry about traffic jams, buy a quality sound system for your vehicle and listen to your favorite music. Careful, though, about fast music: research shows that drivers who listen to heavy metal have a higher rate of accidents. You might also consider

carpooling or taking public transit (I take a bus to work).

- Travel with someone you enjoy, or take an interest in your surroundings (but not too much) as you drive.
- Humor is a good outlet for reducing negative driving emotions. Laugh at other drivers who would otherwise annoy you.
- If another driver cuts you off or impedes you, don't take it personally: he or she doesn't even know you! Give other drivers the benefit of the doubt—they may be coming home from a funeral, on the way to an emergency or just having a bad day.
- If you become angry at another driver, don't try to punish him. Resist the urge to strike back. If you were outside your vehicle, you probably wouldn't even consider acting aggressively.
- After an accident, don't get emotional. Get all the details, such as everyone's name, license number and insurance. In certain jurisdictions, you may not have to report a minor accident to police.
- Keep your driving skills sharp, perhaps with a defensive driving course to keep you prepared for hazardous weather. Older drivers may want to be retested because reaction times can decrease with age. Be sure everyone in the car, including children, is wearing a seat belt.
- Keep your vehicle in top shape and remember to rotate your tires.

A MANTRA TO TELL YOURSELF: *"Shift into neutral."*

The Facts Are With You:

For every 100 million miles driven in North America, there is less than one fatality.

References:

Road Rage and Aggressive Driving by Leon James and Diane Nahl, Prometheus, 2000

LearningMethods, www.learningmethods.com

See: fear of not having control, fear of illness or pain, fear of invasion of territory or privacy, fear of death, fear of aging, fear of enclosed spaces, fear of travel, fear of oneself

Fear of Dogs and Animals

cynophobia (fear of dogs)	*Some are mad if they behold a cat.*
zoophobia (fear of animals)	—WILLIAM SHAKESPEARE, *THE MERCHANT OF VENICE*

Characteristics: Some people avoid certain places (such as relatives' homes) or refuse to have pets because of this fear. The most common fears are of dogs, cats, horses and (ugh!) rats. In extreme cases, some people won't leave their homes for fear of encountering a dog on the street. Others are allergic to animals. Some people fear that birds will attack them (ornithophobia). Others fear that rats and mice carry dirt and disease (suriphobia).

Background: As humans, it is natural for us to be at least cautious about other species. At one time, we were at the mercy of aggressive animals and harbored intense fear of them. Today, a certain amount of fearful respect for them remains.

Fear of animals is often developed in childhood through bad experiences or lack of contact. A United Kingdom study showed that 59 percent of people feared lizards and 51 percent feared rats. French emperor Napoleon Bonaparte was afraid of cats. Fear of animals tends to run in families.

Strategies:

- Gradually expose yourself to the animals that frighten you. Start by looking at pictures of them, then view them in pet stores or humane shelters, then go to the home of someone you know who has access to them. Consider buying yourself a pet that isn't too threatening.
- Try to understand your fear. Ask relatives if you had a bad experience with animals as a child, then tell yourself it's time to deal with it.
- If an aggressive dog lives in your area, politely report it to the owner; if that doesn't work, go to the humane society or the police.

- If an uncontrolled dog approaches you, ignore it, stand still and look off in the distance. Some animals will sense if you are afraid. If that doesn't work, point at it and shout. If it tries to bite, pick up something to use as a shield or weapon. If a dog is leashed, don't assume it's safe. Allow it to come close slowly and sniff you.
- Get bites immediately checked at a clinic or hospital. Get witnesses and the name and address of the owner.
- Remember that some of society's fears about animals are unfounded: bats don't deliberately try to entangle themselves in your hair, bee stings are rare, and horses are not waiting to kick you. And most domestic animals like humans.
- No matter how much he squeals, don't let a monkey take over the wheel of your car (from David Letterman's Top 10 list).
- Cats are usually docile, but don't allow a strange feline to come to you unless it approaches you in a friendly manner. Be aware of your allergies if you visit a home with a cat.

A MANTRA TO TELL YOURSELF: *"Most dogs have more bark than bite"* OR *"Caution without panic."*

Reference:

Understanding Dogs by Clinton R. Sanders, Temple University Press, 1999

See: fear of snakes and spiders, fear of illness or pain, fear of embarrassment, fear and stress in children, fear of not having control, fear of enclosed spaces

Fear of Snakes and Spiders

arachnophobia (fear of spiders)

ophidiophobia (fear of snakes)

We fear serpents with a destructive hatred purely and simply because we are taught so from childhood.
—NATURALIST W. H. HUDSON

Characteristics: With their unusual appearance and movements, it's hardly surprising many people are squeamish about spiders and snakes. People's anxiety, rapid breathing or nausea can be set off by just seeing a picture or thinking about the creatures. Some people are afraid they might bite. Others even fumigate their homes and are reluctant to eat outdoors or vacation in certain areas. Sufferers may think they will faint, but they rarely do.

Background: Humans have harbored a fear or distaste for spiders and snakes since prehistoric times, when they were out in the open and exposed to poisonous creatures. Today, most people with fear of snakes have had no direct contact with them, leading experts to believe this fear is innate. It can be activated for some people just from thinking about snakes or hearing stories about them.

Fear of snakes is often latent; children under two don't seem afraid, but the fear emerges at ages three or four. It can also be acquired through teaching; in the Bible, the devil appeared as a serpent. Fear of spiders is often caused by an incident in childhood. Some people's fear of snakes and spiders is actually a disgust they have for the creatures' appearance.

Strategies:

- Gradually expose yourself to spiders and snakes. First, look at pictures of them or simply think about them, but when doing so, do not see them as a threat to you. When you are ready to confront them, slowly approach a snake or spider. Maintain some distance while you relax in their presence. Give it as long as you want, and don't force yourself to conquer your fear all in one day.
- Educate yourself: most snakes and spiders are not poisonous. Unless provoked, most will not attack humans. Think of how ugly, huge and threatening *you* appear to *them*.

- Learn more about the characteristics and habits of snakes and spiders and their value to nature. They did not evolve just to give you the heebie-jeebies.
- If this fear inhibits your lifestyle, see a doctor or psychologist.
- In areas inhabited by rattlesnakes, wear long, loose pants and calf-high leather boots. Rattlesnakes are usually not aggressive toward people unless startled or cornered.
- To discourage snakes from moving into your yard or home:
  - Eliminate cool, damp areas; remove brush, tall grass and rock piles; and keep shrubbery away from foundations.
  - Control insect and rodent populations to dry up their food supply.
  - To keep them out of basements and crawl spaces, seal all openings with mortar, caulking compound or hardware cloth.

The Facts Are With You:

Of the 34,000 species of spiders, only 12 are poisonous.

References:

Snake: The Essential Visual Guide to the World of Snakes by Chris Mattison, DK Publishing, 1999

Phobias Cured
4838 Delridge Way SW, Suite A
Seattle, WA 98106
(206) 721-8751, keith@phobiascured.com

Dr. Brenda Wiederhold
Virtual Reality Medical Center
San Diego, CA 92121
1-866-822-VRMC, bwiederhold@vrphobia.com

See: fear of dogs and animals, fear of illness or pain, fear of death, fear of embarrassment, superstition or fear of the supernatural

Fear of Water and Swimming

hydrophobia (fear of swimming)	*People wish to learn to swim and at the same time to keep one foot on the ground.* —MARCEL PROUST
ablutophobia (fear of bathing)	

Characteristics: Many people are apprehensive about swimming in deep water, bathing or boating. Some people are embarrassed about their body shape and don't want to be seen in a bathing suit. Others feel a fatal attraction to rushing water, as Marilyn Monroe did while filming the movie *Niagara*.

Background: In our evolution, we've become land creatures more than sea creatures. Some experts believe that the fear of water can be linked to our ancestors the monkeys, who were poor swimmers. Some people fear water after they are traumatized by being involved in or seeing a near-drowning. People afraid of deep water often fear loss of breathing and physical control; in some cases, they fear water creatures or seasickness. Frederick the Great, King of Prussia, was so fearful of water that he rarely washed. Actress Natalie Wood, who was afraid of the water, drowned.

Despite the many people who fear water, it is worth noting that humans can easily get used to water; babies can learn to swim at age three. Many people who seek help for this fear respond well to treatment, and they often even manage to overcome traumatic experiences involving water.

Strategies:

- With regard to swimming, understand that the water is buoyant and ready to keep you up, no matter what your weight is. It is almost impossible to sink if you relax. Proceed slowly. Get used to the water by first dangling your feet from the side while breathing deeply and trying to relax. Consider using a flotation device.
- Take swimming lessons. When you have mastered a technique, it will give you confidence and allow you to get out of a situation if you panic. Or go in the water with a buddy.
- Tips for learning to swim: try a stroke easiest for you, perhaps the breast stroke, where you don't have to put your face in the

water; don't anticipate the worst; keep your mind on your technique, not the possibility of sinking and your proximity to the wall; don't panic; remember that you have more time to react than you think; don't take this book in the water.

- Remember that water is our friend—without it, we wouldn't be here. We can float in water and see and hold our breath under water. Our ears even close instantaneously when we jump in. The human body is made up mostly of fluids, and we came from water in our mother's womb.
- For babies afraid of getting their hair washed, be careful to keep water out of their eyes and ears. Wash with water from a glass rather than from faucets, which can scare some babies. Try to distract the child with a game or music.
- For seasickness, pills and acupressure wristbands show results.
- If you worry about how you look in a bathing suit, remember that others are worried about how they look to *you*.
- If you have a home swimming pool, always have a latched gate to protect children and keep appropriate safety devices on hand. Most child drownings occur in swimming pools.

A MANTRA TO TELL YOURSELF: *"I won't sink."*

Author's Two Cents:

I have been apprehensive about swimming all my life, and I used to think I was a *sinker*. That sensation of water going up my nose was awful. At age 49, I finally taught myself to swim in a condo pool; two years later, I helped to save my wife from drowning by channeling the energy of my fear into my swimming stroke in order to reach her.

Reference:

Researcher Sheri Stein, Sheristein@hotmail.com

See: fear of death, fear of not having control, fear of embarrassment, fear of falling, fear of panic attacks in public, fear of your appearance

Fear of Loud Noises

acousticophobia or ligyrophobia (fear of sounds)

When I tried to lead a session in science, some of the students raised their voices. I had to raise my volume and soon it was a shouting match and I couldn't stand the noise. I hit the panic button. Now I have to avoid those situations. —AN ALBERTA HIGH SCHOOL TEACHER

Characteristics: Some people fear machines, sonic booms, popping balloons, emergency sirens, thunderstorms and even vacuum cleaners because of their noise. They might avoid car races, airports, factories and the outdoors. Others fear music (musicophobia), partly for its noise, or rock music for its brashness and rebelliousness. Victims of car crashes may remember only the noise and may subsequently fear loud noises.

Background: This is one of the basic genetic fears. It serves a useful purpose because an unexpected noise could mean an emergency situation. All animals react sharply to loud noises. Soldiers or accident victims may respond to sounds that remind them of trauma. Children may fear vacuum cleaners, saws and emergency sirens. This fear could also be the result of sensitive hearing. Many people recoil at the sound of their car horn going off (especially accidentally) in a parking lot. Others fear the embarrassment of their reaction because they see that others are just laughing at the noise.

Strategies:
- If you live in a high-noise area, try to anticipate loud noises from train whistles, ship horns and sirens.
- Desensitize yourself to noises by going to airports, factories, truck stops or fireworks displays. Make a tape recording of the noises that frighten you and replay them at various levels. Consider using earplugs in factories and at rock concerts.
- Most noises in Western society are controlled; if you hear an unusually loud noise, there may be a reason to become alert. Perhaps something has exploded or is collapsing. Check the immediate area.

- Telephones can sound alarming because of the possibility that bad news might wait at the other end. Soften the phone's ringing sound.
- Noises can not only be frightening, they can also be serious distractions when you are trying to concentrate on something. Learn to respect the sounds and noises you hear and try to tune out those that distract you unnecessarily. You will want to be in tune with your child's cry, even though at times it may be unnecessary and annoying. Baseball players are famous for tuning out the screams of enemy spectators while focusing on hitting a 90-mile-per-hour fastball. Golf is often a game of distractions, but Tiger Woods' father taught him to ignore them by deliberately shouting when he was about to swing.
- If you have new neighbors, tell them politely if loud music or noise bothers you. As a last resort, call the police.
- If you always jump at noises, examine your hearing or your anxiety levels and the pressures on you in daily life.
- Move into a condo with thick walls.
- If you have a pet with sensitive hearing, expose it to low-volume noises while giving praise or food, then gradually increase the noise level. Provide a safe place for the pet to retreat to when it hears a frightening noise.

A MANTRA TO TELL YOURSELF: *"Noises won't hurt me."*

Reference:

Facing Fears by Ada P. Kahn and Ronald M. Doctor, Checkmark, 2000

See: fear of the unknown, fear of disorder or untidiness, fear of death, fear of illness or pain, fear of weather, fear of crowds

Fear of Weather

astrapophobia (fear of thunderstorms)

chionophobia (fear of snow)

Not even God can hit a 1-iron. —GOLFER LEE TREVINO AFTER BEING STRUCK BY LIGHTNING

Characteristics: This is the preoccupation with weather and weather forecasts, not so much because of health concerns but with regard to driving, property damage, travel and outdoor activities. Some people feel a loss of control in storms, yet others can be exhilarated by them. Many seniors retire to the south to escape northern winters.

Background: Primitive people were so frightened of severe weather that they thought it was evil or sent by the gods to punish them. Many cultures made a god of the sun, which heavily influences the weather. Even today, fear of weather is somewhat healthy because weather can be unpredictable. In some cultures today, the end of the world is supposed to come with a snowbound winter. Eight million Americans suffer from inordinate fear of storms and other weather events.

Strategies:

- Put things in perspective; these days, although weather can change quickly, severe surprise weather is rare. It can usually be predicted and announced over the media. Listen to a radio or television station that has periodic and reliable weather reports.
- Convince yourself that you can tolerate the weather, because, in most cases, you can. Fear of weather can be like fear of terrorism; in both cases, people's fears are often disproportionate to the actual threat. How many people in your area are injured by weather? You're more apt to get a stress-related illness from worry.
- Use common sense in exposing yourself to the elements. Prepare for the sun with sun block, and for rain and snow with a jacket. In cold weather, dress in layers and wear a hat. If you use a cane, buy one with an ice pick for a tip.

- Keep your vehicle in top condition, and make sure it has the right equipment. While driving, use caution without dallying. Some people take defensive driving courses, which are good preparation for heavy weather conditions. In winter, keep road salt and a shovel in the back of your vehicle.

- Tips for getting caught in a thunderstorm: if you can hear thunder, you are close enough to the storm to be struck by lightning. Find shelter in a building or car and keep the windows closed. Go to a low-lying place away from trees, poles and metal objects. Squat low to the ground, but do not lie flat. If caught in the woods, take shelter under shorter trees. If boating or swimming, get to shore immediately.

- If you are inside during a thunderstorm, unplug appliances and turn off the air conditioner. Telephone lines and metal pipes can conduct electricity. Avoid using running water. Draw blinds and shades over windows to prevent glass from shattering due to objects blown by the wind.

- Buy a nature CD with sounds of storms and winds and play it frequently. Go to a local science center that has simulations of weather patterns and get to understand them.

A MANTRA TO TELL YOURSELF: *"I can't control the weather, but I can control my reaction to it."*

Reference:

The Weather Network, www.theweathernetwork.com

See: fear of not having control, fear of death, fear of illness or pain, fear of the unknown, fear of loud noises, fear of falling, fear of travel, fear of driving

Fears of the Ego

Fear of Embarrassment

erythrophobia (fear of blushing)

tremophobia (fear of trembling)

We are terrified of being terrified.
—Friedrich Nietzsche

Characteristics: People with this condition worry about becoming self-conscious, blushing, stuttering, trembling, freezing under pressure, passing wind in a group of people or being stared at or singled out, perhaps after making a mistake. Serious sufferers may avoid meetings, crowds, criticism or compliments, leadership roles, emotional circumstances or potentially embarrassing situations.

Background: Even the most confident people get embarrassed occasionally. We all like to feel we are in control. Everybody tries to protect their ego, pride or reputation to some extent, but that isn't always possible. Some people get embarrassed easily because they are too sensitive or lack confidence. Blushing is a recent development in human evolution, linked to the development of our brains, self-consciousness and pride. Animals never blush. "Man is the only animal that blushes," said Mark Twain. "Or needs to." Fear of blushing is more common in women than men, yet research shows that those who fear blushing actually do not blush more than people who don't worry about it.

Strategies:

- Try to establish how easily you get embarrassed. Do you get flushed easily in social situations? Do you hesitate to have your photograph taken, to ask for directions when you're lost, to speak your piece in a group or to show your emotions? Do you feel that people are always watching you? This is called the spotlight effect, but research has shown that most people are not watching others to judge them.
- Don't fear making errors or being human; others don't care as much as you do if you have goofed up. If you make a big deal out of your mistakes, you'll make more of them and bring on more embarrassment.

- Accept that you will get embarrassed from time to time, and that it may even be good for you. Laugh it off.
- Learn to raise your panic or discomfort threshold by ridiculing yourself while alone. Say aloud to yourself, "You dummy, how can you be like that?" See how you react, and learn not to take barbs personally.
- Practice embarrassment by bringing attention to yourself in a crowd or by admitting a weakness. On the golf course, deliberately dribble the ball off the tee and smile it off. In each case, watch not only your reaction, but the reaction of others. You will quickly learn that people don't pay that much attention to you, and that you will survive your embarrassment.
- Keep your expectations about yourself reasonable, and don't keep activating your nervous system by defending your weaknesses. We all have our weak spots. Be humble without being self-deprecating. This attitude can take a lot of the pressure off and reduce the situations in which you may feel embarrassed.
- If you get embarrassed easily, you might have to consider the state of your confidence and self-esteem. Talk to someone about it. Consider seeing a therapist.
- If you get embarrassed while you are alone about something that happened when you were with people, chances are that you did something you shouldn't have. For example, if someone said in passing that you might have cheated or "fudged" in the board game Scrabble and you still feel embarrassed when thinking about this later on, chances are you really did cheat.

A MANTRA TO TELL YOURSELF: *"Who cares?"*

Reference:

Beyond Shyness: How to Conquer Social Anxieties by Jonathan Berent, Simon and Schuster, 1993

See: fear of not having control, fear of making mistakes, fear of what others think, fear of getting a compliment, fear of showing emotions, fear of public speaking, fear of singing or dancing

Fear of Failure

atychiphobia (fear of failure)

atelophobia (fear of imperfection)

Failure is just another opportunity to more intelligently begin again.
—HENRY FORD

Characteristics: This widespread fear involves an insecurity or nervousness about a task or a relationship through fear of failing at it. It can lead to worry, indecisiveness, tension, poor productivity and problems in relationships, especially during a pressure situation.

Background: Fear of failure can improve effort and productivity, yet it can also be the parent of many orphans: fear of rejection, fear of loss of control, fear of making mistakes and fear of loss of self-esteem and status. Perfectionists are particularly susceptible. This fear may be learned in the early years, particularly if a person is hounded into doing well or is constantly ridiculed. It can also breed if a person doesn't get recognition for successes or comfort for failures. Some people with obsessive-compulsive disorder have a fear of not doing everything right. However, studies show that failure can actually breed success if it is accepted and viewed in a positive way. Getting something right the first time can actually inhibit creativity!

Strategies:

- If you fear failure at a certain task, it may be simply that you don't have the required physical, mental or emotional resources to meet the challenges and pressures of that task. Upgrade yourself and you'll increase your confidence and expertise.
- Examine whether you are afraid of failing or whether you are really afraid of something else. For instance, your intense anxiety about an upcoming test or job interview may actually be rooted in fear of what your parents or a close friend will think if you don't succeed.
- If you are afraid of failing in *many* areas, examine your ego or confidence issues: are you concerned too much about what others will think if you fail?

- Put your fear into the preparation for a task, not in the task itself. Then focus on the task, your skills and the solution, not on the fear. For example, if you are afraid of an upcoming mathematics test at school, study hard, but when the big day comes, trust yourself and focus on the answers, not on the possibility that you might fail.
- Don't be so hard on yourself. Do you expect to be perfect? Mistakes are not terrible. Everybody makes them. Get on with life. Laugh at yourself without demeaning yourself.
- If you often procrastinate, examine the possibility that, rather than simply being lazy, you might be afraid of failing.
- Don't let failure sap your motivation. Winston Churchill said that success "is going from failure to failure without loss of enthusiasm."
- Up to 70 percent of successful people express feelings of failure, sometimes believing they are fakes or imposters, but this feeling increases their drive to succeed and to prove that they are legitimate.
- If you fail at something important, like an exam or a work project, do something pleasurable to distract yourself from the trouble. Studies show that if you think about failures and problems in a negative way, you come up with fewer solutions.
- In the big picture, if you work hard enough and have enough patience, it is difficult to fail in North America.
- So what if you flunk from time to time? You should only regret failing if you don't get something out of it.

A MANTRA TO TELL YOURSELF: *"Most of the time, I'll succeed."*

Reference:

Overcoming Social Anxiety and Shyness by Gillian Butler, New York University, 1999

See: fear of making mistakes, fear of criticism, fear of rejection, fear of what others think, fear of embarrassment, fear of not having control, fear of taking chances, fear of success or happiness, fear of competition, fear of choking in sports, fear of exams

Fear of Making Mistakes

| *atelophobia* (fear of imperfection) | *Inside of a ring or out, ain't nothing wrong with going down. It's staying down that's wrong.* —MUHAMMAD ALI |

Characteristics: This condition involves being hesitant about a job at work, school or home, or about issues in one's personal life, for fear of making a goof of oneself. It can create self-doubt and a reluctance to take chances, and it can prevent people from setting and achieving goals. It can also cause shaking, which would be especially bad for people who work with their hands or fingers.

Background: Fear of making mistakes is the short-term manifestation of the deeper problem of fear of failure. Fear of making mistakes can have its roots in insecurity and low self-esteem. Because society tends to be judgmental, we fear that mistakes will bring us criticism or negative evaluation. Fear of accidents may lead people to hesitate, which can actually make them more susceptible to accidents. On the plus side, fear of making mistakes can motivate us to organize our work and to make a better effort. This fear is often rampant in perfectionists.

Strategies:
- Don't enter a project expecting a guarantee that you will not make mistakes. That is an unrealistic attitude, perhaps even an arrogant one. If you think that way, you'll likely put too much pressure on yourself and make more mistakes.
- If you are involved with an important or high-pressure project, stop worrying and use your talents and training to focus on the task. This mindset will result in fewer errors.
- If you make a serious error, don't use the "I'm not perfect" excuse. If you do, it makes you even less perfect.
- Guess what? The last thing another person wants to see is someone who is perfect. People who are "too perfect" tend to be dull, and the rest of us find them intimidating. Perfection won't bring you many friends.
- Unsuccessful people are those who, fearing mistakes, don't go for the gold. It's okay to make blunders; in 2001, Barry Bonds

hit a record 73 homers but he struck out 93 times! ("Never let the fear of striking out get in your way," said another home-run slugger, Babe Ruth).

- Learn from your mistakes or you may repeat them. Give yourself credit when you bounce back.
- Try to establish whether or not you are a perfectionist by listing the number of times you become anxious over control issues, and why. If you establish that you are a perfectionist, you may want to back off a little. Perfectionism is the fear of being human. Being good is good enough for now. Says clinical psychologist Monica A. Frank, "As you overcome your fear of making mistakes, you will be able to take risks, which allows a person to be successful in career and personal relationships."

What to Tell Children about Mistakes:

- Tell your children it's okay to make mistakes.
- Admit your own mistakes and show how you can learn from them.
- Talk about mistakes made by famous media figures.
- Help your children to learn positive self-talk and to label the mistake—not themselves—as the problem.
- Develop a strategy for dealing with the next mistake.

References:

Behavioral Consultants P.C.
13230 Tesson Ferry Rd.
St. Louis, MO 63128
(314) 843-0080
Monica Frank, Monica@behavioralconsults.com

Education consultant Michele Borba, Michele@moralintelligence.com

See: fear of failure, fear of taking chances, fear of criticism, fear of not having control, fear of the unknown

Fear of Success or Happiness

cherophobia (fear of happiness)	*God would never let me be a success. He'd kill me first.* —GEORGE COSTANZA ON *SEINFELD*, AFTER HEARING THAT HIS PROJECT HAD BEEN UNEXPECTEDLY BOUGHT BY NBC TV
successophobia (fear of success)	
euphobia (fear of hearing good news)	**Characteristics:** This condition is akin to fear of failure, but not as common and certainly more subtle and harder to detect

in a person. Some people don't realize there is such a thing as fear of success; in a way, it sounds ridiculous. Who wouldn't want to succeed? Yet some people hold back in their job, at school or in social settings for fear of becoming more successful or happy. Others fear having pleasurable feelings (a condition known as hedonophobia).

Background: Some people fear success because they think it might set them up for failure at a higher level. Some are afraid of the trappings of success because they have seen how it has changed others. People may also fear that if they are successful, fate will come crashing down on them shortly thereafter, perhaps because they harbor a feeling that they don't deserve success. Others may feel guilty for achieving happiness when they feel that others don't get the opportunity that they have had. It's a frightening thought sometimes, but nature doesn't want us to be happy as much as it wants us simply to survive. Talk about being complicated beings with a complex background and history!

Strategies:

- If you feel some guilt over success or happiness, try to establish where it comes from and how to change it. Is there an inner voice in your head that keeps telling you that you are not good enough? Ask it for some evidence. Who's to say that you're not worthy of success or contentment? You? If you feel this way, you should heed the words of ex-South African president Nelson Mandela: "We ask ourselves—who am I to be brilliant, gorgeous, talented and fabulous? Actually, who are you not to be?"

- Don't easily dismiss the possibility that your failure may be related to worry about succeeding. It wasn't until golfer Ian Leggatt realized he might be suffering from the fear of success that he finally won his first PGA Tour event at age 36 in 2002.
- Put things into perspective. With the right amount of time and effort, there's no reason you can't reach success.
- Don't intentionally set yourself up for a setback, or give a mediocre performance in a job, just to avoid the agony that you feel may be ahead once you succeed.
- There is no "cosmic" fate that will hit you with failure as soon as you succeed. But if you think there is, you could create a self-fulfilling prophecy.
- Life is short enough as it is; allow it to be sweet when the chance arises. Go for the gold. Other people might want the opportunity you have, but never get it. However, don't feel guilty for others who don't have the opportunity you have; just make the most of your chance.
- If you worry that success will bring more attention to you, develop your people skills so that you will be better prepared to handle it.
- Let's turn this scenario around. It's funny, but when things are going badly, we don't suddenly expect the best to happen, do we? (Maybe we should.)
- The actual definition of happiness may scare people. Happiness is a long-term achievement involving work, sacrifice and love. If you think of it as a short-term feeling, you might be more prone to fearing it will slip through your fingers.

Reference:

Toward a Psychology of Being by Abraham Maslow, John Wiley and Sons, 1998. Maslow makes this point: "We fear our highest possibility, as well as our lowest one. We are generally afraid to become that which we can glimpse in our most perfect moments."

See: fear of failure, fear of taking chances, fear of criticism, fear of embarrassment, fear of what others think, fear of asking for a raise or promotion, fear of getting a compliment

Fear of Criticism

enissophobia (fear of criticism)

criticophobia (fear of critics)

Find the grain of truth in criticism—chew it and swallow it. —DON SUTTON

Characteristics: Fear of critical remarks from others affects us all from time to time. Some people allow stinging criticism to stay in their system for days or weeks, like a virus. Fear of evaluation or criticism leads some people to take fewer chances in everything from their job to their landscaping at home to their choice of clothes. Many people get defensive when they believe they are going to be criticized.

Background: By nature, we all have defense mechanisms set up to protect our psyche from harm. In some people, these mechanisms act like armor that tries to repel everything that comes its way. Because many people are negative and reluctant to balance criticism with praise, we have learned to brace ourselves for the worst. But sometimes, this fear is caused by fear of the truth and all that truth represents, including change. We can make criticism work for us if we accept it as a helpful tool for self-improvement. It's human nature to be more critical of others than we are of ourselves; for example, we may hold a higher standard for a neighbor to be friendly with us than we have for ourselves to be friendly with him.

Strategies:

- Learn to distinguish between destructive and constructive criticism. The first thing to say to your critic is "Thank you." Then step back and analyze the remark. Accepting criticism can build character, encourage growth and keep the ego in check.
- Don't take everything personally. Most criticism is not aimed at you as a person. Look on all criticism as helpful in one way or another. It can tell you what you need to improve, or it can tell you about the source of the criticism. Some critics are people who can't deliver the goods themselves. They may be unhappy and looking to release their frustration on someone else. But if their criticism is about an important subject, get a second opinion.

- Don't adopt a defensive attitude; you'll only *invite* criticism that way.
- If you strike back at a critic out of reflex, examine your attitude and defense mechanisms. Are you defending yourself for the sake of it? Will the truth suffer just to protect your pride or reputation? On the other hand, if you accept all criticism without dialogue, perhaps you are trying to please others too much.
- Get used to hearing critical phrases like: "I didn't like the way you did that," or "I thought your idea was not productive." When no one is around, criticize yourself out loud. "Boy, you goofed on that one!" Or ask people you feel comfortable with what they'd like to see changed. Your ego is like your immune system: it needs exposure to criticism to get stronger and more resilient.
- The fear or anger you feel when you are criticized becomes hormonal energy. It feels negative, but you can channel it into your work or other parts of your life.
- Understand that the more successful you become, the more you'll be criticized. Criticism is a sign that you and your ideas have a stage.
- If you are criticizing others, ask for their input first; this will minimize their defensiveness. (Much of the time when we are being criticized, we are thinking of our rebuttals even before the critic is finished.)
- Try to make your criticism constructive, emphasizing what the recipient is doing, or can do, rather than what he did.

A MANTRA TO TELL YOURSELF: *"What I am afraid of?"* OR *"Can I use this?"*

References:

Elbert Hubbard's Scrap Book by Elbert Hubbard, Firebird Press, 1999. He writes, "To avoid criticism, do nothing, say nothing, be nothing."

The Power of Positive Criticism by Hendrie Weisinger, Anacom, 2000

See: fear of rejection, fear of what others think, fear of embarrassment, fear of failure, fear of showing emotions, fear of taking chances, fear of not being loved, fear of singing or dancing

Fear of Rejection

athazagoraphobia
(fear of being
ignored)

What doesn't kill you makes you stronger.
—Friedrich Nietzsche

Characteristics: Fear of rejection is deeper and often more painful than fear of criticism—it can be viewed as the fear of being left out of something. This can lead to a self-degradation, shyness and even avoidance of social situations. A person may hold back for fear of not getting approval. When you feel rejected by someone close to you, it can really wound your soul.

Background: It's human nature to want to be accepted and liked. Extreme cases could come from childhood rejection or abandonment. People who are very sensitive and people with low self-esteem often suffer from harsh fear of rejection.

Strategies:
* Keep things in perspective. Criticism of your work might be meant as a simple critique with constructive components, not as all-out rejection of you or your work.
* Keep plugging along. A young Elvis Presley was told he couldn't sing by his high school teacher and by the club manager at his first performance, who told him to go back to truck driving. Good thing he didn't!
* Don't let rejection from someone else define you as a person; you're worth more than that. At the same time, do accept your occasional failures as part of who you are—an imperfect being trying to get better.
* If you want to get some experience with rejection and thus develop a thicker skin, get into a job or volunteer position in which you have to make cold calls. People may be gruff with you and even hang up the telephone, but you will learn not to take it personally.
* If you avoid a situation for fear of rejection, you may have regrets later.

- If rejection results in self-pity, you may have self-esteem issues to examine and deal with.
- Gaining approval and acceptance for your skills or your personality is often a journey and a risk. Some people will like you, others won't. Learn about yourself from both.
- Psychotherapist Harry Frith-Smith was not close to his father and developed a type of emotional hole as a result. He attempts to close this hole by playing pickup basketball and poker, by singing in a jazz band and by helping others with their own emotional holes.
- Remember that if someone wholeheartedly rejects you, the issues may be about them, not about you. Or it may be about both of you.

A MANTRA TO TELL YOURSELF: *"Sticks and stones will break my bones, but names will never hurt me."*

Author's Two Cents:

Before my first book was published in 1999, I had received approximately 2,500 consecutive rejections over 32 years. The first 100 were the toughest to take, so I used them to wallpaper my office.

Reference:

Friedrich Nietzsche, The Man and His Philosophy by R. J. Hollingdale, Cambridge University Press, 1999

See: fear of criticism, fear of what others think, fear of failure, fear of taking chances, fear of dating, fear of not being loved

Fear of Getting a Compliment

doxophobia (fear of receiving praise)

I can live for two months on a good compliment. —MARK TWAIN

Characteristics: Some people worry about getting into situations in which they could receive a compliment. Although this condition may be subconscious, it may prevent them from trying hard for fear of getting a compliment and subsequently becoming self-conscious about it. It may also cause them to avoid award ceremonies at work for fear of embarrassment or blushing.

Background: If this sounds a lot like the fear of success, it is. Many people receive a compliment and don't know how to respond. We live in a fairly judgmental society and so we are perhaps more used to getting barbs than bouquets. We've also been conditioned to be modest. Some people fear that receiving a compliment at work might lead to higher expectations for them in the future. Nonetheless, a compliment can give a person a warm, motivating feeling when it's accepted properly. If it is not accepted with grace, the giver might not come back with a future compliment, and thus the circle of self-doubt would continue.

Strategies:

- Get used to the sound of your name being exalted. Compliment yourself aloud when no one's around: "You did a good job with that." Give yourself a pat on the back and don't feel sheepish about it. Smile and show emotion. Then rehearse a possible scenario whereby you respond to the compliment with a thank you and keep the conversation going for a while.
- When a person gives you a compliment, accept it without conditions and without downplaying it. If you say you don't deserve it, you may come across as falsely modest. Receiving praise is a bit like receiving a gift—you should accept it with good grace. If it sounds sincere, you may also want to return a compliment, perhaps by saying: "Coming from you, that's a real compliment."

- If others are entitled to your compliment in some way, name them, and explain why. If the praise comes from your superior at work, thank him or her for putting you in a position to succeed in the first place.
- Receiving and giving compliments are ways to develop greater rapport with people. Give compliments to others. Be sincere and specific, but if they don't respond, don't get irritated or act coldly. Perhaps they have inferiority—or even superiority—issues.
- Be prepared to face the fact that you might lack confidence or even have an inferiority complex. Talk to someone you trust about it. Why shouldn't you be worthy of praise? On the other hand, you might have a superior attitude. Perhaps you feel you should receive more praise than you get, or you may feel that the person giving you praise is not worthy of you.
- If you still feel uneasy getting praise, tell that little nagging voice in your head to please keep quiet. Then give it a compliment: "Thanks, anyway, for keeping me in mind."

Reference:

Beyond Shyness by Jonathan Berent, Fireside, 1993

See: fear of embarrassment, fear of criticism, fear of success or happiness, fear of showing emotions, fear of invasion of territory or privacy

Fear of What Others Think

allodoxaphobia (fear of others' opinions)

scopophobia (fear of being looked at)

ego defense (author's definition of how we protect our ego)

In this case, the truth will set you free.
—PSYCHOLOGIST KENNETH SAVITSKY, COMMENTING ON RESEARCH SHOWING THAT FAR FEWER PEOPLE NOTICE OUR MISTAKES OR JUDGE US HARSHLY THAN WE BELIEVE

Characteristics: It is common to feel insecure about how others view you or your work or to feel inadequate in others' eyes. This condition can result in poor performance and can even prevent people from seeking jobs or realizing their dreams. Some people are afraid of being stared at. Some people who worry intensely about what others think can develop a phobia of being imperfect. But this fear can also spur a person to greater heights.

Background: As social creatures, it's natural for us to seek the approval and acceptance of others. A desire to impress someone can be a sign of a healthy relationship, but becomes destructive when it is exaggerated. Those who want to impress others too much often come from homes in which they were not loved enough. This fear can be a good motivator; research shows that people try harder when others are watching—even joggers, who speed up when they believe people are observing them.

Protecting our ego has become important to us in a competitive society. Defending our ego or pride sets off the same fear defense system that is activated by physical threats. Our nervous system has problems differentiating the two; in each case, powerful hormones and energies are released to help us deal with threats. Many high achievers perform incredible feats because they are overcompensating for lack of attention as children. On a smaller scale, fear of what others think motivates us to take care of ourselves and acquire social graces; if we didn't care, many of us would stay in our pajamas all day or pick our noses without guilt.

Strategies:

- Recognize that it is important what *some* people think of you, such as your boss or the people you care about, but it is unimportant what most others think, particularly about trivial issues.

- This is worth repeating: be aware that your nervous system has a hard time distinguishing between a physical threat and a threat to your ego. If you worry too much about others' opinions, you can become anxious and driven by adrenaline.
- If you are trying too hard to please others, examine your motives and attitudes, perhaps even your values. If you want revenge on those who doubt you, you might be able to use this emotional drive productively. "I wanted revenge," actor Anthony Hopkins once said. "I wanted to dance on the graves of a few people who made me unhappy. It's a pretty infantile way to go through life—I'll show them—but I've done it, and I've got more than I ever dreamed of."
- If you do make mistakes, understand that most people probably don't care that much. As psychologist Kenneth Savitsky points out, "You can't completely eliminate the embarrassment you feel when you commit a faux pas, but it helps to know how much you're exaggerating this impact."
- In the end, ask yourself, "Am I going to live my life according to other people's expectations or my own?"
- Make sure you pay attention to your own needs.
- As with many other fears in this section, it's a good idea to practice embarrassing scenarios. You will get used to not caring what others think about inconsequential situations.
- There will always be people who don't like you. If you try to please everyone, you might end up pleasing fewer people, perhaps even no one.
- If you want to impress someone with a job, prepare for it well, and don't make your expectations too high or you might become overly nervous.

A MANTRA TO TELL YOURSELF: *"People's opinions of me are not that important."*

References:

Pressure Golf by Michael Clarkson, Raincoast, 2003

Six Pillars of Self-Esteem by Nathaniel Branden, Bantam, 1994

See: fear of criticism, fear of failure, fear of making mistakes, fear of rejection, fear of not being loved, fear of people, fear of public speaking, fear of embarrassment, fear of showing emotions, fear of what friends think

Fear of Invasion of Territory or Privacy

aphenphosmphobia
(fear of being
touched)

Good fences make good neighbors.
—ROBERT FROST

Characteristics: This condition relates to defending one's territory at work, at home or in public. People with this fear may protect their privacy or personal space, if only through body language. Its effects are often seen in traffic; drivers, believing they are anonymous, are more likely to act out against other drivers who have cut them off. Some people get fidgety standing in a line when they feel someone is gaining an advantage over them. Many nonsmokers get irritated if smokers bother them with second-hand smoke.

Background: Defending territory is a strong and deep-seated animal instinct with roots in our Stone Age past. In our civilized society, many people subdue this instinct until a part of their lives they hold dear is threatened. For example, I know a quiet, mild-mannered man who sometimes acts out in his car because he believes other drivers have entered his personal space. A man whose golf is important to him may get angry if someone in another foursome breaks etiquette and hits the ball near him. Fear of being touched may relate to sexual fears. In many situations, it is difficult to establish where one person's rights begin and another's end.

Strategies:

- Examine the boundaries you establish in your life. Are you too protective in some areas and not enough in others? Are you defending your ego too much? Are you too touchy about criticism?
- Set your borders firmly and fairly, then stand up for the rights you have established.
- Don't protect your rights and territory at the expense of others or at the expense of truth.

- Allow people inside your private space once in a while, if only to learn to become less defensive about it. By *intentionally* letting people go ahead of you in a shop or while driving on the highway, even if they don't have the right of way, you might raise your threshold for tolerance. You should also raise your tolerance levels for others who may be from different backgrounds and who may not share your beliefs about territorial boundaries.
- If someone "trespasses" on your realm at work, don't take it personally; try to find a polite way to let them know. Shift your mindset to neutral and evaluate the situation as objectively as possible.
- If you find yourself overreacting to others in traffic or perhaps in an amateur sports competition, it could mean that you don't have enough control in other areas of your life. While playing a pickup game of basketball at the YMCA, a man started a fight over a foul call. He later apologized, explaining that he felt he was letting someone control him in a personal relationship.
- After all the above has been said, psychologists add that it's okay and even healthy to keep a private space for yourself, even if you are happily married. It could be a quiet time each day or a hobby or a trip that you sometimes take by yourself.

Reference:

Diagonally-Parked in a Parallel Universe: Working Through Social Anxiety by Signe A. Dayhoff, Effectiveness-Plus, 2000

See: fear of other races, fear of strangers, fear of not having control, fear of intimacy or love, sexual fears, fear of driving, fear of solicitors and telemarketers

Fear of Losing Status

kakorrhaphiophobia
(fear of defeat)

I don't want that *dress.* —A SOCIALITE TO
A DRESSMAKER, COMMENTING ON A WARDROBE
DESIGNED FOR ANOTHER WOMAN WHOM SHE FELT
WAS BENEATH HER

Characteristics: This condition involves anxiety about one's status. For a variety of reasons, people may be reluctant to give up their level of power or achievement or their level of financial, academic, social or career status. When people feel that they are losing status, they may become angry, withdrawn or depressed; conversely, they may become highly motivated and focused. Some people may become rude or disrespectful toward others they believe are not in their class.

Background: Wherever pecking orders or class systems (even subtle ones) are in place, this fear will be important, if sometimes subconscious and unspoken. The baby boomer generation may suffer from this fear more than its predecessors did. In a society in which competition is a driving force, pride is often at stake. Whenever a standard has been set, people find it difficult to drop below it. It's natural for people to hang onto what they have; few people willingly accept a lower quality of housing or food, and few people want to give up travel and vacations. This fear has its benefits, though, and keeps people on their toes, striving to reach another level, or at least to stay on the level they've reached.

Strategies:
- Consider the areas in which you might be reluctant to give up your status, and think about whether or not that's healthy for you and those around you. You might not want to give up your position at work because this would lead to a loss of power or salary, yet you might be willing to relinquish authority in a relationship if you are smothering the other person.
- Make a list of your priorities and keep them in perspective. There's not necessarily anything wrong with congratulating yourself if you've worked hard to give your family the best and encouraged them to remain humble and appreciative about it.

A certain amount of pride can be healthy, but do you keep a lot of status symbols—shiny cars, walls filled with plaques, bumper stickers saying "My child is an honor student"— merely to impress people?

- Don't overwork yourself just to keep up with the Joneses. Your desire for status may be unhealthy if it makes you distressed, tired and run down, or if it makes you neglect your friends and family.

- Talk to people who have gone through the process of gaining wealth and status, and who have accepted a leveling or even a decline in these as they got older. You can learn from them.

- Don't be afraid to swallow humble pie once in a while. It can make you grow as a person. To keep your head from swelling, take a volunteer job, perhaps in a soup kitchen. You are no better than anyone else; you may have had a different upbringing and support system, more resilient genes, and a different set of opportunities and talents that allowed you to be more productive than others.

- Examine your issues of ego and self-consciousness. What is your reaction when your neighbor parks his new SUV near your five-year-old sedan? Does materialism play too large a role in defining who you are?

- At work, if your competitors drive themselves too hard to get the upper hand, that's their problem; don't allow it to become yours.

A MANTRA TO TELL YOURSELF: *"Remember priorities."*

Reference:

No Contest: The Case Against Competition by Alfie Kohn, Houghton Mifflin, 1986

See: fear of invasion of territory or privacy, fear of competition, financial fears, fear of what others think, fear of what friends think

Fear of Oneself

autophobia (fear of being alone)

phonophobia (fear of one's own voice)

I have more trouble with myself than any other man. —EVANGELIST DWIGHT L. MOODY

Characteristics: People may avoid situations from fear of how they might react. For example, many people avoid relatives because of potential confrontations; others avoid singing or dancing for fear of blushing. On a deeper level, some people are afraid to confront the truth about themselves and may be in denial about such things as their own rudeness, depression, alcoholism or anger. U.S. General George S. Patton once said, "I don't fear failure. I only fear the slowing up of the engine inside of me which is pounding, saying 'Keep going, someone must be on top, why not you?'" Many people with this fear do not like to be alone because it gives them too much time to think about themselves.

Background: We rarely think about being afraid of ourselves because confronting this feeling may be embarrassing or mean we have to change. That's why denial is so popular. Nevertheless, it may be worth overcoming this fear because there may be important issues that need addressing. Many people don't like themselves enough, and most are not as self-aware as they should be. In the words of psychotherapist Nathaniel Branden, "Most human beings are sleepwalking through their own existence."

Strategies:

- Get to know what makes you tick, explore why you act or react in a certain way and figure out whether that is good or bad. Write down your attitudes, motives, beliefs, needs, reactions—and then evaluate them. Be prepared to explore your inner feelings and perhaps your past.
- Explore your weaknesses. Are you afraid of a situation because you might panic, be lazy, or become angry or too frank? You might avoid leadership because you worry that you don't have the confidence to confront colleagues. As the philosopher Aristotle puts it, "I count him braver who overcomes his desires than him who conquers his enemies, for the hardest victory is over self."

- It is okay to be imperfect and even to fib once in a while. No one is so self-assured that they don't misrepresent themselves at times. Each of us is a work in progress. Be kind to yourself and you will learn to respect yourself more. A.J. Mahari, who has been treated for a personality disorder, says: "One of the most beneficial gifts you can give yourself is the ability to sit with yourself being who you are and accepting that, all your mistakes, shortcomings and weaknesses included."
- Assess whether you avoid competitive situations at work, home or school because of the fear of your own potential reaction.
- By exploring your fear, you'll develop greater understanding of yourself and the possible routes to self-growth. Most often, we change only when change is forced upon us. What if we *volunteered* to change?
- Before you try to improve, learn to love or at least to understand rather than fear yourself. Get to know your strengths as well as your weaknesses.
- If you fear in advance how you might react to a situation, it may be a sign that a defense mechanism is helping to hide one of your faults. I sometimes avoid pickup basketball games with younger players because I worry that the ugly side of my ego will come out. When I catch myself thinking this way, I make myself join the game and work on building a healthier ego.
- If you are angry with yourself, assess the situation, but after it is over, heed the advice of author Alexander Chase: "To understand is to forgive, even oneself."
- Deepen your spirituality by putting less emphasis on yourself and your needs and more on others'. Volunteer your time.

    A MANTRA TO TELL YOURSELF: *"Knowing me can only help me."*

References:

The Road Less Traveled by M. Scott Peck, Simon & Schuster, 1998

The Six Pillars of Self-Esteem by Nathaniel Branden, Bantam, 1994

See: fear of embarrassment, fear of competition, fear of showing emotions, fear of being alone

Fear of Showing Emotions

angrophobia (fear of anger)	*People who never get carried away should be.* —MALCOLM FORBES, ART COLLECTOR, PUBLISHER
counterphobia (fear of fearful situations)	

Characteristics: This condition often involves a reluctance to cry, laugh or show anger, embarrassment or other emotions. People may become expressionless or rigid in reacting to situations, or they may avoid potentially emotional situations. Some people fear laughter (geliophobia).

Background: It is hard to define exactly what emotions are, but one definition is that emotions appear when needs are not being met or have recently been met. We often hide our emotions for fear of looking weak or out of control, or for fear that others will be able to read us. Some people see emotions as inferior to reason and thought. Many men fear that by crying, they'll appear effeminate. Members of older generations and of certain cultures (including Western cultures) discourage the showing of emotions and encourage always being in control. A person who had problems showing emotions as a child will likely have the same trouble as an adult because his or her emotional suppression will become automatic.

Strategies:
- Gauge how you react to certain people and situations, and why. Are your needs being met, or do you sometimes need to hug someone and still hold back? Do you withhold a belly laugh when one is called for?
- Try to let go once in a while and experience the buzz of emotions, including their highs and lows, their cleansing effects, and the freedom they give you from your hangups. On the other hand, if you cry at the drop of a hat, you may be out of control, in which case you'll want to raise your emotional threshold in certain areas.
- Don't believe that crying is always a sign of weakness, because the reverse is often true. Crying shows that you are not afraid to show how you feel, or that perhaps you are but you go

ahead and do it anyway. That takes courage and humility, both of which build character.

- You may be afraid to let your emotions come out because you fear the truth. Often we don't want to reveal our true feelings to others. We may be afraid to show that we are sentimental, that we care deeply for someone, or even that we despise someone.

- Remember that the most attractive men and women in entertainment, such as actors Mel Gibson and Julia Roberts, have a vulnerable quality to them that endears them to their fans.

- Try to be less focused on yourself, especially in your concern for how others view you. As clinical psychologist Gillian Butler says, "The less self-conscious you are, the easier it is to be yourself, and to join in spontaneously with what is going on around you."

Author's Two Cents:

A stiff upper lip helped my British ancestors get through two wars and the Depression, but it gave some of us emotional problems. I was finally able to cry in front of my kids when they were in their early teens—when Canadian sprinter Ben Johnson was caught cheating at the Olympics. My sons put their arms around me. I felt not ashamed, but liberated. Later, when my first grandchild was born, I was not only pleased when my son cried, I joined him.

References:

Facing Fear, Finding Courage by Sarah Quigley, Conari, 1996

Managing Your Mind: The Mental Fitness Guide by Gillian Butler and Tony Hope, Oxford, 1997

See: fear of singing or dancing, fear of not having control, fear of intimacy or love, fear of embarrassment, fear of criticism, fear of what others think, fear of confrontation or conflict

Fear of Having a Photo Taken

camera shy *eisoptrophobia* (fear of seeing oneself in a mirror)	*When you smile for the camera, smile not just with your lips but with your eyes. Tap your source of joy from within by thinking happy thoughts, remembering loved ones or happy moments.* —PORTRAIT AND FASHION PHOTOGRAPHER DOMINIQUE JAMES

Characteristics: This condition involves fear of cameras. It's common for people to act unnatural or to pull a face in front of a camera. Some people avoid group pictures or even throw their hands over their face or leave the room.

Background: Many people are simply self-conscious. Others have a difficult time suddenly "turning on" before a camera. Camera-shy people may worry about their appearance or try to look the way they think other people think they should look. On a deeper level, they may have image or self-esteem issues. The recent popularity of video cameras has made many people loosen up about having their pictures taken.

Strategies:

- Take a look at some of your photos. Are you satisfied with them? Do you look the way you think you should look?
- When you make a fuss for a photographer, you bring more attention to yourself than if you just relaxed and let her shoot. The only person who is conscious of your being self-conscious is you, and this self-consciousness can give you a reputation for not wanting your picture taken.
- At picture time, take a few seconds to compose yourself and relax your facial muscles. Put your chin down to eliminate your neck. To hide a double chin, extend your neck slightly forward toward the camera.
- Remember that an amateur photographer is not focusing so much on you as he is on the mechanics of getting the picture done.

- If you don't perk up, the picture will turn out badly and you'll be documented for history as grumpy. Remember that people will pay more attention if you *don't* smile. Laugh for the camera while thinking about this silly fear or pretending that the birdie is someone who makes you chuckle. Or look at the lens like it is a mirror. In fact, practice by smiling at yourself in a mirror.
- Imagine the best-case scenario: you may wind up in a studio in the mall as a picture of the month, along with those angels and perfect weddings.
- Act naturally. The camera is just another eye looking at you. People tend to make too much of it.
- Buy yourself a camera and shoot other people. When you realize what it's like from the other side, getting your picture taken won't be so painful a process.
- If you don't like pictures of yourself in a group, cut your head out.
- Photos are great! They're a record that you lived.

References:

Overcoming Anxiety by Reneau Z. Peurifoy, Owl, 1997

Kodak PhotoNet Online, www.photonet.com

www.takegreatpictures.com

See: fear of embarrassment, fear of what others think, fear of your appearance, fear of criticism, fear of getting a compliment

Fear of Choking in Sports

anginophobia (fear of choking)

author's definition of choking: When emotions have a negative effect on an athlete's performance.

It's okay to have butterflies in your stomach, just get them flying in formation.
—ANONYMOUS

Characteristics: From time to time, most athletes fear failing in clutch situations. Some remain underachievers because they seize up under pressure, often losing their self-confidence and feeling anxious and tense. Some athletes fear crowds. Others thrive on pressure and use their fear hormones to improve their performance.

Background: When an athlete feels intense pressure, the fight-or-flight response causes her muscles to become tense with an overload of adrenaline and her fingers to shake as blood is diverted to the large muscles. Fine motor skills can break down, along with focus, but emotional drive and skills involving strength can improve. There may be more choking these days in elite amateur sports because of the pressure of gaining professional status or a university sports scholarship. A survey of 1,000 Americans showed that 44 percent feared embarrassing themselves in a sport. At the same time, there are more sports psychologists and teachers than ever before to help athletes with these kinds of emotional issues.

Strategies:

- If you're playing for fun, don't get too psyched up and don't put your ego on the line; that attitude just ruins everyone's game. What is there to prove?
- If you prepare your skills in advance, emotions can enhance your performance in competitive sports, especially if you train with pressure or simulated pressure. Pretend that a game is on the line and that your effort will make the difference.
- If you feel that your emotions will affect your performance, use visualization before the event. Picture everything. Imagine that mistakes or problems come up along the way, but visualize yourself dealing with them and attaining victory. Some athletes even imagine the sounds and smells of an event; when the action starts, they feel they've already been there.
- Stay in the present and focus on the task rather than on the

potential results, allowing your hormones to sharpen your skills.

- Some star athletes have used their insecurity and "I'll show you" attitude to produce record performances. They channel their insecurity and fears into their preparation, then focus tightly on their skills during the event.
- Try to stay in an optimal or manageable level of arousal during the performance. Optimal levels of arousal for various sports are as follows (5 being the highest): 5, football blocking and tackling, 220-yard and 440-yard runs, weightlifting; 4, long jump, sprints, swimming, wrestling; 3, most basketball, soccer and gymnastic skills, boxing, high jump; 2, baseball pitching and hitting, football quarterbacking, tennis; 1, archery, bowling, golf short game, basketball free throws.
- Serious athletes can raise their optimal levels of arousal over the course of a career, especially if they train under pressure.
- If you get too worked up during the action, use deep breathing or positive self-talk to keep oxygen in your system and relax you. In special instances, you can divert the "fear hormones" by briefly getting angry and putting them directly into your skills. Other strategies include looking at your task as a challenge or using a mantra, such as "Just do it!"
- Find a cue, such as a mantra or thought, that brings you back to an optimal level of arousal. Olympic gold medal diver Greg Louganis thought of his mother when he was nervous.
- If you make a mistake, forget it for the time being or it could lead to further frustration. Pretend to flush it down a toilet.
- If you choke from time to time, admit it. It doesn't mean you're a choker. The world's best athletes choke under pressure once in a while.

A MANTRA TO TELL YOURSELF: *"Focus!"*

References:

Competitive Fire by Michael Clarkson, Human Kinetics, 1999

Mental Training for Peak Performance by Steven Ungerleider, Rodale Press, 1996

See: fear of failure, fear of not having control, fear of what others think, fear of competition, fear of illness or pain, fear of confrontation or conflict, fear of crowds, fear of making mistakes, fear of success or happiness

5

Fears at Home

Fear and Stress in Children

In many ways, children resemble phobic adults, with simplistic, generalized reasoning and an unsophisticated linking of cause and effect. —Rush W. Dozier, in his book *Fear Itself*

Characteristics: Children get nervous about many things—other people, the dark, being alone, monsters, going to school, and not living up to parents' or their friends' expectations. Youngsters are dependent on others for survival. Some may feel "separation anxiety" when they are away from their parents, and it may keep them from joining activities. Research on children aged 5 to 12 shows that 20 percent fear ghosts and the supernatural, 15 percent fear being alone, in the dark or in strange places, 14 percent fear people or animals, and 13 percent fear being hurt, ill or in pain. About 25 percent of children between 6 and 12 have nightmares.

Background: Children have more fears than adults because they haven't had enough experience to rationalize or adapt to many of their fears. It can be scary when you are doing things for the first time. Today's kids have lots of demands. Both parents may be working, leaving a void in the nurturing process. Young girls may fear they are not as attractive as teenagers in fashion ads. As they get older, children become more afraid of social harm and getting their feelings hurt. Inhibited children may be highly reactive and have an increased heart rate. Most children outgrow most of their fears.

Strategies:
- Don't smother your children and make all the decisions for them and do all their worrying. Kids should be allowed to face their fears gradually through experience and education.
- Reassure your children about life by telling them you love them, but more importantly, show them you love them by your actions.
- If children have specific fears, encourage them to gradually face the fear, but don't do it all at once with a sink-or-swim approach.
- Be aware of what is available at your child's school. Many middle schools in the U.S. are putting stress management skills on their curriculum. Some Girl Scout groups have a badge for taking a stress reduction course.

- If children get nightmares, monitor their television and movie watching. Even some cartoons are scary. Don't belittle your children's fears. They are real to them.
- Children fear failure just like adults do, and they feel inadequate when they fail. Once they start a project or join a club or group, encourage them to see it through. Tell them it's okay to fail once in a while.
- If a child develops an inferiority complex, encourage him to keep his expectations in perspective and accept his limitations. Help children to respect and love themselves.
- Many children pick up distress and mindsets from their parents. Show affection and respect toward your spouse when your children are around, and avoid serious confrontations in front of them. Their feelings and fears about the world are often conditioned by the level of conflict in the family.
- A family pet is a great way to relieve stress and keep children active, but make sure it doesn't run the house.
- Make sure your kids have quiet time and fun and don't push them too much into organized activities. Research shows that from 1981 to 1997, children's leisure time dropped from 40 percent to 25 percent. "The baby boomers want to give their kids everything and have their kids be in everything: soccer, swimming or piano," says child psychologist Sharon Post. "The kids may feel there just isn't a lot of joy in accomplishment. There's more pressure."

A MANTRA TO TELL YOURSELF: *"Help them face their fears."*

References:

Cool Cats, Calm Kids: Relaxation and Stress Management for Young People by Mary L. Williams and Dianne O'Quinn Burke, Impact, 1996

Keys to Parenting Your Anxious Child by Katharina Manassis, Barron's, 1996

See: fear of change, fear of not being loved, fear of making mistakes, fear of being alone, fear of the dark and all of the fears at school

Fear for Your Children's Safety

Healthy children will not fear life if their elders have integrity enough to not fear death. —PSYCHOLOGIST ERIK ERIKSON

Characteristics: This is the worry about the health and safety of one's children. It can affect every aspect of life, from concern about their day care or school to worry about the safety of the playground or about them getting the flu bug. This fear can make some parents overprotective, even paranoid. Some parents don't even allow their children to take healthy risks or to develop relationships, and may keep them out of activities and organizations. One survey showed that parents worry more about their kids driving safely than about drug and alcohol abuse or pregnancy.

Background: Most parents fear for their children, and this fear may last their whole lives. Since parents are children's primary caregivers, this is nature's way of ensuring our survival as a species. Throughout the animal kingdom, parents are usually overprotective; that's why visitors in forests fear bears when the cubs are nearby. In fearing for our kids, though, sometimes we fear for ourselves. We worry about how we would react if something happened to them. And we fear that if our children come to harm, we might get the blame.

Strategies:
- Teach your kids to be street-smart, to be friendly but cautious and intelligent about their choices of friends and activities.
- Don't make your kids grow up in a bubble. Your children will never be as safe as you think they should be, and sometimes we show a double standard by not allowing them to take the chances we would take. If you overprotect, they may not learn to be self-sufficient when they need to be, and they will likely become fearful adults. However, remember that inhibited children may need more reassurance for challenging situations, such as leaving the house or joining an organization.
- For parents who constantly worry when their children go to school or a playground to be with friends, understand that it is usually safe. In fact, the chances of your child being abused by

someone are very small. Be wary of sensational media reports of crimes against children. In recent years, the mainstream media have sometimes made it appear that there are rashes of child abductions when, in fact, they have simply chosen to focus on that subject for a while.

- If they are not allowed to take some chances, children will be set up for a boring life and perhaps develop an inflexible mindset. Do you want them to be unfulfilled?
- Don't leave young children alone. Have them walk to school with an older child or take them yourself. If they are home alone, tell them not to answer the door and to tell callers that their parents are unable to come to the phone. Monitor your children's Internet use and caution them not to meet strangers after exchanging e-mails.
- Teach children how to use 911 and leave phone numbers of relatives and friends near the phone. As they get older, teach them solid fundamentals about things like sex, driving and drug abuse.
- When selecting a good day-care program, make sure that it has: a good child-to-adult ratio, experienced staff, proper and updated physical facilities, a low staff turnover rate, and high-quality interactions between staff with children.
- If your children take too many risks and do not take legitimate safety concerns seriously, such as following rules and regulations on schoolyard apparatus, they may have an underactive nervous system and not realize the dangers involved.

A MANTRA TO TELL YOURSELF: *"Street-smart, but friendly."*

References:

Protecting the Gift: Keeping Children and Teenagers Safe (and Parents Sane) by Gavin de Becker, Dell, 2000

Two Jobs, No Life by Peter Marshall, Key Porter, 2001

www.thefamilycorner.com

See: fear of the unknown, fear of not having control, fear of responsibility, fear of terrorism, fear and stress in children, fear of becoming a parent, fear of bullies, sexual fears, fear of children leaving home, fear of driving

Fear of Children Leaving Home

empty-nest syndrome: a feeling that can envelop parents when their children grow up and leave home

There is nothing more thrilling in this world, I think, than having a child that is yours, and yet is mysteriously a stranger.
—AGATHA CHRISTIE

Characteristics: When children leave for university or move out of the family home, many parents feel some anxiety; some even become depressed. But the children's departure can also bring a sense of relief and fulfillment after years of responsibility and hard work.

Background: A parent's desire to protect his or her children never wears off. Nature has programmed this into us. When someone has lived with you for two decades or more (children tend to stay home longer these days), it is natural to feel sadness when they leave and to miss them deeply. Some people also feel as though they are suddenly living in a vacuum. This feeling strikes more women than men, but that may be changing as parenting roles evolve.

Strategies:
- Don't let the empty nest sneak up on you. Prepare yourself for the time your children will leave home by starting something new, perhaps a hobby or a paid or volunteer job. Renew old friendships. Begin to look on the empty nest as a transition period to a new time in your life.
- Congratulate yourself. Feel proud that you have helped your child graduate into the big world. Hold a party or buy a gift for yourself or your child.
- When your children start living away from home, don't show up at their place every day or even every few days; if you do, they won't learn self-sufficiency. But try to be close enough at hand that they can still seek you for comfort or advice.
- If you feel an emotional or physical void, try something you've never done, something exciting, like skydiving or coaching a Little League baseball team.

- Spend time with other people whose children have recently moved out of the family home.
- Don't sit at home fretting about your children leaving, and don't exaggerate the way life was with them. It's hard to focus on life if you are always weeping sentimental tears.
- If you are married, this is a time to rediscover one another and get a second wind in your relationship. You now have time to devote to each other, which you didn't have with a full house. But don't smother one another because your children are suddenly gone.
- However it turns out, don't despair—the birds will fly home again, perhaps with their own children. That will bring you a whole new set of wonders and challenges to deal with and enjoy.

  A MANTRA TO TELL YOURSELF: *"Hold them close, then let them go."*

References:

How to Survive and Thrive in an Empty Nest by Jeanette and Robert Lauer, New Harbinger, 1999

www.thefamilycorner.com

See: fear for your children's safety, fear of not having control, fear of change, fear of the unknown, fear of being alone, fear of not being loved

Fear of Becoming a Parent

lockiophobia (fear of childbirth) *fear of storks!*	*There are at least two advantages to having a baby—homeless people will not sift through your trash anymore and your tolerance will develop for loud, piercing shrills.* —FROM WWW.THEFAMILYCORNER.COM

Characteristics: Some people are apprehensive about having children, for a variety of reasons—health issues, financial constraints or the drastic change of lifestyle. Others fear they will be too anxious or overreact as parents or do too much for their kids. This fear can make people avoid friends or relatives who have children.

Background: Who wouldn't have some concerns about bringing another human being into the world and raising him or her? What a responsibility! This fear can make people consider whether they are fit to be parents, but it might also make qualified parents more anxious than they should be. Being a parent takes, patience, strength, knowledge, compassion and financial responsibility, but all of these qualities can be strengthened by actually going through parenthood. There is really no manual for how to be a parent, but by tapping into their common sense and strengths, people can learn to become effective full-time caregivers. Some people don't respect parenthood enough and have children without properly caring for them.

Strategies:
- Talk openly with your partner if you want to have a child. Discuss whether you are responsible and financially and emotionally stable enough. Don't feel pressure to have kids just because most people in your family or circle of friends did. Not everyone has to be a parent; the human species will carry on.
- If you are unsure whether you can be an excellent parent, ask your doctor or midwife to refer you to a social worker for information. Talk to family members and friends who have children.
- Prepare yourself for a roller-coaster ride. It takes hard work and patience and a willingness to learn as you go along. But you will grow and earn a greater understanding of life.

- All babies are different—even those from the same parents—and they don't come with a user manual. Raise them as such (although you will want to keep the same standards for all your children, which is another issue).

- If you are pregnant, channel your anxiety into constructive behavior: start prenatal care early; eat well and learn about nutrition; avoid drugs and stop smoking or cut down; get regular exercise; read a book about raising children; prepare your home for the newborn; go to childbirth education classes; sing to your baby.

- Remember that serious problems during pregnancy and with a newborn are rare. Before the baby arrives, discuss with your partner the sharing of responsibilities.

- Have patience, tolerance and desire. We are born with parenting skills; they may be latent, but they can be developed.

- In the early days of parenthood, make time for yourself and occasionally leave the child with someone you trust. It will relieve some of the pressure of being together all of the time. Expect some strains between you and your partner as you make the transition into parenthood; a new mother may be occupied with the child and the father may feel ignored.

- If you are thinking about becoming a parent after the age of 30, be aware that many experts believe that when parents are more established in their careers, children are less of a threat. Older men tend to be better fathers, and both parents are generally calmer, more patient and better able to go with the flow.

A MANTRA TO TELL YOURSELF: *"Am I up to the job?"*

References:

The Eight Seasons of Parenthood by Barbara Unell and Jerry Wyckoff, Random House, 2000

The ABCs of Pregnancy, www.abcbirth.com

Child and Youth Health, www.cyh.com

See: fear of the unknown, fear of responsibility, fear of commitment, fear of change, fear of intimacy or love, fear of invasion of territory or privacy, fear of illness or pain, fear for your children's safety

Fears for Your Marriage/Partnership

A great marriage is not when the perfect couple comes together.
It is when an imperfect couple learns to enjoy their differences.
—HUMORIST/AUTHOR DAVE MEURER

Characteristics: Worry about whether one's marriage or partnership will last is quite common. There can be numerous negative consequences, such as people becoming too close to their children, being possessive or distrustful of their partner, or feeling distress and withdrawal. One person may try too hard to compensate for the other. Some women overlook physical abuse to maintain a relationship. But healthy worry can create more effort, compromise, intimacy and ultimately a stronger relationship.

Background: There will always be changes, swings and even fears in partnerships. If kept manageable, this is a good fear and motivates people to work on their bond. When a marriage is not healthy, at least one person's needs are not being met and at least one person is not putting in enough effort. Most arguments are about money and children. About half of today's marriages end in divorce, and often there is more than one reason for it. In recent times, the number of marriages has steadily decreased in North America.

Strategies:

- Be on the lookout for signs of trouble: Is communication breaking down? Is one person or both people losing interest? Are disagreements and distrust becoming more frequent?
- Become close friends. You're together every day. Talk, talk, talk—about things big and small and sometimes inconsequential. Find out what the other person wants and needs. Have fun and socialize with others; double-date.
- Don't put too much pressure on the other person to change or to compromise. Respect your partner and give him or her the freedom to think for themselves, and give them *time* to themselves. Even in the closest friendships, we are still individuals.
- Keep responsibilities close to 50-50, although that may not be possible in some areas.
- Men, be aware that, because of their social conditioning and perhaps genetic programming, women generally do more than you

in parenting and keeping relationships working. Pitch in and take off some of the load in this new age when most women are also working outside the home.

- One definition of love is when two people's needs come together (or is that knees?). But love often comes after marriage and takes work, commitment, sacrifice and genuine caring. As psychologist/author Stephen Covey says, "Love the feeling is a fruit of love the verb."
- Draw on one another's strengths, but don't judge weaknesses too harshly. Be prepared to discover that the thing that annoys you about your partner may be a flaw that you also have.
- Tend to the little things that show you care—for example, leaving a note behind when you go on a trip or doing an unscheduled chore without taking credit.
- If you have children, allow them to bring you together, not to pull you apart. That means working together, often with some compromise, on your parenting approach.
- Work on keeping your sex life healthy. That is not easy if both of you are busy, but you must make time for pleasure.
- If you have serious problems, see a counselor or discuss them with people you trust.
- After fights, kiss and make up. Don't break up without having put in a solid effort.

A MANTRA TO TELL YOURSELF: *"What's right for us?"*

References:

Making Love Last Forever by Gary Smalley, Word Publications, 1997

The Five Love Languages: How to Express Heartfelt Commitment to Your Mate by Gary Chapman, Northfield, 1992

www.dearpeggy.com (advice on how to deal with an affair)

www.sexualmarriage.com (for sexual issues)

www.marriagebuilders.com (for general issues)

See: fear of not being loved, fear of sex, fear of intimacy or love, fear of rejection, fear of becoming a parent, fear of the opposite sex, fear of being alone, fear of commitment

Fear of Family Get-Togethers

syngenesophobia (fear of relatives)

soceraphobia (fear of parents-in-law)

[At a party] think about sharing friendship and happiness, and how you fit into all of it, rather than trying to do what you think everyone else wants you to do.
—ANXIETY RESEARCHER CATHLEEN HENNING

Characteristics: Some people are reluctant to attend family gatherings, especially when certain people are expected to be there. Others may feel anxious and shy at a party, or become confrontational with others, especially if there is baggage in the relationship. This fear can keep relationships in the family from growing.

Background: You can choose your friends, but you can't choose your relatives, so the old saying goes. Families are thrown together, for better or for worse, and there will always be discomfort and personality clashes in some cases, especially if one person views another as controlling or rude or sees them as competition. Some people don't want to get too close to relatives because of the work entailed in a relationship. But the family is a natural phenomenon, and we can learn a lot about ourselves from our family.

Strategies:
- Approach a get-together with the idea that you are going to give something or learn something. The more selfish or self-conscious you are, the less likely you are to have a good time.
- Make a family tree. Family is important and deep-rooted in human evolution; don't let yours dissolve easily. We all have some responsibility for maintaining harmony in the extended family, if only to give the children a chance to have relationships. But don't force family structure on those who don't buy into it.
- If you are a guest, take something special for the hosts, such as an unexpected box of sweets or a house gift.
- Think back to parties you dreaded; they rarely turned out as badly as you had anticipated. You might have even had a laugh or a memory to cherish.

- Lower your expectations with relatives, especially if you see them rarely. Remember that we are often more critical of other people than we are of ourselves, particularly if they have a fault similar to one of ours. To ease the pressure on get-togethers or holidays, try to keep in touch with relatives throughout the year. Schedule periodic family reunions.
- If you have a serious problem with a relative, get it out into the open when you are alone with them, if only for your peace of mind. If you share it in front of others, it could damage your relationship further.
- Try not to drag your problems along with you on family vacations. Organize a variety of settings and activities so everyone can let their family issues go for a day or two.
- If you host a party, use common sense: have a variety of activities and food; if possible, have indoor and outdoor areas; make rules for smoking; provide accommodation or cabs for drinkers. Then relax—it's up to the guests to enjoy themselves. You'll never please everybody.
- Consider the fact that maybe you are too shy and need to work on your people skills. Hey, maybe it's not them, it's you!

A MANTRA TO TELL YOURSELF: *"Make an effort."*

References:

How to Entertain People You Hate: Tips on How to Have a Good Time with Bad Company by Ari Alexandra Boulanger, CCC Publications, 2003

Why Bother? Why Not? A Hollywood Insider Shows You How to Entertain Like a Star by Laurin Sydney, Cliff Street, 2000

See: fear of what others think, fear of criticism, fear of people, fear of singing or dancing, fear of not having control, fear of responsibility, fear of confrontation or conflict, fear of not being loved, fear of intimacy or love, fear of oneself

Fear of a Break-in

scelerophobia (fear of burglars)	*I feel depressed. I'm scared. I can't sleep all night. I go into my bedroom and I know somebody has been there.*

—ZEZA, VICTIM OF A BREAK-IN

Characteristics: It's common for homeowners and residents to worry about someone breaking into their home and stealing their valuables or harming them. This fear can cause some anxious people to rarely leave their home, particularly if they have already been a victim. Some people, fearing a home invasion, are reluctant to answer their door. Others feel traumatized for years after an incident.

Background: A break-in is an invasion of physical and personal privacy. In the United States, there is one burglary every 15 seconds. Although there is no foolproof way to protect our homes, 90 percent of break-ins can be prevented through common sense and a little thought. This fear motivates us to protect our loved ones and possessions.

Strategies:
- Your fence should be see-through (with no thick hedges in front) so that burglars who get inside can be seen from the street. Clear shrubs and "hiding places" away from doors and windows.
- Make sure you keep porch, garage and rear lights on all night.
- If you live in a high-crime area or near a highway, consider motion-detector lights. Burglars hit 40 percent more often within three blocks of major "getaway" thoroughfares.
- Lock all doors and windows, even when you're home. An unlocked second-floor window can be entered. Keep ladders locked away.
- Don't hide a key near a door; that's one of the first things burglars look for. And don't leave notes on the door when you're away.
- Install deadbolt locks on entrances. Glass panels on sliding doors can be easily smashed, so use Plexiglas.

- Keep money and valuables locked up or hidden well. Make a list of your valuables, even take photos of them. If they don't have serial numbers, put your driver's license number on them, making them easier to track if they're stolen.
- Make everyone in your house streetwise and wary of suspicious characters in the neighborhood.
- Inform your neighbors when you will be away and ask them to watch the premises. And don't advertise your absence. Have someone pick up your newspapers and mail, and don't leave a message on your answering machine referring to your absence.
- Once you have done all of the above, relax. Remember that when you have done everything in your control, there is no point worrying.

A MANTRA TO TELL YOURSELF: *"Safety first."*

Reference:

Keep Safe! 101 Ways to Enhance Your Safety and Protect Your Family by Donna Koren Wells and Bruce C. Morris, Hunter House, 2000

See: fear of the unknown, fear of invasion of territory or privacy, fear of being mugged, fear of being alone, fear of the dark, worry at night and sleeplessness

Fear of Delivering Bad News

An important part of leadership is the ability to deliver bad news. Unfortunately, it's as unnatural as the embouchure for the oboe (trust me), so we usually flub it on our first time out.
—BUSINESS CONSULTANT BOB LEWIS

Characteristics: Delivering bad or sensitive news can cause anxiety for a lot of people, especially if it is about an illness, downsizing, or the fact that the person didn't get a job or is being let go. Some people pass the buck to others to deliver the news.

Background: We are rarely comfortable with the feeling of fear, whether it is our own fear or that of others. And we know that delivering bad news to others usually evokes a negative emotional response. Telling someone about an emergency or the death of a relative is a job that police never get used to. Many medical schools still don't train students in how to tell patients and relatives about serious illnesses. Most people are uncomfortable talking about death, and many emergency services personnel use gallows humor to deal with it. In general, we deal poorly with emotional issues.

Strategies:
- Try to pick the right environment to tell someone bad news, and try to make it a private, face-to-face meeting.
- Plan carefully what you are going to say and how you will say it. Make sure you are calm; use deep breathing or meditation, perhaps even visualization as you rehearse what you are going to say. Unlike good news, bad news should not be delivered spontaneously.
- If you're having trouble making the decision to do it, remind yourself that this is a great chance to show responsibility and leadership. Draw on your inner strength. Seek the advice of others, who may know something about the person you don't know. If you always pass the buck about telling bad news, work on your people skills. You might have to toughen up mentally.

- If the news is deeply sensitive, touch the person first. It helps you connect with them, and vice versa. Have them sit down (some people can faint). Speak softly, slowly and confidently; the person may pick up on your anxiousness. You may have to repeat the bad news because some people immediately freeze upon hearing it.
- Be frank and to the point, and try to avoid sugarcoating the news. Begin with, "I have some unpleasant news," or "I'm sorry I have to tell you..."
- Be prepared for an emotional reaction and try to detach yourself from it. If the person reacts badly—even if they take it out on you—remember that it has nothing to do with you. You are the messenger and sometimes messengers get the brunt of the reaction. If you are worried about a potential violent reaction, prepare in advance for your own safety and have a witness or alert security.
- Once the reaction has subsided, provide the resources the person will need, such as contacts or phone numbers. Help them focus on the positive.
- If you have to give bad news to a group, beware that you may get more negative feedback, as emotions may gain momentum.
- There is always a silver lining, and there are people who care— you, for one, who had the courage and empathy to deliver the bad news. Reassure the person that you are there for them. Help them prepare for what they must do next, beginning with a phone call or a ride.

A MANTRA TO TELL YOURSELF: *"A messenger is important."*

References:

Business consultant Bob Lewis, Bob_Lewis@csi.com or www.info world.com

Physician/writer Elizabeth Heubeck, eheubeck@physicianspractice.com

See: fear of showing emotions, fear of confrontation or conflict, fear of the unknown, fear of illness or pain, fear of death, serious worries, fear of ending a romantic relationship

Fear of Disorder or Untidiness

ataxophobia (fear of disorder)

mysophobia (fear of dirt or germs)

You know you have a problem when you fear your house will be burglarized and you worry you haven't had a chance to clean the place up. —ANONYMOUS

Characteristics: This condition involves an intense desire to keep everything proper, such as following a strict schedule, or a compulsion to arrange things in order. Some people may show displeasure with those who don't care about order as much as they do. Others fear dirt or contamination, some to the point that they constantly clean their fingernails or refuse to shake hands with people. At its most severe, this fear leads to obsessive-compulsive behavior, such as the repeated washing of hands.

Background: The desire or need to maintain control is inherent in many people, and in the big picture it helps create civilization and orderly societies. But this need could actually stem from a fear of dealing with others and their different styles and schedules. In moderation, the fear of disorder and untidiness can keep one clean, healthy and on time. Perfectionists can sometimes be compulsive with cleaning and may have self-esteem or ego issues to deal with. Fear of dirt or germs relates back to times when disease was more rampant.

Strategies:

- Without order, there is chaos. If you loathe dirt and lack of structure, however, you might want to examine whether your fears are obsessive and unwarranted.
- Sometimes there's a fine line between order and disorder. Consider your worries out of proportion if:
  - you treat scuff marks on your carpet like footprints to track down a suspect
  - you don't allow kids to play in your backyard
  - you are known only for your appearance and rarely for your spontaneity
  - your vacation plans are a strict itinerary

- Examine other areas of your life where a similar mindset may exist, such as inflexibility in relationships, fear of failure at work or trouble relaxing. Are you a perfectionist? Do you try to control things too much?
- Let go once in a while. Have a jeans-only day, or the audacity to be late for an appointment, and observe how life goes on and you don't get fired. At home, let someone else do the housework or schedule the appointments.
- Look upon your house as lived in. Leave cushions askew once in a while. Let glasses and cups have a living-room life of more than 30 minutes. What would happen if you didn't do the laundry for 24 hours?
- Go to other people's homes and see how they live. It might give you some perspective.
- If you laugh at yourself and your habits once in a while, the rigidity can loosen. Ask yourself, "Do I control my life or does my life control me?"

A MANTRA TO TELL YOURSELF: *"Do I want to live in a sterile world?"*

Reference:

Anxiety Disorders and Phobias by Aaron T. Beck and Gary Emery, Basic, 1985

See: fear of not having control, fear of change, fear of criticism, fear of what others think, fear of making mistakes, fear of embarrassment, fear of family get-togethers, fear of strangers

Fear of Solicitors and Telemarketers

hobophobia (fear of beggars)	*If you get one of those pushy [telemarketers], just listen to their sales pitch.*

When they try to close the sale, tell them you'll need to go get your credit card. Then set the phone down and go do the laundry or something. —FROM WWW.FAKECRAP.COM

Characteristics: People with this fear are reluctant to answer the telephone or the door because they may have to confront someone who will try to sell them something or convert them to a religion. Some people may become irritable, even angry. Others are sheepish or intimidated when they walk past panhandlers.

Background: Most people are territorial by nature and habit, and suspicious of strangers coming onto their property. Some may feel their privacy has been trespassed when unauthorized people call or come to their door. A home is a person's castle and refuge. If we had no apprehension at all, we'd be letting everybody into our homes. Telemarketing has become more popular than door-to-door solicitation, but many people still see it as an invasion of privacy, especially at mealtime or late at night.

Strategies:

- Don't be so quick to shoot the messenger—solicitors usually work for a company or organization. Be kind—do you think they like setting themselves up for rejection or derision?
- Have a preset dollar figure in mind for your charitable contributions for the year and the type of charities you want to give to.
- If you are against solicitation, put a sign up: "No Solicitors Please," or "My Dog Doesn't Bite but My Spouse Does."
- Hard-sell tactics or tear-jerk stories could be a tip-off to an unscrupulous solicitor. Watch out for get-rich-quick schemes or company names that sound very close to the name of a well-known charity or brand name.
- At the door, ask for identification and perhaps a brochure on the group. (In some areas, door-to-door solicitors need a license.) You can read it and send a donation later.

- If you hire someone to do work around your house, ask for references. If you're unhappy with the work, call the Better Business Bureau.
- Pay by check. Don't give cash or your credit card number.
- Get a feeling for the *other side* by volunteering to go door to door or solicit over the phone for a charity.
- Try to be tolerant of religious groups. Remember that some religious groups believe one of their mandates is to go door to door to spread their message. If you want them to respect your beliefs, respect theirs. It doesn't mean you have to let them in.
- Telemarketers have developed a reputation for fast talk and con artistry, but people are buying; it's estimated that $230 billion in goods and services are sold over the phone each year in the U.S. If you are against telemarketers, keep a note near your phone, clearly stating your position. Screen calls and hang up on auto-dialers. Or get an unlisted number.
- If you consider buying something from a telemarketer, ask for written information on the product (or charity). Scammers will not send you written material.
- To avoid junk mail, think twice before entering sweepstakes and draws.
- To avoid solicitations, have your number placed on a do-not-call list in accordance with the Telephone Consumer Protection Act (in the U.S.).
- How to deal with panhandlers on the street is sometimes an ethical decision. Yes, you work hard for your money, but don't dismiss them as lazy bums; they may be mentally ill or destitute.

A MANTRA TO TELL YOURSELF: *"Be nice, but fair."*

References:

The Alliance Against Fraud in Telemarketing and Electronic Commerce, www.fraud.org

See: fear of strangers, fear of invasion of territory or privacy, fear of confrontation or conflict, fear of a break-in, fear of oneself, fear of embarrassment

Worry at Night and Sleeplessness

noctiphobia (fear of the night)	*Sometimes I lie awake at night and I ask, "Where have I gone wrong?" Then a voice says to me, "This is going to take more than one night."*
somniphobia (fear of sleep)	—CARTOON CHARACTER CHARLIE BROWN

Characteristics: Many people lie awake at night, tense or worrying about what happened during the day or what might happen tomorrow, or whether there is a burglar on the prowl. They may worry about getting to sleep and how that might impact their energy the next day. Some people fear sleepwalking. "The variability of their sleep drives people nuts—they [lie awake] and wonder, 'What's it going to be like tonight?'" says Jack Edinger, a professor of psychiatry and behavioral sciences at Duke University. "It's a crapshoot." Children may not sleep for a variety of reasons and fears, including bedwetting (I was an occasional bed wetter until age 11).

Background: We are vulnerable to anxiety when we lie in bed, with nothing to do but attempt to sleep. When we are fatigued or tense, issues are often exaggerated and turn into worries. Little wonder that prayer is so popular at the end of the day. Sleep disorders have been common throughout history; up to 10 percent of the population suffers from insomnia. Shift workers are particularly vulnerable to night worry and sleep problems. In some people, this condition relates to the fear of death; they are afraid they won't wake up.

Strategies:
- If you constantly have problems sleeping, limit the time you spend in the bedroom. Use the bedroom for sleep only.
- If you have issues or worries that need dealing with, tell yourself you will tend to them in the morning.
- If you have an active mind at night, worry about things over which you have some control, then sleep on it. Some research has shown that when you awake in the morning, you might have been thinking about an answer in your sleep.

- Keep a pad by your bed to write down ideas. Or talk to your partner about your concerns.
- "White noise" can calm you—turn on an air purifier, a house fan, an air conditioner or soothing music you wouldn't ordinarily listen to. If you have a tendency to look at the clock, turn it around or cover the face.
- If you really can't sleep, get up and do something. In the short term, getting only four or five hours of sleep won't hurt your performance the next day. Don't panic if you average only six or seven hours of sleep a night. Everyone is different in their sleep needs. As well, older people tend to sleep more lightly.
- Watch your lifestyle: drinking too much caffeine or having catnaps during the day can keep you sleepless at night.
- Be aware that you might be suffering from depression, anxiety disorder or physical problems. See your doctor.
- In some cases, sleeping pills may be necessary. Consult your doctor. Many sleep experts argue against their use for more than a few weeks because they can increase the risk of auto accidents and memory or confusion problems.
- Nightmares may be expressions of waking fears. People who have nightmares tend to have other forms of sleeping disorders.
- If your child awakes from a nightmare, calm him or her. Later, draw the dream with the child, helping him or her see it from a different perspective. Then make up a happy ending for the dream. About 25 percent of children 6 to 12 have nightmares.

A MANTRA TO TELL YOURSELF: *"Count your blessings instead of sheep."*

References:

Sleep Thieves: An Eye-Opening Exploration into the Science and Mysteries of Sleep by Stanley Coren, Touchstone, 1998

Solve Your Child's Sleep Problems by Richard Ferber, Fireside, 1986

See: fear of the dark, fear of death, fear of the unknown, fear of not having control, sexual fears, fear of religion, fear of a break-in, fear of oneself, fear for your children's safety

Fear of Being Alone

isolophobia (fear of solitude) *monophobia* (fear of being alone)	*Many people become anxious or fearful if they are not always in a crowd of people, socializing...we might feel left out of something.* —LAUREN WOODHOUSE, AUTHOR OF *LAUGHING IN THE FACE OF CHANGE*

Characteristics: People with this fear may constantly feel the need to be around others, may easily get bored or sad being alone, or may not like their own company. Just thinking about being alone can cause anxiousness, vulnerability or even depression. When alone, their other fears tend to become exaggerated. Many children fear being alone because they feel helpless and worry their parents will never return. We tend to feel loneliness more when we get tired or when our resources are depleted.

Background: Humans are generally social creatures built and conditioned for interaction, so we often feel vulnerable alone. Many of us don't spend enough time alone to be comfortable with it (although this may be changing in our increasingly insular society). Some people don't like to be alone because they don't like themselves very much or they don't want to face the truth about themselves, which may involve mindsets and behaviors they have to change. This fear tends to affect women more than men, perhaps because of their sensitivity to or possible need for companionship. It also can increase with age, especially if a person's relatives or acquaintances die or are ill. Victorian author Charlotte Brontë wrote, "My mind has suffered somewhat too much; a malady is growing upon it—what shall I do? How shall I keep well? Sleepless I lay awake night after night, weak and unable to occupy myself."

Strategies:
* Learn to be your own best friend. If you don't like yourself enough to be in your own company, take steps (small ones, at first) to correct that. It's a great way to find out things about yourself. Don't be too dependent on others. Learn to entertain yourself. If you find yourself alone, talk aloud to yourself. Laugh with yourself.

- Write your feelings down or try to do something creative when you feel lonely. If you are lonely because you have lost a loved one, a job or a routine, help to fill that loss by connecting with something else.
- Don't mope or lull into self-pity—it may turn off others.
- Stay active. Exercise. Reading a book opens up another world with other characters. Get a pet. When you are engaged in something, it's hard to worry. Meet people with interests and needs similar to your own. Join a club or volunteer. Look up an old friend. Have a regular walking route and say hello to everyone you pass. Don't be afraid to strike up conversations.
- Use your favorite music to take the stillness out of silence. Music also can inspire you or put you in a state of flow, connecting you with ideas and with others, even though they are not there.
- Keep a journal. Briefly review your life and your plans and goals for the future. Tend to the things you might not do with others around: improving hygiene, thinking through complex issues and projects, writing, or tending to a pet's needs. Your most creative work may be done alone. Learn to treasure your time alone. Remember that other people are always close by through telephone, e-mail, letter or photo album.
- If you fill loneliness with drinking, drugs, aggression or overwork, it can make your situation worse.
- If you form intimate and nurturing bonds with others, you will feel inner support even when you are alone.

A MANTRA TO TELL YOURSELF: *"Hello, me."*

References:

The Tao of Music by John M. Ortiz, Weiser, 1997

Dr. Luann Linquist, psychologist
P.O. Box 13172
La Jolla, CA 92039
(858) 581-1122, DrLuann@deletestress.com

See: fear of intimacy or love, fear of oneself, fear of death, fear of the dark, fear of your children leaving home, fear of retirement, fear of aging

Fear of the Dark

achluophobia (fear of the dark)	*I overcame my fear of the dark and put it into my books.* —TOMI UNGERER
phasmophobia (fear of ghosts)	**Characteristics:** Sufferers may avoid dimly lit areas or even stop going out at

night. Children often confuse fantasy and reality and may be afraid to sleep for fear of monsters. Some adults may avoid being alone at night. Others are spooked by shadows or they fear that their mind will play tricks on them in the dark.

Background: This is a perfectly natural fear from our days as hunter-gatherers, when the real danger of predators lurked in the dark. Since we cannot see well in the dark, this is nature's way to help us to be more alert. This fear is closely related to the fear of the unknown. We are sometimes conditioned to fear the dark; remember the line from that childhood prayer, "If I should die before I wake"? Sometimes this fear surfaces after a traumatic event. The benefit to small children is that such fears keep them cautious at an age when they are vulnerable. Fear of the dark usually dissipates when the child is able to understand how the world works, but if the child continues to be afraid of going into a dark room, it could be that it has turned into a phobia, and may even spread to refusal to going into a basement or outside. On the positive side, this fear makes everyone more alert when visibility is not good.

Strategies:

- Understand that most of your fears of the dark are probably unjustified; trees do not turn into monsters after sunset and ghosts do not wait until then to appear in closets. Muggers usually do not target middle-class areas. However, use common sense in strange areas; stay out of high-crime areas at night.
- Desensitize yourself to the dark by sitting alone at home with most of the lights off, then all of them. If you feel anxious, breathe deeply, meditate, or listen to music.

- Talk about your fear or write about it, as author Anne Rice did in her novels about vampires.
- If you or your child has a fear of ghosts, remember that there is no proof they exist. Is it just a coincidence they are only seen in the dark or when we are half-asleep and our brains are not functioning 100 percent? If fear of ghosts persists, it could be you have an unresolved issue with a dead person.
- If you walk or jog after sunset, wear bright clothes. If you bicycle, have lights and take extra precaution with motorized vehicles. If you drive, be more cautious.
- If your children fear the dark:
  - let them know you are nearby and available to them
  - put a nightlight in their room or leave the door slightly ajar
  - don't make a big deal out of their fear of monsters; reassure them and don't tell them they're wimpy
  - some parents allow their kids to sleep in their bed under certain circumstances
  - offer the child some input on how to solve the problem; get them to talk about a monster and what it could do to them; if something in the room looks frightening, ask how to make it less so
  - limit scary movies and TV shows

A MANTRA TO TELL YOURSELF: *"I'm a night creature, too."*

References:

Keys to Parenting Your Anxious Child by Katharina Manassis, Barron's, 1996

See: worry at night and sleeplessness, fear of the unknown, superstition or fear of the supernatural, fear of being mugged, fear and stress in children, fear of enclosed spaces, fear of being alone

6

Fears in Social Settings

Fear of People

anthropophobia (fear of people)
scopophobia (fear of being looked at)

Man is a social animal. —ARISTOTLE

Characteristics: People with this condition are often shy and will avoid one-on-one situations, eye contact with others, eating in public, crowds, or gatherings at work, school or with family. They may be embarrassed or blush through self-consciousness or from fear of appearing silly or inadequate. Shyness can prevent people from making friends, especially close friends, and it can lead to depression or drug use and heavy drinking. Shy people may believe that no one is interested in them, and they may have a distorted view of relationships or feel lonely. Some shy people overcompensate for their feelings and are actually assertive or aggressive in public. Many become performers so that they can act out in a structured environment.

Background: Some 93 percent of people experience some sort of shyness from time to time. About 7 percent of North Americans have a type of person-related phobia. Some species of animals, including humans, use *staring* to intimidate. Many people fear being observed; in serious cases, this fear can be permanent unless treated. This form of shyness could be genetic (children with the same upbringing can have opposite reactions to people) or stem from bad experiences or lack of exposure to people. Such fears increase as our society becomes more insular and as we communicate more and more through computers. Social phobias usually peak in a person's late teens.

Strategies:
- Come to this quick conclusion: most people don't bite. And if they do, get a civil lawyer fast.
- If you are uncomfortable around people, try to establish why and come up with solutions. Do you sometimes have a low opinion of yourself, or are you very sensitive to criticism? Are you just lazy and don't want to talk or develop a relationship?

- If you or someone you know has such a social phobia, it can be treated by a therapist, perhaps by improving your view of the world and of yourself. Start by getting help from a family doctor or member of the clergy.
- Tips for developing communications skills: make eye contact, don't talk too softly, stand close enough to people to show confidence, don't apologize or belittle yourself, use open-ended questions, learn to be assertive and to be a good listener. Think about the good things you have to offer other people.
- Medications, such as Neurontin, are available to help treat intense shyness.
- A shy patient of Los Angeles psychologist Gary Emery developed the following strategies for meeting others:
  1. I look straight at the other person, eyes fixed.
  2. I hold my ground and let him move toward me, rather than rushing to him.
  3. I keep my body straight and balanced, projecting presence.
  4. I communicate openly, keeping my arms down rather than in a defensive position.
  5. I keep my head erect rather than nodding or looking away.
  6. I speak confidently in a clear, direct way, rather than qualifying excessively, apologizing or overexplaining.
  7. I ask questions about the person and call him by name.
  8. I'm friendly but quiet and sincere.
  9. I'm dressed in a way that allows me to feel good about myself.
  10. I'm really enjoying meeting the person.

  A MANTRA TO TELL YOURSELF: *"I'm important, too."*

Reference:

The Shyness and Social Anxiety Workbook by Martin M. Antony and Richard P. Swinson, New Harbinger, 2000

See: fear of strangers, fear of crowds, fear of what others think, fear of embarrassment, fear of criticism, fear of panic attacks in public, most fears in Part 4 and Part 6

Fear of Panic Attacks in Public

agoraphobia (fear of crowded public places)

> *While a person cannot always immediately overcome the first level of fear, he can stop frightening himself over the anxiety itself.* —GARY EMERY, DIRECTOR OF THE LOS ANGELES CENTER FOR COGNITIVE THERAPY

Characteristics: This is the fear of having a panic attack in what one considers an unsafe place. It is the fear of fear itself. At the same time, it is a complex and sometimes generalized fear that could pertain to a number of situations. Sufferers may avoid crowded highways or stores because they worry about panicking and being unable to escape, or bringing embarrassment upon themselves in their anxiety. They may shake, perspire, hyperventilate or even believe they are having a heart attack. Some people feel this way when at home alone, but it commonly occurs when people are far away from home. This condition is often accompanied by, or leads to, depression.

Background: This fear is often passed along in families. It can also begin if a person grows up with an overprotective or perfectionist parent. About 80 percent of agoraphobics are women (leading to the phrase *housebound housewife syndrome*), although this percentage has been dropping in recent times. The onset of panic disorder usually occurs between late adolescence and the mid-30s.

This fear is believed to be related to early humans' fear of being caught out in the open and vulnerable to attack. It served to keep vulnerable people close to their protectors. Charles Darwin described his occasional panic attacks as a "sensation of fear... accompanied by troubled beating of the heart, sweat and trembling of muscles."

Strategies:

- Gradually expose yourself to the situations that you fear and that tend to make you panicky. You might want to go with a trusted companion at first. Get used to crowds and trips to the country. Start by using visualization to imagine the situation, then do it in real life.
- Learn to make your thinking more realistic, and don't allow

your imagination to get the better of you. This situation cannot harm you, but your catastrophic thinking can make you tense and sick.

- Learn to relax by using breathing techniques, humor, music on a portable player or meditation. Say calming things to yourself both before and while you're in what you consider to be an unsafe place.
- Stop worrying about what others think of you. If you feel panic or embarrassment coming on, no one else knows but you. And no one else cares.
- Don't panic about your panic. If you become dizzy, calm yourself by remembering that agoraphobics rarely pass out. If you constantly feel threatened or tense, you may have a hair-trigger nervous system and need medication. See your doctor.
- Consider therapy. A study of people who suffered panic attacks revealed that only 19 percent who were treated for it subsequently suffered depression, compared to 45 percent of those who were not treated. Researchers concluded that detecting and treating panic disorder may reduce the risk of depression.

A MANTRA TO TELL YOURSELF: *"Slow and slower."*

References:

The Anxiety and Phobia Workbook by Edmund J. Bourne, New Harbinger, 2000

The Encyclopedia of Phobias, Fears and Anxieties by Ronald M. Doctor, Ada P. Kahn and Isaac Marks, Facts on File, 2000

Agoraphobic Foundation of Canada
P.O. Box 132
Chomeday, Laval, Quebec
Canada H7W 4K2

Agoraphobics in Action Inc.
P.O. Box 1662
Antioch, TN 37011
(615) 831-2383

See: fear of people, fear of crowds, fear of what others think, fear of strangers, fear of embarrassment, fear of not having control, fear of the unknown, fear of enclosed spaces, fear of doctors or dentists

Fear of Public Speaking

glossophobia

topophobia (stage fright)

The essence of public speaking is this: give your audience something of value, to walk away feeling better about themselves or some job they have to do. Even if you pass out, get tongue-tied or say something stupid, they won't care.
—PHYSICIAN, AUTHOR AND PROFESSIONAL SPEAKER MORTON C. ORMAN

Characteristics: Many if not most people suffer anxiety when speaking before a group of people or even when engaged in a social affair. Sufferers report dry mouth, stumbling voice, trembling fingers and loss of confidence. Some people are so fearful of being evaluated, looking silly or making a mistake, they never speak to a group or go to a party.

Background: As we have evolved into sensitive, self-conscious creatures, fear of public speaking has come to rival fear of death among humans. About 75 percent of North Americans report experiencing this fear; in some surveys, more people say they are afraid of speaking than say they are afraid of dying. This fear can set off your emergency fear system, with its increased heart rate, blood flow and adrenaline. Sufferers have included former presidents Ronald Reagan and Franklin Roosevelt and singer Barbra Streisand. On the positive side, some people say they actually perform better when anxious, because their fear gives them increased focus and a feeling of power.

Strategies:
- Get some experience with speaking to groups of people. Even if your first steps are small, you'll still grow in confidence.
- Use your nervous energy to help you organize and prepare for your talk. The extra effort will give you confidence in your knowledge of your topic. Know your audience as you prepare your content. Have a theme and structure to your presentation, but make only two or three major points.
- Keep things in perspective and don't become obsessed with an upcoming talk. If you see a presentation as too much of a threat, your emergency fear system will make you overly anxious and tense and you may not be able to control your nervousness.

- Look upon the talk as an information-giving session rather than as a performance. If you worry about how a performance will be perceived, you have a greater chance of letting your ego come into play and you may feel more anxious and defensive.
- Remember that the audience, even if it is just a few coworkers at an office presentation, wants one thing—the information you are giving them. They want you to succeed in giving it.
- Conceptualize your message. Don't memorize, because if you do, the moment one section is forgotten, your whole session could break down.
- When the time for your presentation comes, if you feel overly scared or tense, take a few deep breaths and visualize what you are going to do. If your mouth gets dry, drink water or press your tongue against the roof of your mouth.
- Use humor, especially self-deprecating humor, which releases endorphins into your system and relaxes you. Audience members want to laugh and like to know that you share their sense of humor. Laughter is a way of connecting.
- If you want to become a performer or a professional speaker, take a speaking course. And don't be afraid of being critiqued or of asking others' opinions about your stage presence.

Author's Two Cents:

In my first professional speaking engagement in 2002, I received a poor mark. My ego was bruised for 12 hours and I contemplated quitting. But the next day, I organized my speech better and added humor. At the next conference, two weeks later, I received the second-highest mark among 21 speakers.

References:

In the Spotlight: Overcome Your Fear of Public Speaking and Performing by Janet E. Esposito, Strong, 2000

See: fear of what others think, fear of failure, fear of embarrassment, fear of making mistakes, fear of criticism, fear of not being loved, fear of strangers

Fear of Crowds

enochlophobia (fear of crowds)

agoraphobia (fear of open or public places)

I hate crowds and making speeches.
—ALBERT EINSTEIN

Characteristics: People with this condition may avoid shopping malls, sporting events and theaters for fear of strangers, of what others think of them, of being crushed or trampled, of pickpockets or of contracting a virus. Some people may feel a loss of their identity or feel alone in a crowd, or they may fear getting lost. Others get very anxious or aggressive or feel like they are having a panic attack. Many people live in the country or suburbs because they are intimidated by the crowds and traffic in cities.

Background: Traditionally, humans tended to live in groups of no more than 75 people. Humans also have a history of sometimes getting caught up in mob mentality and acting differently, perhaps even violently, in large crowds. Women tend to suffer from fear of crowds more than men. If one of your relatives suffers from this condition, you are three times more likely than the average person to suffer from it as well. If you have low self-esteem or suffer from a traumatic disorder, you may feel insignificant or lonely in a group of people. Others may be afraid of crowds because they are in poor health and worry about falling and getting crushed.

Strategies:

- Go to a shopping mall, a sporting event, a movie theater or another crowded place—perhaps with someone you feel comfortable with—and gradually get used to rubbing elbows with people in crowds. Pin up photos of big crowds in your home.
- You may be simply shy. Talk to others more often. Go to group activities and interact with people. Consider taking a leadership role, even if it is just a small one at first.
- If you are physically afraid of groups of strangers, tell yourself that you're actually pretty safe in a crowd. That's why criminals (except for pickpockets) rarely try anything with others around. Too many witnesses.

- Avoid crowded situations in which intense emotions come into play, unless you can desensitize yourself to often noisy fans at sports stadiums. If you cannot, don't do anything to inflame your condition.
- Don't quickly dismiss or judge people who live in cities; you may do so out of a subconscious fear of crowds or traffic.
- Crowds can actually be fun! People at sports events or in theaters can enjoy doing the "wave" or singing together ("Take Me Out to the Ballgame") or giving a standing ovation at the opera or a rock concert.
- If you fear crowds, you're in some elite company—singer Frank Sinatra was uncomfortable being around a lot of people. And actor Clark Gable didn't like crowds.
- If you find yourself in a tight, claustrophobic situation around people, breathe deeply, think of your loved ones, use humor or music in a portable player or force yourself to keep perspective.

A MANTRA TO TELL YOURSELF: *"Blend in"* OR *"No one will harm me."*

Reference:

The Hidden Face of Shyness: Understanding and Overcoming Social Anxiety by Franklin Schneier, Avon, 1996

See: fear of people, fear of strangers, fear of other races, fear of the unknown, fear of illness or pain, fear of being mugged, fear of invasion of territory or privacy, fear of panic attacks in public, fear of enclosed spaces

Fear of Strangers

xenophobia (fear of foreigners or strangers)

Fear makes strangers of people who should be friends. —SHIRLEY MACLAINE

Characteristics: This fear often results in avoiding people one doesn't know. In serious cases, it keeps people housebound. Some people avoid crowds or parties. Some even avoid new jobs or moving to new regions or neighborhoods because they are apprehensive about talking to people they haven't met. Others won't ask directions from strangers on the street.

Background: There may be more fear of strangers in recent times because our society is becoming increasingly insular. Many people spend a lot of time on their computers and don't develop close relationships. Sometimes we make a snap decision about a person based on looks and decide we don't want to get to know him or her. This fear also relates back to primitive days, when strangers were potential attackers. When we're in strange areas, this fear keeps us alert.

Strategies:
- Keep an open mind and heart toward others. A stranger may be just a friend you haven't met, not someone out to fleece you.
- When approaching someone new, there's nothing to break the ice like a smile or a hello to encourage a conversation or to ward off confrontation. Take the initiative in conversation. Strangers don't have anything up on us; they're just as in the dark about us as we are about them, and perhaps just as apprehensive.
- If you rarely strike up a conversation with a stranger, it may be a sign that you are shy or that your confidence needs a boost. Volunteering or joining a club will help you deal with this fear.

- Go to a restaurant or bar in a region or section of town you are not acquainted with, perhaps with a person you know. Or take a cruise with new people you must mingle with for a week or two. Always try to make new friends. A relative of mine wondered how I could walk onto a playground and start playing pickup sports games with strangers (as I sometimes do); I told him you get used to it and sometimes you look forward to it.
- Don't be a couch potato, and don't conduct your relationships on the Internet. Get out more often. Remember that meeting new people introduces you to fresh ideas and styles. You may learn a different way of dancing, of tying a shoelace or of baking a cake.
- If your baby cries around strangers, don't panic. It's normal for infants to be afraid of strangers, especially when they're around eight months old. This is often just a sign that the baby feels comfortable with familiar faces.

A MANTRA TO TELL YOURSELF: *"I am a stranger to others."*

Reference:

Beyond Shyness by Jonathan Berent, Fireside, 1993

See: fear of other races, fear of the unknown, fear of terrorism, fear of intimacy or love, fear of religion, fear of crowds, fear of public speaking, fear of change

Fear of Other Races

xenophobia (fear of foreigners or strangers)	*There can be hope only for a society which acts as one big family, not as many separate ones.* —FORMER EGYPTIAN PRESIDENT ANWAR EL SADAT

Characteristics: This condition involves fear or dislike of people from a different region, culture, race, religion, age or color. Sufferers may avoid them, form stereotypical attitudes toward them, or even shun them or become hostile toward them. Some people believe other races are more violent or less worthy than their own.

Background: We are all programmed with a gene that makes us suspicious of other groups of people. This is sometimes called the us vs. them gene, which nature originally gave us to protect us from unknown tribes that may wage war against us. Nowadays, we know much more about other "tribes" and we are relatively good to one another, yet this fear still causes much grief in the world and was one factor in the tragedy of September 11, 2001. We often fear others and sometimes become angry toward them when we don't understand them. Real problems can occur if we start to consider others less human than us, or if we believe another race will contaminate our own. This fear, which appears more when we are under stress, is prevalent in politics, in which right-wing people may despise left-wingers and vice versa.

Strategies:

- Don't be so quick to assess or judge others who are not like you. When we oversimplify or stereotype other people, we open the door for resentment and fear.
- Educate yourself and get to know someone from another race. "When we have fear of the unknown, we kill the unknown. That is a natural instinct," said Randall Tetlichi, speaking to the Canadian Royal Commission on Aboriginal Peoples.

- Try to find common ground with others; you'll probably discover that you share similar hopes and attitudes. If put in a similar situation to yours, most people would probably react in a similar manner.
- Try to avoid raising your self-esteem by becoming part of a group, such as a winning team or a particular race, just to defeat or put down another group.
- Don't feel a sense of entitlement over new immigrants. Originally, we all came from someplace else. Should we close the door now that we are inside the gates?
- In politics, when you examine attitudes and beliefs, right-wingers are not that far apart from the left-wingers; don't always exaggerate the differences to prove a point. For example, don't assume that all conservatives are intolerant or that all liberals are undisciplined. You won't be able to defend yourself when presented with evidence to the contrary.
- Although 9/11 was an inexcusable attack on civilians, try to understand the mindset of radicals and the danger of lumping them together with others from their culture. Sheldon Solomon, a professor of psychology at Brooklyn College, points out: "For the radical Islam represented by Osama bin Laden, the West is evil and must be eradicated. On the other side, President George W. Bush declared this conflict a crusade, suggesting that our god is better than theirs."
- Practice tolerance. A tolerant society may be a higher form of society.

A MANTRA TO TELL YOURSELF: *"They're more like me than I think."*

Reference:

Tolerance (Cultures of Peace) by Dominique Roger, UNESCO, 1995

See: fear of terrorism, fear of religion, fear of the unknown, fear of strangers, fear of rejection, fear of homosexuality

Fear of Singing or Dancing

phonophobia (fear of voices or speaking aloud) *chorophobia* (fear of dancing)	*I am terrified of dancing. Any social situation where I may suddenly be cajoled into strutting my self-conscious, inhibited, middle-class stuff scares me stiff.* —MICHAEL STEPHENS, GUITARIST AND MUSIC COLUMNS EDITOR AT WWW.POPMATTERS.COM

Characteristics: People with this condition avoid singing or dancing in front of others for fear of embarrassment, comparison or criticism. Even if they attempt it, they may experience dry throat, nausea, tension, sweaty palms, or lack of rhythm or confidence. At parties, people may drink heavily to lose their inhibitions before they have enough confidence to sing or dance.

Background: Fear of singing or dancing in front of others is one of the most common fears. People may worry that their voice will break or sound flat, or that others will think less of them if they fail. Or they may worry that others won't like their choice of music. Those who fear dancing may fear embarrassment or may have problems with balance and coordination.

Primitive man may have been less inhibited and may have had more rhythm than we have; social evolution has made some societies more rigid and self-conscious. Music could be more important to our society—if we allowed it to be, if we didn't keep it to ourselves. One theory is that there is a connection between social rhythm and physical rhythm. For example, Italian people tend to be rhythmic in dance and in their social connections. Music is good for your health; research shows that people who keep the beat or sing along in a 30-minute music session have a greater increase in antibody concentrations than people who only listen to it.

Strategies for singing:

- Host a party with people who like to sing; invite a friend experienced in playing piano or guitar. Buy a karaoke machine and practice alone, or go to a karaoke night where you are anonymous.

- Take singing lessons (I'm thinking about it) or buy an instructional CD or tape (I did). Practice will strengthen your vocal chords, which are muscles like those in your arms.
- If you must, have a few drinks to take the edge off your nervousness (but not too many!).
- Start out by humming or whistling. Let the rhythm and the harmony take you; focus on the words, and don't be distracted by other people in the room.
- Lower your expectations; others won't expect you to sound like Sinatra. But if you show the courage to sing, you could become a leader and discover that others want to sing along.
- Many people who became famous singers were initially afraid, such as Perry Como and Barbra Streisand. Others without strong voices made it big, including Madonna and Bryan Adams.

Strategies for dancing:

- Do you have two left feet? Who doesn't? Few people are great dancers because most of us don't dance enough to get really fluid at it. Dance at home to build up some rhythm and confidence.
- Surround yourself with fun people, particularly if they are not judgmental. Even if you are a bad dancer, they won't care that much, and they certainly won't see you as less of a person.
- Take dance lessons, perhaps with a partner, but be sure you are signing up for lessons that teach the type of dance you want.
- Let your defenses and inhibitions down and take your coat and tie off. To deny your inner rhythm is to inhibit yourself unnecessarily. This is a personality trait you may want to improve.
- Don't deny yourself one of life's joys.

A MANTRA TO TELL YOURSELF: *"Let my rhythm flow."*

References:

Learn to Sing Harmony by Cathy Fink, Marcy Marxer, Robin Williams and Linda Williams, Hal Leonard Publishing, 2001

Video: *Learn to Dance in Minutes* by Cal Pozo

CD: *Learn to Sing Like a Star* by Ava Tracht Landman

See: fear of embarrassment, fear of making mistakes, fear of criticism, fear of what others think, fear of showing emotions, fear of falling

Fear of Dating

sarmassophobia (fear of love play)	*A man can be short and dumpy and getting bald, but if he has fire, women will like him.* —Mae West

Characteristics: Many people experience this condition. They feel nervous about the social or sexual consequences of going on a date with someone, or simply fear being with a new person all evening. People can feel pressure to make a good impression or to have others like them immediately. The fear of rejection from a date can be powerful; we may react to it very personally. Multiple failures can result in a person becoming gun-shy and avoiding relationships, or he or she may start to feel inadequate or unattractive.

Background: Dating is always unpredictable because of the differences in people and their needs and motives. One person may want to have fun and the other to get married. Experts are still not sure what makes a perfect date, never mind a perfect match. Nature wants to keep us procreating, so the sexual desire in people who date remains strong. This can add to the fear and pressure of a date.

Strategies:
- It sounds geeky at first, but try going on a date with a relative to reduce your fear.
- Ask for advice from a parent, friend, teacher, relative or confidante, particularly someone with lots of dating experience.
- Be open and honest with your date. Admitting your fear and sensitivity often makes you more attractive to the other person.
- Always start dating slowly. The relationship may grow or it may not. Relationships are unpredictable. If you are too enthusiastic, you may scuttle your opportunity.
- If you want to start a relationship on the first date, don't go to a high-class type of venue just to impress because you may never go there again. You want to find somewhere you'll enjoy again and again. If you try to be someone you're not, the truth will eventually come out.

- Be wary of kissing on the first date, never mind jumping into the sack. Don't be so superficial as to endanger others' feelings or your future. Seek something more than sex, and let the other person know your attitude toward this issue.
- Be a good listener and try to have fun. It's just a date. Do not force yourself to determine feelings about the other person too quickly.
- What looks like a fear of dating may actually be a fear of the opposite sex, of intimacy, of having sex or even of other people in general. Analyze your fears and your motives.
- Remember that opposites may attract, especially in their personalities, but this kind of attraction can be superficial and temporary. People of similar values and interests are more likely to bond over the long haul. If you are looking for a long-lasting relationship, seek out someone you can be friends with.
- What is the worst that could happen on a date? Is your self-esteem so insecure you couldn't withstand rejection? Could your date bite off your nose?
- Go the cliché route: don't put all your eggs in one basket. There are lots of fish in the sea.
- Learn something from every date you have, and leave the other person with something.

A MANTRA TO TELL YOURSELF: *"At least for now, it's only a date."*

References:

Fearless Loving: 8 Simple Truths That Will Change the Way You Date, Mate and Relate by Rhonda Britten, E.P. Dutton, 2003

The Worst-Case Scenario Survival Handbook: Dating and Sex by Joshua Piven, David Borgenicht and Jennifer Worick, Chronicle, 2001 (careful, this book's a little in-your-face)

The Romance Page, ww2.best.vwh.net/romance.html

See: fear of commitment, fear of rejection, fear of intimacy or love, sexual fears, fear of the opposite sex, fear of embarrassment, fear of the unknown, fear of oneself

Fear of the Opposite Sex

heterophobia (fear of the opposite sex	*Men mistakenly expect women to think, communicate and react the way men do;*
androphobia (fear of men)	*women mistakenly expect men to feel, communicate and respond the way women do. We have forgotten that men and*
gynephobia (fear of women)	*women are supposed to be different. As a result, our relationships are filled with unnecessary friction and conflict.* —JOHN

GRAY, AUTHOR OF *MEN ARE FROM MARS, WOMEN ARE FROM VENUS*

Characteristics: This condition creates discomfort, anxiety or even conflict about the opposite sex in social, professional or intimate situations. This fear may affect behavior and decisions in business, making some women feel discriminated against and some men feel threatened. Such fears may result in prejudices and stereotyping.

Background: Men and women have probably misunderstood each other since the beginning of time. We tend to fear things we don't understand, and until recently, we have not openly discussed the differences between men and women. In many areas, we've tended to treat men and women as identical, and we've often been frustrated when they've reacted differently. Heredity plays a part in this fear, but so does environment (for example, boys and girls are often warned by adults to stay apart). This fear may be related to the fear of sex, fear of a parent, or strong, repressed feelings.

Strategies:

- We need to better understand the trends and traits of the opposite sex: men tend to be more rational, objective and goal- and work-oriented. Women tend to be more emotional and subjective, eager to talk about their feelings and interested in developing relationships.
- The above having been said, men and women should be aware that they also display traits from the opposite sex, and they should try to develop the positive ones (men should be more open, cuddly and cooperative; women should think things through before relying on their emotions and shouldn't be afraid to compete).

- Be prepared to challenge stereotypes: are all men really unsentimental? Are all women really afraid of mice?
- Try to understand the evolution of the opposite sex. If you're a working woman, try to be dispassionate and see the Old Boys' Club as a natural progression of men's having long had most of the power in the world. If you're a man, try to examine why many women seem more drawn to spirituality, even to psychic and supernatural things. For a long time, many men didn't take such things seriously, but many women sought peace in them.
- Sit down and have a serious conversation, and don't be afraid to bring up these issues. Lack of communication is often behind fear and poor relationships.
- Don't criticize or judge someone of the opposite sex who reacts with different emotions than you. Says marriage counselor William F. Harley Jr., "The five most important emotional needs of men are usually the least important for women, and vice versa...the two sexes lack empathy."

Author's Two Cents:

My wife is from a family of boys. Our first date was to a Buffalo Bills game. Sometimes I ask her if we always have to watch football on Sunday. She wonders why I sometimes wear more jewelry than she does. I consider our relationship healthy because we allow each other to break gender stereotypes.

A MANTRA TO TELL YOURSELF: *"Understand a different way of thinking."*

References:

He Says, She Says: Closing the Communications Gap Between the Sexes by Lillian Glass, Putnam, 1993

Men Are from Mars, Women Are from Venus by John Gray, HarperCollins, 1992

You Just Don't Understand by Deborah Tannen, Ballantine, 1990

See: fear of intimacy or love, fear of not being loved, fear of rejection, sexual fears, fear of responsibility, fear of commitment, fear of becoming a parent

Fear of Commitment

gamophobia (fear of marriage)

We have to make a conscious decision for commitment. That means choosing not to have affairs, choosing not to make another person as important as our partner, choosing to talk to our partner rather than someone else when we're angry, choosing to listen, choosing to see things through.
—AUTHOR AND CONSULTANT REX BRIGGS

Characteristics: This condition keeps people from committing to others for such reasons as an inability to trust or to take responsibility. Those affected may not want to go steady or get engaged or married; they may even balk at having relationships. This fear can leave people with sad lives and few close friendships.

Background: We live in an increasingly fast society in which commitment often takes a back seat. Indeed, 50 percent of marriages fail. But without commitment, can there really be true love? Some people just won't take a chance to come out of their comfort zone. People who lack commitment in one area, such as romance, may not in another area, such as a job or an organization.

Strategies:
- Commitment may sound like a kind of straitjacket, but if both parties compromise, it won't be too tight or too foreboding. Talk openly about the relationship, and get to know what each person needs and expects from the other.
- Be aware that this fear may be a sign of immaturity. It may also indicate that you lack the patience, passion or discipline required in a healthy relationship.
- It may, however, simply be a sign that you don't want commitment with a certain person, or that you don't love them or don't see yourself developing love for them. Think it through. Maybe there is something about the other person you don't like, or would like to see improved. Talk to them about it.
- If someone is willing to make a commitment to you, consider taking it as inspiration to increase your own effort.

- How can you tell if he or she is Mr. or Mrs. Right? No one is ever completely sure of such things.
- Don't fool yourself: making a full commitment, especially to marriage and perhaps children, is a life-altering decision.
- Maybe you want to stay single. Who said there was anything wrong with that? Well, lots of people, but it doesn't mean they are right in every instance.
- If you don't get into a relationship because you don't trust others, consider the words of therapist Robert Epstein: "Yes, people sometimes cheat and lie, but they sometimes are also faithful and truthful. Trust is a matter of interpreting what people do positively. You decide—trust or live in isolation."
- If you have trouble committing to things in other areas, such as in work, family life or school, you might have to develop the same type of patience, passion or discipline required in a relationship. Sign up for a course or an organization in which you have to stay the course for at least several months; if you can't do it alone, do it with a friend.

A MANTRA TO TELL YOURSELF: *"I'll take a stand on taking a stand" (make a decision on whether to make a commitment).*

Reference:

Transforming Anxiety, Transcending Shame by Rex Briggs, Health Communications, 1999

See: fear of taking chances, fear of the unknown, fear of intimacy or love, fear of responsibility, fear of the opposite sex, sexual fears, fear of becoming a parent, fears for your marriage/partnership

Fear of Ending a Romantic Relationship

neophobia (fear of anything new)

There are no cut-and-dried answers, merely accumulated feelings that show it is time to end a relationship.

—BARRY LUBETKIN AND ELENA OUMANO, AUTHORS OF *BAILING OUT*

Characteristics: People with this fear often stay in stale or abusive relationships because of apprehension or guilt over a breakup, or through fear of hurting the other person's feelings. They may even fear physical reprisal or reprisal against friends or children caught in the middle. Others are just lazy or don't want to give up familiar surroundings.

Background: Breaking a bond, especially a long one, can be very difficult physically, emotionally and spiritually, particularly if people are married with children. We all form bonds that we are reluctant to break, out of concern for either our own needs or the other person's. We may be very needy and have emotional holes from a poor home life or an earlier relationship. And we may fear that we'll never get another relationship if this one ends. In general, most people are afraid of the type of confrontation a breakup can create. People may also be afraid of giving up the friends or the perks that came along with their partner. Many spouses of powerful people or celebrities stay in poor relationships because they don't want to give up the high life.

Strategies:
- Be certain that you want to end the relationship. Many bonds simply need more commitment, compromise and work.
- Look for warning signs that the relationship may be on the way out: Are you feeling disconnected from the person or have you stopped caring? Do you feel you can't trust him or her anymore? Are you being abused physically or emotionally? Have you become too critical? Are you looking for excuses to be apart? Have you been to counseling and decided it cannot help?

- Find the right time and place to break up. Usually, it's best to break up when no one else is around, but if you feel it may spark an emotional or physical reaction, you may want to do it in a public place or with witnesses.
- Once you have decided on ending the relationship, tell the person why. Don't blame one another. Breakups are complex and usually occur for more than one reason. Be respectful and kind, even after the relationship is over. Don't end it with a bad taste in your mouths. Anger is often a counterproductive emotion.
- Understand that the other person will likely feel hurt or sad. Perhaps you'll both feel that way and it may take some time to get over.
- If you are married, don't be so quick to end the relationship. You may later regret it and find it is hard to patch up. But if you do end it, protect your rights and see a lawyer.
- In the early days after the breakup, expect a range of emotions. Try to keep busy. And don't jump into another relationship right away. There may be chances for reconciliation.
- Don't stay around just for the sex.

  A MANTRA TO TELL YOURSELF: *"I'll do what must be done."*

Reference:

Crucial Conversations: Tools for Talking When Stakes Are High by Kerry Patterson, Joseph Grenny, Ron McMillan, Al Switzer and Stephen R. Covey, McGraw-Hill, 2002

See: fear of not being loved, fear of what others think, fear of change, fear of failure, fear of the opposite sex, fear of delivering bad news

Fear of Homosexuality

homophobia (fear of homosexuality)

The biggest problem we've got is the primitive, age-old fear and dehumanization of people who are not like us.

—PRESIDENT BILL CLINTON, TO GAY AND LESBIAN SUPPORTERS IN 1999

Characteristics: This is the fear, anxiety, anger, discomfort or aversion that some heterosexual people feel toward gays and lesbians. Some people discriminate against or harass gays and lesbians; in extreme cases, people even commit acts of violence against them. Others fear they are attracted to members of the same sex or worry that they are perceived as gay or lesbian themselves.

Background: Homosexuality exists throughout the animal kingdom and is a natural phenomenon. But surveys show that up to 70 percent of the American public is homophobic. Many people fear what they don't understand or what they feel threatens them or their beliefs. Other factors accounting for homophobia include rigid gender roles, social pressure to fear and hate gays, institutionalized heterosexism and homophobic religious beliefs. Some research suggests that homophobia is sometimes the result of repressed homosexual urges that a person is either unaware of or denies.

Strategies:

- Ask yourself how open you are about others' sexuality and about your own. Think the issues through and don't be afraid of them.
- Keep an open mind and be receptive to new research. Much of what we have been taught has been colored by bias, stereotyping and misinformation or has been based on lack of information. We're still finding out new things, partly because gays and lesbians have been reluctant to come forward with information.
- Be aware that most serious research points to genetics and not environment as the cause of homosexuality, although this question remains open to debate. "Mental health professionals used to consider homosexuality a type of mental illness, but now it's seen as a normal condition that is at least partially determined by genes," says psychologist Robert Epstein.

- Get to know an openly gay man or woman and listen closely if they talk about their attitudes and life. Discuss yours with them.
- Refrain from hating homophobics. Understand that some people genuinely see homosexuality as a threat to procreation, world health (through AIDS) or their religious beliefs.
- If you discriminate against someone because of sexual preference, think of how you would feel if someone did the same thing to you.
- Understand that many men and women who appear to be gay are not.
- Some of the most creative, productive people are openly gay: Olympic gold medal swimmer Mark Tewksbury, singer kd lang, tennis legend Martina Navratilova, actors Ian McKellan and Ellen DeGeneres, to name but a few.

A MANTRA TO TELL YOURSELF: *"Understanding and tolerance."*

Author's Two Cents:

While conducting two major investigations into AIDS for newspapers, I found gay men to be generally nonthreatening, sensitive and caring. This discovery made me less intimidated by them.

References:

And the Band Played On by Randy Shilts, St. Martin's, 2001

Homophobia: How We All Pay the Price by Warren Blumenfeld, Beacon, 2002

See: fear of other races, sexual fears, fear of religion, fear of what others think, fear of the unknown, fear of the opposite sex

7

Fears at School

Fear of School

scolionophobia (fear of going to school)

sophophobia (fear of learning)

Nearly all children will have some reluctance and fear going to school. They eventually get over it with encouragement and support...stay calm and tell them you love them.

—FAMILY PSYCHOLOGIST MICHAEL G. CONNER

Characteristics: Up to 10 percent of children suffer from a mild form of fear of school, and about 1 percent have a serious form of it. Some children may fake illness or throw tantrums or have tension or stomach cramps. They may stay away from school or complain about the teachers, the principal, the curriculum, classmates or bullies, or they may fear being punished. Even children who like school may get stressed going back after summer vacation. Some children are afraid of getting undressed for gym or going to the bathroom. Healthy fear or respect can make some lazy students try harder.

Background: There may be many reasons for fear of school: some children are afraid of leaving home (separation fear); others are afraid of teachers, of having to work hard, of not living up to parents' expectations, of not being accepted or popular, or of other students or bullies. This fear can last an entire academic career, or it can come and go, depending on the circumstances of the student or the school. In some cases, fear may be related to not liking school—many children do not like structure or being told what to do. A British study of students 7 to 16 years of age showed that 46 percent of them were stressed about doing well at school, 43 percent worried about coming into contact with drugs and alcohol, 40 percent feared being bullied, 37 percent worried about future education and 34 percent worried about friendships at school.

Strategies:

- All children grumble about school occasionally, but be wary if your child constantly complains about school, teachers or classmates. Examine if the fear is specific—students may fear a certain teacher or course, they may fear bullies, peer pressure or the prospect of looking stupid, or they may fear the pressures of exams or competition, of speaking before a class, of hard work or of having to get a job when it's all over. Whew!

- Maybe the fear is academic, or the curriculum is not suited to the individual. Maybe the student believes he or she is not allowed to be expressive or creative. If this is the case, see a counselor or trusted teacher.

- Don't coddle your children too much—they'll become too dependent and fearful. On the other hand, if you pressure them too much academically, they may rebel or quit.

- If you believe your child suffers from separation anxiety, slowly desensitize her to the situation by going with her to class for a brief time, and then gradually decrease that amount. Talk about this condition with the teacher. If the child still refuses to go to school, find ways to help boost her confidence. Children will eventually adjust to school when they realize they can handle it by themselves.

- Encourage your child to join a club, a sports team or an activity. Consider becoming a volunteer. Motivation in one area can spill over to another, such as the academic field.

- It's possible that a health issue is involved. Perhaps the student is allergic to something or there is poor circulation in the building.

- In any type of serious case, get the teachers and school nurses or counselors involved. Counselors are there not only to guide students about education and career choices, but also to help them with lifestyle and stress issues.

A MANTRA FOR PARENTS: *"With my encouragement, my child will be fine."*

References:

The School Years by Benjamin Spock, Simon & Schuster, 2001

David A. Gershaw, psychologist, Arizona Western College, DAGershaw@aol.com

See: fear of change, stress and fear in children, fear of strangers, fear of religion (in some private schools), fear of bullies and all the school fears

Fear of the First Day of School

separation anxiety syndrome (children's fear of being separated from their parents, which can also occur the other way around)

September finds more than one parent walking away from a preschool or elementary school classroom with misty eyes...for women, separation anxiety actually begins at birth and continues through various stages.
—PARENT EDUCATOR ELAINE M. GIBSON

Characteristics: Apprehension in children and/or parents about the first day of school is natural and common. Signs of nervousness may appear before or during that day, including dry throat, trembling or lack of confidence. There may be a lot of crying and clinging to parents for at least the first few days. Parents may feel guilty that their child is put into a situation where he or she is afraid.

Background: Nature creates a tight bond between parents and child to ensure the child's survival and care. When a young child's parents have always been close by, it can be traumatic to be suddenly without them and among strangers at school. Letting go of a lifeline is sad, but necessary to the development of both child and parents.

Strategies:
- At an early age, get your children gradually used to your occasional absences. Until the age of three, most children can't understand the concept of time. When you leave briefly, they may think you are gone forever.
- Improve your child's social and play skills. Get the child used to other relatives and visitors and make visits to others' homes. Show your children love and security, but teach them skills in getting along with others and give them some freedom.
- At first, ask to occasionally sit in on school activities and see how your child interacts with teachers and classmates.
- Make sure your child has sufficient verbal skills to communicate with others. Read age-appropriate books with them.
- Before the big first day, tell the child that he will be going to school and reassure him that it will be a good experience. Use role playing or puppets to act out the first day. Consider riding the bus with your child the first day. Let the child bring a security object (a stuffed toy) or your photo to class.

- Don't overreact if your child cries and refuses to leave your side. Most teachers will allow you to stay for a while. When you leave, don't sneak out; it may make the child feel abandoned.
- If you are anxious, don't show it in front of your child, who may pick up on it. Learn to deal with your own issues of separation and try to trust other adults with your child's needs.
- With each step, children gain freedom and independence on their way to growing up. And parents learn to relinquish some of their control for the benefit of the child.

Author's Two Cents:

We put our shy three-year-old Kevin in preschool too young. He accumulated a softball-sized clump of tear-soaked tissues and planned on stealing a tricycle to sneak home. We pulled him out, but even two years later, he was afraid when we dropped him off at kindergarten. Later in kindergarten, his mother and older brother had to stay with him in class through part of the morning for several weeks. Finally an understanding teacher got him through it. Kevin slowly developed his social skills and now shows leadership in groups.

A MANTRA FOR PARENTS: *"Take a deep breath, then go"* OR *"She's not a baby anymore."*

References:

My First Day of School by P.K. Hallinan, Ideals Children's Books, 2001

When You Go to Kindergarten by James Howe and Betsy Imershein, Mulberry, 1995

Life Advice, www.lifeadvice.com

See: fear of not having control, fear of school, fear of your children leaving home, fear of the unknown, fear of showing emotions, fear and stress in children, fear of being alone, fear of strangers, fear of panic attacks in public

Fear of Appearing Stupid

asthenophobia (fear of weakness)	*Zeal will do more than knowledge.* —AUTHOR WILLIAM HAZLITT
catagelophobia (fear of ridicule)	**Characteristics:** Nobody wants to look stupid or inadequate. But some students suffer from serious anxiety or withdrawal

because they believe others—classmates, friends, teachers or smart students—think of them as academically inferior. Some students may lose motivation, exaggerate their prowess or even cheat because of this condition. In extreme cases, this fear can lead to depression, antisocial behavior and substance abuse.

Background: In an education center such as a school, much of the focus is on intelligence and the ability to learn; hence, the popularity of tags such as nerd, geek, brain, dumbbell, clueless and professional student. A healthy fear of appearing inadequate can sometimes motivate a student through a school career that may span 15 years or more. A student's home environment and circle of friends can have a heavy influence on this fear. If people are constantly told they are stupid, they might start to believe it. In our society, we are constantly aware of how we measure up to others, and we worry if they look down on us. This fear can make one try hard, but it can also make one try *too* hard.

Strategies:

- Step back and gain some perspective. Just because you think you appear stupid to others doesn't mean others actually feel that way. If you have this mindset, it may be that your family or friends continually talk down to you.
- We all have an inner critic—a little voice in our head that is constantly giving us advice and often judging us. Challenge the inner voice if it keeps putting you down. Ask yourself where it comes from and how much credence you should give it.
- Upgrade yourself through study and discipline. The best revenge against critics is living well, or in this case, learning well. Examine your level of academic competence and ask yourself if you are where you want to be.

- Don't be afraid to ask for a tutor. A little extra help, or just bouncing your thoughts and ideas off a tutor, can take you to another level academically and boost your confidence.
- Remember that everyone is different. People peak and learn at different ages; boys, especially, tend to be late bloomers academically.
- Don't hang around with negative people who constantly run others down. Praise others for their knowledge. While alone, praise yourself.
- If you worry too much about what others think or if you constantly compare yourself with others, maybe you need to develop your confidence and determination.
- If you're a parent, don't put all your emphasis on the three Rs. Encourage your kids to think for themselves and to understand ideas, to learn cooperation and empathy for others, and to familiarize themselves with the behaviors of other cultures as well as their own.
- If you flunk out, try to bounce back. But remember, Joan of Arc was illiterate, comedian Jack Benny was expelled from high school after failing, and Benjamin Franklin attended school for just a few years and was largely self-taught.
- If nothing else, establish some structure and discipline; you'll need it as an adult.

A MANTRA TO TELL YOURSELF: *"I might not become Einstein, but I am intelligent, and I can develop it."*

Reference:

Test Taking Secrets by Steve Frank, Adams Media, 1998

See: fear of embarrassment, fear of failure, fear of criticism, fear of rejection, fear of what others think, fear of what friends think, fear of exams, fear of teachers, fear of your appearance, fear of dating, fear of the opposite sex

Fear of Exams

testophobia

Pressure can be a good thing in small doses. —JAY BAGLIA, TEACHING ASSISTANT, UNIVERSITY OF FLORIDA

Characteristics: Some students freeze or perform poorly when they write tests. Others feel anxious, tense or depressed about exams right from the first day of school—even good students who prepare well for them. Some are so afraid of failing, they cheat. A track record of low marks can add to the fear.

Background: For just about everyone, it's natural to be apprehensive about being tested or evaluated, whether at home, at work or at any level of school. Up to 25 percent of college students have what has been termed *math anxiety*. Students might fear failure, loss of job opportunity, or what their parents, teachers, family or friends might think. Indeed, upbringing has a large effect on a student's apprehension toward tests; demanding mothers or fathers can push children to great heights, but can also burden them with too much pressure. On the other hand, overly casual parents may leave students without the respect for curriculum and exams they need to be successful. Teachers' expectations also provide pressure, or lack of it.

Strategies:

- When approaching an exam, try not to put too much pressure on yourself; keep your goals realistic. A test may be important, but it won't be the end of the world if you don't attain the mark you seek. Show respect to the wishes of your parents and teachers, but make your goals your own. Some students set their own academic standards too high or are too hard on themselves.
- Test yourself prior to the exam, or have someone test you, then mark you critically. Simulating a type of pressure in advance allows you to get used to the feelings of tension and anxiety. Then, when the exam day comes, you'll feel as if you've been through it already. Some schools give test-taking practice; check to see if *your* school does.

- Study intensely over an extended period, but don't cram. Conceptualize the work, the theories and the ideas. Don't memorize: if you do, you take the risk of your structure breaking down if you forget one section.
- Before an important test, make sure you get the right amount of sleep and exercise and eat a balanced diet.
- Remember that a *manageable* amount of pressure and intensity can actually bring out the best in you, as long as you are well prepared. You don't want to be too casual or you might not be mentally sharp. The hormones released by your nervous system can help you concentrate at a higher level if you remain calm or direct the energy into your work.
- The start of a test is important. Take a few deep breaths and do the easier questions first. If possible, take short breaks. Close your eyes and relax. Even 30 seconds of deep breathing can reduce distress.
- Put yourself on automatic pilot and let your subconscious and your knowledge take over. If you try too hard, you'll get in your own way. Focus on the process, not the potential results. After you receive your marks, review and analyze everything, including your strategies. Think of your errors as an opportunity to grow and learn.
- If these strategies don't work, it's possible that your daily anxiety levels are too high. You may have too many pressures in your life, or may not be managing your pressures properly. You might want to see a school counselor.
- Parents, monitor the attitudes and tension levels of your children throughout the year and especially at exam time.

A MANTRA TO TELL YOURSELF: *"I'm not perfect, but I'm ready."*

References:

Take the Anxiety Out of Taking Tests by Susan Johnson, Publishers Group West, 1996

Sylvan Learning Center, (866) 732-3438, www.educate.com

See: fear of the unknown, fear of not having control, fear of failure, fear of making mistakes, fear of criticism, fear of appearing stupid, fear of what friends think, fear of not having or getting a job, fear of losing status, dealing with deadline pressure

Fear of Teachers

tyrannophobia (fear of tyrants)

dikephobia (fear of justice)

When you make peace with authority, you become authority. —ROCK STAR JIM MORRISON

Characteristics: Nowadays we often hear about lack of respect for authority and teachers. Yet many students still fear teachers, or at least worry about going to school or a class because a teacher is harsh or unfair, or makes students look foolish in front of the class or work hard. Some students worry that a teacher will give negative appraisal to their parents.

Background: Fear of authority is common among children, especially those who have harsh, overprotective or argumentative parents. It's natural for a child, even a teenager, to be in awe of someone with so much knowledge and power. If a child feels the teacher is not meeting his or her needs, this awe could turn into distress. But *healthy* fear of or respect for a teacher can boost student production and discipline and make going to school challenging, even pleasurable.

Strategies:

- Realize that if a teacher seems critical, it's probably not personal; teachers are human and have different personalities and even prejudices. Some teachers are more authoritarian than others. They also have lots of pressure with increasing workloads and class sizes. What a job! One day, try to volunteer for sessions in which you are given authority, or pretend you are the teacher and put yourself in their shoes.
- Don't engage in anti-teacher talk with other students. This will lower class morale, could erode your relationship with the teacher and may make you more cynical.
- Understand the changing climate; society has less respect for authority than it had in the past. This can cause frustration in teachers who grew up in a different era. Do your small part by trying to foster more mutual respect.
- Consider the possibility that you are more afraid of the subject than of the teacher. Let the teacher know if you need special

help. Talk through problems and issues with the teacher one-on-one, or involve your parents or counselor.

- Do something nice for your teacher, even if he or she isn't nice to you. Volunteer on a class trip or clean up after a group experiment.
- If you constantly blame a teacher for your failures, chances are you will blame authority figures in other stages of your life. Learn to take responsibility.
- If you continue to be a good student, chances are you will eventually develop a good relationship with the teacher. You are together every day; why not try to get along?
- Parents, don't allow an issue between you or your child and a teacher to rob the child of a proper education. If you suspect that legitimate problems exist between your child and a teacher, initiate a meeting and volunteer to be a go-between to deal with the issues. Consider becoming a volunteer at the school.

A MANTRA TO TELL YOURSELF: *"The teach is human."*

Author's Two Cents:

As a sports coach and school volunteer for 20 years, I found that any problems I had with children under me and their parents usually had to do with communication. I occasionally held group and individual meetings to get the issues out in the open; I also encouraged the children to come to me one-on-one. If the kids were afraid of me, I wanted to find it out from them.

Reference:

www.teachers.net

See: fear of not having control, fear of criticism, fear of embarrassment, fear of failure, fear and stress in children, fear of strangers, fear of school, fear of appearing stupid, fear of the boss, fear of confrontation or conflict, fear of responsibility

Fear of What Friends Think

peer pressure

Peer pressure can be frightening for kids and parents in adolescence when the young are challenging so many basic values: demanding the right to sexual freedom at younger and younger age periods and becoming involved increasingly in pregnancies, experimenting with drugs and alcohol.
—Dr. Benjamin Spock

Characteristics: This condition involves excessive concern for the esteem of friends. People who change their behavior or appearance to suit their friends—for example, by smoking, drinking or disrespecting teachers—could be overly afraid of what their friends think. Some students become depressed. Sometimes, though, peer pressure can be a positive thing and can result in people upgrading their marks or getting involved in school activities.

Background: Friends are very important to a young person, especially in the teenage years when identities are being molded. Youths sometimes rebel against their parents and look for independence and, ironically, acceptance from others at the same time. The people they get involved with could have a major impact on them and they make take on their mannerisms, even if only subconsciously. Students are particularly impressionable in the first years of middle school, high school and college, when they don't fully have their bearings at a school. Students who develop confidence and a strong sense of identity at home have less chance of being heavily influenced by peer groups.

Strategies:

- Assess how much influence your friends are having on your schoolwork, your personal life and your attitude, and ask yourself if it is positive. At what expense do you want to be liked? If you're a student, school is pretty much your job. Are you willing to let others screw it up, or screw up your future?
- Five years from now, the people you are trying to impress likely won't be involved in your life. But the decisions you make could still be affecting you. In reality, your friends probably don't care as much about what you do as you think they do.

Most people are focused more on themselves, or worried about what *you* think of *them*.

- As pals, influence one another in a productive way; join a school club or a sports team or study together.

- We all want to be liked and accepted by our friends, but we should also try to win the respect of our other classmates, our parents and our teachers.

- Be wary of "friends" who want to try borderline things and justify their own behavior by getting other kids (perhaps ones with stronger values) to go along. But don't forget to have a blast once in a while, as long as it is not at others' expense.

- Don't stay in a negative relationship for fear of what friends and family might think if you break up.

- If you are a parent, listen with compassion, not judgment, when your child talks about friends, but don't back down from your values. Look upon this as a time to solidify your relationship with your children, while understanding that they also need others to balance their lives. Get to know the parents of your child's friends. Monitor TV and telephone time.

- You can't avoid the media hype and consumerism, but if you refuse a request for a peer-pressure item or clothes, explain your reasons. Maybe you can't afford it, or you think your child is too young, or you think it's dangerous or mean-spirited. Don't give in just because you feel guilty about not spending enough time with your child.

- Teach your children to stand up for themselves in disagreements with friends and praise them for doing the right thing.

A MANTRA TO TELL YOURSELF: *"I'm me"* OR *"Real friends will accept me for me."*

References:

The Complete Idiot's Guide to Surviving Peer Pressure for Teens by Hilary Cherniss and Sara Jane Sluke, Alpha, 2001

Parent Guidance Workshops, New York, founder Nancy Samalin, www.samalin.com

See: fear of what others think, fear of not being loved, fear of rejection, fear of cliques, fear of appearing stupid, fear of confrontation or conflict

Fear of Cliques

enochlophobia (fear of crowds)

Everybody sticks together in these dirty little goddam cliques. The guys that are on the basketball team stick together, the goddam intellectuals stick together, the guys that play bridge stick together. Even the guys that belong to the goddam Book-of-the-Month Club stick together. —HOLDEN CAULFIELD, IN J.D. SALINGER'S CATCHER IN THE RYE

Characteristics: Individuals or groups may be suspicious or antagonistic toward other groups who may not share their attitudes, dress, music or behavior. This may appear as a dislike of another group, but deep down it might be a fear that stems from mutual intimidation.

Background: This fear is similar to the fear of other races or any people who are different from us. We are all hardwired with an us vs. them gene, which protected us from strange tribes when we were primitive people. This fear can be potent because students are confined in the same building every day. Of course, joining a group can have benefits when it gives a student some positive direction. Students often join subcultures such as the hip hop, punk, skater, raver, goth, metalhead or alternative scenes because they want to become accepted by others or join a common cause. Although such group affiliation can be healthy, it can sometimes cause rivalry with other groups.

Strategies:
* Fear of other cliques often comes from lack of understanding. Start by communicating with students or groups of students who are different from you. Encourage communication; perhaps start with the most approachable member of a group or, if the climate is acceptable, hold a "clique party." At one point in my newspaper career, I brought together numerous subcultures in a high school for an article and, after they had openly discussed their attitudes and desires, they went away with a better appreciation and understanding of one another.

- On the other hand, be suspicious of groups who are always negative or destructive. You won't change them, but they may change you.
- Examine your attitude; it's possible that you dislike people only out of arrogance. You may look down on them and believe they are not worthy of your attention.
- If you are part of a clique, be conscious of it and don't make others feel like outsiders. Don't provoke other cliques or try to accentuate your differences from them.
- Don't judge individuals who are part of a group. They may not even agree with the group they are associating with; rather, they may be lonely and just want to be accepted.
- If you are a parent or teacher, monitor the student's situation, but always remember that children are looking to develop their identities, and that means associating with people other than adults. Sometimes it's hard for parents to accept that.

A MANTRA TO TELL YOURSELF: *"Deep down, they're probably like me."*

References:

Cliques: 8 Steps to Help Your Child Survive the Social Jungle by Charlene C. Giannetti and Margaret Sagarese, Broadway, 2001

Cliques, Phonies and Other Baloney by Trevor Romain, Free Spirit, 1998

See: fear of what friends think, fear of rejection, fear of other races, fear of confrontation or conflict, fear of strangers, fear of homosexuality, fear of your appearance, fear of bullies

Fear of Your Appearance

obesophobia (fear of gaining weight) | *Not being beautiful was the true blessing...it forced me to develop my inner resources. The pretty [person] has a handicap to overcome.* —Golda Meir

Characteristics: Worry about body shape, facial looks or clothes can lead to anxiety, stress, missing school, ill health and even eating disorders. Some people develop distorted views of their appearance, believing they are ugly or fat when they're not. Many are afraid of how they look in their gym clothes. Plastic surgeons report instances of children as young as 14 coming in with their parents to request surgery. A mild form of this fear can encourage people to take pride in themselves and their appearance.

Background: Everyone wants to impress others to some degree and to put on the best possible face while covering up their weaknesses. It seems a sad indictment of our society (indeed, of our history as human beings), but the pretty people often get more attention, while some others retreat and even suffer self-esteem problems. The fashion industry taps into society's obsession with looks; many ads now have teenagers in sexual poses.

How you feel about yourself, your shape and your appearance has a lot to do with how you were raised and how your parents felt about themselves. The teen years are filled with self-discovery and self-doubt. As we grow older, we realize that appearance is just a small part of who we really are.

Strategies:

- Keep this fear in perspective. Intense focus on your appearance can lead to a superficial, distorted attitude. You can start worrying more about your clothes than your intelligence, personality, skills or other things you have to offer.
- Do you feel you are inadequate because you don't have a perfectly round face or Michael Jordan basketball shoes? Get your priorities in order—it's who you are as a human being that counts. Being a nice person and helping and inspiring others is a lot more important than looks or shoes.

- Make the most out of what you've got while being as natural as possible. Be yourself, but don't be sloppy. When you dress in a "presentable" way, you look professional, even if you're still young. But be cautious about buying expensive clothes just because your friends have them. If they have a hang-up with materialism, that's their problem.
- Have fun with your look! Overload with jewelry one day, or wear jeans if appropriate. Having a fun attitude might take the pressure off trying to keep up with your peers.
- Eating a balanced diet and staying in shape have many benefits, but if you are concerned about your physique, don't go overboard. Metabolism is an individual thing; some people retain fat more than others, while others burn their blood sugar more quickly.
- If students continually tease you about the way you look, beat them to the punch by poking fun at yourself. This can take the sting out of their comments. If you are afraid of losing friends over your looks, those may be friends not worth having.
- If you fret about your body shape in gym class, look around; people come in different shapes and sizes. Would you look down at someone with a body shape you didn't like? Then don't look down at yourself.
- If you believe you have an eating disorder, see a trusted teacher or school counselor. And, of course, talk to your parents about it.
- Parents, talk to your teenagers about the importance of appearance, but do a lot of listening and don't try to impose your standards on them.
- If you continually try to prove yourself through your appearance, you might have an inferiority complex. Remember the words of former first lady Eleanor Roosevelt: "No one can make you feel inferior without your consent."

A MANTRA TO TELL YOURSELF: *"I'm cool."*

Reference:

Smart Eating: Choosing Wisely, Living Lean by Covert Bailey and Ronda Gates, Houghton Mifflin, 1996

See: fear of what others think, fear of what friends think, fear of criticism, fear of rejection, fear of not being loved, fear of embarrassment, fear of having a photo taken, fear of getting a compliment

Fear of Bullies

scelerophobia (fear of being hurt by a wicked person) *For a lot of years I've taught at the university, and I always ask my classes how many felt an impact from bullying, and probably a third raise their hands and say, "You know I'm still carrying with me a sad or frightened memory about someone doing something to me."* —CHILD SAFETY EXPERT DAVIE SCRATCHLEY

Characteristics: Fear of bullying is widespread. Students may become anxious or depressed and avoid situations or classes because they fear physical or verbal harassment or robbery. If bullying continues, it could have a long-term effect on self-esteem and confidence and result in physical injury.

Background: Bullying is a worldwide problem that has lately received more attention. Bullies, often victims themselves, know that psychological intimidation can be as fierce as physical force. Bullies may be jealous of others, insecure, afraid of being unpopular or unable to show their feelings. They may act out because they are trying to "find themselves," to prove something to others or to themselves, or to get the attention of a group they want acceptance from. Boys tend to bully with force while some girls engage in sophisticated forms of aggression such as gossip, backbiting and social isolation. These days, however, girls are increasingly getting involved in physical bullying. A Gallup poll revealed that 47 percent of parents feared for their children's safety at school.

Strategies:

* Whenever possible, try to ignore teasing, nasty comments or getting drawn into an argument. If you show you're upset, it may spur the bully on. If someone insults your appearance, abilities or race, ignore it. Resist the temptation to meet force with force. The law of the jungle where only the strongest survive is not the law of civilized society.
* If you are afraid, hang out with people you trust.
* If the bullying is a sudden, isolated incident, assess the situation and respond accordingly. Simply walk away or stand up for your rights or possessions—but don't do it at the expense of a beating. Learn to shout "No!" and walk confidently.

- If you are harassed for your possessions by someone who may become aggressive, give them up without fighting back, then report it to teachers and the police.
- If bullying continues, talk to a trusted teacher or your parents about it. In certain cases, you might want to confront the bully yourself. Some kids who are nice to your face may pick on you when they're in a group. Get them alone or on the phone and ask them why they gang up on you.
- Consider taking a self-defense course, or gain physical confidence through sports.
- Parents, be aware of signs that your child is being bullied. If a child is unhappy or gets stressed at the same time every week, hates going to certain places, has mysterious cuts or bruises, has become sullen or nervous, cries at night or when alone, or keeps losing possessions, he or she may be a victim of bullying.
- Make sure your child is not worsening a situation by countering bullying with insults or abuse. Teach your children to avoid bullies, explaining that the bullies are the ones with the problem, but also teach assertiveness and positive self-talk. If nothing helps, get involved through the teacher or even the police.

A MANTRA TO TELL YOURSELF: *"Don't get even, get help."*

References:

The Bully, the Bullied and the Bystander by Barbara Coloroso, HarperResource, 2003

Kids Help Phone (in Canada, a 24-hour phone counseling and referral service for children and youth), (800) 668-6868, www.kidshelp.sympatico.ca

National Association of School Psychologists, Bethesda, MD, (301) 657-0270, www.nasponline.org

See: fear for your children's safety, fear of being mugged, fear of illness or pain, fear of embarrassment, fear of cliques, fear of strangers, fear of confrontation or conflict, fear of invasion of territory or privacy, fear and stress in children

Fear of Not Having or Getting a Job

There are no wrong jobs. Every job is a learning experience and there is no one clear path to glamour and happiness.
—HEIDI MILLER, CHIEF FINANCIAL OFFICER OF CITIGROUP

Characteristics: Many people worry about not having a job. Students may feel pressure to get a good job—even one that can buy them a house—right out of school. This fear can affect their work habits, and add pressure during exams. Adults feel pressure to maintain their standard of living. This pressure can lead to overwork and distress, even depression and broken families. Many laid-off workers get distressed or depressed.

Background: There are few things more important to humans than providing for themselves, their future and their family. Until recently, many men were defined by their job and became depressed if they were out of work. Now women have joined the workforce in droves and have similar concerns. "It's a complicated topic, but many men still haven't been taught the skills of coping," said management consultant Jane Baddeley. "Women deal with things differently and express their feelings more. And, if a woman loses her job, she may look on it as an opportunity to stay home with her children." A fluctuating economy and unemployment rates and the specter of downsizing all add to fears and uncertainty. But many people have become motivated by this fear and have used it to make a better life.

Strategies:
- There are probably more ways to find a job now than ever before—through the Internet, newspapers, headhunters, professional journals, trade magazines, unemployment offices, cold calls and word of mouth (not to mention relatives).
- Here's how to write an effective resume: before you begin, assess your skills, abilities and goals, and jot these down on paper. Put your contact information (telephone, e-mail address and mailing address) at the top of your resume. Be specific about the job you want, but tailor your objective to each employer. Using action words, give your work experience and responsibilities. Indicate you will give references upon request. Have your resume reviewed by a career counselor.

- Develop a relationship with your school's career counselor and be sure to look out for trends or openings. Keep an open mind about your career choice.
- Keep your education and training upgraded. It's a competitive world and others are looking for the same job you are.
- When starting out, toss a wide net and don't be too choosy; you may have to work in entry-level positions before you get the job you want. Gradually try to become good at one thing. Plan your schedule of looking for work, but don't let it take over your life. Make sure you balance things with recreation, and keep taking care of your health.
- When career planning, determine the things that constitute your dream job, pinpoint companies that fit and don't allow discouraging economic news to temper your enthusiasm.
- Be open to change and trends in the workplace.
- If you have just lost your job, don't fall into anger or resentment. It happens to thousands of people. If you've left a job you didn't like, you'll eventually feel a sense of relief. Seek friends and family to support you emotionally or see a counselor.
- Losing a job or changing jobs are two of life's most stressful events. But if it is done properly, career transition can be one of life's biggest learning opportunities, a time for self-exploration and reflection. You can come out of it with a better perspective and a hungrier attitude.
- Don't let your job—or lack of a job—define who you are. It's an important part of your life, but so is being a son or a mother or a volunteer or a friend.

A MANTRA TO TELL YOURSELF: *"I will land on my feet."*

References:

The Resume Handbook by Arthur Rosenberg and David V. Hizer, Adams Media, 1995

What Color Is Your Parachute 2003 by Richard Bolles, Ten Speed Press, 2002

See: financial fears, fear of downsizing, fear of the unknown, fear of what others think, fear of failure, fear of exams, fear of losing status, fear of a job interview, fear of quitting

8

Fears at Work

Stress at Work

ponophobia (fear of overworking)

karoshi (Japanese for death by overwork)

If you don't have a job without aggrava-tion, you don't have a job.
—MALCOLM FORBES, ART COLLECTOR, AUTHOR AND PUBLISHER

Characteristics: Who hasn't felt stressed at work, at least occasionally? While some stress is normal, some people feel stretched thin physically, emotionally and spiritually; others feel tense, irritable and unproductive; and others feel dizzy, grind their teeth or have chest pains. Some workers even burn out, particularly people in service jobs, because they are often empathetic towards others and don't take time for themselves. On the other hand, pressure can also be a positive force: we can use it to increase our passion, our physical and mental skills and our efficiency.

Background: Stress, pressure and fear at work can be double-edged swords, at times helping with production and focus through eustress but more often causing tension, poor focus and fatigue through distress. It's estimated that the U.S. economy loses $300 billion annually through worker absenteeism related to distress. This problem seems to have grown in recent years as many companies and workers have been asked to do more with fewer resources, partly because of government cutbacks. And the pace of business has accelerated. Many workers feel powerless and uncertain about their jobs. Peoples' reactions to bureaucracy and office politics are also major contributors to distress. All of these factors combine to create cumulative distress, which may take some time for workers to defuse. The No. 1 stressor in many studies is interruptions; the average interruption experienced by a manager lasts six to nine minutes, and it takes three to 23 minutes to recover. People with physical jobs are generally not as prone to distress because they are able to channel their nervous energy into their work.

Strategies:

- Identify how you react to pressure at work—do you generally focus better under the gun or do you choke, letting your emotions interfere with your production? Understand that you may do both at various times, depending on the circumstances and your energy levels. Try to improve in the areas in which you most often perform poorly.

- Examine whether you are putting too much pressure on yourself by setting expectations too high.
- Without overdoing it, lose yourself in your work by focusing on the task and your skills, not on results.
- Talk with your coworkers or superiors about having more input and power in your job.
- See to your needs. Keep your energy levels up with a balanced diet and enough sleep. Exercise, breakfast and a shower before work are beneficial.
- Keep your commute to work manageable by rising a little earlier in the morning and using relaxation techniques while driving home, such as music and positive self-talk. Carpooling is a great idea.
- When hassles and tension appear, it's how you react that defines whether you are an effective worker. Find one or more "letting go" techniques that work for you: music, meditation, daydreaming, humor, exercise, stretching or taking breaks. Your mind and body need recovery after intense periods of work.
- "Master your breathing and you'll be able to find calm sanctuary in even the most stressful work environments," writes Paul Wilson in his book *Calm at Work*. "Take air through your nostrils and expel it through your mouth. Breathe slowly, six to eight breaths a minute."
- Don't drink more than two cups of coffee or tea in a day. Try herbal tea or hot water with lemon.
- Make good use of your time. Some surveys show that holding too many meetings is the No. 1 time waster and a cause of distress in many businesses. Another problem is too much socializing. Consider using a headset for the phone, allowing you to do other things with your hands. Don't feel that you have to answer all e-mails immediately.
- Sharpen your focus and streamline your tasks: prioritize, stay on schedule, reduce paperwork and cut down on distractions by telling coworkers if you don't have time to socialize or you

really can't help them with a question. Organize your work station so that you feel you have more control.

- Allow time to think; for conceptual thinking, you need quiet. Set aside an hour or more daily when you will not be reached by phone. Keep a private e-mail address for the more important notices and make it available only to a select few. If possible, do some work out of the office.

- Pace yourself. If the workload becomes too heavy, prioritize, delegate and learn to say no. Balance your expectations with the hours and resources you have; people who work more than 50 hours a week usually are not efficient. Don't be on call unless it's necessary. Learn to identify the signs of burnout: lack of incentive, energy or ideas.

- Take regular recovery breaks. Connect with a coworker for lunch, exercise or chill out. Take enough time off throughout the year. Don't take your work or your problems home with you.

- Many offices have found that production improves when music is played—music can even regulate the employees' heart rates. However, musical tastes are subjective, so you might want to use a headset.

- Take care of your posture and make sure your work station is ergonomic. Physical tension leads to more distress.

- If you get distressed through boredom, try to be more creative, but also consider the words of M.C. McIntosh: "Every job has drudgery. The first secret of happiness is the recognition of this fundamental fact."

- If you make mistakes, choke or have occasional spats with others, welcome to the club. Everybody does. Laugh at yourself. The average child laughs 300 times a day, the average adult only 17 times. We're too serious! Encourage periodic dress-down days.

- Be sure to have stress control on Sunday nights and Monday mornings; research shows that Mondays are the most stressful day, triggering more strokes and heart attacks than other days of the week.

- We live in a job-based culture. In the big picture, assess how much of your identity and time goes into your work and how much balance you have with your personal life.

Most Stressful Jobs: teacher, U.S. president, police officer, stockbroker, secretary, laborer, air-traffic controller, inspector, office manager, administrator, waiter, farmer, physician

Less Stressful Jobs: scientist, architect, programmer, librarian, civil engineer, professor, lineman

A MANTRA TO TELL YOURSELF: *"Balance everything, including pressure."*

QUOTABLE: *"Oh, you hate your job? Why didn't you say so? There's a support group for that. It's called EVERYBODY, and they meet at the bar."*—comic Drew Carey

Author's Two Cents:

At two jobs I had, I was able to find a group of noon-hour basketball players at the local YMCA. After a 30-minute sweat, we went back to work not only more relaxed, but with more "calm" energy. After the games, I had a light lunch with no alcohol. If such games become too competitive, however, they can be counterproductive and kick in your ego defense system and cause more distress.

References:

Stress Management for Dummies by Allen Elkin, IDG Books, 1999

Surviving Job Stress by John B. Arden, Career Press, 2002

See: fear of not having control, fear of the unknown, fear of failure, fear of making mistakes, fear of what others think, fear of criticism, financial fears and the other work-related fears

Financial Fears

peniaphobia (fear of poverty)

chrometophobia (fear of money)

Robber: "Your money or your life."
Comedian Jack Benny: "Let me think about it."

Characteristics: Insecurity or worry about having enough money to pay the bills, to keep up a certain lifestyle or to send children to school is common in our society. Many people lie awake at night worrying about income and bills. Some even get ulcers over it. One survey of 1,000 Americans showed that 57 percent feared the Internal Revenue Service, while just 30 percent feared God. People who've lived through troubled economic times may develop a mindset of thriftiness or deny themselves gifts and pleasures. Some people work two jobs or become workaholics. Others may hoard their money.

Background: Because financial matters are related to powerful human needs, they produce substantial pressure and fears. Even many successful people remain insecure; comedian Jackie Gleason always kept $10 in the pocket of each suit he owned in case his riches suddenly collapsed. Personal bankruptcies hit an all-time high of 1.5 million families in 2002. Research shows that women tend to get stressed by financial fears and men by work. Despite these fears, the quality of life in North America remains high. Some people believe they are afraid of never having enough money or material goods when their *real* fear is over what others think of their lifestyle ("keeping up with the Joneses").

Strategies:

- Have regular family discussions about money. It is not talked about enough. Teach your kids how to save and budget. Get into the habit of saving. Stash money aside regularly in a variety of mutual funds and stocks or in a savings plan.
- Ease up on credit card purchases, using them only for safety and convenience. Be cautious about using them for online purchases; your identification number can be vulnerable to theft.
- Unless it is an emergency, don't borrow money from friends or family. It could later cause problems in your relationship.

- Don't let money, or lack of it, define who you are as a person, especially if you must sacrifice family life for it. People with self-doubt often fill the void with materialism.
- Cut back on take-out food and eating out. Last year, those sucked up 46 percent of American families' food budget. Pack a lunch for work.
- Prepare for your retirement by checking what pension benefits you may be eligible for. Social security will provide only about 40 percent of your total retirement income. Save in advance. When you get a raise, save it.
- Watch out for the effect of taxes; take advantage of tax-deferred and tax-exempt investment opportunities.
- Teenagers should try to save their summer cash. Bankrate.com has a test to see how good teenagers are with money.
- Get insurance coverage for your home, even if you are renting.
- If you have problems motivating yourself to work, or to make extra cash, think of your loved ones, who would benefit from it, or target something you want to buy and work toward paying for it.
- Don't panic or make drastic decisions if you face money problems; there are enough social safety nets in our society to catch you until you can get back on your feet.

A MANTRA TO TELL YOURSELF: *"It's only money... if you have enough."*

QUOTABLE: *"To be satisfied with what one has, that is wealth. As long as one sorely needs a certain additional amount, that man isn't rich."*—Mark Twain

Reference:

Consumer advocate Clark Howard, www.clarkhoward.com

See: fear of not having control, fear of the unknown, fear of asking for a raise or promotion, fear of downsizing, fear of retirement, fear of quitting, stress at work

Fear of a Job Interview

testophobia (fear of being tested)   *The only difference between a date and a job interview is that there are not many job interviews where there's a chance you'll end up naked at the end of it.* —JERRY SEINFELD

Characteristics: Fear of job interviews is very common. This fear can make a candidate appear less qualified than he or she is for a job. A candidate may be nervous or sweat before an interview, stammer, or show lack of concentration or confidence. Some people may avoid an interview entirely or show up late. Others, however, "turn on" for such an event with heightened personality, confidence and focus, bringing out the best in themselves.

Background: Being tested or evaluated in any way usually makes people nervous, if not downright scared. Apprehension over a job and your future is quite understandable. Someone who doesn't get a little nervous may not be that interested in the job and may not be alert enough to make a good impression on the potential employer. There is more pressure on an applicant these days because of increasing competition in a declining workforce. You know that if you flub, someone else is probably waiting in the wings.

Strategies:
- Research the company you are applying to. Familiarize yourself with what the employer wants from you, as well as with its goals, such as a plan to increase mergers, to expand sales or to solidify a market. Just as importantly, know yourself and what you want. Many people are not clear about what they want to do, or even about what they *currently* do for a living.
- Prior to the interview, get proper diet, exercise and sleep. That sounds simple, but your health can affect your performance and your mood. Practice the interview at home by simulating pressure and having someone play the part of the interviewer. Try to anticipate the type of questions that will be asked.
- On the day of the interview, visualize the entire process. Imagine yourself driving to the appointment, sitting down and presenting yourself well. Imagine the interviewer reacting well to you and offering a second interview or the job.

- It's natural to be keyed up for an interview; if you aren't nervous at all, you may come off flat, and the employer may not see the enthusiasm and passion he or she is seeking.
- Wear clothes that make you feel good but that won't offend anyone. You may want to bring a favorite piece of jewelry that you can touch from time to time if you get nervous.
- Tell yourself that you will deliver. If you're troubled by nervousness during the interview, use cue words to snap into focus ("Get it done!") or get mad at yourself briefly without showing it, then focus on the interview again.
- Get off to a confident, but not aggressive, start. Interviewers usually make up their minds about a candidate in the first five minutes. But don't try to be perfect. It's your expertise, ideas and work ethic that employers are looking for. Make sure you don't look too anxious or eager (by sitting on the edge of the chair, for example).
- Look the employer confidently in the eye and explain why you are a good candidate and how you will contribute to the company.
- If you don't get the job, don't take it personally. As psychotherapist Susan Britt says, "It may have little to do with you and a whole lot that you look like the interviewer's ex-wife or perhaps you worked for a company which once turned down the interviewer for a loan." And it's not the end of your world. Allow yourself disappointment, but quickly pick yourself up and get back at the job search. Write down the good and bad points of your last interview and learn from both. Perhaps ask the interviewer what he or she thought of you.

A MANTRA TO TELL YOURSELF: *"Prepare."*

Reference:

Best Answers to the 201 Most Frequently Asked Interview Questions by Matthew J. Deluca, McGraw-Hill, 1996

See: fear of failure, fear of making mistakes, fear of the unknown, fear of what others think, fear of embarrassment, fear of the boss, financial fears, fear of rejection, fear of confrontation or conflict, fear of losing status

Fear of Downsizing

the pink slip
syndrome

Downsizing creates a whole new set of dynamics in a company. Workplace survivors *feel a deep sense of loss, a severing of close friendships and a fear of the future.*

—AUTHOR AND CAREER DEVELOPMENT COUNSELOR BARBARA BOWES

Characteristics: Many workers feel worry, doubt or anger that they or fellow employees will be let go. This fear can cause anxiousness, nausea, tension and many health problems, including migraines, ulcers, and even disease and heart problems. Some workers worry they will be replaced by a computer. Even the word *downsizing* can cause distressful symptoms. Seeing coworkers get laid off can cause uncertainty and resentment with the remainder of the staff and can be demoralizing and hurt productivity. On the positive side, this fear can spur greater productivity and commitment.

Background: What makes downsizing doubly hurtful to workers of the new millennium is that, not so long ago, there was job security in our society and a person might stay at the same job for life. Many companies were good to their employees and protected them with benefits. Now the focus of many companies is on the bottom line. Some firms treat their workers impersonally, said Larry More, an engineering designer, who blamed his ulcer on a layoff: "They treat employers like used toilet paper and put pressure on them to quit or they just throw them out. You get dejected if you think you got a raw deal."

Strategies:
- If you keep doing a good job with an honest effort, chances are that if downsizing comes, you will be a valuable commodity and your firm will try to keep you. But you might have to find ways to become more versatile.
- Don't expect a lot from big companies, even good companies. Even those people who perform long and well can be susceptible to cutbacks these days. Downsizing can be used as a strategy to make a firm's bottom line more attractive to a prospective buyer or to increase profits for shareholders.

- If you feel daily anxiety, use a calming method that works for you—perhaps a combination of deep breathing, meditation or prayer, music, humor and exercise.
- Find out if your company has support groups, counseling or job-search services. If you have a union, keep on top of issues through your local representative.
- If you are released, don't ask "Why me?" but "What's next for me?" and don't let the experience embitter your future. This is an opportunity to reassess your goals. It might be the trigger to make that career change you've always thought about, or to gear down to part-time. Allow yourself a transition period, perhaps starting with a vacation and a funny book. Millions of people are unemployed; why not start your own support group?
- Getting released is also a chance to become what Harvard professor Juliet Schor has termed a *downshifter*, a new breed of professional who trades income and long hours for more leisure and a better quality of life.
- Managers, reduce uncertainty by letting employees know ASAP if downsizing will affect them. For those remaining, give them a vision of where your company is going and ask them for ideas on how to cut costs and create more efficiency.

A MANTRA TO TELL YOURSELF: *"It if happens, I'll be ready."*

References:

Are You a Corporate Refugee? A Survival Guide for Downsized, Disillusioned and Displaced Workers by Ruth Luban, Penguin, 2001

Career development counselor Barbara Bowes, barb@bowes-group.com

For senior executives, team leaders, HR directors and consultants: *Charging Back Up the Hill: Workplace Recovery After Mergers, Acquisitions and Downsizings* by Mitchell Lee Marks, John Wiley and Sons, 2003

See: fear of the unknown, fear of change, financial fears, fear of not having control, fear of failure, fear of losing status, fear of the boss, fear of rejection, stress at work, fear of retirement, fear of embarrassment

Fear of Retirement

gerascophobia (fear of aging)

The harder you work, the harder it is to surrender. —LEGENDARY FOOTBALL COACH VINCE LOMBARDI

Characteristics: People approaching retirement age often feel anxious, restless, irrelevant, or even depressed or ill. Their reasons are many and complex, ranging from concern over not having enough pension money to losing their colleagues at work to fear of getting bored to worry about suddenly being at home all the time. Some people may put retirement off. After retirement, some people become isolated and depressed, but others feel rejuvenated and free.

Background: It's common to feel a big letdown at retirement after spending 40 hours or more a week at something for all of one's adult life. If a person's self-esteem has been largely wrapped up with who they are at work, as is often the case with men, they will likely have problems after the work is finished. The goal of retiring early has become ingrained in our psyche, leaving many with lots of free time. Many retirees take part-time jobs or continue to lead active lives. Seniors and baby boomers are generally more fit than they've ever been—more than 250,000 people annually take part in U.S. regional competitions for the Senior Olympics (for those over 55).

Strategies:
- Before you retire, get your finances in order: start saving early and don't expect to keep up the same lifestyle you have had if you rely only on social security. Participate in your employer's retirement plan. Save in a tax-deferred account. Diversify your investment portfolio.
- Also prior to retirement, while you are still fully covered by health insurance, get a thorough checkup at the doctor's, have your eyes examined and your teeth cleaned and checked.
- Write down your retirement goals and strategies. There were probably some things you wanted to do while you were working, but didn't have the time for, such as starting a garden or taking up golf. Now is the time.

- Take part in the gray-power revolution. You'll only be "put out to pasture" if you allow society to do it to you. There are lots of opportunities for volunteering, part-time work or getting involved in community activities. If you were not in a leadership role at work, perhaps try one now. Don't worry about being bored—there is as much to do as you want to do.

- Develop your spirituality by making new friends and keeping in touch with old friends and work colleagues through golf, cards, church groups, volunteering and simple get-togethers. Take part in your children's lives (without interfering) and develop your career as a grandparent.

- Don't underestimate what seniors' residences have to offer, especially in terms of social contact with people of your generation. It's fun being around other people who might share your interests and experience.

- Look back on the work you did! If you are not happy with it, examine other ways you can still make a contribution. You've got lots of time left yet—life expectancy is near 80. You can do more!

- Moderate exercise is necessary to maintain your health in retirement. While you were working, the demands of your job probably helped keep you fit. A balanced diet, low in fat and with plenty of fruits, protein and vegetables, is recommended.

- This is a good time to reflect and document your life and that of your family. Talk to relatives and put together a written family history or organize photo albums.

- You're never too old for anything, except maybe bungee jumping.

A MANTRA TO TELL YOURSELF: *"Free to do as I wish."*

References:

The Ultimate Safe Money Guide: How Everyone Over 50 Can Protect, Save and Grow Their Money by Martin D. Weiss, John Wiley and Sons, 2002

Analyze Now (for retirement planning), www.analyzenow.com

See: fear of the unknown, fear of change, fear of not having control, fear of aging, fear of death, fear of success or happiness, fear of being alone, fear of losing status

Fear of Technology

cyberphobia (fear of computers)

mechanophobia (fear of machines)

I don't fear computers, I fear the lack of them. —ISAAC ASIMOV

Characteristics: Many people feel intimidated about learning to operate new machines, particularly computers. Others—especially older people, who tend to experience a decline in short-term memory, focus, processing speed and problem solving—may feel frustration, anxiety and difficulty concentrating with an overload of technology. Some people fear health problems from electromagnetic fields associated with computers and monitors. Others feel that computers will take their jobs. Some fear that by getting caught up in the Information Age, we risk neglecting ideas and overlooking more meaningful aspects of life.

Background: It isn't surprising that technological advances make some people uneasy. Things are changing so rapidly, it's hard to keep pace these days. More than 50 percent of the workforce uses high-tech equipment—e-mails, faxes and cell phones. Employees of Fortune 1,000 companies send and receive on average 178 messages each day through technology. Our brains have difficulty with such overload. If we are older, we may have trouble being flexible and attempting new things. If our cave ancestors could see the amazing things we are doing at such a fast pace, the hairs on their backs would stand up.

Strategies:
- Don't panic, but if you don't keep up with the changes in technology, you'll be left behind. The good news is, there is lots of help out there, and computers are getting simpler to operate every day. And they'll help you do your paperwork quickly and allow you to communicate with others across the globe.
- If you are having trouble adjusting to computers, use your tech-support person at work. Ask him or her to format your desktop with shortcuts to the programs and files you use on a regular basis.

- If you are having problems learning, practice using your computer and upgrade your training. Don't be afraid to ask someone younger than you; children pick up technology fast.
- Make sure you take periodic breaks at your computer to keep your stress at a manageable level. Organize yourself and go at your own pace, not at the machine's pace; otherwise, your metabolism may speed up and your attention span could shorten. Try to alternate repetitive computer tasks with other jobs that are unrelated.
- Improve your lighting (it should be over the computer, not behind you) and reduce neck and back problems by having your screen at about eye level.
- If you get headaches, attach an anti-glare shield to your screen.
- Keep your work environment as quiet and as undistracted as possible.
- Elderly people may want to consider using eyeglasses while using a computer.
- Beware of getting preoccupied (perhaps subconsciously) by the rush of information that comes across your desk or computer. Don't let technology crowd out creative, philosophical and ethical considerations. It's easy to get caught up in the cyber rat race and to become more superficial in one's thinking. If things become a blur, stop and get off for a while!

A MANTRA TO TELL YOURSELF: *"Machines will help me."*

References:

TechnoStress by Larry D. Rosen and Michelle M. Weil, John Wiley and Sons, 1998

The Internet for Dummies, Eighth Edition by John R. Levine, Carol Baroudi and Margaret Levine Young, John Wiley and Sons, 2002

See: stress at work, fear of change, fear of the unknown, fear of not having control, fear of embarrassment, fear of making mistakes, fear of taking chances, fear of appearing stupid

Fear of Asking for a Raise or Promotion

doxophobia (fear of expressing opinions or receiving praise)	*Asking for a raise ranks up there with getting a tooth pulled.* —Detroit journalist Jennifer Bott

Characteristics: Many people are reluctant to ask for a raise or promotion. They may work themselves into a tizzy just worrying about what to say or how the boss will react. They may feel unworthy or believe that the company can't afford it. But if workers can't bring themselves to at least ask, their incentive can decline and their work might suffer.

Background: Many people are afraid to blow their own horn, even when it's warranted, partly because our society teaches us to be humble. Others may be afraid of getting turned down or being exposed as inadequate at their job. Paradoxically, some workers refuse to ask for a raise out of arrogance, because they believe they are worth much more and that their employer won't give it to them.

If you are reluctant to ask for a raise or promotion, it could mean that your skills or work ethic need improving or that you're afraid of your boss or that you lack initiative or courage.

Strategies:

How to ask for a raise:

- If you think you're worth a raise, take a stand. If you don't stick up for yourself, who will? Very few of us have agents or public relations representatives.
- Research what others in similar jobs are getting and be reasonable in your request. Know your company's policy on incentives and raises. And find out if your company tends to give raises at certain times of the year. Make an appointment with your boss a day or two in advance and treat it like an important meeting. Close the door and discourage distractions.
- Don't come right out with, "I deserve a raise." You might deserve one, but sometimes the world isn't fair. And don't say *why* you need the extra money; it doesn't mean much to your employer. Probably most people in your company also believe they deserve or need a raise.

- Make a case for your job performance by outlining how you've benefited the company. Your boss may not recall all of your achievements. Many firms have no tools in place to measure performance.
- Negotiate rather than ask for a raise. You have a service to offer and you are simply asking a good price for it.
- If your company has just had a poor quarter, consider other things you can negotiate—incentive compensation, stock options, an extra vacation week, personal days or education benefits.
- If you don't get the raise, be grateful for what you have, and let the boss know it—not only with words but with continued good performance. The boss may remember your grace and the raise may come a little later.

How to ask for a promotion:
- It may be easier to ask for a promotion than a raise because, if you are turned down for the promotion, you can then ask for a raise.
- If you believe you are ready to take on more responsibility, make it clear to your employer. It shows him or her you are ready to grow with the company.
- Always make it seem like you are offering something rather than requesting something. In other words, the company will be getting something more in return for your promotion.
- Try to come up with a new initiative in which you serve the company. Employers like initiative and are always eager to reduce middle-management tasks.
- If you are passed over for a raise or promotion, don't take it personally. Put things in perspective by talking to a trusted friend or relative.

A MANTRA TO TELL YOURSELF: *"I'm worth something."*

Reference:

How to Say It at Work by Jack Griffin, Prentice Hall, 1998

See: fear of not having control, fear of rejection, fear of confrontation or conflict, fear of the boss, fear of success or happiness, fear of taking chances, fear of responsibility, fear of losing status, fear of what others think, stress at work, fear of competition

Dealing with Deadline Pressure

choking (letting your emotions negatively affect your work)

flow (being in the zone of optimal performance)

Coffee is only for closers. —ALEC BALDWIN'S CHARACTER TO UNDERACHIEVING REAL ESTATE SALESMEN IN *GLENGARRY GLEN ROSS*

Characteristics: The pressure of deadlines and important tasks can make people tense or excited. Pressure often leads to shaking fingers, flustered concentration and apprehension, as well as decreased productivity. On the other hand, pressure can lead to increased focus, drive and efficiency. A person may deal with pressure well on some days, while on other days, their wheels may fall off. Some people avoid jobs with intense deadline pressure, while others seek them out.

Background: Some people are hardwired for good production under pressure and are adrenaline sensitive. They may produce seven hours of work in just four. Others are not able to control their adrenaline production. Age, upbringing and experience all come into play.

If you have your ducks in a row physically and mentally, you can actually perform better under pressure because your "arousal hormones" can add to your concentration and your energy levels. If you can get into the zone at work, time seems to slow down and everything seems to be happening smoothly in a type of flow.

Strategies:

- Keep your pressures from reaching unmanageable levels. Prior to a task, prepare yourself physically and mentally.
- If you keep your desk uncluttered, with resources at hand, you'll have a feeling of control. Organize your time and, if possible, allocate a certain amount of time to a certain amount of work.
- See the job as a challenge, not a fearful situation. If you feel nervous, see it as a sign that you are geared up for the challenge and your emergency fear system has kicked in. Let it help you.
- Don't worry too much. Trust your skills, stop resisting the pressure and get out of your own way. Your subconscious and your muscle memory, which you've trained, will come through.
- Visualize what you want to do and imagine yourself doing it successfully and on time.

- Make sure your posture is good, particularly if you're at a computer.
- Don't get too keyed up. Try to keep a level of arousal that you can control. If you begin to lose control, take deep breaths, use cue words such as "Easy does it" or get up and take a break. If you lose motivation, remind yourself of the importance of the job and use cue words like "Just do it!"
- With confidence and focus, it's possible to redirect high arousal directly into your work. Stay in the present, focusing not on the end result but on the task. Check on the time periodically, but not every few minutes or you'll get distracted.
- Take breaks and allow recovery time after an intense session.
- If you miss a deadline or are not satisfied with a job, learn from it and move on.

How Physiological Arousal and Your Emergency Fear System Affect Skills:

The average heart rate is 70 beats per minute. When engaged in fine motor skills (those involving dexterity or hand-eye coordination), you can perform well at low to medium levels of arousal, with up to 115 heartbeats per minute, but this will lessen the dexterity of your fingers. When engaged in complex motor skills (those involving a series of muscle groups and movements requiring hand-eye coordination, precision, tracking and timing), skills begin to deteriorate at 145 heartbeats per minute. Gross motor skills (those involving the large muscle groups and strength and speed activities) actually improve as your level of arousal rises.

A MANTRA TO TELL YOURSELF: *"Focus and get out of your own way."*

Reference:

Intelligent Fear by Michael Clarkson, Key Porter, 2002

See: fear of failure, fear of making mistakes, fear of what others think, fear of criticism, financial fears, fear of not having control, fear of the boss, fear of choking in sports, fear of exams

Fear of the Boss

tyrannophobia (fear of tyrants) *poinephobia* (fear of being punished)	*In apologizing for accidents and errors, never tell your boss how he or she should feel about it.* —COMMUNICATIONS EXPERT JACK GRIFFIN

Characteristics: Most people probably have some apprehension about their boss. They might fear the power he wields or what he might do if they fall out of favor. Some people are so anxious that they rarely talk to or challenge their boss, and that can be bad for everyone. Some people even quit because they don't like or fear their superior.

Background: Most employees have always feared, respected or hated their superiors because of the power they wield. Some people fear authority figures because of their own insecurity or self-esteem issues. In this age of downsizing, the boss may seem more formidable than ever. Because of human nature, bosses can sometimes condescend to their subordinates, and workplace relations can turn into a type of class system. However, a healthy fear of authority can keep a workplace running effectively. Some people actually fear or hate their work and turn their angst toward their boss. People who suffer from this fear may have had argumentative parents.

Strategies:
- If your boss is critical, try to put a positive spin on it. She may be right. Thank her and find ways to improve.
- If you goof, admit it. Show your superior that you actually learn from your mistakes.
- If a compliment comes, accept it with gratitude and grace. Perhaps share it with others who helped you.
- If things are never good enough for your boss, see it as an opportunity. If you want to prove something, focus your energy on your work, not in belittling your boss.
- When talking with your boss, always keep eye contact and be confident.
- To show you are a team player, when talking to your superior, use the words "we" or "us" rather than "I."

- If given an assignment you don't like, don't grumble, but tell him you'll approach it with a good work ethic. If it is an important task, ask if it's possible to take some time to digest it and get back to him ASAP.
- Keep small and big communications lines open; for important issues, ask for a closed-door meeting. You probably shouldn't be buddy-buddy with your boss, but develop an open relationship by occasionally going for coffee or lunch with her.
- If she is unreasonable, talk to your employee-assistance rep or a trusted colleague about it, but don't gossip. It may get back to her.
- If your boss is a monster, his bad attitude is probably not personal. Cut him down in your mind by imagining him as a child acting out his fantasies. Smiling at him could improve his demeanor with you. Try to get something positive out of your situation—having a disagreeable boss is a good way for you to raise your tolerance and toughness levels.
- If your boss is an empire-builder, he may be impossible to deal with, so try looking the other way. As anthropologist Michael Maccoby writes in his book *The Productive Narcissist: The Promise and Peril of Visionary Leadership*, "Don't invest your ego in the relationship. Don't look for empathy, interest in your life or praise. You won't get it...you may have to let him or her take credit for all of your good ideas and accept blame for all his bad ones. It's the bargain you make working for a visionary."

A MANTRA TO TELL YOURSELF: *"Fe, fi, fo, fum..."*

References:

Competitive Strategy: Techniques for Analyzing Industries and Competitors by Michael E. Porter, Free Press, 1998

Awesome and Awful Boss Hall of Fame, www.meaningatwork.com/boss/awfulpage3.html

See: fear of not having control, fear of failure, fear of criticism, fear of making mistakes, fear of downsizing, fear of confrontation or conflict, fear of teachers, stress at work, fear of asking for a raise or promotion, fear of quitting

Fear of Quitting

| neophobia (fear of anything new) | *Tell people that you have an opportunity more in line with your goals and one that you cannot pass up.* —BEVERLY RILEY, |

HUMAN RESOURCES REPRESENTATIVE, TEXAS INSTRUMENTS

Characteristics: Leaving a job can be traumatic and complex. It can also make people nervous, anxious and even ill with headaches, stomach problems or ulcers. Some people quit inappropriately and suddenly because they are afraid of confrontation with bosses or coworkers.

Background: Most people want security and are afraid of change, especially in today's uncertain job climate. The larger a person's family, the more reluctant he or she may be to quit even a bad job. Some people feel too loyal to quit, or too tied to their coworkers or the job itself. Those reasons, however, are not always poor ones. Fear of quitting can inspire people to try harder and to try to make their job more tolerable.

Strategies:

- If you decide to quit, be sure that you *want* to quit. Think about the reasons and write them down. Can you live with the issues that trouble you at your present job? Give it a fair chance because you don't want to jump from job to job. Perhaps you just need to put in a bit more effort to like your job more, or perhaps you should talk to your superiors about nagging issues, and they may do something about them.
- Be certain that you have other irons in the fire before you quit. Have another offer, or a resume and references ready to go.
- If you are certain you want to leave, write a resignation letter, then make a formal appointment with the boss. Keep the meeting respectful, but friendly.
- Keep things positive and progressive. Even if you can't function in your job anymore, you have learned from the experience and from your employers. Write down these positive lessons and leave with a good taste in your mouth.

- If you have an offer from another company, tell your boss the money you will get and the conditions that make the potential job attractive. If he makes a counteroffer, tell him you want to think about it overnight.
- Check your rights and conditions with the company you are leaving. Will you lose retirement funds? Vacation? Will your new employer offer security?
- Give plenty of notice, if possible, and allow for your transition to go smoothly. Don't go out in a tantrum. Remember that if you burn your bridges behind you, the swim back will be difficult. "First impressions may be important," says career counselor Jean Ann Cantore. "But your last few weeks in a position are what really shape employers' and coworkers' opinions of you. Remember to handle the situation tactfully. Leave your work and files organized and don't tell coworkers you will be back to visit often if you can't keep the promise."
- Make good use of your exit interview. Offer constructive criticism to your employer. Start with what you liked about your job, discuss problems briefly and then end with a positive remark about the job or coworkers.

A MANTRA TO TELL YOURSELF: *"I'll do what's best."*

References:

It's a Job, Not Jail by Robert M. Hochheiser, Fireside, 1998

Quit Your Job and Grow Some Hair: Know When to Go, When to Stay by Gary N. Rubin, Impact Publications, 2003

See: financial fears, fear of the unknown, stress at work, fear of change, fear of the boss, fear of asking for a raise or promotion, fear of confrontation or conflict, fear of failure, fear of what others think, fear of delivering bad news

Fear of Firing an Employee

Firing someone with dignity takes thoughtfulness, sacrifice and skill. It's never, ever easy, but it can be done well. —Diane Tunick Morello, an official with the research firm Gartner

Characteristics: Unless they're cold-blooded, who relishes the idea of terminating someone? Just the thought of it can make an employer anxious or tense. Some bosses may be too sensitive or forgiving to do it, and that doesn't necessarily make them a good boss.

Background: Just like employees, most bosses like to be accepted and liked. Being up in an ivory tower is not much fun, and they don't pay enough for this kind of task. It's a painful chore to fire someone when you know their livelihood is in your hands. A boss may avoid giving a worker the ax for fear of triggering a harsh reaction, a lawsuit or fallout with the rest of the staff, or for fear of hurting the company's image. But it may be bad for the company and bad for morale to keep someone who is dragging his or her feet or is incompetent. Not many people are cut out for, or have the experience for, such a confrontation.

Strategies:
- Closely examine why you feel the employee might be terminated. It's a big decision. Consider all the ramifications, including the fact that if a poor employee is not released, it could affect the performance and morale of some of the staff.
- Firing someone usually takes several steps and may not come as a surprise to the employee. But before it comes to that stage, you may want to put the employee on warning and perhaps discipline him or her.
- Prepare well for the firing with valid reasons and perhaps evidence of the employee's inadequacy or offense.
- Treat the employee with fairness and respect. Don't make it personal. You are disappointed with the performance, not the person.
- Have the employee leave on the best terms possible. Give positive remarks to help the person the next time, such as, "I know

it didn't work out here, but I liked some of the things you did [detail them] and I'm sure you will improve upon them with another firm."

- A letter informing the employee of the termination and the effective date of the discipline is the most usual method of telling the employee about the organization's decision. If possible, let the employee go immediately, with two weeks of added pay to ease the blow and to avoid worker's compensation difficulties.

- See this confrontation as a chance to grow as a boss or manager. Don't take it personally if the fired employee takes it out on you. He or she may be embarrassed and not want to admit failure or be worried about the family consequences.

- If you are the one being fired, try not to discuss the issues immediately with the boss, except to get all the relevant details. Tell the boss you want a few days to digest the news. If you feel that the firing is unjust, seek your union representative or a lawyer. It may not be personal, but merely a matter of downsizing. Ask under what possible conditions you might stay with the company.

A MANTRA TO TELL YOURSELF: *"Do what's best."*

References:

From Hiring to Firing by Steven Sack, Alliance House, 1995

www.hrzone.com (human resources guide)

See: fear of confrontation or conflict, fear of quitting, fear of taking chances, fear of downsizing, fear of responsibility, fear of criticism, fear of delivering bad news, fear of ending a romantic relationship

Fear of Harassment

With harassment or discrimination, explore all your options; you have more power than you think.
—JOHN B. ARDEN, AUTHOR OF *SURVIVING JOB STRESS*

Characteristics: People may become nervous at work if they are harassed, offended, intimidated or humiliated by a coworker or a boss. It's not uncommon for people to face discrimination based on race, age, religion or sex. Some people are offended by wolf whistling, stereotyping and off-color jokes. People get upset if malicious rumors about them are spread around the office. At the very least, such problems create workplace distractions and may lead to high rates of absenteeism and employee turnover.

Background: Sexual harassment is quite common in workplaces, where people get much of their regular social contact. Many relationships begin at work, but others are thwarted. Many people don't complain about harassment for fear of embarrassment, for fear of being seen as a complainer or for fear that nothing will be done about it. Harassment is sometimes about a person or a group of people using power inappropriately over another person or group. This can cause poor morale or poor employee relations and give the company a bad reputation. Companies are not permitted to discriminate, but it does happen. In North America, most governments have antidiscrimination and equal opportunity laws that protect people in the workplace, but these often differ from region to region.

Strategies:
- Before you take any official action against someone at work, make your displeasure known to the person who is harassing or offending you or discriminating against you.
- With sexual harassment of a minor nature from an older person, consider the age and background of that person, who may be from an era in which offhand sexual comments were common and often laughed off. In other words, remarks such as "Aren't women supposed to be the ones making coffee?" may not have been personal. This doesn't make the person's attitude right, but it may make it easier to understand. You might want

to respond, while you are chuckling, "Aren't men supposed to be the only ones working outside the home?" Don't be politically correct to the point of losing your sense of humor.

- Make sure you don't create a possible opening for sexual harassment by flirting with a person, perhaps even subconsciously. Learn to read other colleagues' body and verbal language and respond accordingly.
- Examine your company's policies on harassment. Follow them and make sure you document an incident, preferably with witnesses.
- If someone verbally bullies you, ask for him or her to repeat it, especially in front of witnesses. The person, forced to hear his or her own tone again, may then realize what has been said and back off.
- Try to avoid bullies at work whenever possible. Giving them a taste of their own medicine often escalates a situation.
- If a supervisor orders you to do a task a certain way and you know it doesn't work, ask him or her to show you the way. If it fails, don't rub it in.
- Employers should remember that it is in their interest to promote a safe, healthy and fair environment for their workers.

A MANTRA TO TELL YOURSELF: *"I'll get protection when I need it."*

Reference:

Workplace Sexual Harassment by Anne C. Levy and Michele Antoinette Paludi, Prentice Hall, 2001

Note: Complaints can be lodged with the (U.S.) Employment Equal Opportunity Commission, which investigates cases of harassment and discrimination. The Labor Commission oversees labor law and ensures that nonunionized employers abide by basic labor standards.

See: fear of invasion of privacy or territory, fear of solicitors and telemarketers, fear of bullies, fear of not having control, fear of confrontation or conflict, fear of being mugged, sexual fears, fear of enclosed spaces, fear of embarrassment, fear of the opposite sex

Fear of Competition

kakorrhaphiophobia (fear of defeat)

testophobia (fear of being tested)

The best way to motivate people is to pit them against one another. —J. Watson Jr., former CEO of IBM

Characteristics: This condition involves anxiousness or avoidance of jobs or projects that have goals or quotas. It also involves fear of comparisons or competition with other employees or business rivals. It can lead to lack of confidence and even illness or depression prior to a project or event. It can also drive people to great heights as they improve themselves and try harder and prepare better for fear of losing.

Background: A competitive nature is inbred in humans, who have had to struggle for survival of the fittest. (At the same time, early humans survived partly through teamwork and cooperation.) Partly because of this drive, humans have conquered the world. Our competitive nature can show itself even before birth— twins have been photographed fighting for space in the womb. In a society that often values status, becoming No. 1 is important. This fear can be related to fear of rejection or failure—some people won't even play Scrabble for fear of losing—and the fear of being on a team. But some people avoid competition because they don't want to belittle or defeat others.

Strategies:

- Be competitive in the areas you need to be and let go in others. If you are fighting for a contract, you will need to give it a full effort. If you are competing for attention from a coworker or a relative, you might want to assess how far you want to go.
- Compete with yourself first, challenging yourself to make improvements, even if they are small but continual.
- If you have an intense fear of looking silly when losing a competition, examine your ego and self-esteem issues. Maybe you take losing too personally. False pride is not worth it.
- Maybe you are more cooperative than competitive; there's nothing wrong with that, as long as it isn't affecting your job.
- If you must compete intensely, learn teamwork and respect for others. If you are part of a team, praise others to raise

collective pride. And learn to be a good loser; for one thing, you learn a lot about yourself and your character.

- Be sure to compete only to get ahead at work or to have fun in your hobbies, not to prove something or diminish somebody. Unfortunately, many high achievers take this route; it may lead to improved job productivity, but it also harms their personal lives and keeps them from forming many close relationships. On the other hand, don't judge people who are ultra-competitive. While their attitudes and personal lives may not be what you seek, such people can create a lot of progress and good in the world.
- Think positively. Research showed that optimists sold 29 percent more insurance in their first year than their more pessimistic peers and 130 percent more in their second year.
- If you want to get to the top in any profession, you must embrace competition, because your competitors certainly will.
- Remember that healthy competition usually produces a better product and a tougher and smarter person.

A MANTRA TO TELL YOURSELF: *"What am I afraid of?"*

From Another Angle:

"Life for us has become an endless succession of contests. From the moment the alarm clock rings until sleep overtakes us again, from the time we are toddlers until the day we die, we are busy struggling to outdo others. This is our posture at work and at school, on the playing field and back at home. It is the common denominator of American life."—Alfie Kohn, in his book *No Contest: The Case Against Competition*

Reference:

Michael Porter on Competition by Michael E. Porter, Harvard Business School, 1998

See: fear of failure, fear of what others think, fear of success or happiness, fear of losing status, fear of not having control, fear of confrontation or conflict, fear of choking in sports, fear of embarrassment, fear of getting a compliment, fear of exams, fear of a job interview

Serious Worries and Ways to Relax

Serious Worries

It makes no difference how deeply seated may be the trouble,
How hopeless the outlook,
How muddled the tangle, how great the mistake.
A sufficient realization of love will dissolve it all.
—EMMET FOX, IN *THE GOLDEN GATE*

Characteristics: Most people experience moderate to serious symptoms when they are faced with life-changing events such as illness, death or divorce. These symptoms can include anxiety, withdrawal, aggression, anger, denial, grief, sleeplessness or too much sleep, depression, ulcers, hypertension, high blood pressure, disease and even thoughts of suicide. But many people overcome such symptoms to show leadership in times of crisis.

Background: Some worries are legitimate and unavoidable. These include serious illness and death, job loss, divorce, massive change, problems with family, and general worries over issues like terrorism, global warming or the spread of AIDS. Fear of death is hard to cope with because we live in a repressed society when it comes to grieving and worrying about our demise. At first, these worries may seem overwhelming, but we do have resources to deal with them, beginning with our own character and our support network of family, friends and coworkers.

Strategies:

- If you have a serious problem, don't allow yourself to add chronic worry to your burden. You can choose to put your worry to good use by planning strategies and finding solutions, or you can allow yourself to slide into depression or self-pity.
- If you develop your sense of well-being and your self-esteem, large problems will not be overwhelming. If you practice love and compassion in your daily life, you will feel less pain when something bad happens.
- Be open to your pain and face it. But then let it go, even laugh at it. It helped me deal with my uncle Gordon's tragic death when my last words to him in hospital were: "You look like s——." And his reply, through a chuckle, was "I feel like s——."

- Sometimes it is hard to reduce mountains to molehills, but dwelling on a big problem can make it even more ominous.
- A big worry is important, but it is only part of your life. Your life remains complex, with numerous issues, people and responsibilities, including the responsibility to yourself. Don't throw them all aside for one component. "The most important thing to remember is that life is a gift," says author Richard Carlson. "Despite the pain, the troubles, and all the big stuff, life is still a magical experience."
- If you have a serious illness, don't look for someone to blame. Says clinical psychologist Hap LeCrone, "As an alternative to thinking, 'My pain is all the fault of my employer, doctor, family, etc.,' one might instead consider, 'Unexpected things sometimes happen in life, but I am confident that I can learn to deal effectively with unexpected events.'"
- It's impossible not to spend at least some time worrying about the future, but stay in the present and enjoy it as much as possible.
- If someone close to you dies, allow a grieving period, but don't allow yourself to become a victim of self-pity. Nature gave you grief partly to get you to focus on the deceased and all the issues that need attending to when someone dies (such as funeral arrangements).
- For big worries, seek help and advice from others. "Trouble is a part of your life, and if you don't share it, you don't give the person who loves you a chance to love you enough," singer and philanthropist Dinah Shore once said. Consider professional help, spiritual help or medication. Also consider a support group for people with similar problems. In fact, share other people's real problems. It's an opportunity to grow stronger together.
- Try to remain optimistic. Studies show that optimists who suffer setbacks attribute them to external causes that are temporary and can be changed. When Mozart suffered the deaths of four children, serious illness and repeated financial disasters, his optimism actually rose.
- Understand that everyone has serious worries. As Ann Landers said, "When life's problems seem overwhelming, look around and see what other people are coping with. You may consider yourself fortunate."

MANTRAS TO CONSIDER: *"My family loves me"* OR
"Thankfully, my life will go on."

Author's Two Cents:

My wife, Jennifer, is an inspiration to all around her. In 2002, she had a knee replacement, suffered three dizzy spells a day, and discovered she had an incurable blood disorder. Using mental toughness, humor and compassion for others, she made it easier for the rest of us to support her. Rather than quitting work, she set a record for sales. On one occasion, I tried to get depressed about her condition, but how could I?

References:

What About the Big Stuff? by Richard Carlson, Hyperion, 2002

Clinical psychologist Hap LeCrone, hlecrone@aol.com

See: fear of illness or pain, fear of death, fears for your marriage/partnership, fear for your children's safety, fear of delivering bad news, fear of retirement, fear of downsizing

How to Relax

- Examine and manage the pressures in your life so that your nervous system does not constantly kick in. Try to avoid overloading yourself with responsibilities at home and work.
- Identify and eliminate exaggerated thinking. You may be an obsessive thinker and make mountains out of molehills.
- Raise your "anxiety threshold" so that you don't become anxious over unimportant things.
- Learn to express your feelings without constantly bottling them up.
- Get regular aerobic exercise, eat balanced meals and get as much sleep as you need.
- If you have a phobia, slowly expose yourself to what you fear.
- Cope with worry by focusing only on the problems you can control.

- When you feel anxious, breathe deeply from your abdomen, or use mantras such as "Relax" or "Stop it now!"
- Learn to relax through meditation and spirituality. Think about things beyond yourself. Volunteer.
- Build a good network of family, friends and coworkers.
- Get a pet and talk to it. Pet owners have fewer visits to the doctor.
- Change things once in a while. Routine and boredom can make you anxious.
- Prescription medications can help. See your doctor.

Note: More serious anxiety disorders not covered in this book include panic disorder (although we've discussed agoraphobia, the fear of having a panic attack, on pages 154–55), post-traumatic stress disorder and any generalized anxiety disorder that persists for over six months. If you feel that you or someone you know has one of these disorders, see a doctor or therapist.

A MANTRA TO TELL YOURSELF: *"What is going to hurt me?"*

Author's Two Cents:

I was not good at recognizing my own anxiety until one day, in my 30s, I got numb all over my body for two weeks. I went to my family doctor and his diagnosis was that I had too much pressure in my life and that I needed to manage it more effectively. After that, I stopped worrying about some of the things I couldn't control and my numbness left.

References:

The Anxiety Disorders Association of America
11900 Parklawn Drive, Suite 100
Rockville, MD 20852-2624
(301) 231-9350
www.adaa.org

The National Institute of Mental Health (offers pamphlets and a list of resources)
(888) ANXIETY (269-4389)
www.nimh.nih.gov

See: Most of the fears and phobias in this book have at least some anxiety as a symptom.

How to Cope with Pressure

- Control your external pressures before they become unmanageable by keeping your resources high. Keep your energy up through proper diet, sleep and exercise. Upgrade your job skills: if you can type only 50 words a minute and the job calls for 60, you will feel pressure unless you upgrade.
- Control your internal pressures by keeping your goals in perspective.
- Don't worry so much about what others think, unless you can channel your worry into motivation.
- Learn to delegate some of the pressures.
- Be aware that these days, women generally feel more pressure than men because of the duties they take on at work and at home. Women must learn to delegate and not feel guilty when everything doesn't get done. Men must learn to help take some of the pressure off them by pitching in with the children and relationship issues.
- By performing more under pressure and by training with pressure, you can raise your threshold and learn to feel comfortable when under strain.
- Stay cool under pressure or your emotional reaction may cause more pressure.
- Music and humor can keep pressure at a manageable level.

Reference:

Positive Under Pressure by Gael Lindenfield and Malcolm Vandenburg, Thorsons, 2000

See: how to deal with stress, dealing with deadline pressure, fears at school and fears at work

How to Deal with Stress

It's not stress that kills us, it's our reaction to it.
—PIONEER STRESS RESEARCHER HANS SELYE

Strategies:

- Keep stress levels manageable by keeping your life and your work in perspective. Taking on too many challenges sets off strong reactions from your emergency fear system.
- Examine the things in your life that you see as a threat and that thus set off your nerves. Some of them may create healthy challenges.
- When we feel nervousness or tension, we can defuse this energy or, if we are working, we can try to redirect it into whatever it is we are doing. In most situations, we will want to defuse it and calm down our fear reaction.
- Situations in which we may want to defuse our stress: when talking to people, when worrying, when reacting to a putdown or when a pressure situation is too much for us to handle. Situations in which we may want to redirect our nervous energy or tension: during an intense project or deadline pressure, during a sports competition or theatrical performance, when faced by a physical challenge, or anytime we feel confident that we can perform better with adrenaline in our system.
- To defuse stress, find one or more of the traditional methods that help you wind down: deep breathing from the abdomen, meditating and putting your issues into perspective, listening to music or talking to and laughing with someone you trust.
- If stress buildup is too high, you may want to walk away from whatever it is you are doing and take a break. Our bodies need a recovery period after too much fear reaction. Exercise also eases the stress buildup.

- To redirect stress energy, focus intently on whatever you are doing. If the stress distracts you, change your mindset briefly to anger or look upon the situation as a challenge, using a cue phrase such as "Go for it!" This will change your emotional chemistry to a more proactive mix of hormones. Then focus intently again.
- Remember Hans Selye's words on the previous page. Reacting negatively to stress can make you ill and ruin your efficiency. Up to 70 percent of visits to doctor's offices are stress-related.
- If you have chronic stress, you may want to examine problems with your job, your home life and how you view yourself and the world.

References:

Don't Sweat the Small Stuff by Richard Carlson, Hyperion, 1997

The American Institute of Stress
124 Park Avenue
Yonkers, NY 10703
(914) 963-1200
stress124@earthlink.net

www.stress.org

The Canadian Institute of Stress
P.O. Box 665, Station U
Toronto, ON
Canada M8Z 5Y9
www.stresscanada.org

See: Stress is a component of most if not all fears in this book. Especially see how to cope with pressure, fear of the unknown, fear of change, fear of embarrassment, fear of failure, stress at work

How to Deal with Anger

- If you are angry, analyze what has triggered this reaction and think about whether your anger is justified. Anger is not a force you want to unleash for every situation. If you are angry over a situation that legitimately threatens you, such as someone giving facts that misrepresent you, you might feel justified. But if you snap at someone just to protect your pride or reputation, your anger can be counterproductive, especially if the facts don't support you. In the long haul, anger can seriously hurt you. You might be using it as a defense mechanism to cover up your deficiencies. Ask someone you trust if you get angry too much; it's hard for you to be objective.

- If you're faced with a real danger and you feel justified in using anger, you can still be civilized about it. If you just explode in a primitive tantrum, your anger can be like an acid that erodes everything nearby, and your message can lose its effectiveness.

- On rare occasions, you may *have* to show primitive, visible anger—if it's hard to get your message across in any other way. In a pickup hockey game, if someone constantly hits you with a stick and the referee is not protecting you, you might have to show anger to ward your opponent off. You might face a similar situation in a relationship if a person keeps harassing you and doesn't heed warnings to back off. But don't hold onto anger longer than necessary.

- If you have an anger problem, don't look on it as an issue of *anger management*. It's really about *anger production*. You are the one who is activating your emergency fear system. Monitor and manage your anger production. There are probably just a few circumstances in which you need to produce anger. Stop seeing so many things as threats; there's no need to get upset if the driver in front of you is too slow or if someone criticized you over something unimportant. Do you really want to produce cortisol and testosterone to get revenge on a faulty computer?

- Be wary of the short-term, feel-good symptoms of anger. Yes, anger can intimidate others or make them respect you for standing up for yourself, and it can give you a sense that you are doing something about what stresses or frustrates you.

However, it can also make you seem out of control to others.

- If you consider using anger as a performance tool from time to time, be certain that you have mastery over your skills. During the job, use anger as a very short-term fuel to jump-start your task, then focus intently on your skills. For example, if you are failing at deadline work, briefly get angry with yourself (perhaps using a cue phrase like "Stop letting yourself down!") and focus the extra energy into beating the clock.
- If anger is affecting your life or health, learn to relax. Don't take things personally. Get a better perspective on life and use deep breathing, humor or your favorite music to defuse the emotion. Raise your anger threshold by driving behind the slowest truck or hanging around someone who annoys you. It will also raise your tolerance and patience thresholds.
- If you are constantly angry, identify and deal with your feelings. Perhaps there is an unresolved issue you must approach. On a larger scale, examine your confidence and feelings of self-worth. You might want to talk to someone, perhaps a counselor, about it.

A MANTRA TO TELL YOURSELF: *"Is this worth getting angry about?"*

References:

Anger: The Misunderstood Emotion by Carol Tavris, Touchstone, 1989

Stress Management for Dummies by Allen Elkin, CDG Books, 1999

See: how to deal with stress, how to relax, fear of oneself, fear of not having control, fear of downsizing

When Nothing Works

You know you need professional help when nothing has worked, when you feel depressed, anxious or agitated, when you are unable to carry out your obligations. But the most important point is to select someone with professional credentials and experience, referred by a reputable person or organization.
—DR. TERRY MIZRAHI,
PRESIDENT OF THE NATIONAL ASSOCIATION OF SOCIAL WORKERS

If the strategies in this book don't help you, and if discussing your fears, phobias and problems with family, friends and peers haven't helped, you may want to seek further help, perhaps starting with your family doctor or a therapist. Group therapy—sharing your concerns with people like you—can also be effective.

There is no shame in seeing a psychologist or a psychiatrist (I've been to both). Why should we go to doctors for physical issues only? Check in your yellow pages for psychologists or mental health centers, especially if you suffer from depression. Sadly, less than 25 percent of Americans with anxiety disorders receive any kind of treatment.

"There is a wide range of warning signals that could indicate the need for therapy," says Dr. James Morris, president of the American Association of Marriage and Family Therapy. "That includes marital or family relationship dissatisfaction or distress, alcohol or drug abuse, loneliness, depression, sexual problems, unexplained physical problems, employment difficulties, or an inability to set or attain goals."

Counseling can be helpful for phobias you cannot shake on your own. Counselors can also help you face a transition period in your life or your job, or deal with the pain of separation or loss.

You may need medication from time to time to balance your biochemicals, especially if you suffer from depression (I was on the antidepressant Paxil and it worked). In certain situations, it is healthy for children and teenagers, especially those with generalized anxiety disorder, to receive anxiety medication.

Therapists can deal with your phobias by tailoring their strategies specifically to you, or they may use elaborate or high-tech methods such as virtual reality programs that provide simulated exposure to your fears.

Psychotherapy can change your life, not only by teaching better techniques to cope with your pressures, fears and stresses, but by increasing your self-esteem and improving your view of yourself and the world, which is often at the root of such issues.

References:

The American Psychological Association
For referrals to psychologists, call (800) 964-2000, www.apa.org

Be Your Own Therapist, www.psychologyhelp.com

When You Don't Fear Enough

hypophobia (absence of fear, or a fear of not being afraid)

Those without normal levels of anxiety may lack basic caution and end up losing jobs and getting into fights where others simply sidestep trouble.

—HELEN SAUL IN *PHOBIAS: FIGHTING THE FEAR*

Characteristics: Some people actually don't worry or become anxious or alert enough about real threats or the future. People who don't worry about the consequences of their behavior may get into trouble when they speak up. Others have problems getting inspired for exams or important projects, and their lack of focus or effort can scuttle relationships. Children who fear too little are prone to accidents. Some adults with this condition are called apathetic.

Background: This lack of fear may result partly from an underactive nervous system or from attitudes and beliefs developed in childhood. Not much is known about this condition because "sufferers" don't come forward for help and may not even realize they have a problem. If we didn't have a certain amount of fear for what others thought of us, we'd probably walk around like slobs with poor work habits.

Strategies:

- Take notice if you are continually getting into trouble at work or in relationships for speaking before you think or for not considering the consequences of your actions.
- If you often get injured, you may suffer from lack of fear rather than from lack of coordination or other physical problems.
- Find something you like to do and develop it. The passion could rub off in other areas of your life.
- Network with others, especially enthusiastic people. They can introduce you to mindsets and activities that could light your spark.
- Set goals and stick by them. Look upon them as a challenge.
- Exercise and become physically passionate about life. Get involved in sports or an aerobics class. Play more with your kids.
- Realize that if you are rarely active, if can affect others around you.
- Learn to recognize life's real challenges and threats: your family's health and welfare, financial security, close relationships, career issues, spirituality and the chance you could fall into apathy.

A MANTRA TO TELL YOURSELF: *"Heads up."*

QUOTABLE: *"Nerves provide me with energy. It's when I don't have them, when I feel at ease, that I get worried."—film director Mike Nichols*

Reference:

Fears, Phobias and Rituals by Isaac Marks, Oxford, 1987

Other Phobias

alektorophobia: fear of chickens
anthrophobia: fear of flowers
arithmophobia: fear of numbers
ballistophobia: fear of missiles or bullets
bibliophobia: fear of books
caligynephobia: fear of beautiful women
cibophobia: fear of food
coulrophobia: fear of clowns
deipnophobia: fear of dining or dinner conversations
dishabilliophobia: fear of undressing in front of someone
eleutherophobia: fear of freedom
ephebiphobia: fear of teenagers
frigophobia: fear of cold or cold things
heliophobia: fear of the sun
homilophobia: fear of sermons
hoplophobia: fear of firearms
koniophobia: fear of dust
liticaphobia: fear of lawsuits
macrophobia: fear of long waits
maniaphobia: fear of insanity
methyphobia: fear of alcohol
misophobia: fear of being contaminated with dirt or germs
novercaphobia: fear of your step-mother
nudophobia: fear of nudity
ommetaphobia or *ommatophobia:* fear of eyes
panophobia or *pantophobia:* fear of everything
paraskavedekatriaphobia: fear of Friday the 13th
peladophobia: fear of bald people
phalacrophobia: fear of becoming bald
psellismophobia: fear of stuttering
pyrophobia: fear of fire
rhytiphobia: fear of getting wrinkles
scoleciphobia: fear of worms
tridecaphobia: fear of the number 13
vitricophobia: fear of your step-father
xenoglossophobia: fear of foreign languages

Acknowledgments

I have tried to make the complex subject of fear as simple and understandable as possible by writing in layman's terms. Some of the research I have done myself since 1988, including thousands of interviews with psychologists, psychiatrists, researchers, phobics and people caught or working in pressure situations. But much of the background and strategies have come from other sources, such as the publications and reputable websites mentioned throughout this book.

I would like to thank some specific people whose research and studies have brought us to this point in our quest to understand fears and phobias, beginning with pioneers in psychology such as the father of psychoanalysis, Sigmund Freud (1856–1939); stress researcher Hans Selye (1907–1982) of McGill University in Montreal; psychologist Abraham Maslow (1908–70), who studied the hierarchy of needs; psychologist Maxwell Maltz (1899–1975) for his work on the mind-body connection and visualization; and Norman Cousins (1915-90), whose work on positive thinking and health was groundbreaking.

In recent years, universities, colleges and health centers have been doing wonderful research, which is available to writers like me. Thank you to Redford Williams, M.D., head of psychiatry and behavioral sciences and medicine at Duke University, for his research on hostility and anger control; Herbert Benson, M.D., Harvard Medical School, for his theories on the relaxation response; psychiatrist Edward Hallowell, M.D., founder of the Hallowell Center for Cognitive and Emotional Health in Sudbury and Andover, Massachusets, for his work in several fields, including worry; Massad Ayoob, director of the Lethal Force Institute in Concord, New Hampshire, for his cutting-edge work on emergency fear; David H. Barlow, Ph.D, professor of psychology at Boston University, for his research on anxiety; Julian Hafner, Ph.D, associate professor of psychiatry at Flinders University in Adelaide, Australia, who studies the effect of anxiety on relationships; Graham Davey, Ph.D, professor of psychology at the University of Sussex in England, who has found that cultural beliefs contribute to things like fear of spiders; and Robert Thayer, Ph.D., professor of psychology at California State University, who studies emotions.

Thanks also to psychologist Jaylan Turkkan, Ph.D, for her work on behavioural biology at the Johns Hopkins University School of Medicine; S.J. Rachman, Ph.D, in the department of psychology at the University of British Columbia, for research on the biology of emergency fear; psychologist Steven Berglas, Ph.D, for his work at Duke University on success-induced burnout; Richard Earle, Ph.D, director of the Canadian Institute of Stress, for his work on workplace fears and stress; British psychotherapist Frances Wilks for her work on using emotions intelligently; Michael Davis, Ph.D, professor of psychiatry and behavioral sciences at Emory University School of Medicine in Atlanta, who led his department's research to find medicine to help deal with phobias; Mihaly Csikszentmihalyi, Ph.D, an expert in concentration and the flow state at Claremont Graduate University in California, who conducted earlier work at the University of Chicago; clinical research psychologist Steve Fahrion, Ph.D, who studies biofeedback at the Life Sciences Institute of Mind-Body Health in Topeka, Kansas; Sue Johanson, R.N., a founding member of the Planned Parenthood Federation of Canada, for her work on sexual fears; and evolutionary psychiatrists Randolph Nesse, M.D., at the University of Michigan and Isaac Marks, M.D., at London University, who have researched fear as a survival instinct.

Thank you to Clare McKeon and Meg Taylor at Key Porter Books; to my unflappable agent, Robert Mackwood of Seventh Avenue Literary Agency; to my booking agents at the National Speakers Bureau/Global Speakers Agency; and to my editors at the *Toronto Star*.

On a personal note, thanks to my immediate family for their love and support—my wife, Jennifer; my sons, Paul and Kevin; my daughter-in-law, Tanya; my granddaughter, Skye; my mother, Irene Clarkson; my late father, Fred Clarkson; and my in-laws, Tony and Kathleen Vanderklei, and their family, along with my brother, Stephen, and his family.

And thank you to the many other people who have contributed to this book over the years, from people I have interviewed and worked with to the writers, psychologists and researchers who have inspired me. It is their book, as well.

Index

Sources of fears are in **boldface** type.

abandonment, 63, 124, 146
accidents, 81, 88
accidents, 58–61, 78, 98
    dystychiphobia, 58–59, 80–81
adrenaline, 4, 16, 21, 120, 216
affection, 40–41
aging (gerascophobia), 68–69, 210–11
agoraphobia, 6, 154–55, 158–59
airplanes, 52–53
anger, 9–10, 59, 116, 237–38
anger (angrophobia), 80, 116–17
animals (zoophobia), 82–83, 124
anxiety, 5–6, 233, 239
attackers, 54–59, 78, 148
attention, need for, 40–41, 104–5
attention (scopophobia), 108–9,
    152–53
    lack of (athazagoraphobia), 104–5
authority figures, 186, 218–19

bad news, delivering, 138–39, 222–23
bathing (ablutophobia), 86–87
bats, 83
bedwetting, 144
bees, 83
beggars (hobophobia), 142–43
behaviorism, 11–12
birds (ornithophobia), 82
blood (hemophobia), 7, 58–61
blushing (erythrophobia), 94–95, 106, 114,
    152
body image, 118, 192–93
boredom, 210
boss, 218–19
break-ins, 136–37
breakup, 172–73
bullies, 178–79, 194–95, 224
burglars, 144
    harpaxophobia, 56–57
    scelerophobia, 136–37, 194–95
burial alive, 72
burnout, 200, 202

cameras, 118–19
cars, 78–81
cats, 82
change (tropophobia), 32–33, 212–13
childbirth (lockiophobia), 130–31

children, 99. *See also* parenting; teenagers
    fear and stress in, 124–25, 145, 161,
        186
    and school, 178–81
children
    leaving home, 128–29
    safety of, 126–27, 194
choking (anginophobia), 120–21
claustrophobia, 72–73
cliques, 190–91
commitment, 170–71
comparison, 164
competition, 178–79, 226–27
compliments, 106–7
computers (cyberphobia), 212–13
conditioning, 11–12
confidence, 107
confinement, 72–73
conflict, 38–39
confrontation, 38–39, 114, 172, 220, 222
control, 48–49, 99, 216
control, loss of, 80, 90, 96, 140
    physical, 68–69, 76, 86
cortisol, 4, 10, 16
counseling, 239–40
criticism (enissophobia), 80, 102–3, 152,
    164
critics (criticophobia), 102–3
crowds, 72, 78, 120
    enochlophobia, 158–59, 190–91
crushing, 158

dancing (chorophobia), 164–65
darkness (achluophobia), 124, 148–49
dating, 166–67
deadlines, 216–17
death from overwork (karoshi), 200–203
death (thanatophobia), 62–63, 68–69, 144,
    148, 230
defeat (kakorrhaphiophobia), 112–13,
    226–27
defense mechanisms, 14, 102–3
dentists (dentophobia), 60–61, 66–67
depression, 239
destiny, 48–49
dirt and disease
    mysophobia, 140–41
    suriphobia, 82
discrimination, 224
disorder (ataxophobia), 140–41

distress, 8–9, 16, 200
doctors, 64
doctors (iatrophobia), 60–61, 66–67
dogs (cynophobia), 82–83
dopamine, 14–15, 21, 44, 59
downsizing, 208–9, 218
driving, 80–81

ego, 13, 140, 226
ego defense, 108–9
embarrassment, 88, 94–95, 106, 116, 154, 164, 224
emergencies, 58–59
emergency fear, 3, 4, 7–9
emergency fear system, 7–8, 10, 16, 56, 217
    coping with, 20–21, 237
emotions, 120–21, 138
emotions, showing, 116–17
empty-nest syndrome, 128–29
enclosed spaces (claustrophobia), 72–73
endorphins, 15, 157
enemies, 56–57
eustress, 8–9, 16
exams. *See* tests

failure (atychiphobia), 96–98, 100, 125, 141, 184
    in sports (anginophobia), 120–21
falling (basophobia), 68–69, 74
    down stairs (climacophobia), 76–77
fate (Zeusophobia), 44–45, 48–49
fatness (obesophobia), 192–93
fear. *See also* emergency fear
    awareness of, 24–25
    in children, 124–25, 145, 161, 186
    coping with, 2–3, 15–21
    lack of, 75, 240–41
    physical effects of, 8, 14–15, 60, 217
    reactions to, 4, 14–15
    sources of, 10–15
    specific, 6–7, 18–19
    types of, 3, 13
    uses of, 20, 120–21
fear, 154
fear defense system, 4, 108–9
fearful situations (counterphobia), 116–17
fight-or-flight response, 8, 56, 59, 120
fires, 58–59
firing an employee, 222–23
flying (aviaphobia), 52–53, 78, 79
foreigners (xenophobia), 28–29, 46–47, 54–55, 160–63
friends' opinions, 188–89
future, 28–29, 231

gays, 174–75
generalized anxiety disorder, 233, 239
genetics, 11, 12
germs
    mysophobia, 140–41
    suriphobia, 82
getting lost, 158
ghosts (phasmophobia), 44–45, 124, 148–49
gods (theophobia), 46–47
good news (euphobia), 100–101

happiness (cherophobia), 100–101
harassment, 224–25
health, 64, 231
heights (acrophobia), 74–75
helplessness, 146
high objects (batophobia), 74
homosexuality (homophobia), 71, 174–75
hormones, 14–15, 120
horses, 82–83
hospitals, 60–68
humiliation, 56–57, 96, 182–83, 224
hypochondria, 64–65
hypophobia (lack of fear), 75, 240–41

ideas (ideophobia), 34–35
illness, 62–65, 124, 158
imperfection (atelophobia), 96–99, 108
inferiority complex, 107, 125
injury, 56–57, 60–63, 68–69, 80, 124
in-laws (soceraphobia), 134–35
insecurity, 108, 121
insomnia, 144
interviews, 206–7
intimacy, 42–43, 70–71, 167
invasion of privacy, 110–11, 136, 142
isolation (autophobia), 114–15

jinxes, 44–45
jobs
    interviews for, 206–7
    losing, 196–97, 208–9, 220
    quitting, 220–21
jumping (catapedaphoiba), 74–75
justice (dikephobia), 186–87

karoshi, 200–203

laughter (geliophobia), 116
lawsuits, 58–59, 222
layoff, 208–9
leadership, 36–37, 114, 138, 158, 211
learning (sophophobia), 178–79
lesbians, 174–75

lizards, 82
loneliness
    autophobia, 68–69, 114–15, 124
    monophobia, 146–47
looking stupid, 178–79, 182–83, 226
looking up (anablepophobia), 74
love, 40–41, 133, 170, 230
love (philophobia), 42–43
    lack of, 40–41, 70–71
love play (sarmassophobia), 166–67
luck, 44–45, 49, 101

machines (mechanophobia), 212–13
marriage (gamophobia), 170–71
    breakdown of, 132–33
masturbation, 71
medical situations, 60–61
medications, 19, 153, 239
memory loss, 68–69
men (androphobia), 167, 168–69
menopause, 68–69
menstruation, 70
mice, 82
mistakes, 96, 98–99
money (chrometophobia), 204–5
muggers, 56–59, 148
music (musicophobia), 88

narrow places (stenophobia), 72–73
needles, 67
new things (neophobia), 172–73,
    220–21
night, 144–45
nightmares, 124, 125, 145
noises (acousticophobia, ligyrophobia),
    88–89
noradrenaline, 21

obesity (obesophobia), 192–93
observation, 108–9, 152–53
obsessive-compulsive disorder, 96, 140
old people (gerontophobia), 68–69
open places (agoraphobia), 6, 154–55,
    158–59
opinions
    of friends, 188–89
    of others (allodoxaphobia), 108–9,
        158, 184
opposite sex (heterophobia), 167, 168–69
other people, 108–9, 158, 162–63, 184,
    188–90
other races, 162–63, 190
overwork (ponophobia), 200–203

pain, 6, 230, 231

pain, 58–59, 80, 124
    algophobia, 64–65
panhandlers, 142–43
panic attacks, 154–55, 158
panic disorder, 233
parenthood, 130–31
parenting, 124–27, 180–81, 184, 187, 189,
    194–95
parents-in-law (soceraphobia), 134–35
peer pressure, 178, 188–89
peer pressure, 178–79
people (anthropophobia), 124, 152–53, 167
perfectionists, 96, 98, 108, 140–41
performing (topophobia, stage fright),
    156–57
phobias, 3, 6–7, 242
    dealing with, 7, 18–19
photography, 118–19
pickpockets, 158
pink slip syndrome, 208–9
pleasure (hedonophobia), 100
post-traumatic stress disorder, 12, 233
poverty (peniaphobia), 68–69, 204–5, 210
powerlessness, 30–31, 48–49, 200
praise (doxophobia), 106–7, 214–15
pregnancy, 131
pressure, 8–9, 120, 216–17
    coping with, 234–35
    from peers, 178, 188–89
pride, 10, 112, 113, 192, 226–27
    as ego, 8, 14, 20, 94, 103, 108
privacy, loss of, 110–11, 136, 142
promotion, asking for, 214–15
public places (agoraphobia), 6, 154–55,
    158–59
public speaking (glossophobia), 156–67,
    178–79
punishment (poinephobia), 178, 218–19

quitting work, 220–21

racism, 11–12. *See also* tolerance
raise, asking for, 214–15
rats, 82
rejection, 40–41, 96, 104–5, 166, 214–15
relationships, 152, 166–71
    breakdown of, 132–33, 172–73
relatives (syngenesophobia), 134–35
relaxation, 232–34
religion (theophobia), 46–47
responsibility (hypegiaphobia), 36–37, 170
retirement, 210–11
revenge, 109, 182
ridicule (catagelophobia), 182–83
riding in cars (amaxophobia), 78–81

risk, 34–35, 126
road travel (hodophobia), 78–79
robbers (harpaxophobia), 56–57, 136–37,
    194–95

school (scolionophobia), 178–81
seasickness, 86
self, 114–15, 146
    appearance of, 192–93
    in mirror (eisoptrophobia), 118–19
self-consciousness, 118
self-esteem, 118, 194, 210, 230
    and ego, 13, 140, 226
self-esteem, loss of, 96
self-image, 118, 192–93
separation anxiety, 124, 178–81
seratonin, 20
sex, 133, 166–67, 173–75
sex (erotophobia), 70–71, 110, 167
sexual harassment, 224–25
sexual inadequacy, 68–71
shyness, 152–53, 158
singing, 164–65
singlehood (anuptaphobia), 40–41
sinning (peccatophobia), 46–47
sleep, 144–45
snakes (ophidiophobia), 84–85
snow (chionophobia), 90–91
social harm, 124
solicitors, 142–43
solitude (autophobia, isolophobia, mono-
    phobia), 114–15, 146–47
sounds (acousticophobia, ligyrophobia),
    88–89
speaking (phonophobia), 114–15, 164–65
    in public (glossophobia), 156–67
spiders (arachnophobia), 84–85
spotlight effect, 94
stage fright, 156–67
status, loss of, 96, 112–13
stereotyping, 162, 168–69, 174, 224
storms, 90–91
strange places, 124
strangers (xenophobia), 28–29, 46–47,
    54–55, 158, 160–63
stress, 8, 9, 16
    in children, 124–25
    dealing with, 124, 235–36
    at work, 200–203
success (successophobia), 100–101, 106
suffocation, 86
supernatural, 44–45, 124, 148–49

superstition, 44–45
swimming, 86–87

teachers, 184, 186–87
teamwork, 226
technology, 212–13
teenagers, 188, 205
telemarketers, 142–43
terrorism, 54–55, 78
testosterone, 59
tests (testophobia), 38–39, 184–85, 206–7,
    226–27
therapy, 18, 19, 239–40
thinking too much (phronemophobia), 5
thunderstorms (astropophobia), 90–91
tolerance, 143, 224–25, 238
    racial, 46–47, 55, 111, 163
touch (aphenphosmphobia), 42–43, 110–11
trampling, 158
trauma, 12–13, 15, 57, 136
travel
    airplane (aviaphobia), 52–53, 78, 79
    road (hodophobia), 78–81
trembling (tremophobia), 94–95
tyrants (tyrannophobia), 186–87, 218–19

ugliness, 192–93
unemployment, 196–97, 208–9, 220
unknown, 28–29, 44, 148
untidiness, 140–41

vasovegal reaction, 60
virginity, loss of (primeisodophobia), 70–71
visualization, 18
voice, own (phonophobia), 114–15, 164–65

water (hydrophobia), 7, 86–87
weakness (asthenophobia), 30–33, 182–83
weather, 90–91
weight, gaining (obesophobia), 192–93
witchcraft (wiccaphobia), 44–45
women (gynephobia), 167, 168–69
work, 178–79
worry, 2–3, 4–6
    coping with, 17–18
    financial, 210
    health, 64
    at night, 144–45
    serious, 230–32

xenophobia, 28–29, 46–47, 54–55, 160–63

W9-AGF-522

1 - TOP 10 BOOKS ON THE ISLANDS
-Island Sun 6/13/97

What they are saying about Sean Michael Dever's BLIND PASS:

"Sean Michael Dever has an extraordinary grasp of his material-especially for a first time writer. He knows the ins and outs of his characters, his plot and his locale. A significant first work."
-Jackie K Cooper Reviews

"An excellent read...Dever is a natural storyteller who knows how to pique the readers imagination...I dare anyone to put down the last fifty pages!"
-Harold Hunt, Cape Coral Breeze

"A real page turner from the start! It lets you get involved in the dark side of otherwise sunny South Florida. A great read for the beach...or anywhere else for that matter!"
-Chris Paul 13 WMAZ-TV Mornin' Show

"...a hit thriller..a 244 page act of revenge."
-Todd Bishop, The Philadelphia Inquirer

"A very talented young writer!"
-The Del Ward Show

"A touch of Clancy, Grisham..."
-Jill Tyrer, Sanibel Captiva Islander

"..A whirlpool of events and the reader is sucked into them as they swirl and spiral to a final conclusion...a mystery along the lines of a John D. MacDonald or Lawrence McNalley thriller."
-The Daily Sun

"Colorful, fast-moving...great beach reading.."
-Ft. Myers News Press/Sun-Press

A NOVEL BY

SEAN MICHAEL DEVER

BLIND PASS

Duchess Publications

Cape Coral, Florida

BLIND PASS
Copyright 1995
Sean Michael Dever

ISBN 0-9658180-0-4

Published by, and copies may be obtained from:
Duchess Publications
P.O.Box 150053
Cape Coral, Fl. 33915-0053
See order form at the back of this book for additional copies. Blind Pass may
be obtained by retail outlets at special rates.

This book is a work of fiction. The characters, names, incidents, dialogue, and
plot are the products of the author's imagination or are used fictitiously. Any
resemblance to actual persons or events is purely coincidental.

Copyright© 1995, 1997, 1998 by Sean Michael Dever
All rights reserved. No part of this book may be reproduced or transmitted in
any form or by any means, electronic or mechanical, including photocopying,
recording, or by any information storage and retrieval system, without the
written permission of the Author, except where permitted by law. For
information contact Duchess Publications, Cape Coral, Florida.

123456789
Cover Art and Design by S.M. Dever and Tram G.Pham
Photo: Laura Ann Martin

**Contact Sean Michael Dever online at:
FLWRITR1 @ aol.com**

For Laura,
> *Thank you for believing in me and showing me how to follow my dreams. I miss you very much.*

To my parents and family,
> *Thanks for all your love and support,*
> > *and I'm glad I surprised you. (I surprised myself!)*

To my readers,
> *Thank you for the inspiration to continue telling stories. As long as you'll read 'em, I'll write 'em.*

And thank you to all the people I have known over the years who convinced me my writing was worth something and that have encouraged me to stick it out including: Tom Reilly, Rev. Bruce Martin and Family, Dr. Erica Kobylinski, Kim Maheuron, Laurie Romonov, Richie Patrick, Spencer Franklin, Steve Perry, Christopher Murry, Jack Chinn, The Kohler Family, Harold Hunt, Jackie Cooper, Chris Middlebrooks, Martha Ambrose, Dr. David Kirby, Steve Beck at Sanibel Island Bookstore, Barbara Keene at Barnes and Noble, Macon, Ga., Kelly Sonnanstine at Books A Million, Ft. Myers, and so many others.

Acknowledgments:

This is a work of fiction, but in order for any work of fiction to be believed, it must be based on truth. I would not have been able to complete this story without the help of the following :

Special Agent James Rorten, US Drug Enforcement Agency (DEA)
Special Agent Mark Leon, Federal Bureau of Investigation (FBI)
Dr. William McConkey, Florida Senate
Janey Hoover, Florida Dept. Of Law Enforcement (FDLE)
ETC Lauton Collins, US Navy
Mr. Greg Scott of the Federal Election Commission
Mr. Owen McCaul, Asst. State Attorney, Florida 2nd Judicial Circuit
Mr. Joe Bizzaro, Public Information Director, State of Florida, Office of the
        Attorney General

In addition to help with the technical aspects of my story, I need also to thank the people who gave me the inspiration to write. Their belief in me was what kept me writing day after day. First, I'd like to thank Mr. Tom Reilly. Even though Tom's life is hectic enough as one of the busiest first assistant directors in film, he took the time to not only read my stories, but to comment on them as well. Next, I thank my parents who have always encouraged and supported my writing. Finally, to Laura Ann Martin whose patience and understanding made this possible. She made my words and thoughts clear enough for others to understand.

SEAN MICHAEL DEVER
BLIND PASS

Duchess Publications

Cape Coral, Florida

1

Thursday, August 31

"The sure way to be cheated is to think
one's self more cunning than others."

Francois de La Rochefoucauld

The soft moaning of the woman was not discernible against the rattling of palm fronds in the breeze, not that anyone would have heard if it were. Across the bay, the lighted resorts of Fort Myers Beach defined the shoreline in the darkness, but the sands of Sanibel were empty, except for the few creatures who lived in the surf. The sounds of music and laughter drifted across the water toward the sliding glass doors of the bedroom facing the Gulf. Inside, the moonlight reflecting in the tide cast wild shadows on the bleached white walls. They danced along the dressers covered with photos, brushes, and makeup cases, over a bikini top hanging on the back of a chair, then jumped to a desktop, where the matching bottom was draped over plastic amber prescription bottles scattered like bowling pins.

On the bed, two silhouettes embraced, frosted light surrounding them as their bodies pressed together into one indistinguishable mass. Their movement was rhythmic, passionate. The moaning became louder, cutting through the misty night air. Occasionally, moonlight slid between the two, revealing the strong muscular back of a man and the perfectly rounded breasts of the woman below him. The couple moved as graceful as dancers on a private stage. After a few minutes, the synchronicity started to disappear. It was slight at first; an observer would hardly have noticed the fluidity of the movement changing. It looked unnatural and forced. No longer did it appear that the two worked together in this sexual frenzy.

He strained his head back and bit his lip as his body began pounding against hers. The thrusting and grinding of the two quickened, becoming almost violent. The low growl of his breathing grew, matched by the couple's intense movements. Her moaning was replaced with short quick breaths. The word "Stop" formed on her lips, but did not escape as her body responded to the feeling between her legs. Her breasts glistened as beads of sweat rolled to her stomach, then down onto the bed. He pushed deep into her as every muscle in his body strained. Then, with a shudder, he rolled off and turned onto his back. Turning his face to her, he watched as she continued to move, grinding her hips, searching for him. She arched her back high into the air, oblivious to the fact that he was no longer inside her. The muscles in her stomach were visible as her body started to spasm. She tilted her head back, and let out a cry. The sound was not long, nor loud, and she ended it by clamping her jaw shut, biting through her tongue in the process. Dark red blood ran down her mouth and neck in small streams, while her convulsions continued. Her arms began to flail about, slamming his chest with sharp slaps, until, finally, she let out a gasp and her body relaxed. Drained, she turned her head toward him. Her eyes open, she stared at him, but was completely still. As he leaned over the edge of the bed, she exhaled deeply.

Sitting up on the king size bed, he reached down and unfurled the dark blue diver's wet suit that he had worn earlier. After pulling it on, he leaned over and lightly stroked the woman's wrist with his finger. Getting no response, he lifted her arm just a few inches, then let it go, watching it drop to the sweat-covered linen. She still made no sound. She still did not move. Pulling a pencil beam flashlight from the pocket of the suit, he traced the circle of light along her body, stopping at her face. Her deep brown eyes reflected the circle of light, but could no longer see.

Satisfied, he pointed the instrument down to the floor and searched. Under the bed, the light focused on a condom wrapper and syringe. Reaching down, he retrieved the items. After placing a tiny blue cap on the needle, he dropped them into a small bag, sealed it and attached the bag to his dive belt. Startled by a knock on the door leading into the house, the diver tensed, and became perfectly stationary. Standing as quietly as possible, he closed his eyes and concentrated, trying to picture what was on the other side of the hollow wood door, hoping it was his imagination. A voice pierced the silence, "I'm going to bed." It was a man's voice; her husband's voice. The diver quickly slid his hand down to the plastic sheath on his belt and gripped the handle of the stainless steel blade. The door handle jiggled. "Damn!" the diver thought, cursing himself for not checking the lock. His heart thumped so loud in his chest, he was sure it could be heard through the door. "Good night," the husband repeated more softly this time, the despair and disappointment shining through the words.

The metallic clicking of the brass handle stopped, and the footsteps retreated down the hallway assuring the intruder that there would be no more interruptions. He relaxed the grip on his dive knife and noticed his knees were shaking. He tried to steady himself by leaning on the desktop, but as he placed his hand down to steady himself it slid, knocking over some plastic videotape cases that

*had been stacked there. He froze for a second time, and listened. When he was sure
that no one had heard, he bent down to retrieve the videos.*

*Shining his flashlight, he noticed one of them had opened when it impacted the
floor. He lifted up the tape from inside, and read the label. He pulled the video from
its cover, and smiled. His eyes were drawn back to the woman. Standing over her, he
moved her hand so that it rested on her body.*

*A few moments later, the intruder emerged from the doorway onto the sand-
encrusted patio. Picking up his fins and tank, he made his way across the sand. He
adjusted his mask and disappeared into the warm, black, salt water.*

*

Ten hours later, and roughly 90 miles to the east, the Gulfstream IV corporate
jet began its takeoff roll at Ft. Lauderdale Executive Airport. The two-engine plane
belonged to the Grand Key Bank and Trust of Miami, and on board was Francis "Frank"
Menceti, Chairman and CEO of GKB. Along for the ride to the Virgin Islands were
Tanya, Frank's latest twenty-year old girlfriend, her dog, a little tan mutt she
adopted from animal control, and Jeffrey Strata. Frank was reviewing an album of
Jeff's work. As he flipped through the pages, he occasionally commented on how
powerful the images were. But, for the most part, he seemed disinterested in Jeff's
art.

"What's this go for?" Menceti asked, pointing down at the page.

"Eight grand. I sold it last week," Jeff answered. Menceti grunted,
unimpressed. Eight thousand dollars was not even a day's pay. The next print was the
very gruesome and surreal image of a mother and child, both decapitated. The Angel
of Death was carrying away their skulls.

"What about that one?"

"I still have that, I completed it last year."

"Very nice," Menceti said, "I might like..." He was interrupted by the dog,
which let out a high pitched screeching bark. "Woman, what the hell are you doing to
that animal!?" Menceti screamed. Tanya and the dog both cowered at the anger in the
man's voice. Jeff waited for someone to say something, but the only sound was the
whine of the jet engines outside. He felt no pity for the girl; she knew what she had
gotten into. But he was afraid for the puppy, for Jeff knew Menceti well, and figured
the dog would not live to see the trip home. Jeff tried to help by drawing the man's
attention towards the artwork. He cleared his throat loudly, causing Menceti to
break his icy stare at Tanya.

"You know Frank, art is a great investment," Jeff said, trying to divert the
banker's anger. "The IRS can't tell you what it's worth, just what you've paid for
it."

"I mean, it's a good place to keep money, maybe even hide money." Menceti
turned back towards the artist, but looked up occasionally at Tanya. She nervously
squeezed at the green tennis ball that the dog used for a toy. The puppy sensing the
tension was gone, reached up with his paws and tried to take it away. Tanya, though,

was too nervous to let go.

"Are you going to play with that damn dog or what?" Frank said. "That's why I bought him for you."

She threw the ball down the aisle between them and curled up into the seat. The puppy went down to where the ball had stopped, sniffed it, picked up the ball and trotted back to Tanya; but the woman was too frightened to move. The puppy dropped the ball and sat quietly under the her seat. Satisfied that there would be no more interruptions, Frank turned his attention back to Jeff.

"You should paint a portrait of me," Frank said.

"I've never done a portrait. Maybe I could paint you and Tonya."

"Hell no,"Menceti said drawing a dirty look. " Maybe me and that damn dog. I have a feeling that mutt will be around longer than that stupid bitch." Jeff watched Tonya look away.

"Not really my style," Jeff replied, hoping the subject would change.

Frank closed the portfolio and handed it back to Jeff. "I'm sure we can work something out." Jeff understood what that meant. With Francis Menceti working it out meant you did what Frank wanted.

The fifty-two year old banker stood and walked to the back of the plane. He motioned to Tanya, who quietly joined him. They retired into the private quarters and closed the door.

Jeff watched the small dog sniff at the base of the door, looking for its master. The G-4 was the size of a small airliner and had every amenity one would find in a deluxe hotel suite. Jeff knew he could get used to it, but this was big money, real money. Money he just didn't have. Not yet, anyway. He stretched out in the seat and figured he might as well enjoy himself now. The trip back would be different. Menceti was staying a week, but Jeff had to be back in two days, which meant a cramped, noisy commercial turboprop. He was not looking forward to it.

The artist turned and gazed at the midnight blue water five miles below him. There were no small tropical islands, no white capped waves, nothing to give his attention to except the deep blue Atlantic. He leaned back and relaxed, but dared not close his eyes. He had learned that he could live on only four hours of sleep a night, and even that was more than he would like. Any longer and the images he put down on canvas visited him, as they had every day since his mother's death.

2
***
Saturday, September 2

The cries of a wailing saxophone hung in the humid air as Susan Ranson turned into the driveway of the Sands Golf and Tennis Club. As she reached the clubhouse parking lot, she read the banner that had been stretched over the entrance, "WELCOME TO THE 15TH ANNUAL TASTE OF JAZZ." Below the sign, an elderly parking attendant, distinguishable by his Day Glo Orange safety vest, sat in a lawn chair under a large green and white umbrella. He wiped the sweat from his forehead with a handkerchief and put down his cup of ice water when she turned into the lot. Susan did not see the five orange cones that blocked her path, and knocked down three of them as she hit her brakes.

Susan did not really want to be there, but she had no choice in the matter. Being the wife of the Lee County District Attorney required such appearances, especially now that David was going to run for Congress. She could care less whether he was a D.A. or the President of the United States for that matter, she still wanted to leave him. But it would have to wait until after the election, at least that was what David had insisted on. And she had promised to stay until then. It was not that she was opposed to being a politician's wife, she had enjoyed it. The attention was nice, as was the social life, and the access she was given helped her get the job at the paper. She simply was opposed to being Mrs. David Ranson.

The attendant stood up and slowly walked over to the cones, picking up each one, then placing it back in line with the others. When he finished, he went to the left side of the gold Lexus coupe and tapped on the driver's window. Susan pressed a button on the armrest and the glass lowered into the door, allowing the air conditioning to escape into the old man's face. He enjoyed the cold air for a moment before speaking.

"I'm sorry, parking is for VIP's only, Miss."

Susan pulled out the green and white press pass issued to her by the Sheriff's department and handed it to him.

"I'm with the Sanibel View."

The old man reached into his pocket and took out a pair of eyeglasses. He placed them in front of his face and examined the card. After deciding it was genuine, he walked back to the cones and moved them out of her way. With a nod and a smile, he waved her through. She made her way up the drive, under the clubhouse carport, and parked between a convertible BMW and a local TV news van near the golf cart barn.

She loved the annual festival with all the people, the mellow music. It gave life to the private club, which in her opinion desperately needed it. Susan was not a tennis player or a golfer; in fact, the only reason she was a member was because of David. And he hated seeing the course torn up by the crowds. Maybe that's why she liked it so much, she thought. Susan smiled to herself in the mirror and placed her press pass back in her purse. She wasn't on assignment for the paper, but it allowed her a great parking space.

"Who knows? I might write something,"she thought, justifying herself. She pulled out her makeup case and gave herself the once over. She teased her hair with her hand, then with a brush, but the humidity was getting the best of the long brown locks. Frustrated, she finally pulled it back into a ponytail. Susan adjusted the straps on the brightly colored sun dress, which, not coincidentally, highlighted her glistening, freshly-shaven legs. Though not conceited by any scale, she knew she could pass for twenty-three, and smiled at the thought of how many times she had been carded at the local clubs. Susan enjoyed the surprised looks of the bouncers when they saw her true age.

After a few minutes she was ready to be the sweet, loving, public wife of the Lee County District Attorney, and the thought almost made her sick. "This time next year, you'll be a free woman," she told herself. She popped the trunk and opened the door.

Susan had walked to the back of the car when the skinny, little, platinum blonde came through the tinted double glass doors of the Sands Clubhouse.

"Let me give you a hand!" Wendy Richardson yelled as she ran across the lot to the struggling reporter.

"Thanks." Susan pulled blankets and pillows from the trunk.

"I was looking for you. David said you were right behind him."

"I stopped for gas," Susan replied. "Where is he?"

Wendy pointed to the clubhouse, "At the bar with Doc Whitmore and Larry. I don't know why you two don't ride together." Susan patted the black plastic device on her purse strap, "Two beepers, two cars."

Wendy bundled the blankets in her hands and headed over to the stage; Susan closed the trunk and quickly caught up. The two women sauntered up past the side of the flatbed trailer filled with lights and speakers, and out to the eighteenth green. No longer a golf course, the perfectly manicured front nine looked more like a carnival. The large stage was set off the first tee. The driving range and paths leading to it were covered with families sitting on blankets and relaxing to the cool jazz flowing out. A few of the club's die-hards were still smacking little white balls into the lake behind the crowd, but most had ceded the area to the once-a-year invaders.

"Where to?" asked Wendy.

"Over towards the right side of the stage to that sidewalk. I love sitting in the grass, but the fire ants eat me alive. Last year I had twenty-two bites when I got home." They headed over near a sign that read "Carts Only On Path" and dropped Susan's things.

"Did you bring something for the no-see-um's? I have some lotion if you didn't."

Susan pulled a bottle of repellent lotion from her bag, "All set." She opened the bottle and rubbed the warm lotion on her legs. She looked around and noticed a bunch of guys playing touch football near the tee off point. " I see that the view is as good as ever," she said.

Wendy looked over, "That's nothing; wait until you meet Jeff. Gorgeous and talented. I'd do him right now if he'd ask me."

Susan gave Wendy an unapproving glance, "That's what I like about you, Wendy. Your sense of romance."

Wendy ignored the comment, " I'll meet you up there. It's the second tent on the right."

Susan continued to rub the lotion in, "Second tent, gotcha."

"You'll know it," Wendy told her, " It's got all kinds of weird paintings and stuff out front." Susan waved her away, and watched her head up the hill to the eighteenth hole. They weren't what she considered *friends*. She and Wendy worked at the same paper, and they had some things in common, but not enough to base a friendship on. No, it was just mutual companionship. Wendy was from a poor family also, but was not well educated. Some would call her white trash, in fact most people did, until they saw the images. Wendy was one hell of a photographer, which was why she was hired. Susan thought it was funny how natural talent in art, any art, suddenly erased any class standings. Women who would not let Wendy clean their bathrooms suddenly became a dear friend when they saw the photographs. But Susan also thought Wendy was very naive, and ignorance, at least in this case, was bliss.

Of course Susan also didn't fit in with the women that lived or vacationed on the island. She was only a friend by association with her husband. She knew she would need someone to talk to after the election was over.

Near the green, huge, colorful tents covered every bit of grass from the clubhouse, to the pool, to the tennis courts. Just about every restaurant in the area had set one up, and they were trading tickets purchased at a little wooden booth for samples of their cuisine. Scattered among the food tents were others that offered T-shirts, temporary tattoos, and face painting. Some local artists and writers were also there, signing their work and selling their creations.

Wendy came out of the bright yellow tent just as Susan topped the hill. "Over here," she yelled.

*

The deep green carpet accented the brass and polished oak fixtures of the private lounge. The thirty-five foot bar had two television sets hanging over it, but the three patrons sitting there were not interested. Most of the excitement was outside the huge windows that lined the back of the wall. The temporary food court and market had replaced the usual serene beauty of the golf course. The musicians on stage could not be seen, but the vibrations of the glass assured the three club members that the band was still there.

Closest to the lounge, David Ranson was sipping on a Jim Beam and Coke, looking for his wife through the window near the bar. In his mid-forties, he still had dark brown hair, though it was starting to thin. At six foot two, two hundred pounds, he was very intimidating, especially in a courtroom. He knew this and used it to his advantage when he had to. He also had a temper. This fact was well known to both his friends and adversaries although he could be downright charming if it suited him. And right now charming suited him.

On the stool next to him sat Dr. Willard W. Whitmore, a friend of the District Attorney, but more importantly, a prospective contributor to David's political campaign. For the past hour David had been trying to get the old man to write a check for his run at the House of Representatives. But at present, all the Doc was interested in was watching the shapely young bartender as she fixed his drink.

"Never happen, Doc," David teased.

"You never know."

"What do you think, Larry ?"

"She's young enough to be his daughter."

"Leave me alone," the doctor grumbled as he blew a paper wrapper from a straw across the bar. Larry Kindle ducked as it sailed past, then laughed at the drunk old man.

"What kind of behavior is that from a man of your stature?"

"Humph," Whitmore snorted, and turned his attention back to the bartender. David, sensing the Doc was in no mood to hand out money, turned around and stared out the large picture windows. The food vendors were close enough that he could smell the chicken wings cooking, and his stomach growled.

Larry whistled, and the bartender grabbed the glass mug in front of him. She pulled a clean frosted one from the freezer and stuck it under the tap.

"Hey, Doc, where's your wife?" Larry asked loudly when the bartender was close enough to hear. The young woman smiled as she placed the freshly drawn draft on a napkin and took Larry's money.

"David, tell the young man to mind his own goddamn business."

"The doctor wants you to mind your own goddamn business, Larry," David said without turning around.

"Thank you," Whitmore grunted as he sipped on his vodka tonic.

Doc Whitmore was thirty years Larry's senior and showed every bit of it. His hair had turned white long ago, and what was left of it was normally hidden under a wide-brimmed hat. His eyeglasses were thicker than most, yet he still practiced medicine. He was once a prominent orthopedic surgeon, and in his prime he was making over seven figures, and had been a partner in five different clinics.

But that was twenty years ago, when he was young. All he had cared about was money and prestige. Aging changed his priorities. His friends spent less time with him and more with their own families. The photos and stories of children, and then grandchildren became too much to bear. He sold his stake in the clinics for more money than he could ever spend, then married a much younger woman and set about making a family. But it was not to be. He had gotten more than he bargained for with his new bride, and they had more than their share of troubles. So the Doc went back to doing the only thing he knew. He opened a small office on Sanibel and started a pro-bono family practice for the less privileged on the island. He started drinking and spending less time at home. The work he did at the clinic wasn't very challenging, but it kept him busy and away from his wife.

Larry Kindle, on the other hand, was retired from the Merchant Marine and did very little of anything. He was not officially retired; he had actually served only five years. Assigned to an ocean going tug in Mayport, Florida, he and some shipmates had converted all their paychecks into lotto tickets and hit the jackpot. His share had made him an instant multi-millionaire. At twenty-seven he left his life on the sea, intending to build his fortune into a huge financial empire. But all he managed to do was hire a trustworthy accountant and run up a big bar bill. He, too, was on the list of potential supporters of David's ambition.

Larry went over next to David, who was now standing at the windows.

"Whatcha lookin' at?"

David kept his eyes focused out the window, "Where the hell is she? Wendy said she was coming right back, right?"

"Haven't you learned that a woman will do what she wants, when she wants? Relax."

David turned back to the window. "Yeah, well, Susan knows better!"

"It doesn't look that way to me, how 'bout it, Doc?"

The doctor was watching the bartender bend down for ice in front of him. She knew he would try to look down her shirt, and she wore it loose enough to keep interest but tight enough to keep the rich old bastard wondering. As she stood up, Doc Whitmore quickly turned to the window. She put down his drink and picked up the ten dollar bill, knowing he would not expect change.

"Isn't that your wife?" The old man pointed out the window.

"Where?"

"Next to that yellow tent, near the light pole."

David saw her standing with Wendy near a small canvas tent. A man was next to them, and when he disappeared under the tarpaulin, Wendy followed.

"Yes it is," David said without taking his eyes off Susan, "I'll see you guys later."

David never looked back, but made his way along the windows to the door. He did not look at anything except Susan, and ran into a waitress on his way out, knocking over a tray full of drinks in the process. He neither stopped, nor apologized, he just made a beeline for his soon to be ex-wife. Whitmore squinted as he looked through his glasses, "Who's that fellow she was talking to?"

"Got me by the balls, Doc," Larry answered watching, "But that boy better watch himself. He's a candidate now. He's got no place for a temper."

*

The vibration against his leg could only mean one thing. Brian Doyle reached into the pocket of his J.C. Penney, pin-striped, ninety-nine dollar-on-sale suit and turned off his beeper. Touching his wife, Sarah, on the shoulder, he leaned over and whispered in her ear. She nodded and quietly picked up her pocketbook from the pew. Without a sound they turned and walked out while the minister led the First Baptist Church in a prayer for the newly married couple still standing at the alter.

Outside the small white building, Brian Doyle put his imitation Ray Ban sunglasses on, and took his wife's hand as they walked past the two young boys decorating the groom's car.

"I'm sorry," he said to his wife.

"For what?"

"Because you're going to miss the reception. Because it's Saturday and I should be home with you and Jenny."

"It's not your fault," she said, "After twenty years as a policeman's wife, you get used to these things." Detective Doyle squeezed his wife's hand lovingly, knowing the sacrifices she had given up for him over the years. The big as well as the small.

After unlocking the car, he opened both car doors and felt the heat that had built up inside hit his face. The couple waited a minute while the light breeze circulated the air in the vehicle. His forehead was already dripping with sweat when he reached inside to remove the cardboard sunblock jammed against the windshield. He turned the ignition as his wife strapped on her seatbelt. He flipped on the air-conditioning, which immediately triggered a loud whine from the fan belt of the little four cylinder engine. He backed out of the parking space as Sarah retrieved the car phone from the floor of the back seat. She plugged the cord into the hole where the cigarette lighter had been. She then handed the phone to her husband, who dialed while he waited to pull out onto US Route 41.

"This is Doyle. You paged me." He listened, then gestured to his wife for something to write with. She opened the glove compartment and took out a pad and pen. He switched the phone over to his left ear, squeezing it up to his head with his shoulder, and wrote an address on the notepad held by his wife.

"Let them know I'm on my way. I'm not on the island so it may be a while."

Sarah took back the pen, paper and phone. After tearing off the page with the writing on it, she returned the items to their proper storage place.

"What is it?"

"I'm going to have to drop you off at the house; it's going to be a long day," Brian Doyle sighed.

*

David was halfway across the putting green when his beeper went off. Susan was standing near the open flap of the tent when she heard the annoying electronic sound. She turned around and saw David quickly coming toward her. She stepped over to him, and put on her best smile. He scooped her up in his arms and hugged her tight. He put his lips up to her ear.

"Where the hell have you been?" He asked.

The words had no hint of affection or caring. She turned her head and looked at his face, the smile was gone. She squirmed as he squeezed her ever tighter. He saw the fear in her eyes; she found the familiar coldness in his. Susan struggled in his grip, but he just held on, watching the pain start to register. She freed her right arm and tried to slap his face; he let go. She dropped to the ground hard, almost losing her balance. She adjusted her dress and backed away from her husband.

"I was out here!" She talked through clenched jaws, not loud, but stern. She did not like the accusation, nor did she deserve it.

"You were supposed to be following right behind me," David replied mocking her by clenching his teeth. She straightened the straps on her dress. She knew the routine, but until recently it had stayed private.

"I had to stop for gas! Where do you think I went?" She did not even try to stop her anger or the flow of tears. Susan was about to start a very loud, very public argument right there on the spot, shattering the sweet All-American family image of the campaign commercials. But then Wendy stuck her head out of the tent.

"Look who I found!" Wendy said straining to pull a tan shirtless man out from inside the canvas behind Susan. Wendy's grip slipped, causing her to hit Susan's back from behind. This in turn caused a collision between David and his wife. The District Attorney fell back, barely missing a wooden telephone pole. Susan's head hit David's jaw with a thunderous crack!

Oblivious to the accident she caused, Wendy had already disappeared back inside the tent. Susan's head hurt, but she found a sense of satisfaction when she saw David rubbing his bruised chin.

"I want you to meet someone!"

The couple heard her before they saw the bosomed blonde emerge from under the canvas. She ran over to David, and pulled him by the arm up to the tent, where Wendy's new found interest was standing. Wearing only beige shorts and black sandals, the artist looked more like a shipwreck survivor than a noted painter.

"This is David Ranson, our next Congressman. David, this is Jeff Strata. He's an artist!"

"We've met," said Jeff flatly. David said nothing, just stood, rubbing his chin. The moment was awkward for everyone. Finally, Jeff offered his hand.

"It's been a long time, David. Or is it Congressman now?"

David stood there, staring, not moving a muscle. Jeff lowered his hand. The two women were puzzled by David's reaction. Jeff shifted his eyes to Susan, then back to David.

Wendy tried to break the tension, "It's not Congressman yet, but everyone I know is voting for him!" Both men shifted their eyes to her, then back to each other. Then a big grin came over Jeff's face.

"If you're going to represent me," Jeff said, "You're going to have to work on that bedside manner, Davey." He started laughing loudly, slapped David on the back, then turned around to go back in the tent. David did not like being embarrassed. He reached out and grabbed the painter's shoulder.

"Don't you turn your back on me!"

The smaller man quickly took hold of David's arm and spun him around, expertly twisting it behind his back. Then, before David knew what was happening, he found himself up against the wooden pole.

"We're not kids anymore, David. Now, please, don't make me hurt an old friend!" Jeff growled.

He held David's face harder against the pole to drive in the point. Susan and Wendy stood there, astonished, not knowing what to do. David's beeper went off again, and Jeff gave him a final shove for emphasis. David turned to him. Scrapes were on his face, his white polo shirt was caked with tar from the pole. The pocket of his blue shorts hung down, ripped from its seam. Looking around, he saw a crowd of people had gathered. As David eyed each face, they slowly went back to whatever they had been doing.

"I'm going to have your ass arrested for assault!" David threatened.

"I did not assault you, I defended myself!"

"That's not what they saw, was it?" David waited for words of support, but Susan and Wendy did not make a sound. They had never seen anyone stand up to David like that before. The beeper went off a third time, Jeff glanced down at the device on the DA's belt.

"Are you going to answer that or what?!" Jeff asked.

David stood defiantly for a moment, then reached down and silenced the little black box. He turned toward Susan, who just looked at him, speechless. "I'll see you at home tonight!"

David then turned to Jeff, "You're lucky I have to go. This isn't over!"

Jeff smiled and waved an exaggerated good-bye as David turned and walked down across the grass.

*

A thousand miles away, two men stood on a pier in front of a small warehouse, watching a crane unload a large, steel container from the Lady Salstedor. Sally, as her crew called her, was a container ship of English registry, but it had been a long time since her crew had been to England. She operated between Hong Kong and the Virgin Islands, delivering toys, canned goods, sporting equipment, most anything that could be placed in the thirty-foot long, steel and aluminum containers that were stacked on her deck. The two men were part of the crew. They had never been on board, except on paper, but that was all that mattered. And, for the money the captain was being paid, he'd swear on the shipment of Bibles in Compartment C5 that the men had sailed the seven seas by his side.

The two called themselves James and Alvin, but of course those weren't their real names. No one used his real name in this line of work. James was from Sydney, though he told people he was born in London. Alvin, the short one with red hair, was from Dublin, Ireland. He never told anyone where he was from. They were standing at the dock alongside a giant container ship that flew an English flag.

"Who are those blokes?" Alvin asked.

The two Americans turned slowly and followed Alvin's eyes to three men grouped near a taxi about a hundred yards away.

"They've been there a long time," Luis commented, "I noticed them when we drove in." Jack, the other American, didn't like it. He had noticed them earlier, and thought they too, might have been waiting for a container to be off-loaded. But the men never even looked at the ship. Not once.

"Too long for a taxi," Luis said, and lit a cigarette.

Alvin also pulled a cigarette from his pocket and lit it. A second later the cellular phone in his pocket buzzed.

*

David Ranson stormed out to the parking lot and over to the black convertible Porsche 930. He ripped off his shirt and wiped his face with it. He looked in the mirror on the door and cleaned the smudge of pine tar from his cheek. Popping the trunk release, he took out a new shirt that was still in the wrapper. He put on the shirt, throwing the dirty one in the compartment, and slammed down the lid. He stuck his key in the door and tried to turn it. The lock jammed.

"Fucking piece of shit!" He kicked the side of the sixty-thousand dollar car. "I fucking hate this fucking thing!"

As David screamed obscenities, two toddlers hid behind their father, whose white belly poked out from under a light blue T-shirt. Both parents watched as the well dressed man beat on a car worth more than the family's house. As the mother whispered something to her husband, David noticed them staring at him.

"What the fuck are you looking at!" he said to them.

The whole family turned their heads and quickly walked to the cart path. David yanked hard, and the door lock released its grip on the key. The District Attorney got in the car and started it. Looking over toward the tents, he thought he could see Susan still talking to the man who had just made a fool of him.

He didn't need this shit, especially with the pressure of an election coming up. He slammed the car into gear and dropped the clutch. The tires squealed, leaving black marks and white smoke, as he pulled out of the parking space. At the end of the lot, David had to turn hard to avoid three teenagers on bicycles. He fish-tailed the German sports car, nearly sideswiping a Sanibel Police Jeep Cherokee parked in front of the clubhouse. The old man wearing the orange vest jumped up on to the curb as the speeding convertible sped through the barricade, knocking the cones all over, and dragging one almost a hundred feet down the drive.

David's head was throbbing. He didn't like being made a fool of, especially in public. Especially by little Jeffrey Strata. He would deal with him another day. He would deal with his wife when he got home.

*

"What the hell is going on?" Special Agent Chris Murry, FBI, wondered aloud as he watched the four men. "This is taking too long."

They watched Alvin put the phone back in his pocket. Murry watched as all four men turned and looked over in their direction.

"I think we're blown. We're going to have to break off," Special Agent John Bender said. He was worried. Taxis on Charlotte Amalie, Virgin Islands, rarely came out to the cargo docks, especially on Saturday. Even when they did, they stayed mostly down at the other two piers where the cruise ships docked and freight offices were. The orange and blue car was the perfect cover for most surveillance jobs, but they had really screwed the pooch this time. It just didn't belong there, especially not this long.

"The other team should be here soon. They'll be in a red Mercedes truck," Agent Eddie Dark told them as he put away his cellular phone.

"I'm getting a bad feeling," Murry said again to no one in particular. The three watched as Alvin and the others casually walked over to the two black 4x4's and hopped inside.

"We're moving!" Agent Bender said. As if on cue, Eddie suddenly fell to the ground. Blood was splattered on the taxi's paint. Plunk! Plunk! Two holes appeared in the fender of the car. It took a few seconds for the agents to realize someone was shooting at them. Bender turned to help Eddie, then felt a stinging sensation in his shoulder. Murry had his weapon out and ducked down behind the open car door. He scanned the area, looking for the gunman. Plunk, Plunk, Plunk! They were pinned down.

"Dammit, someone's shooting at us!" Bender yelled.

"I know! I know! I'm looking!" They hadn't heard a gunshot, but someone was definitely putting holes in the car. Both Murry and Bender now held their automatics as Eddie crawled inside the vehicle and called in on the radio. Murry ran around to the other side of the car; the door glass shattered above his head as he jumped inside. The FBI agent turned the ignition and stepped on the accelerator, trying to get them out of the line of fire.

Alvin and James sped past the bullet riddled taxi, followed closely by the two Americans. The sniper they had hired would keep the three federal agents busy for a while. He was using a silencer on the end of the rifle and he would be hard, if not impossible, to find.

*

"I apologize about that," Jeff said.

"No, it was me. David's my husband," Susan said.

"Well, hell! If you married David Ranson, then I really am sorry," he replied.

"Do you know him?" Susan asked.

"I'm a disgruntled friend from way back."

Susan cracked a smile. Wendy had been watching both of them since David had left. Jeff had not noticed anyone except Susan. Jealousy took hold of Wendy and she reached out and took Jeff's hand in her own.

"Let's just forget about it and go buy some frozen Margarita from the Fat Tuesday's tent."

"I'm not thirsty," Jeff said as he pulled his arm back, and gave Wendy an annoying glance. He reached in his pocket and took out some tickets, "But you guys go and have a drink. On me."

Wendy grabbed the tickets from his hand and turned to Susan. "Come on Susan," she ordered.

"No," Susan had not taken her eyes off Jeff, "I think I'm going to stay here and look at Mr. Strata's handiwork. If that's all right?"

"I'd love to show you my collection," he replied with a smile.

"Fine!" Wendy said, then stomped away in a huff. The two did not watch her leave; instead, Jeff put his arm around Susan and walked her into his tent. Once inside, he led her over to a large display of paintings. Although some were bright and colorful oils of marine life, the majority were dark and lonely, portraying single subjects, greatly distorted.

"Welcome to my humble gallery."

Susan was overwhelmed. Not an art aficionado by any means, his works somehow reminded her of the pain and suffering that she held inside herself. They spoke to her in a way she had never felt before.

"These are, well..." she tried to find the words, but they would not come. Jeff smiled, he was used to the reaction.

"My work seems to either speak to people or it doesn't," he explained, "There's very little middle ground."

"It does, it does," she said softly as she studied a canvas that portrayed a very distorted female figure screaming in horror. Jeff saw her reaction and lifted the painting from the easel. He handed it to her, but she pulled her hands away.

"What are you doing?" Susan asked, puzzled.

"Here, take it," Jeff said, and held it out to her.

"No, I couldn't."

"Of course you can," he told her, "I saw how you reacted to it. That's why I paint, to see a reaction like that. Take it." Susan reached into her purse and pulled out a checkbook.

"Don't insult me, please."

"But that's how you make a living."

"I think I can spare one painting."

Susan saw his sincerity and accepted the gift.

"Besides," Jeff added, "My real masterpiece is back at my boat, in the cabin, above my bed."

"I'd like to see it sometime," Susan teasingly replied to the innuendo. She might as well enjoy herself now, because at home she knew there would be hell to pay.

*

Detective Brian Doyle had driven past the familiar landmark hundreds of times, and admired its beauty. But this would be the first time he turned into the driveway. Passing under the large spider webs that connected the trees on either side of the crushed shell entrance, he wondered what the three inch long banana spiders sitting in the center of them thought about all the noise that destroyed their tranquil resting place. Pulling around a sharp bend in the drive, he saw it loom up through the trees.

The pink stucco house was both unique and ordinary for Sanibel Island. A one-of-a-kind design, the architects intended for it to withstand tidal surges and hurricane winds. Built in 1985 after the original home was destroyed by fire, it had been through two hurricanes without suffering so much as a lost shingle. It had also graced the pages of several magazines and had been featured in a Hollywood film. But magazine editors were not the only ones who praised the house. Many local boaters welcomed the sight of it as well. The property bordered on both the Gulf of Mexico and the entrance of the channel that led to Pine Island Sound and the many marinas that lined it. The large structure greeted the pleasure craft that used the waterway, and symbolized home. To tourists and visitors of the island, the brightly colored home was a monument that showcased the skills of the local construction trade. Building this house, and others like it, had allowed more than a few of the local building contractors to afford homes of similar stature. In a way, it was almost ordinary, for multi-million dollar homes were now the norm on this part of the island.

But the large pink structure was also unique. Unique because it had one thing the others did not have. Within its walls lay the secrets to a murder.

*

James and Emily Druknol had been walking their dogs, Duke and Duchess, along the beach, as they had every morning for the last five years. The two Dobermans ran ahead, as most dogs do, sniffing and investigating every shell, branch, and blade of grass they could find. The dogs headed up to the patio of the pink house, then disappeared inside the open doors. It was not the first time they had gone inside the house uninvited, and James expected his neighbor to come out and walk with them, as she often did. She liked the dogs, and they seemed to enjoy playing with her. She would occasionally feed them treats and scratch their ears. The dogs loved that. So when they did not come out, the Drucknols were not too concerned.

The couple continued their stroll, figuring the owner chose to stay inside. They worried about her, she seemed too young to be sick all the time. She was in her early forties now, and had been very athletic up until the last two or three years. But the last few years they saw her less and less. Emily believed she had cancer or some other equally horrible disease; James figured that the woman was just getting older.

About fifteen minutes later, the Druknols came back by the house. They were on their way back to their own home, and it had already started heating up outside. His wife was tired of waiting, so James was sent up to retrieve the dogs. He called the animals from outside the door, and Duke and Duchess came running out the sliding glass door, darting past their master and out to the surf. The retired plant manager was about to leave, when he heard the buzzing coming from inside the bedroom. He called the woman's name, and hearing no reply, he walked inside. That was when James found her on the bed. He yelled, and Emily called the police.

*

"Who would have thought it would have been so long?" he asked himself. Brian Doyle was the one and only Homicide Detective for the city of Sanibel. There was just no need for more. The Sanibel Police Department was a small organization, with a relatively quiet history. There had been only a handful of investigations involving deaths, none of them questionable. Most fatalities on the island were natural, from old age. There was the occasional car accident, and one or two drownings at the resorts, but they had all had reasonable explanations, and none had even the hint of malice or foul play. Except one.

The "Blind Pass Murder" was the first, last, and only murder on the island since the turn of the century. Officially, it was not even a murder case because no suspect or weapon had ever been found. Even the cause of death remained unknown. In 1972, Marjorie Johnson, 31, had been found by a fisherman. This was back when Sanibel was a little known resort, before the great invasion of snowbirds. The man's fishhook had snagged her body at Blind Pass while he was angling from the bridge that joined Sanibel and Captiva Island. The naked body had been in the water for a couple of days, and state investigators later thought it lucky to find her when they did. The undercurrent of the pass would probably have taken her body into the Gulf when the tide went out that night. An autopsy revealed that she had cocaine in her system, but, due to the decomposition of the body and the fact that fish had been feeding on it, nothing else was known. Actually, until Sam Hardson, editor of the local paper, had started writing about it, police were baffled as to the identity of the woman. No one except for the police and fisherman had even known about the body. Luckily, someone had read about it in the View, which at that time was nothing more than a newsletter for island residents, and only an anonymous call to the paper had identified her. Johnson lived alone. Unemployed and new to the island, noone police had spoken with even remembered what she looked like. When Sam ran the story, he used a photo of her house; no usable photo of the victim could be found. After a month of pleading, the state sent investigators down to look into the case. But with no leads after seven months, they ruled it a boating accident and packed their things.

The locals were not satisfied, but many resorts were just moving on to Sanibel, and the last thing the developers needed was an unsolved murder in paradise. Using their influence, and with the support of many long-time residents, the developers convinced the city council to form a police force. Up to that time, they had been protected by the county sheriff's department. But politicians wanted the tourist dollars, so a resolution passed. Because so much was at stake, the resorts kicked in financially. They went on a nationwide search to form the best law enforcement agency money could buy. They especially wanted to create a homicide unit to ensure that if, God forbid, there was a next time, they would not have to beg for an investigation.

They recruited veterans of the top agencies and police forces in the country. Most were happy to come. The unrest over Vietnam, the riots in Watts and Chicago, and other events made being a cop hazardous duty in the early seventies. Over a thousand applications were received for the thirty positions that would be filled. While other cities cut police department budgets, Sanibel offered a policeman's dream: starting salary of twelve thousand dollars which was unheard of in 1972, a brand new fleet of air-conditioned cruisers and four-wheel drives, one per officer that could be taken home. Caribbean Plantation, one of the new large resort communities, went so far as to offer free housing for up to one year. Also, a large national bank, whose CEO lived on Sanibel, made a deal for low interest mortgages for the small condos after that year was up. Even a helicopter and two twenty-foot Sea Ray boats had been leased for the new department.

Within six months, the Sanibel Police Force was second to none. The Homicide division had the latest equipment and was manned by five former FBI investigators. The youngest was twenty-seven-year-old Brian Doyle.

The detective thought about the changes over the last quarter century. It didn't seem that long . He could still picture all the guys in the department. One by one, the homicide division had shrunk as men retired. Concern had turned to apathy, then to complacency as the residents and the city, sheltered by the fact that no serious crimes had been committed, assumed that they would not need investigators anymore. Most of the incentives were gone. And although Doyle and his family still lived on Caribbean Plantation, the resort had become too valuable and expensive for a police officer's salary, even with a low-interest mortgage. The Sanibel Police Department had become average. Brian Doyle felt like the last of the Mohicans: he was the only original left. And now this.

*

"She doesn't look like a lawyer." That was what people said when she was introduced. She was chunky, not fat. She had a very pretty face, her cheekbones gave away the Native American heritage. But most people never noticed that. They just looked at the one hundred-eighty pounds she carried on her small frame. Shirley Lamina would never be accused of sleeping her way to the top, but she liked it that way. She had paged her boss on a Sunday, and she knew what she was in for. She didn't even think he would answer the page. And if he did, she knew David Ranson would come in the office raising hell, asking her why he needs a Senior Assistant District Attorney if they call him every second. She had prepared herself. She would wait him out, wait until he calmed down enough to tell him why she interrupted his weekend. But when the call came, David had not yelled. Never even raised his voice. He simply stated he would handle this one himself. Shirley was beside herself.

*

The body was found spread across the comforter, naked, uncovered. The police photographer was still shooting film to record the condition of the room when Detective Doyle called from upstairs. When he walked through the hallway to the living room, the detective was surprised to see the District Attorney himself at the scene, and so quickly. Doyle had met the man only a handful of times, though he knew all about him from the various prosecutors he routinely worked with. Then Doyle remembered that this was an election year.

"I was told you are in charge here." David said as they approached each other.

"Yeah, for this part anyway," Doyle offered his hand, "Until your office gets it. I must say, I'm surprised to see you here."

"I was paged by one of my assistants, and I live on the island. There's no sense in one of them driving forty miles out here if I'm only five minutes down the road. Has anyone called the press, or have they shown up yet?"

Politics, Doyle thought, definitely politics. He wanted to get his picture in the paper. "I'd rather find out what we have before we make statements to reporters, if you don't mind," the detective said.

"Sounds like a good plan. Don't want another fiasco, right?"

The detective looked over at the D.A. and just shook his head in disgust, "Yeah, right." Doyle led him down the hall and into the bedroom of the house. As they entered the room, the stench of the body was overwhelming, and hung in the humid air. Flies continued to land on and around the corpse, annoying the two Florida Department of Law Enforcement investigators as they started their work. David felt a lump in his throat, then ran over to the open patio doors and threw up, much to the chagrin of the two FDLE officers. He wiped his mouth, and asked where the closest bathroom was so he could get some water.

A few minutes later, David returned to the room. He took some ointment from one of the officers and rubbed it under his nose. The white cream smelled like ammonia, but it was better than the stench from the corpse.

"So what have you got?" he asked.

"Everything's preliminary right now. Some fingerprints, some hairs, we'll probably find more. We believe the body has been here for two or three days. It was found by a couple walking their dogs this morning, a James and Emily Druknol.

Neighbors, they live down the beach. They called us."

"I know the couple," David said while nodding. Everyone knew everyone on the small island.

"Her panties are over there," the detective pointed towards the floor in front of the television, "We think the perp might have come and gone through the patio door."

"Why?"

"Well, the interior door was locked, and the patio door was wide open," Doyle answered. It was an obvious conclusion.

"Maybe she locked it. Do you have any proof that someone came in from the beach?" Doyle looked over at the District Attorney annoyed. Typical politician, he thought. No professional training or experience in police work, yet this guy was questioning the judgment of a veteran detective and former FBI agent. He'll go far, Doyle concluded.

"You can see the sand that was tracked in," Doyle said. The District Attorney studied the carpet; he even bent down and picked up some grains of sand in his hand. Of course, he then wiped his hands off on his pants. He stood up and briefly glanced at the body, then walked out the door. He reached down and grabbed a handful of the white sugar sand near the patio and studied that. David looked out to the small breakers beyond the beach.

"What do we know for sure?"

Doyle pulled the thin notebook from his coat pocket. "Not much. No sign of forced entry, no bumps or bruises, no sign of trauma. The jewelry and other valuables were left sitting in the open. Nothing except one dead woman." Doyle let the last three words linger.

"Could be a suicide."

"Could be, but I doubt it," the detective answered firmly, "Someone was here, either as it happened or right after."

"You said you found some hairs?"

"We are still working on that. A lot of people were in here before us, including those dogs. There was some blood on the sheets..."

"Blood?"

"Yeah," Detective Doyle went to the body, "Let me show you." He pulled some rubber surgical gloves from his pocket and snapped them on. He then lifted the victim's head and pointed to her mouth. Blood stains were clearly visible. "It looks like she bit her lip; it must have been close to the time of death because it pooled in there," he pointed to the inside of her mouth, "The lab guys are going to check it out."

"It still could be a suicide, couldn't it?" Ranson asked.

"Yeah, maybe--at this point it could be little green men from Mars. But look at this," Doyle went over to the footprints, laying his shoe over one. The print was visible all around Doyle's size eleven shoe. "This foot is not hers. Someone else was here."

"Druknol?"

"No, we checked," Doyle answered.

"Detective!" One of the technicians yelled as he came in from the hall. Doyle went over to him and signed some paper work. David stared at the dead woman. At the ring on her finger.

"Has anyone contacted the doctor?" the D.A. asked quietly.

"We haven't found him yet," Doyle answered without looking up, " We'd like to find out why he didn't call us."

David walked back over to the bed, and touched the dead woman's arm. It was strange how people look different after they've died, he thought.

"Tell them to try the lounge inside the Sands. I saw him there a little while ago. I doubt he knows what has happened."

*

Ten minutes later, two police officers walked into the clubhouse and over to the bartender. She pointed to Doc Whitmore, sitting at the bar, tossing Cheez-its at Larry.

"You act like a twelve-year-old, you know that," Larry said, ducking the small orange projectiles.

Doc Whitmore just laughed as he continued throwing the crackers.

"I can't believe you're a doctor," Larry whined as a cracker hit him on the forehead, to the amusement of the bartender. "Watch it, you could poke my eye out!" This caused the old man to let out a bellow so loud that it startled the two women sipping wine at the other end of the bar.

The officers walked over toward the two men. Larry saw them coming and warned his friend, "Knock it off! Someone called the cops!"

But the Doc just continued his act. The policemen stepped up to the doctor. The senior officer, wearing sergeant stripes and a badge reading Sanibel Police, tapped Whitmore on the shoulder. The old man ignored him and continued throwing the little orange squares. Larry tugged at the officer's arm.

"He's drunk, officers. Been that way for about an hour. I'll take him home; we don't want to cause any problems." Larry went over and tried to help Whitmore off the chair, but the old man just knocked a bowl of pretzels on the floor as he clung onto the corner of the mahogany bar. Larry gave up and let his friend go, thereby causing the doctor to fall from the chair onto the floor. Tears flowed from his eyes as he was turning red from laughing. The two women at the bar watched the show with contempt.

"Is this Dr. Willard W. Whitmore?" the police sergeant asked Larry.

"It was," the Doc replied, trying to sit up on the carpet. Whitmore threw some crackers at the policeman and fell back laughing even harder. Larry grabbed the doctor, and he and the other officer helped the old man into a chair.

"I'm sorry," Larry apologized, "He isn't always like this. He's had a bad week."

"It's about to get worse," the policeman replied.

*

David walked over to the panties near the television and picked them up. He saw the flashing LED display that read "EJECT."

"Has anyone been playing with this?" he asked out loud. No one spoke up. Doyle and a uniformed officer watched as David pushed the eject button on the VCR. After a whir and some clicks, a video tape popped out. David held it up, reading the title.

"What have we got here?"

The tape was an adult title. Triple X. S & M. David tossed it to Doyle who read the title, then examined the tape. "Lifestyles of the rich and famous?" Doyle replied.

"Maybe she was lonely?" the D.A. said.

"Granted, I've seen some weird things, but I don't believe the woman was *that* lonely," the detective replied.

"What, detective, only men watch these?" David said sarcastically, "This is the electronic age, everyone rents this stuff now."

"Maybe she was watching them with whoever left the footprints?"

"No way Doyle," David went to her body, "Look at where her hands are." The detective looked over at the body being attended to by the FDLE.

"She was alone, I'm tellin' you!" David said.

"You moved her arms," Doyle argued, "I watched you."

"But I put them back. She's so stiff, I couldn't change their position if I wanted to," the D.A. replied. Doyle looked over at the FDLE technician.

"He's right. This one's stiff as a board, detective," the investigator agreed as he pulled prints of the dead woman's fingers. The woman's left hand was placed on her left breast. Her right hand was laying between her legs. He knew what the District Attorney was insinuating. It was plausible to the homicide detective. But something was wrong with the picture.

"If she didn't die from a gun shot wound or other weapon, which we can assume since there are no marks consistent with that, then we need to assume it was cardiac arrest. At least for now. I don't know what caused her heart to stop but it did," Doyle talked slowly, thinking of each word, allowing his mental picture to take shape.

"Yeah, that's pretty obvious," David answered. The technicians stopped working, and listened to the detective as he spoke.

"When you have a heart attack, you grab your chest like this," Doyle held his hands over his heart simulating a heart attack, "It supposedly feels like an elephant is stomping on your chest."

"Maybe she was," David, "Look at her right hand."

Doyle tried to move the hand to her heart, but it would not stay. "No. This hand was on her breast when she died. See the fingers." The woman's nipple fit perfectly between her right thumb and index finger.

"Maybe she orgasmed herself to death," an FDLE investigator joked.

"I wish it were possible," his female partner added. Everyone laughed except

Doyle, who sat in silence as he went over every detail in his mind. He was missing something, something that was probably so obvious that he didn't give it a second thought. He scanned the room with his eyes.

"Here's two more!" The uniform cop held up two black plastic video cases in his hand, "They were over there next to her medication."

"What medication?" Doyle asked, his thinking pattern interrupted.

"These, on the desk," the officer said as he lifted the swimsuit. Underneath lay a pile of clear amber containers. The DA and detective inspected the bottles. Doyle opened one of them and poured its contents into his gloved hand. He inspected one of the small pills.

"I don't recognize them," he turned the bottle with his fingers, "Maybe it wasn't a who, but a what that helped her?"

David was looking at the others scattered on the desk. "None of them are labeled. Shouldn't these have have names and dosage on them somewhere on them? There are supposed to be labels on a prescription bottle, right?"

"They look like painkillers or something."

Doyle placed his bottle with the others and turned to the officer, "I want these taken down to the lab. Find out what it is."

"Yes, sir." The uniformed policeman pulled out a plastic bag with the word "EVIDENCE" printed on it, and placed the bottles inside. He then labeled the sealed bags with the date, time, and other pertinent information and walked out.

"If she took enough pills, she wouldn't even know that she was having a heart attack," the female technician said.

"How do you figure ?"

"Because she could be in a dream-like state, and, if she was aroused, her heart would pump harder anyway. Of course that depends on what the drugs are."

Doyle asked the FDLE people to take a break for a minute so he and the District Attorney could talk in private. It was now just Doyle, David and the corpse. He closed the door and turned to the DA.

David thought Doyle wanted to hear his opinions but did not want to ask in front of "the help."

"What are you thinking?" the detective asked.

"I'm thinking that we need to speak to her husband," David replied, smiling.

"Do you want to know what I'm thinking?" Doyle's tone of voice was all wrong. It was almost suspicious." I'm thinking that I want to know how you knew where to find her husband?"

"I told you, I just left him. I was at the festival at the Sands when I was paged."

"Do you know him?"

"I know a lot of people. This is a small island."

"That's not what I mean, and you know it," Doyle was aggravated; he did not need this kind of problem. "Now be straight with me. Do you know him, and, more importantly, did you know the victim!?"

"Yeah. So?" David was not liking this, not at all, "Are you insinuating something?"

Doyle ignored the question for the moment, "I just realized that you were here almost a full thirty minutes before you even mentioned you knew them. Doesn't that strike you as odd? It does me." Doyle let that sit for a moment, "You know what, never mind that, I have a more important question..."

"What?" David was really not liking the direction this was leading to now!

"Why is a big shot like you taking over a case like this?" Doyle spoke calmly, efficiently, no accusation in his voice at all, "I mean, a death is a big thing on Sanibel, but not in Lee County. I don't buy the *I just happen to be here* theory. You didn't personally prosecute the case when that sheriff's deputy was killed last year, did you?"

"Look, I..." David started to answer but was cut off.

"I didn't think so," the detective injected. David was steaming.

"Listen, all right! I've heard things!"

"What things?"

"Problems. Marital. Drugs. Cheating. I owe it to the Doc to check it out, okay?! I didn't want to say I knew them. So what, I recognized the address! And so I knew the victim! Fine. I admitted it, and it sure as hell isn't even relevant to the case regardless!" David was rolling," I wanted to see that everything is done right; is that okay with you, Lieutenant?!"

Doyle walked over to the window, his arms behind him, hands locked casually together, "Are you sure you don't have a conflict of interest here, Mister District Attorney?"

"Positive!" David snapped. His arms were folded in front of him, his right foot was tapping on the floor.

The homicide detective turned and faced him."Then you wouldn't mind if I ask *you* some questions?"

"Shoot," Doyle watched him for a moment. He saw the anger, but there was something else, too. Intuition told the detective that something else was hiding, and he made a mental note to check up on the District Attorney.

"Friends?"

"Yes. For a long time. What are you getting at?"

Doyle looked around the room, and spread his arms, "When was the last time you were here?"

"About a week ago, why?"

"How close were you to the Whitmores?"

"I am not a suspect here! Dammit, this is my case! Do you realize that, Officer Doyle?! If you want to know about my personal relationship with Cathy or her husband, ask them!"

"I'd like too, but one of them's dead," Doyle said, and pointed to Cathy's body. David looked away. The two men stood silently. Doyle studied David Ranson. Except for the smell, the man had not seemed affected by the fact that the wife of a friend was lying dead just a few feet away.

"I'm not worried that you will affect the investigation, I'm worried about," he paused. "Okay, yes, I'm worried about how it will affect the investigation. Your judgment. How the media presents your involvement. It just does not seem proper. And more than that, I don't like it." Doyle smacked his hand on the desk, a rare show of anger that stirred a cloud of white dust from where fingerprints had been lifted. Brian Doyle did not enjoy getting dressed down by a politician. David knew the detective was right, it didn't look proper. David needed the police to work with him, not against him. Not now, and certainly not during the election.

"Are you done, sir ?" David asked, trying to throw in an air of respect for Doyle.

"No," Doyle continued, "One more thing. I decide who is the suspect, not you, or the mayor, or even the President of the United States. This isn't your case yet, not until I give it to you. Let's just get that clear right now." David waited to make sure the detective was finished before he spoke.

"You're right, I was out of line. You have some well-intentioned and valid concerns, granted. But the fact is that I am the District Attorney, and it is up to me who prosecutes and investigates this for my office. And it will be me. I am sorry if you don't like it, but we need to accept it and move on."

It was obvious that the Doyle didn't like it. But he gave the man time to let the fact sink in. "All right then." The detective could not accept the change in attitude so quickly, but decided to play along, at least for a while.

"I'll accept that. But you need to be honest and forthright from now on. If you know something you say so. I don't like pulling teeth, agreed?" Doyle demanded.

"Agreed," David answered.

"I think she OD'd. Did she have a history of drug use?"

David looked at the body, then at the detective, "You think her husband gave her drugs?"

Doyle shrugged, "You knew them, not me. She wouldn't be the first doctor's wife with a substance abuse problem."

David walked back over to the open doorway. The breeze off the water blew back the sheer white curtains on each side of the opening. The laughter of sunbathers and sparkle of the Gulf of Mexico contrasted with the conversation.

"That sand could have been dragged in by the Druknols; Cathy might have left it open." David theorized as he ran his hand along the door frame.

"I leave my door open occasionally," Doyle said.

"Everyone does, the breeze is nice this time of year," David stood mesmerized by the waves. Maybe this would work out; he hadn't really thought about using it, but, hell, it might even help his campaign. Only if he did it right. He turned and faced the detective.

"Yes," he stated,"Cathy had a problem. I knew that. Not first hand, but I had heard the old man complaining. He said she was getting help, so I left it alone."

"Evidently, he was the one helping her," Doyle commented.

"What we need to know -- and prove -- is that he was giving her the drugs," David said. He had set the bait, would he catch something? He waited for Doyle's reply.

"It's worth looking into," the detective agreed after thinking it over a moment. The doctor could be, probably was involved. David was ecstatic. He had a bite, now to land the sucker.

"Can I tell you my theory?" David asked.

"Go ahead," Doyle replied. This ought to be good.

"This is what I think happened," David started, "I think that the doctor knew his wife was an addict, and he supplied her with the drugs."

"Why?" asked Doyle, playing Devils advocate.

"Because it would be safer for both of them. She would not need risk being caught buying the drugs, and he could control what, and how much she used." As he listened, Doyle sat back and wondered why David would be trying to implicate his own friend.

"But, why is she dead if he controlled it? He is a doctor." There was a knock on the door and David opened it. A plain-clothes officer, wearing a blue wind-breaker that had "POLICE" written on the back, walked into the room and over to Doyle.

"Detective, FDLE needs to get back in the room."

"Oh, I'm sorry," Doyle apologized, not realizing how long they had been in there alone, "Tell them to come in."

"Oh, yeah," the officer added, "Sergeant Bond told me to tell you that they have the husband at the station. He just arrived."

The detective peeled off the gloves and looked over at David, "Why don't we go speak to Doc Whitmore before this goes any farther?"

"That's not a good idea. He's really out of it," the officer said.

"What do you mean 'Out of it?" David asked.

"He is higher than a kite. We haven't even told him about his wife yet."

Doyle told the officer to contact the police station and to keep someone with the doctor at all times, but not to tell him about his wife. When the old man had sobered up Doyle was to be called. No one was to talk to Whitmore before the detective arrived.

"I have to get to the office." David handed over his business card, "My beeper is on there also."

"I'll contact you before we question him," Doyle said.

"Thanks," David picked up the video tapes. "I'll return these to the rental place, it's on my way home."

"Don't you think we should hold on to them?"

"They're rentals. I'll bet there are over a hundred sets of prints on them. I'll let the video store know we may need them again. Go see what Doc Whitmore has to say."

Doyle followed David up the stairs and out to the yard. A young woman in a white lab coat and rubber gloves yelled to them. They stopped as she ran up.

"The medical examiner wants to get started."

"Tell him he can do whatever he needs; we're done with her."

"Any special requests?" the woman asked.

"Make sure this is his number one priority," David said. "And tell him to call me when he's got a report."

"Just ask him to look for any drugs in the body, anything that could be prescribed in pill form."

"Okay, I'll let him know."

"Also, I'd like a rape kit done on her, you never know," Doyle added. The lab technician turned to leave. David stopped her.

"I don't think that's necessary. We know she wasn't assaulted. Our case is against the doctor."

"It won't hurt," argued Doyle, "We found her without any clothes on."

"I don't want to wait any longer than we have to," David argued. "Let's go with what we know." David turned to the technician, "Test for drugs, and don't worry about anything else right now."

*

The sun was setting over the trees as Susan placed the straw in her lips. The frozen daiquiri slid over her tongue, and, as she swallowed, goose bumps formed on her skin. The steel drum band on stage was just finishing up a set, and she closed her eyes, settling back into the lounge chair. Wendy was off somewhere. Probably picking up some guy, thought Susan. She felt sure that the young photographer would be dead from AIDS before she turned thirty. She was always telling Susan about the men she met. Married, single, divorced- Wendy didn't seem to care. She would go into detail with Susan about her sex life. Susan never showed any interest, and tried to ignore it, but working together every day made that impossible.

"Hey there." Susan opened her eyes. It was Jeff, holding two frozen drinks in one hand and a folded lawn chair in the other. "I see I'm too late." His eyes shifted to the drink in her hand.

"You can leave that one too, if you want." She said.

"A two fisted drinker? I'm impressed!" Jeff set the frost covered plastic cups down on the blanket, then unfolded the chair. He pulled a towel from Susan's bag and spread it on the chair, then took the bottle of her lotion that was sitting in the grass near her chair. Susan watched with amusement.

"Please, just make yourself at home," she said.

"I thought I was?"

Jeff sat down, put his feet up on the red and white cooler in front of him, and relaxed. He unbuttoned his shirt and laid it on the ground. She slid her sunglasses from her hair down to her eyes. The setting sun was directly in Jeff's eyes, so he shut them and let his mind drift as the music started up again.

Susan studied him through the dark lenses. She watched his chest move up and down to the rhythm of the music, a true artist. He was tan, his whole body was. It must be nice to do nothing but paint pictures and sail boats your whole life, she thought. He had made her nervous at first. She definitely thought he would be different. The rumors about him had circulated for as long as she could remember, and Susan had bought into them just like David had.

But that was before she met him. After spending three hours talking, she was having second thoughts. She actually found out she liked him. He was talented, but it was more than that. She felt comfortable near him. And safe-- no doubt that had something to do with the way he handled David. Jeff, she found, had a way of making everyone around him feel good. It was like a gift. So easy-going when they met, she hadn't realized how muscular he was until that little episode with David. *That was great, wasn't it?* she thought.

*

Jack Sutton, Special Agent in Charge of the Miami office of the Federal Bureau of Investigation walked quickly down the yellowed and cracked tiled hallway. The secretary heard the footsteps and watched the agent on the video monitor on her desk. He walked passed her desk without a word. She was expecting him. The electronically-locked door buzzed right as he reached for the handle. He walked into the office without missing a beat, followed by three more FBI agents.

Elizabeth Hobbs sat behind her desk. As the senior DEA agent in Florida, she had called this meeting after the report from the two field operatives landed on her desk.

"Sit down, please."

The four federal agents sat in the low-backed swivel chairs as Hobbs picked up the manila folder marked CONFIDENTIAL from her desk. She handed it to Sutton, who scanned it and passed it to Special Agent Chris Murry. He turned red with anger, but did not say a word as he passed it down the line. Laura Wilson, the temporary Agent In Charge of the Key West and Southwest Florida Office was the last to read the file.

"We have a problem. How can we solve it?" Hobbs asked.

*

"What?" Jeff sat up quickly, almost spilling out of the chair. He rubbed his eyes and looked around to get his bearings. The dream had seemed real, a little too real. Susan was startled by his reaction, she had just slightly touched his arm. He shaded his eyes with his hand, and reached down to get his sunglasses that had fallen on the ground.

"Are you okay?" she asked, concerned.

"Yeah, yeah," Jeff told her, "Just a, a bad dream, that's all." He regained his composure, stretched out his arms, and yawned. He looked down at his empty wrist, then at Susan. "What time is it?"

She reached into the bag next to her and pulled out her watch. "Seven."

"I shouldn't have fallen asleep," he said while reaching down and picking his cup off the ground. He took a sip of the no longer frozen drink. "So did I miss anything?"

"I was just listening to the music and thinking."

"What do you have to think about on a day like this?"

"I was thinking about my husband," she said, "I really don't feel like dealing with him when I get home."

"So don't go."

"It's a little more complicated than that. I'm not free to just go and do what I want without worrying about anyone else, like you."

"I was like you once."

Susan eyed him suspiciously, "You were married?"

"Engaged, it didn't work out." He sipped more of his drink.

"What happened?"

Jeff stretched his arms and sprang up to his feet. He picked up his shirt, and after a little trouble, he managed to button it. "Are you hungry?"

"Tell me what happened?" She was intrigued.

"Over dinner," he said grinning at her, while folding his chair.

"I can't. David would have a fit!"

Jeff shrugged his shoulders and finished his drink. Susan sat up in her lounge chair, her feet on either side. "Oh come on, tell me."

"I'm going to go get cleaned up, and then I am going out to get something to eat. I will also be telling stories of my sorry love life to those who happen by my table at the Pink Pelican Restaurant at 8:30 p.m. tonight." With everything in hand, Jeff stepped over the cooler and off the blanket and started off across the grass.

"I said I can't," Susan yelled to him. She did not rise off the folding chair but watched him walk away. Dammit, she thought. He hadn't looked back, and was walking farther and farther away. "I'm not making any promises!" She yelled after him. He turned around and faced her. Walking backwards he shrugged his shoulders as he waved, a big smile stuck on his face. Then he tripped, almost falling on top of an older couple. She laughed and shook her head.

*

Doyle sat across from Dr. Whitmore, who was sipping a cup of coffee. The ashtray on the table was filled with butts, and the air in the enclosed room had grown stale hours before. Doyle had thought of using the small lounge as a makeshift interrogation room in hopes that the more comfortable surroundings would relax the old man. The detective was not convinced he killed his wife, but there sure were a lot of questions to be answered, the least of which was how a man could live in a house with his wife lying dead for two days and not know about it. So far, though, the police did not have any solid evidence to link him to Cathy's death. At least not yet.

"How were things between you and Cathy?" The old man's eyes were as dead as his wife's as he looked up at the detective, then back at the table.

"I don't know why this is necessary. She's dead."

"I know, and I'm very sorry," Doyle said sincerely, "But, as I've explained to you, we need this information to find out who's responsible."

Doyle looked at the old surgeon. He had been sober for about two hours. The doctor had taken it badly. The detective could still see the tears forming in the old guy's bloodshot eyes. But at least he was answering Doyle's questions. The homicide detective stood up. "Can I get you anything, Doctor?"

"A vodka tonic," the old man said. He wanted to escape his thoughts of her dead as much as he did when she was alive.

"I can't do that, but how about a turkey sandwich and a pop," The old man nodded. Doyle walked over to a doorway and into the hall, closing the door behind him. David was there, as was Shirley, his Assistant DA, and various police officers. Shirley was an expert on drug cases, but they normally involved dealers and smugglers, not this. Doyle gave one of the officers some money and sent him out to get sandwiches. Shirley handed him a red folder.

"Hot off the press. The bottles had Xandrid, it's a type of Benzodiszenes. An anxiolytic." Shirley explained excitedly. Doyle looked at David and the others. They all had blank looks on their faces.

"In English, please," Doyle asked.

"I'm sorry; I'm used to dealing with the DEA. It's a prescription medication."

"I've never heard of it," David said.

"What's it used for?" Doyle asked while reading, but not actually understanding, the lab report.

"It relieves anxiety in people who are really stressed. It's very addictive," Shirley told them.

"How would someone get it?"

"It's widely prescribed, and unfortunately, very often abused." Doyle knew that if it were widely used, then the chances that he could prove where she got them from were slim, even if it was a prescription.

"That's just great," David said.

"It's relatively new. A company in New England came up with it a few months ago."

"So how much is out there? It can't be too widely distributed if it's only a couple of months old."

"Well, that's not exactly true. In order for a drug to be in demand, doctors need to know about it, and Nantech, the developers of it, sent out a ton of free samples. It was picked up pretty quick."

"There's a stock you should have bought into, Doyle." David added. Doyle ignored the comment and listened while Shirley continued.

"But it's a controlled substance, so I'm betting that the DEA would be able to trace it."

The detective looked in at the doctor. He might have given his wife the gun, but did he pull the trigger.

"Could this stuff have killed her?"

"An overdose could cause death, among other things."

"Would she, if she took enough, would she know she was dying?" Doyle asked.

"It depends. People react differently but if you are asking, 'Would she be conscious?', I'd say yes. Probably."

"I believe what the detective wants to know is if she could be sexually aroused, and if so, would she have any warning or sense that she was dying?"

"Yeah, sure," Shirley answered, "In some people the drug exaggerates the senses. Some cultures, especially Asian, use Benzodiszenes to further sexual pleasure. And there have been some people who died using it this way."

"Is death instantaneous?" Doyle asked her.

"There have been cases where the heart explodes during usage. It doesn't literally explode, it just stops. We just had a briefing at the DA's office two weeks ago on this stuff; I can give you the material to read."

"That would be great; thanks." Doyle said, "Any other news?"

Shirley pulled out a manila envelope and opened it. She scanned the page with her finger as she talked, "On the fingerprints, we lifted a couple of unknowns, of course yours and David's--you two should really wear gloves next time- the Druknols gave us their prints to match any we found," she flipped the page, "It says here that they found a partial on the body." She looked up, "That's odd, usually any prints on a body are gone after about twelve hours."

"It's too bad we don't have an AFIS computer to check the print," David said.

"I might be able to get us access to one," Doyle told him, "I still have some friends in the Bureau."

"Super," David said, "So what else, Shirley?"

"Let's see-they found some dog hairs. Well, not some, a lot of dog hairs. They also recovered some others, gray, curly like a beard or something."

"Can I see that?"

She handed the hair report over to Doyle, then continued, "The blood was hers, A positive. Nothing much there really. Um, we are testing the linens now. They were covered with dried perspiration, but no semen."

"When will they be ready?" David asked.

"It will be a few days. Is there anything else?" Shirley asked her boss.

"No, good job," David said, "I'm going to be here, so why don't you head to the office. Page me if you need anything. I'll bring back the lab reports when we're done."

"You got it," she said, then headed down the hall. Doyle finished reading the report and handed it back to the District Attorney.

"If I ask him anything else, we had better Mirandize him," the detective said.

*

Susan searched the den yelling her husband's name. When she didn't get a reply, she thanked God that David wasn't home. The steak she left out had defrosted and she broiled it while she showered. Susan called the Pink Pelican, confirmed that Jeff's reservation was for 8:30, and dressed. She took the London Broil from the oven and quickly whipped up some instant mashed potatoes. She wrote a note saying she had to go out then stuck the food in the refrigerator.

*

David looked through the small window in the door and watched the old man eat. The doctor sat staring at the wall. Every so often he would take a bite. But Willard Whitmore's thoughts were a million miles away.

David knew that the Doc did not kill his wife. But the District Attorney no longer cared. He'd been looking for a boost for his campaign, something that would put his face on the six o'clock news. Now he had one bonafide wife killer and drug dealer. No one else looked at the old doctor that way, at least not yet. But they would. The doctor would pick up the tab for David's Congressional seat after all, it just wouldn't be in cash. They had been growing apart as friends anyway and after it was over, once David was elected, he'd help the Doc anyway he could. It was politics, and he thought the old man would understand. Just politics.

But right now David needed time. Until he had real, solid evidence, there wasn't even a sound bite for the noon news. The little evidence they had was very circumstantial, nothing really to hold him for. Nothing the Doc could not readily explain. Hairs and unmarked prescription bottles. Damn, they needed something a lot stronger than that. The only other option was to let the old man walk. And, in his sorry state, there was no way David was going to risk letting his meal-ticket go home. Whitmore had cried for thirty minutes when David told him his wife was dead, and the old man confided to his supposed friend that he wanted nothing more than to go home and join her. That gave the D.A. an idea.

"I may have something, but I need to make a call," David said, "Where's a phone I can use?"

"Take Mr. Ranson to my office: it's private," Doyle told one of the uniformed officers. David followed him down the hall. They passed the police chief who joined the group outside the break room.

"Are you sure this is your guy?" the chief asked Doyle.

"I think so, the preliminary stuff fits."

"Is there anything you overlooked, something you might have missed?"

"I was a little rushed, and it's been a while. But I'm sure that I didn't miss anything. And the FDLE would find it if I did."

"I don't like havin' that damn politician around here," the chief said, "He just gets in the way."

Doyle watched Whitmore through the glass, "I know what you mean, he gets on my nerves too. But we can't do anything about it." Doyle stepped over to the door of the lounge, "Do you want to try talking to him?"

"Introduce me," the chief said.

The doctor did not look at them when Doyle opened the door. He just bit his sandwich. Doyle and the chief sat down in front of him, and the old man's eyes shifted to them, then back at the wall.

"Where's David?" Whitmore asked quietly.

"He had to go use the phone." Doyle spoke softly, "If you want to talk to him I can...."

"No," the old man interrupted, "I was waiting until he left before I said anything. He thinks I am a senile old fool, but I know what is going on." Doyle and his boss exchanged looks.

"What's going on, Doc?" the chief asked. Whitmore proceeded to explain to the police officers.

"Let's just say it's just like you think it is, Willard," the chief said when the doctor was finished, "That still doesn't explain why you would not notice your wife being dead. Fine, you say you two didn't get along, but, c'mon, three days?"

"It's like I told you," the old man said, "We never talked. We never saw each other. I don't know how else to explain it to you guys. Maybe if I had been a better husband this wouldn't have happened. I don't know." The old man's emotions poured out. His eyes swelled up, and he turned his head away, so they wouldn't see him crying.

"Okay, Doc," Doyle said, "Settle down." The old man tried to regain his composure. "Maybe I did cause it, maybe if I had spent more time, or, I just don't know..."

Doyle placed a box of tissues on the table, and the two officers went out to the hall, to give the old man some privacy, and to give their consciences a break.

"I feel like I'm interrogating my grandfather," Doyle said.

"I know, I felt like we killed her," the chief added.

"What do you think of his story?"

"He could just be upset or trying to mislead us. He may be old, but the guy's a surgeon, he's not stupid."

"I think it's worth checking out."

"Okay, but keep it quiet," the chief told him.

*

The table was covered with appetizers, though neither were hungry after a day in the sun. They sat on the deck of the waterside restaurant on Ft. Myers Beach, watching the boaters come in from the Gulf. The rotating beacon atop the Sanibel Lighthouse was already visible across San Carlos Bay. The sky was a golden color now, the sun had set soon after they had arrived at the restaurant. Susan was dipping a chicken finger into the bowl of honey mustard sauce.

"What is art? I guess to me art is what I saw today, when you looked at my painting," Jeff explained as he leaned back in his chair.

"What do you mean?" Susan asked.

"To me, art only means something when it appeals to one's soul; that is why I paint. That is why I wanted to give you that canvas. It appealed to your soul: and you can't put a price on that."

"But you do put a price on it. I saw those prices."

"That's only for the people who can't feel real emotion. Most people equate the value of art with the value of the dollar. They try to buy the emotional message, but most of the people who can afford to buy my work don't have the least bit of understanding of what it means."

"So, what you're saying is you don't care why people buy your paintings, as long as they buy them?"

"You got it, Babe."

Babe? Susan wondered if he knew how arrogant he sounded. Jeff could see he struck a nerve.

"I know I sound cocky, and I don't mean to. Of course I care, but I also need to make an honest living. Look at what I have achieved, without any help." Jeff stopped talking and ate a forkful of salad.

"I've heard rumors," Susan was almost ashamed to bring it up, but she saw right away that Jeff had been expecting it. He swallowed, then wiped his mouth with the cloth napkin.

"The popular theory that I run drugs and use my paintings to cover my income was not started by me. I have never said that is what I do..."

"But you've never denied it."

"No, I haven't. You're right," Jeff sipped his diet cola, "Look, people invite me to parties, and trips, and all kinds of things because they think I'm some kind of criminal. Hell, I've even gone to the Superbowl. It's a rush for them, and I make a good living from selling something I love to create." Jeff pointed to the huge watercolor on the wall of the restaurant. It showed two Bottlenose dolphins, swimming in the wake of a sailboat.

"Look over there at that watercolor."

Susan turned from him and studied it. "I love those-the way the colors flow-the way you can see under the surface and above it at the same time..."

"Thank you. It's one of mine."

"I'm impressed," she said.

"Don't be. It was nothing, really. I did it in one day." Susan looked at him suspiciously. David continued, "That is an example of an artist becoming too well known."

"How is that a bad thing,"Susan asked.

"Because I sell crap like that! Oh yeah. It took me, oh, maybe five hours. It sold for sixty-five hundred dollars. They buy it because my name's on it. In fact..." he said grabbing a napkin. "I would bet that I could draw a stupid little pen drawing on this and it would sell."

"No way!" She said, amused, but daring him to try it. Jeff asked the waitress for a pen. He drew a small stick figure on it, then signed his name to the bottom. "Watch this,"he said and called the waitress over. He told her to ask the manager if he would accept the napkin as payment for his meal. He explained who he was, and she matched the signature to the painting on the wall.

"No way they will do it," Susan said. But five minutes later the manager was at their table explaining how he was going to frame the napkin. After a few minutes the man took the check and left them alone again.

"That's what I mean. The real art sits because no one looks at that and says, 'That means something to me'? No. To everyone it's just a the signature of an artist."

"You have all this talent, and you grew up dirt poor; yet you're saying the money means nothing."

"Hardly." Jeff said as the waitress brought them their drinks, "I enjoy the money. I enjoy life, for the most part."

"What would you change, if anything?"

Jeff thought a moment, "I'm not proud of everything I've done. I'd make some changes, but we don't know each other well enough yet."

"Is it because I write for a newspaper?"

"What do you mean by that,"Jeff asked, surprised at the suspicious tone of her voice.

"Let me ask you," Susan bent down across the table and spoke quietly, "Are you a dope dealer? Do you smuggle drugs?" Jeff leaned over towards her and smiled. He answered just as quietly. "What do you think?" She stared into his eyes, and at his lips, and then backed away.

"I don't think you would tell me if you were."

"You might be right about that." Jeff leaned back in his chair and picked up another wing. They both were having a good time. He held out a bowl full of them. "Want one?"

"Thank you." Susan grabbed the wing from his hand, and ate it in one bite.

"A girl after my own heart," Jeff teased.

"So, what do your parents think of your reputation?"

Jeff took a sip of water, "I don't talk about my family."

Susan was struck by the tone his voice. It was cold and harsh. "I'm sorry. I didn't mean anything by it." An uneasy silence enveloped the two. Susan looked out the window; she had not meant anything by the question. She wished she could take it back. She looked at him; he was upset. She wanted to make things right, but how?

"Would you like to, I mean you don't have to," Susan began saying as Jeff looked up at her. "I just think that you would be an interesting person to do a piece on. A feature story."

"For your paper?"

"Yes." Susan wasn't sure if she would regret asking him, but his mood instantly reverted to its former arrogance. The dark cloud had been lifted as quickly as it had come.

"About me?" Jeff took a drink from his glass, then chewed on a carrot stick.

"You don't have to, I just thought..."

"No, I think that would be cool." Jeff smiled, "But what about your husband?"

"Whatever problems you two have, they are between you guys. I'm not involved."

Jeff thought of the effect of this on David, "Sure, why not!"

*

Francis Menceti's private jet landed at Tallahassee Airport and taxied over to the transient ramp. After the ground personnel chocked the tires, the pilot shut down the engines. The door opened, and Menceti walked down the stairway to the waiting stretch limousine. The driver took him along Lake Bradford Road and around the main campus of Florida State University. He zig-zagged through the state capital, until he came up to the gates of the Governor's Mansion. The sleek black Cadillac pulled up the circular drive and stopped in front of the century old house. Governor Peter Snelling met his old friend at the door, and they went inside for a private dinner.

*

"The way I see it we have two choices," David explained, "Use the Baker Act. Say he's a danger to himself and others. If we do this we can hold him for observation for a short time, say Monday morning. He admitted to me privately that he wanted to join his wife. I took that as a threat of suicide."

"Or?" A young policeman asked.

"Or charge him with disorderly intox, go for the max of sixty days jail and a fine. But within twenty four-hours he's due a first appearance."

"You can ask for a high bond," Doyle said.

"The judge will want to know why, and if we tell him he's a potential suspect depending on the judge assigned, the whole thing may blow up in our face. Also the media will know we think he killed his wife," David replied. The one thing that no one wanted was a media circus. Not even David. Not yet anyway. He wasn't ready. He needed some time to rehearse his impromptu comments to the press.

"You would need to sign the statement," Doyle said.

"I'm aware of that." David said.

"Let's go with Baker," Doyle agreed. This would give him time to check the doctor's statement.

"It's something," the chief added.

"It's set then," David announced, "Let's do it!"

"Let him finish eating first," Doyle told him. David took a last look at the doctor through the window.

"I don't care, just have him in custody before you leave. I'll call Shirley in Ft. Myers and get the paperwork ready; I'll sign it in the morning. I'm on beeper. Goodnight." David walked down the hall. That had been much easier than he thought.

*

The two men finished their meals and retired to the living room. The Governor asked to be left alone and closed the double hardwood doors so they could speak in private.

"I haven't heard from you in a while, Francis." The Governor had always called Menceti by his Christian name and was one of the few people who could get away with it. Menceti sat down in the soft leather chair.

"I've been busy; I'm out of the country a lot. You know the drill."

"I remember," Snelling said, "But, I'm glad they accepted you as my replacement."

"If nothing else, it has improved my comfort while traveling. A man my size doesn't fit too well in those small airline seats."

"Do you still use the Lear?" Snelling asked.

"Nah. Too small. It couldn't cross the Atlantic. The junior execs use it now. I have a spankin' new Gulfstream four. "

"Gulfstream, huh? Good plane - long legs."

"Oh, yeah. It skips across the pond easily. Paris, London, even Asia."

"And plenty of hidden cargo space for the short hops, too."

"That's why I bought it. You must come for a ride."

"With the election coming up I can't just take off for Europe."

"Don't give me that shit. We could go to the Virgins tonight. Hit some of the casinos, or bring one or two of your special friends"

"I can't do that, not for a while. Voters have this thing about private companies flying their elected officials on junkets. Besides, school's in session."

"Maybe we can arrange a field trip? The last ones were fourteen or fifteen, plenty old enough to miss some classes."

"Maybe, " Snelling thought. "But Zoe doesn't like it, he's been telling me to get counseling before it leaks."

"Fuck Zoe! With the money I pay those kids, it ain't never seeing daylight!"

Snelling laughed nervously. "Francis," Snelling said changing the subject. "I need to talk to you about something else..."

"Peter, if this is about money, don't worry. You've been good to me and my organization, and as long as we continue..." Menceti outlined his needs to the Governor, who listened attentively.

*

The black Porsche drove down Periwinkle, past the restaurants, shops, and other tourist traps. The air was cool, and David had the top down. He figured his wife would be in bed by the time he got there. It wouldn't matter, really, if she was or not. David drove past the beaches toward home. He watched a three-masted schooner quietly try keeping pace with him. The fluorescent plankton caught in the froth of its wake glowed, giving away the path of the vessel in the dark water.

David Ranson had grown up on Sanibel. His father, Gerald Ranson, had brought his wife and two sons back to the island in the mid-sixties. David's dad had grown up in Ft. Myers. His grandmother was a house woman for a prominent family in the area. David's grandfather had died in the great war at the hand of a German POW guard. So when Gerald was drafted, he left to fight the Nazis with a vengeance. After the war, he used the GI Bill to get a degree and settled in New York City. A stockbroker for most of his life, he had also invested in the promise of real estate. A devoted fisherman since his youth, he had bought a small cabin and waterfront land on Sanibel when he started becoming successful. Planning for the future, he had bought more land as time and money allowed. When investors showed interest in his Florida hideaway in the early 1960's, Gerald was keen enough not to sell. In 1964, Gerald Ranson finally was able to retire. By now, he was a wealthy man. His property on Sanibel had increased in value hundreds of times over and was now worth over nine million dollars. He built a new home on the island, and settled in with his wife and sons.

David was in his senior year of high school when a third generation of Ransons was called to war. But David's brother, Gerald, Jr., did not go willingly. Junior, as he was called, had been protesting the war when his draft number was drawn. He had dropped out of college the previous semester to concentrate on the anti-war movement. After delaying his departure for as long as possible, he left for army boot camp. Only seven days after driving his son to the bus station, David's father received a telegram telling him that his oldest son had been killed.

Junior had gone AWOL on his second day at bootcamp. He had hooked up with a local woman whose husband came home, found them in bed, and shot both of them and then himself. While his parents seemed to be drawn closer by the death of their son, David withdrew into himself. He broke up with his girlfriend and stopped going out with the guys from school. He went out at night alone for walks, or stayed locked away in his room for hours. His parents were worried, but because David's grades stayed high, and he wasn't getting in any trouble, they left him alone. David took up sailing. In May of 1972, after graduation, his father purchased a boat for David. The teenage boy would go out in the morning and not come home until late at night.

Even though they had two docks at the house, David kept the craft at the Lost Cove Marina at Tarpon Bay. His parents suspected he had a girlfriend because he would come home smelling of perfume. They thought that he might be meeting her at the marina. Not wanting to disrupt his "secret," his father rented a slip for him to use at the marina.

In July of '72, David's acceptance letter into Princeton arrived. He left in August. In 1973 he transferred to Georgetown, telling his parents that he was thinking of going to law school at Georgetown, and that he thought he'd have a better chance if he finished his undergraduate studies there. David entered Law school in 1974 and started working as a prosecutor in 1976 in South Florida. A steady record of success followed the young, aggressive lawyer. He met Susan Crawford in 1977.

*

"I wish you would stay," the Governor said, "We could shoot eighteen holes tomorrow."

Frank stood up, and shook hands with Snelling. "I have to be back, I have a seven o'clock meeting in the morning, but I'll be in touch." The two men walked to the foyer. Outside, the car and driver were waiting. They joked a few minutes, until, right on cue, Snelling was called inside to answer the phone.

The door was closed behind Menceti after he sat in the car. The driver turned right onto Tennessee Avenue. They drove along, past hundreds of college students gathered in front of and in the bars that lined the road. "The Tennessee Waltz," his chauffeur said. Menceti closed his eyes and leaned back in the seat. He almost wanted Snelling to lose the election so he wouldn't have to come up like this and kiss his arrogant ass. But then he would have to start all over with the next Governor who might not like some of Frank's business practices, or worse, might be even more greedy or perverse than Snelling. If that was possible.

*

David signaled and turned on to the white sand and crushed shell drive. Surprisingly, the lights in the house were still lit. He pulled up under the carport and parked behind Susan's Lexus.

David walked in through the kitchen door and read the note she had leftfor him. He looked down the short hall and could see the television was still on. After heating the steak and potatoes in the microwave, David poured himself a glass of sweet tea and headed to the den.

Susan was asleep on the couch when he sat down across from her. Placing his meal on the coffee table, he picked up the remote control and slowly turned up the sound. He was not particularly interested in the documentary that was showing on the screen, but he found the screeching monkeys to be particularly annoying. David watched his wife as the volume increased. She began to stir, and he laughed to himself.

"Turn it down!" She covered her ears with her hands, before even cracking open an eyelid. When she did, she saw David sitting across from her in the chair, with a big stupid grin on his face. She closed her eyes again.

"You shouldn't fall asleep with the TV on," David said after he adjusted the sound to a more reasonable level. He took his knife and cut a piece of meat. It was dry and tough, it did not cut easily. He placed the food in his mouth, and then quickly spat it out into a napkin. "What kind of shit is this?" He yelled.

Susan opened her eyes, and watched him momentarily. "If you don't want it, cook your own damn food," she told him as she lifted herself off the couch. David threw the wadded up napkin and meat chunk at her. She turned and looked at him through sleepy eyes, then without a word, dragged her body up the stairs and into her bedroom. She closed and locked the door behind her. She did not need this.

*

Detective Doyle phoned the small office on Ortiz Avenue to let them know he was bringing over a patient. Whitmore said nothing when he was informed that he was going to be committed. The detective was sure that the Baker Act was not intended to be used to hold potential murder suspects, but he tried to convince himself that he was doing nothing wrong. The doctor was in bad shape, and where would he go anyway? His house was a crime scene, and the FDLE investigators would throw a fit if they allowed the suspected perpetrator of the crime to stay there. They hadn't been able to find any relatives, except for the dead woman's sister. She was flying down from Quebec, Cathy's original home, and would not arrive until the morning. But he could not silence his conscience.

He arrived at the county run facility, and Whitmore was led back to his room. A nurse handed Doyle a stack of admission papers that needed to be signed. After reminding the detective at least ten times that David's statement needed to be here by the following morning, he finally was able to leave for home.

It was close to two a.m. by the time Doyle had finished having Dr. Whitmore admitted to the mental health facility and driven home. Sarah had long been asleep when her husband walked through the door. After a quick shower, he checked on their daughter and crawled into bed. He tried to sleep, but his mind was racing. He could not close his eyes without seeing Cathy Whitmore's body.

Maybe he should just retire. He had his twenty years in, plus some. Then he wouldn't have to deal with any of it. But he had run away from the FBI, and had always regretted doing so. Doyle thought about what the doctor had told him and the Chief, about David and how everything did not feel right. He wondered if he might have missed something or if he was reading into things too much. He knew he was confused and tired, but that was the only thing he was sure of. He was rusty, and that scared him. The last murder on the island had not been solved, and he was afraid that he was just jumping on the Doc as the first convenient suspect.

Doyle decided that he would call his old partner from the Bureau and bounce some ideas off him. He needed his help anyway with that partial print they lifted. He and John had stayed in contact over the years, and he was due for a call. He would just work it into the conversation. Doyle also decided that he would look at the Blind Pass files to see what mistakes, if any, had been made so he would not repeat them. He wasn't going to let this go unsolved for twenty years.

*

Jeff was sitting and reading in the cabin of his boat when a car pulled into the marina lot. It was the off season, and he was the only live-aboard in Lost Cove Marina. He heard the three men as they walked along the wooden pier out to his slip. They stepped onto his boat without asking permission and entered the cabin.

"Good evening, Jeff," one said standing in the doorway.

"Luis. I figured it was you."

3

***

Sunday, September 3

Rick Cox woke before daybreak and slipped from under the blanket. He went to the closet and dragged out the heavy green canvas seabag. It had been packed the night before. He quietly removed the olive drab flight suit from its plastic hanger and laid it on top of the bag. He closed the door, then tiptoed around the bed. Leaning over, he softly kissed his wife, Laura, on the cheek without waking her. He picked up his gear and quietly left the bedroom, shutting the door gently behind him.

*

Susan headed down to the stairwell to the kitchen. It was already nine o'clock, and she was still not dressed. David was sitting at the table reading the paper. She took a deep breath and stepped onto the tile floor, in view of her husband. She walked over to the freezer and took out a bag of bagels. She would try to ignore him. She hoped he would do the same.

"Did you sleep well?" he asked her with a smirk.

"What are you doing up? Isn't it your day off?" She was surprised at herself, that almost sounded sincere. She did not want a fight.

David sipped his coffee. "That's the nice thing about working as a prosecutor. You don't get a day off."

Susan grabbed the bagels when they popped up from the toaster and set them on a plate. She took the container of cream cheese from the door of the refrigerator and spread a healthy amount on each bagel. She put the dish on the table and walked into the den to turn on The Weather Channel. She turned the TV so that she could watch it from the kitchen. Walking back to the table, she watched David finish the last of her breakfast.

"Was it good?"

"Marvelous; thanks, hon. You really know what it takes to make a good wife."

"You are such an asshole."

It had just slipped out before she could stop herself, and she regretted it. David laid the paper flat on the table. Susan tried to ignore him, hoping he would just let the comment pass. She quickly turned toward the freezer and reached for a bag of waffles. She started shaking when she heard his chair slide out from the table. David walked over behind her. "I'm sorry, was that *your* breakfast" he said. He reached up and twirled her hair with his fingers, "I wonder what people would think about a woman who denies her husband breakfast?"

"What would people think..." Susan cleared her throat, "What would people think if they knew that the DA hadn't slept in the same bed as his wife for five years because he can only get off when he's drunk?!" David pulled on her hair, spinning his wife around. She let out a scream, and he slapped Susan's face, knocking her to the ground.

"Don't ever threaten me again!" David warned, "If you ever threaten me or my career, you will have a major, major problem. And little Jeffy won't be there to save your ass."

She looked up at him and fought back the tears, not giving him the satisfaction of knowing how much her cheek stung. She dared not say a word so as not to provoke him further. She ran upstairs and locked the door behind her. Leaning her back against the door, she slid down to the floor crying. Out in the hall she heard David's footsteps as he came up the stairs and stopped right outside her room. He stood there until he heard her sobbing, then turned and walked outside to his car. Susan did not open her door until she heard his car take off down the drive.

*

The sun had not been visible when Rick Cox drove across Garrison Bright on his way to work at US Naval Air Station Key West. It had just started coming up over the horizon when the Navy Lieutenant started his pre-flight. But that was three hours ago, and now the glare off the Gulf of Mexico made him thankful that he remembered to replace the tinted visor in his flight helmet.

Rick enjoyed flying on Sundays; especially when testing a new system. The pleasure boats were out in full force which not only provided some nice scenery, but mock targets as well. He also liked that they were alone in the airspace. Except for a few Air Force Reserve flights, there was no traffic in the restricted airspace on weekends. During the week, it seemed to Rick as if he could walk through the sky there were so many military aircraft here.

Rick and his crew were testing the Infrared Detection System, or IRDS, in the newly-designed helicopter, and everything was working perfectly. They had already made several runs at some container ships in the area, and now they were flying past a cruise ship. The black and white image on the monitor inside the cabin showed what the gimbaled camera under the nose was pointed at. Rick had it selected to black hot, then moved the toggle to white hot. The image suddenly reversed itself. The heat generating parts of the ship were now displayed in white. The engine room, smokestacks, even the kitchen inside the hull were visible to him. It was like a moving x-ray of the ocean liner.

Unofficially nicknamed "Horny Toad" because of all the bumps and antennas protruding from its sheet metal skin, the ESH-60G belonged to the Naval Air Warfare Center, Detachment Three. Although the Warfare Center was located in Maryland, Det Three was permanently assigned to Key West. Its mission was to test and evaluate systems that were being developed by NAWC. It was an unorthodox relationship, but after Congressional Base closures and re-alignments, the men and women in the command were just happy to still be around. Besides, the system in place worked. The consistent weather--and open water bombing and ASW ranges near St. Croix and in the Gulf-- made NAS Key West a convenient location to test new aircraft and systems. Toad Five, as this particular aircraft was known, used the airframe of the SH-60 Seahawk Lamps MK3. The fuselage was stretched, and more powerful engines were added. Inside, various communication, navigation and other electronics had been added. The purpose of the aircraft was to give the Navy a multi mission platform for its elite forces: the SEALs. Designed with all-weather capabilities, and an assortment of specialized navigation and flight systems, it was to be the next generation sea-based cousin to the Pave Low III of the U.S. Army.

"Let's head back, Flight. We're signed off on this test," Rick said.

"If you're satisfied, we're satisfied," the pilot answered. Rick continued to play with the system as the pilots reversed their heading.

*

The Island View was a small paper, but it was the only one on Sanibel. The few writers it employed all lived on the island, all but one were women, and few of them worked for the money. Like Susan, they were there because they found they needed to be something more than "Mrs. So and So". Most had college degrees, but, due to either inheritance or their husband's success, they hadn't needed or used the education they had obtained. They worked because they did not play tennis or golf, or had played and were simply bored. The editor, founder, and sole stock owner of the View was Samuel Hardson.

A successful publisher "up north," Sam had retired and moved to Florida in 1961, at the ripe old age of thirty-eight. Finding retirement at such a young age less than satisfying, he started a small newsletter in 1962. At the time, Sanibel was known for seashells and fishing. Accessible only by boat, very little happened on the island that was worth reporting. The biggest story up to that time was when residents called the sheriff's office believing the island was going to be invaded. This was right after the Bay of Pigs, and there were reports of machine gun and cannon fire, along with some explosions around the island. Witnesses also said they saw military boats offshore. After a few phone calls, resident's minds were put at ease when they found out it was just some people from Hollywood making a World War Two movie. The area was substituting as the South Pacific, and the boats they saw were surplus patrol boats used in the film.

In 1963, the tollbooth at Punta Rassa began charging three dollars for the privilege of driving across the newly built causeway. The connection by road to Ft. Myers brought an increase of visitors to Sanibel and a greater demand for its one and only newspaper. Subscription service was started, but the ferries BEST and REBEL were now out of service. So the mail-boat SANTIVA, which was still operating, carried the Sanibel View over San Carlos Bay to the mainland and across Red Fish Pass to Upper Captiva.

The View turned into an actual newspaper in the late 60's, when a group of investors saw the potential of a tropical island paradise. It was within the boundaries of the US, and only a few hours drive from the new attraction that a man named Walt Disney had built. Resorts and golf courses invaded, driving the value of the finite amount of land on the island to new heights. People who had for generations barely made a living as fisherman or guides sold parcels of family land to these investors and never looked back.

By the middle seventies, Sanibel was a playground for the rich and famous. In less than ten years, the little speck of soil in the Gulf of Mexico had become a thriving tourist community, with restaurants, world class shopping, and a center for art and artists. Sam expanded the size of the paper to meet the demand as the population increased. Over the next couple of years, the paper's readership had grown, taking the Island View from a two-page newsletter to a large, well respected newspaper in the area.

When Susan arrived Sunday morning, she went right into Sam's office. She closed the door and excitedly told him about the exclusive with Jeff Strata. Sam was an art collector of sorts and had mentioned occasionally that Jeff would be a great story, if for no other reason than the mystery and rumors that surrounded him. Another reason was that the artist never gave interviews. Susan thought Sam would be overjoyed at the prospect. But he wasn't.

"Is that all you did yesterday?" Sam asked. "Talk with this guy?"

"I thought you'd be happy, no one's ever gotten an interview before..." her voice trailed off. Sam held up a copy of the Ft. Myers Press. On the front page was a photo of the Whitmore residence with an FDLE van out front. She took it from him and read it. The Press had scooped the story, thanks to a young intern that actually paid attention to the scanners in the newsroom. No other news agencies had picked up the signal-seven. The veteran assignment editors knew that older people died in their beds everyday on the island, but someone had forgotten to tell the young college student and now every reporter in the area was being asked the same thing that morning, "Where were you?"

"At least the others have a valid excuse," Sam told her. "They aren't married to the District Attorney."

"It was my day off," she replied, "Besides you know how things are with David and I right now."

"There are no days off for a good reporter," Sam said. "Personal problems or not, you should have been there."

"I'm not the only reporter you have, Sam."

"But you're the only one I really count on," he answered, "The others are here for a social club type thing. You are here because you are a damn fine writer, and this is in your blood." Susan knew he was telling her the truth. David was gone most of the time, and she had wanted to go into journalism. She had studied it in college. But when she mentioned getting a job to David, he had "forbidden" it. She met Sam at a fund-raiser for her husband, and the two hit it off immediately. By the end of the night, Sam had offered Susan a job. And because of Sam's influence, both financially as a large contributor to David's campaign; and as the editor of the only paper on the island, her husband could not say no.

"I know the paper is popular because it is known more for soft news than the hard stuff," Sam told her, "But I count on you, Susan, to be there when things happen."

"I know." She was starting to feel guilty. Almost every story that had her byline began on page one. He had been like a father to her, and she did not like letting him down.

Sam asked her to go over to the police station and find out what was going on. She asked about doing the piece on Jeff, and he said he wanted that too, but the Whitmore story came first.

*

"She's at three o'clock." The co-pilot searched the water, while the pilot in the left seat concentrated on flying. The boat was about two thousand feet below them.

"Getting close, it looks like a tuna clipper." Rick was adjusting the knobs on the control panel of the IRDS display.

"I see her," the copilot called over the ICS. "About three miles, going away."

"That's her." Cox confirmed. Rick walked up to the flight station and looked over the co-pilot's shoulders. The red and white tuna boat was making good speed.

"About twenty knots, I'd say."

"Not bad for that hunk of shit," the co-pilot observed. The pilot and Rick agreed.

"Doesn't it seem strange that a fishing boat this far out would not have its nets in the water?" Rick asked over the ICS. The pilot moved the collective in his left hand, and they went down for a closer look.

*

Susan gathered her notebook and purse, then went looking for Wendy. After searching through the offices, she found her in the darkroom developing film. Wendy had three stainless steel tubs in front of her filled with chemicals. She placed the 35mm film into the tub. Around the two women in the red lit room, photographs were hanging on wires strung from the walls. The space was cramped, and Susan needed to stand behind the petite, blonde wearing surgical gloves and look over her shoulder. Wendy expertly manipulated the paper as the ghostly images appeared.

"What would you say if I wanted to do a feature about your husband?" Wendy asked her.

"David? Why on earth would anyone want to read about him?"

"He's running for Congress! I think a lot of people would like a first hand account of how someone goes about doing that."

"If you want to hang around with him all day, feel free. That will get him off my back." Susan replied. Wendy removed the last photo from the tub and hung it on the wire with a plastic clip. She put away the tweezers and Xacto knife, and flipped on the light. Then she turned toward Susan. "I was just thinking about it, I haven't even asked Sam yet."

"It's not a good day to approach him," Susan said. She described her earlier meeting and Sam's mood. Wendy peeled the gloves off and threw them in the trash. "I'm ready to go."

*

The FDLE investigators arrived at Dr. Whitmore's free clinic at 10 am. They walked in equipped with a hand truck, empty boxes, plastic bags, and a search warrant. The receptionist, a nineteen year old volunteer, had watched enough cop shows on TV to ask to see the warrant, but in reality, the two law enforcement agents could have shown her a contract to buy a new car and she would not have known the difference. She let them into the office and showed them where the files were. She also showed them where the copy machine was and told them if they needed anything to just ask.

"Dr. Whitmore will be upset when he gets here. Should I just send him back to you?"

"I don't think he will be coming in today, so I wouldn't worry about it," the investigator told the girl.

"Oh, he'll be here. He always comes in late on Sunday," she replied.

"Not this Sunday."

"Oh, I'm sure he will be here any time," the receptionist asked, a puzzled look on her face.

"I doubt it. He's in custody right now, and I have a feeling it will be a long time before he comes back here."

"Oh, no!" she replied."I knew I should have drove him home! I told him he would get a DUI sooner or later!"

"It's a little more serious." the other investigator said.

"His wife was found dead yesterday."

" Mrs. Whitmore? No way!"

"Did you know her?"

"No, not really." She had only met her boss's wife a few times, and Cathy had been rudely cold to everyone in the office, including the Doc. Everyone seemed to know that they weren't getting along well. The receptionist had heard the arguments between Doc Whitmore and his wife. Maybe the woman deserved it, the way she berated the old man in front of everyone.

"What happened?" she asked.

"That's what we're trying to find out."

"Who did it? Do they know?"

"Right now, it looks like your boss; but that's unofficial. Just my opinion."

The receptionist could not believe it, would not believe it. Not Doctor Whitmore, he's such a nice old man. She did not want to think about it, so she looked around for something to do. But without him, there wasn't much. The woman was the only volunteer due in that day, and the waiting room already had five patients in there. She sat and watched the investigators do their work. There was nothing else she could do.

*

"Are you ready for a photo run?" the pilot asked Rick over the ICS.

Rick loaded the new 8mm tape into the camera. Like many Navy aircrew, he always carried his camcorder when he went flying. He liked to video whales and sunsets and, occasionally, the Cuban MIGs that intercepted them when they strayed too close. He often wondered why the small camcorders were not required equipment for occasions just like this one. "Okay, let's make this one from the stern along the starboard side."

The pilot flew the helicopter only one hundred feet above the water, shifting his eyes from the boat to the water off the nose past the windscreen in front of them. The copilot's eyes never left the instrument panel. If the pilot started to descend, he would see any deviations immediately, and hopefully keep the helicopter from flying into the water. Rick was standing at the side window looking through the viewfinder at open water.

"We are coming up on the target. Ten seconds."

Rick hit record, and the red light in the viewfinder verified the tape was rolling.

"Five seconds...Four seconds...Now..Now..Now!"

On the third *now*, the aft end of the fishing boat came into the view of the camera. Rick described what he saw into the ICS. The 24 track magnetic tape recorder behind him preserved his observations. Normally used for ASW operations, it worked equally well for this mission.

"Cruiser stern, red and white hull, name is Martha Ann, US flag. Key West homeport. Lower mast amidships, British type gantry. Nets are not in water. .See two, no three crewmen on deck..Tapered funnel, with red and blue stripes, King post with heavy crosstree and topmast..I see more men on deck..No cargo on deck, I count six electronic arrays on bridge. They appear to be new."

"Do you want me to continue alongside?"

"Yeah, stay with him Flight. I'm almost done. Okay... there are more crew on deck and they...call the Coast Guard, Flight; they are throwing bales over the side. I'm getting all this on tape. Stay with 'em."

"Roger, stand by, I'll call it in."

The pilot switched the radio and notified the Coast Guard who, in turn, relayed the report to the USCG Cutter Antilles. She was the closest Coast Guard vessel in the area. They were on their way, but asked the Navy helicopter to shadow the Martha Ann.

"Flight, I see what appear to be guns, possibly AK47's, being carried by some of the crew, lets pull back." The pilot turned the helicopter away from the boat and settled about one half mile behind and five hundred feet above the smugglers.

"Good eye, Cox." the copilot said over the ICS. That was also recorded.

*

Special Agent Laura Wilson woke up and called the office. She had slept in after getting home late from the meeting in Miami. She notified the duty officer that she would be there in forty-five minutes. She went down stairs to the kitchen and saw that Rick had left his usual mess from breakfast. She doubted he had ever washed a dish. It must be from eating in Navy chow halls most of his adult life, where others cleaned up after him, she concluded. That was one more habit she'd have to help him break now that they were married.

She pulled the box of Fruity Pebbles from the top of the refrigerator and poured the little colored flakes into the bowl. She read the notes from her meeting in Miami while she ate, scribbling ideas into the margins. After she was done eating, she showered and dressed.

One of the benefits of working in the Keys was the casual dress code. It was just too hot to walk around in suits and business attire most of the time. There was also a safety consideration: it allowed the agents to blend in with the general population of sun worshipers. Besides, it was Sunday, and the Agent-in-Charge had the authority to relax the standards, to a point. No swimsuits or Daisy Duke cutoffs, but the bright yellow shorts and striped top she was wearing would be fine. And Laura was the Agent in Charge, at least temporarily, so she was sure no one would say anything.

*

"Bingo!" the investigator yelled. She had been searching through the three drawer cabinet for over an hour before she found the file. She called for the lead investigator of the team and showed it to him.

"It lists Cathy Whitmore's complete history, down to the amounts and types of drugs that her husband gave her."

In the one inch thick file, a chart showed the dosages and dates going back almost the whole ten years of the doctor's marriage. Right at the top of the latest chart the drug Xandrid was listed over 15 times. The notation SAMPLE DOSAGE

ADMINISTERED filled the square next to it. The investigators called Doyle.

"I think you should send them home," the investigator told the girl as he motioned to the waiting area. "Dr. Whitmore probably will not be seeing any more patients."

"Until when?"

"He will probably not be seeing anymore. Period. If I were you, I'd gather my things together and start reading the want ads."

*

"It should be the next mailbox."

"I see it."

Susan turned the Lexus into Dr. Whitmore's driveway around 10 a.m. Yellow police tape still surrounded the house. Combined with the various vehicles in the yard, it looked more like a construction site than a crime scene. Other members of the media were there, including the three local network affiliates, setting up for live feeds for the noon news, but the police allowed no one in the house.

"It's a gorgeous home."

"It's so big, I wonder what it's like on the inside." Wendy wanted a house like this someday.

Wendy went off to shoot some photographs of the home and of the investigators walking in and out carrying bags and boxes.

"Susan, how are you?" the young reporter asked when he saw her. He was sweating, no doubt due to the long sleeve shirt and tie he was wearing in the 90 degree heat.

"Chris, I haven't seen you for a while," Susan remarked. "Except on TV."

"I've been getting more face time since John Douglass went to TLV in Miami. He's making almost twice what he got here."

"Miami's a much bigger market."

"Yeah. I thought about you, I saw your husband at a news conference the other day. He looks good."

"I guess."

She and Chris White had been in some journalism classes together back at USF and had kept in touch after she married David. Susan had helped him get a job with the View. But he was too skilled, and too good looking for the small paper, and he had quickly moved up to the local NBC affiliate as a reporter. He had recently been promoted to weekend anchor, but still worked in the field on the three weekdays he was scheduled.

"Are you still having problems? I thought you would be excited about becoming the wife of a Congressman."

"It's not as great as it looks, believe me."

The cameraman yelled for Chris from the van.

"I gotta go, I have a live feed, I'll call you." He ran back to the truck as Wendy returned.

"I'm glad I brought my zoom lens," Wendy said walking toward Susan. "I saw the door to the bedroom was still open, so I went down onto the beach and got a shot of the inside."

"Could you see anything?"

"I don't know; the curtains on the door were flapping in the breeze," She said while taking a wide shot of the hectic scene in the yard.

"I don't think there is anything here, but I have an idea." They left for a more promising location.

*

"Thanks, Navy, we have it from here."

"Roger, Antilles. Have a good one."

The crew of the helicopter watched the Coast Guard cutter as she trailed the Martha Ann to Key West. The crew were under arrest and being questioned inside the Coast Guard vessel. They had been caught with a couple of tons of marijuana and a few thousand vials of Valium. At least that was what the Coast Guard said it was. The Executive Officer of the Antilles sailed the dope carrier back to US Customs under its own power. Rick and his crew would send them the tape after Rick made an unofficial copy for himself. It was his camera after all.

*

Being the wife of the District Attorney had its privileges, so instead of presenting her press pass, Susan handed the duty officer her husband's card. She asked to speak with the Sanibel Island Chief of Police. He was not available, the officer said, but she could speak with Detective Doyle if she liked. She and Wendy helped themselves to coffee and donuts in the reception area.

Detective Doyle walked out, and, after asking what this was about, he informed Susan, eloquently, but in no uncertain terms, that he did not care who her husband was. He told her that neither he nor the police had any comment at this time.

"I can always just go ask David."

"Feel free," he responded.

"Detective Doyle is it? It's a long drive from here to the courthouse and back, so why not be a sport and save me the trouble. Was it a suicide? I heard drugs were involved. Did she OD? Come on."

Doyle just looked at her. "I'm sorry. I have no comment."

"How is Doctor Whitmore taking it? Have you spoken to him?"

"I am not giving out any information at this time. I am sorry, please excuse me." Doyle walked over to the Duty Officer and softly spoke in her ear. She nodded and Doyle walked out of the station to his car. Susan went to the duty desk and asked if there was anyone else she could talk to. The officer said no, but if Susan would leave a card and a message, she would see that the chief got it.

"Thanks, but no thanks. I'll find someone on my own."

*

Scott Zoe, Chief of Staff for the Governor of the State of Florida, walked into his boss's office. He carried with him copies of various papers from around the state and placed them on the oak desk in the center of the room. The Governor told the lobbyist he was talking to that he would get back to him and hung up the phone.

"I don't even know who the hell that was," Snelling told Zoe, "I used to love campaigning, but now I hate election time."

The Governor picked up the papers from his desk and started to read. "What's this shit?"

"This 'shit'," Zoe explained, "is a preview of who you will be running against. Every paper from Miami to Pensacola is there."

"It's only August; do I need to see this yet?"

"If you were ahead in the polls, no. What I want you to do is look at some of the other races, and see if we can't attach you to some of the stronger party candidates."

"Like who?"

"Representative Cortez from Miami is up for reelection; he's well liked and has no serious challenger. You could go down and 'support' him a few times. The Latinos love the guy. Also the congressman from Orlando.."

"Yibstreth?" Governor Snelling shook his head.

"Yeah, she will be back for another term."

"She's a total bitch! What's that radio guy call her? A feminazi? I can't deal with that woman!"

"I don't want you to sleep with her..."

"That definitely won't happen," Snelling said under his breath. The Governor searched through some of the papers and came to the Sanibel View. The story revolved around David's announcement.

"Who's this guy Ranson?"

"David Ranson? He's the D.A. down in Lee County. Been there most of his life, good record, married, good press. The incumbent is not running against him.."

"What happened to Jordy?"

"He had that heart attack in January. He announced this would be his final term."

"It's about time," the Governor said, "Christ, he's eighty years older than God."

"That's why the AARP adopted him. He's one of their own," Zoe said, "So do you want to set up something with this guy Ranson? I think it's worth checking out." Snelling read the article again.

"Yeah," he told his Chief of Staff, "I'll fly down to him, though. I need to get out of this town for a while."

"I'll set it up. How about this weekend?"

"Let's do it tonight. Can we do it tonight?" Snelling asked as he sat at his desk.

"No, we have that other matter," Zoe said, "Mr. and Mrs. Mathews. Regarding their daughter. And I swear this better be the last one, sir!"

"I know, I know. Dammit, I forgot about that. I will get help."

"How about tomorrow?"

"I can't. I want to meet Ranson tomorrow," the Governor was already reading the notes for the budget meeting he was late for. Zoe gathered the papers and headed for the door.

"Scott," the Governor called out.

Zoe turned. "Yes, sir?"

"Thanks. And see if you can get in touch with Menceti. I would like him to be there, too. And call Rockman in Hollywood, find out if he wants to be there; if not, get the rundown on Ranson from him."

"Yes, sir." Zoe laughed to himself. There was no way that Lance Rockman, the Attorney General of Florida, was going to be caught in the same state as Frank Menceti, let alone the same table.

*

David received the call from Larry reminding him that the fund-raising Beach Party was that night. Larry asked about Doc Whitmore, but David put him off, saying he would fill him in at the party. He hung up the phone as Susan came into the outer office. She was greeted by Donna, David's secretary.

"Good morning, Mrs. Ranson," she said sarcastically as her finger depressed the intercom button. "Mr. Ranson, your wife is here," Donna did not like being called in on weekends.

"Please have her take a seat," the voice on speaker said, "I'll be with her in a minute."

David sat back and put his feet up on his desk. He enjoyed making Susan wait. He pictured her out there, fidgeting while sitting on the couch. She would not come to see him if she wasn't pissed about something. It would have to be really major if she drove all the way off the Island, instead of calling. He wished he could peek out, but there were no windows that gave him a view of that part of his office.

After what he deemed an appropriate length of time, he picked up the phone and placed it to his ear. He then pushed the intercom.

"Donna, would you let my wife know I will see her now."

He had to try very hard not to smile as Susan walked into the office. She did not look happy. He waved her over to a chair. She was really pissed. He hoped he keep a straight face, but he was really enjoying this.

"Can you call me back in a few minutes? My wife just came in," he told the dial tone in his ear. David hung up the phone and leaned back in his chair. The view from his office was spectacular. It looked over the Caloosahatchee River into North Ft. Myers. The remnants of the old Edison bridge were visible, it was now a fishing pier. The new twin spans of its replacement were filled with traffic.

"It used to be the summers here were dead," he said to his wife. "Now look, bumper to bumper and it's not even four o'clock. And it's a Sunday."

"I'm not here to talk about traffic."

"Then why are you bothering me in the middle of my workday, Honey bunch?" Oh, that did it.

"Why the hell didn't you tell me about Willard and Cathy?!"

"Why didn't you tell me how much Sam's paycheck was last week?" David countered.

"What does that have to do with anything?" He had caught her off guard. Susan was confused; David could see that on her face. "It's none of your business what Sam makes, I don't even know what he makes!

"Precisely !" David said.

"Precisely what? Don't change the subject. I want to know why you didn't tell me!" Susan repeated.

"The same reason you don't tell me about Sam," David lied, "I don't bring my work home." *And I knew it would bug the shit out of you,* he wanted to add. Susan was always more aggressive in public, where she knew David could not control her. But she would pay for it when they were in the privacy of the Ranson house. The added benefit was that it also made many people believe his wife was a bitch. That would help in the divorce.

"Bullshit! They were our friends. You should have said something." Susan said.

"They were *my* friends, dear. You have never even been to their house."

"Like you go there all the time."

"Would you have written about it if I had said anything?"

"Of course, it's my job."

"That is exactly why I didn't tell you!"

"You don't mind all the crap I write about your election campaign! No more free coverage, is that what you want?"

"Fine," David looked right into her eyes and spoke slowly, "I can find someone else to write about me. I am sure it won't be difficult to find someone of equal talent."

He watched as his words sank in, and as much as Susan did not want to admit it, the words hurt. If nothing else, he had learned how to push her buttons and make her feel like shit.

"By the way," David added, "We have that dinner tonight. Be ready at seven."

Susan was too upset to argue. She stood up and went to the door.

"Susan?" She stopped, but did not turn around. David continued, "This time, wear something nice."

She slammed the door behind her.

Down at the car, Wendy spotted Susan storming out of the building. She reached the car and threw her handbag in the back. The tears were streaming down her cheek. She hated that man, and she hated him more for giving her the ability to hate someone. She slid in behind the wheel and pulled the car door closed. Wendy was stunned. She had never seen Susan like this.

"What happened?" Wendy asked.

"Never mind!" Susan snapped as she turned the key. Wendy sat quietly as Susan pulled the car out of the lot. Susan did not speak, except to ask for a tissue. The gold luxury car swung into the right lane and up the exit ramp. Susan pushed down the accelerator and merged with the southbound traffic on Interstate 75.

"Where are we going?"

"Shopping," Susan replied as the Lexus Coupe's speedometer climbed past eighty miles per hour.

*

Doyle arrived at the Lee County Mental Health Center just after one-thirty that afternoon. He strolled up the sidewalk to the admissions office. In daylight, it reminded him of a resort. The center was only one year old, and much of the landscaping was still being worked on. It was a relaxing place, with fountains and benches near adolescent cherry blossom trees. It felt like a place of healing, he thought. The white stucco buildings all looked the same, and he watched some of the patients walk around, working out their problems. Of course, the doctor would not be out here. The ones who were dangers to themselves and others were kept indoors and supervised, always supervised.

The next building Doyle came to had a sign reading "Service Entrance" with an arrow that pointed down a sidewalk. He turned and followed it. It led around the back of the building and up a hardwood ramp, ending at a large, windowless door. He stepped up to the solid white door and pushed a button. Above the door, a security camera pointed at him. The detective pulled out his wallet and held it up to the camera so that his gold shield was visible. Although he did not look up, he felt the person examine him and his badge. When the buzzer sounded, he pulled the door and walked inside.

*

Rick ran up to Operations and dropped his flight bag. He then went down to see his Commanding Officer, Commander Chuck Haas. He sat in the outer office and waited for the two pilots to join him. When they arrived, Cox knocked on the CO's door.

"Come in."

The three officers entered the room. After the standard military courtesies, they sat down across from their boss and briefed him on what had taken place.

"Should I fill out a standard Intel brief on this or just have the tape transcribed?" Rick asked his CO.

"Where is the tape?"

"Right here," Rick said handing the black cassette over to Haas. The officer called his intelligence officer who ordered a TV and VCR to be brought up. Rick gave him the adapter for the 8mm tape and they watched the operation. When it was over, the Intel officer took the tape and said he would have copies made up and sent to the Coast Guard, DEA, and other authorized agencies.

"Can I get my original back?" Rick asked him.

"I'm sorry, but this is now government property," the officer said.

"I paid for it. I own the tape, can I at least get a copy?"

"Once again, I'm sorry. You're not authorized for a copy, but we can reimburse you for the tape. You did a good job." The intelligence specialist walked out the room. Rick was visibly disappointed.

"Let me talk to him, and see what I can do, Lieutenant," Haas offered, "Now how did the tests go?"

*

Wendy and Susan stepped across the parking lot and into the mall in Naples, Florida. The community of Naples-Marco Island sat on the Gulf of Mexico about 30 miles south of Sanibel. Its sandy white beaches and beautiful weather ranked it right up with Sanibel, as did the average wealth of its population. Along with million dollar condos and exclusive golf and tennis clubs, Naples also had five star hotels such as the Registry and Ritz Carlton. To appease all this wealth, hundreds of fully staffed shops had popped up, including two huge indoor malls. Naples was the place to be for clothes, jewelry, and other items for the well to do. All the exclusive New York and Rodeo Drive shops were represented here and catered to their customers in the manner they were accustomed to.

"Where to?" Wendy asked as they strolled past store after store in the mall. Susan wasn't sure where to go. She wasn't even sure what she wanted to buy. But she was sure that David's VISA bill would reflect her orders to *wear something nice, this time.*

*

Doyle walked up to the circular linoleum counter. A woman, no older than twenty he guessed, sat behind the desk, typing into a computer. She noticed his presence and told him to hold on as she hit a few more buttons. After a click or two from the machine, she gave the detective her attention.

"May I help you?"

Doyle took out his badge and showed it to her. "I'm here to pick up a patient, Dr. Willard Whitmore. He was brought in here late last night."

"I saw it on the news, it's a real shame. If you stay here a minute, I'll find his therapist. You can have a seat over there." She pointed at a row of five blue plastic stacking chairs against the wall. A television blared along the opposite wall. A daytime soap was showing.

"Thank you."

The receptionist disappeared through a door after unlocking the large silver handle. About five minutes later she returned.

"Dr. Ramirez will be right out," she told the detective, and went back to tapping her keyboard.

Doyle stood and examined the room. It was bright, and as sterile and as uncomfortable as a room could be, right down to the hard plastic stacking chairs against the wall. The door opened with a bang, startling Doyle. He was approached by a bearded man wearing the compulsory white lab coat. The man offered his hand to Doyle.

"Hi, I'm Jack Ramirez, Doctor Whitmore's therapist."

"Brian Doyle, Sanibel Police." They shook hands and sat down on the plastic chairs.

"Doctor, I need to know when Dr. Whitmore can be released."

"I'm not really sure. We just received the paperwork from the D.A.'s office a few hours ago. He hasn't spoken to anyone since being brought in last night. He's been through a very traumatic experience, it will take some time for him to get over it."

"What are we talking about? Hours? Days?"

"At least a couple of days. Maybe longer. Is there some kind of rush?"

Doyle hesitated. "Well, frankly, yes. I came here to arrest him."

"Arrest him? For what?"

"The murder of his wife."

The doctor's voice lowered, "I think you may have the wrong guy. From what I've observed of him he would not be capable. Are you sure?"

Doyle nodded. "Reasonably."

Ramirez shook his head, "Detective, I'm going to give you my opinion. It doesn't mean much but I don't think he killed anyone. I could be wrong, but in his state... if you are intent on arresting him..."

"I am."

"Then I would say," he thought a moment, "and this is just a guess,...I could release him to you in seventy-two hours. You can take him now, he's free to go. But I don't know how he'll react. He may come right back to us. He's not very stable."

Doyle thought about what Ramirez said. He could wait a couple of days. Whitmore wasn't going anywhere, and it would give more time for the test results. But he had better be sure. "May I see him?" Doyle asked.

"He is with his sister-in-law; when she comes out, you can go in."

"I don't think there will be a problem with him staying here, but I need to let the DA's office know. Is there a phone I can use?" The doctor walked him to a phone, shook his hand and walked back into the world behind the door.

*

"No fucking way!" Lance Rockman said into the speaker phone. "Unlike your boss, I want to get reelected. Menceti's got his fingers in everything, racketeering, drugs. Shit, I know of three murders right now that Francis committed himself!"

"Then why haven't you picked him up?" Zoe countered.

"I have a whole state to worry about. You know I don't get involved in the prosecution of one person!"

"Bullshit, Rock. You're an old cop. I know you'd nail this guy, especially since he's in your old stomping grounds."

"Of course I would, but then I would need to tell your boss. And I'm not about to do that."

"Why? What do you think Snelling would do?"

"I think we both know the answer to that, don't we?" Rockman replied, "And I'm sure that the Governor would appoint his own special prosecutor. No, Scott, when I have enough, I'll take this myself."

"I'd love to see that. I thought the Attorney General stayed out of criminal cases?"

"Normally, sure. But technically there's no reason why I can't get involved."

"But why would you?" Zoe asked.

"Because he's a real slick little bastard, and no one will talk against him. I don't understand why your boss even speaks to him."

Scott Zoe was prepared for that. Rockman was straight as an arrow, that was how he managed to keep his job under two different administrations of different parties. If you were friends with Rockman, you were worth the voter's trust.

"The Governor needs to be told of an investigation, you know that?" Zoe said. Rockman turned off the speaker phone, and picked up the receiver. His voice lowered.

"Not if it's federal. Snelling's gonna be history if he doesn't watch his ass. And I'm only telling you that as a friend, Scott."

"Is there something I should know about, Lance?" Zoe asked. Rockman was silent.

"You could solve both our problems if you indicted the son of a bitch," Zoe said. "That is your job."

"In due time, my friend. If I were your boss, I'd be watching the clock."

"Snelling is a big boy, Lance. Frank Menceti is a big contributor and has a lot of friends. Not everybody can be as well liked as you. But I will take it under advisement."

Their friendship was mutual, but the respect was not. Rockman thought that Zoe didn't push hard enough when he had to, although he would never say anything to him. Lance Rockman was an aberration. By *not* playing politics, he had managed to hold on to one of the highest political offices in the state.

"So what else can I do for you, besides say no to dinner."

"David Ranson. From the west coast, Lee County. I need a rundown for the Governor."

The State Attorney General gave his opinion of David Ranson, though he did not know him well. He also gave his opinion of Menceti, Snelling's chances of reelection, and the budget cuts regarding prison overcrowding that had gone before the Florida Legislature earlier that year. The two talked for an hour and then said good-bye. Zoe was disappointed that he had not been promised support for the Governor by Rockman, but at least the guy hadn't told him he was endorsing their opponent. They still had time; unless he found out about Snelling's taste for young girls.

*

"That will be three hundred ninety-two dollars, please." Susan handed over the gold colored credit card to the saleswoman. Even though David was more than financially secure, Susan rarely spent more than fifty dollars on a dress. Never had she done it without David's direct consent. But she did not deserve that remark, and if he wanted to see what it cost to have her look "nice," then she would show him.

"Thank you, is there anything else?" the woman asked as she handed back her receipt and card.

"Not today, thanks."

"It must be nice."

Susan looked over at Wendy. The girl didn't come from money, and it made Susan feel sort of guilty. Wendy seemed easily impressed by wealth, as Susan was when she first met David. She was a journalism student at the University of South Florida in St. Petersburg. Eight years her senior, she was awed by the young prosecutor. Growing up in a Tampa trailer park with her mom, Susan had won scholarships that paid for her education. She had always wanted to be a news reporter, and had interned at the local paper during her junior year. In her senior year, she had visited the Ranson's house on Sanibel for Thanksgiving. Overwhelmed by it all, she accepted David's proposal of marriage that Christmas. Upon graduating from school, she accepted a job at the Tampa Times. She left after only two weeks when David accepted a job in Lee County as an Assistant District Attorney. They moved into the Ranson family residence when David's parents were killed by a drunk driver in a car crash on Alligator Alley later that year. They left everything to David. Not yet twenty-five and it seemed like Susan Ranson had the world. Little did she know.

"How about a make over?" Wendy suggested. Susan thought. That scene in his office had made a mess of her makeup; it only seemed fair.

"If you get one with me," she pulled out her husband's credit card. "David's treat." Two hours later, the two women walked out of the small shop.

"You look good. I never realized how pretty you are," Wendy told her. Susan looked in the mirror. "I do look good," she told herself. At least better than she did earlier. As the two of them browsed the shops, they drew a lot of attention, though most of it was subtle. For the first time, Susan really enjoyed Wendy's company.

"Hey, why don't you come with us tonight?" Susan asked as they exited the mall.

"To the dinner?" Wendy asked, amazed at the offer.

"Sure, I'm positive David won't mind." It would give Susan someone to talk to that David could not accuse her of sleeping with.

"Thanks, I'd love to!" Wendy replied. *Being nice to the wench paid off.* She did not like Susan very much. She thought her ungrateful for having a husband like David Ranson. David was rich, smart, and good looking. Wendy wondered what he saw in Susan besides looks. All Susan ever did was bitch about him. What did she have that Wendy didn't? Maybe tonight, she would have the chance to show him.

*

Dr. Ramirez opened the door and walked out with Lisa McCay, Whitmore's sister-in-law. The therapist motioned for Doyle to join him. The detective hung up the phone and walked over.

Although a few years younger, there was no doubt that Lisa and Cathy were sisters. The same features were in her face, they also shared the same fabulous body. The only difference he could see was the hair color. Lisa's was auburn, while Cathy had been a blonde. Of course, Lisa was also breathing.

"Miss McCay, I'm Brian Doyle. I'm a detective with the Sanibel Police. Can we talk?"

"Sure." The three sat down on the plastic chairs.

"It's about Willard. We believe that your brother-in-law is responsible for Cathy's death. I came here to arrest him." Her face said it all. The tears formed, her mouth opened, and her lips began to quiver.

*

Francis Menceti called his secretary into his office and told her to call the Governor and thank him for the invitation for dinner. Then she was to call and have the jet ready to take him to Ft. Myers.

"Call dispersing and tell them I want a draft in the amount of five thousand dollars in the bank's name to be given as a political contribution to a man named David Ranson."

"How do you spell the last name?" she asked.

"How the hell do I know? Call Zoe at the Governor's office."

"Yes, sir."

"And tell them to vacuum that fucking plane or something. It smells like that damn dog shit in it!"

*

Laura Wilson pulled into the driveway on Southard Street. Due to the Key West sun, the bleached, weather-beaten, eyebrow style home was in desperate need of a paint job. The FBI agent walked up the steps under the overhanging roof. All kinds of ferns and hanging plants adorned the patio, and a thick layer of dirt and spider webs covered the window-sills. She knocked hard on the door, and she heard the familiar voice of her boss.

"It ain't locked," he yelled.

She fought the wooden screen door when she tried to open it. Laura finally got it to cooperate, but managed to break one of the hinges in the process. She carefully laid the door against the house and went inside.

"Where are you?" She looked around, and saw boxes scattered about.

"In here." She followed his voice as it resonated down the hall. The cardboard boxes were spaced about every four or five feet. Most were at least partially filled with books or dishes or some other household item.

"It's Laura. Laura Wilson," she said. She still didn't know where she was going. There were no lights on and the roofline over the front of the house had effectively blocked all the rays of the sun from entering. It must have helped keep out the heat in the unairconditioned home, but it also made it hard to see.

"I'm in the den." His voice echoed off the hardwood floor of the hallway. At the end of the dimly lit passage, she pushed on a semi closed door and finally came into view of the man. "I'm sorry, I didn't mean to yell."

"It's okay," she said, "How are you feeling?"

"Better." He was lying on an old brown couch. Laura guessed it was made in the late 1970's. The room had a very strong, musty odor, and no lights were on. In fact the only clue that there was electricity was the black and white television set sitting on the flipped milk crate in the corner. Her boss had a cast on his leg, and a large white dressing was wrapped around his left shoulder and chest. He was wearing plaid shorts, black socks, and sandals, but the bandage prevented him from wearing a shirt. The Marlboro in his mouth had an ash almost three-fourths of an inch long, and the yellow smoke curled up above it.

"How do you like it?"

Laura looked around. "Are you moving out?"

"You mean the boxes? I guess I never finished unpacking."

Laura looked around and realized all she saw were bare essentials. Everything else was still in boxes, which were covered with dust.

"But you've lived here fifteen years?"

"The wife left me the week after I moved down, and I haven't decided where to put everything." He sounded serious.

It was hard for her to believe this was the same man who graduated sixth in his class at Harvard, and was in charge of all FBI operations in Southwest Florida and the Keys. No wonder he was always in the office.

"So how do you like being the AIC? Did you move into my office yet?" The man tried to laugh, but ended up coughing something into a tissue.

"It's only temporary."

"I don't know, I was hit pretty bad."

"I saw the report. And Chris filled me in yesterday in Miami. We are still looking for the sniper."

"Don't waste your time, he's long gone."

"So what did you want to talk to me about that a phone call couldn't answer?" Laura asked.

"I got a call today from a friend of mine named Brian Doyle. He's a cop from Lee County --Sanibel Island. He wanted your help, well, my help, but I'm asking you since I'm not in a position... He and I go back a long time. I wasn't sure about it, and I wanted to find out your opinion. It wasn't something I wanted to discuss in the office." John Bender lit up another cigarette and told Laura about Doyle.

*

Ramirez closed the door, leaving the two men alone. Whitmore just stared at the wall, and Doyle watched him. After about ten minutes, Doyle decided that Whitmore would stay. The police detective went over to the door and knocked on the window to notify the nurse he was ready to leave.

"Have you looked into it?"

The voice seemed very far away. Doyle turned toward the doctor.

"Excuse me, did you say something?"

"I asked if you looked into it?" The doctor had not moved; his expression had remained the same, but clearly his mind was working.

"Not yet," Doyle answered. "I'm supposed to arrest you, take you in custody."

"I know. Why haven't you?" Whitmore's speech was methodical and soft. There was no remorse, no anger, none of the emotion that had been present twenty-four hours before. It made the homicide detective nervous.

"Your doctor asked me to let you stay a few more days. You have some problems to work out."

"I have no problems. And he's your doctor, not mine."

"I guess he is. You're right." Doyle didn't like being in the room with the man. He wanted to leave, just walk out the door. Any doubts he had about the old man's ability to take someone's life evaporated with every spoken word.

"Are you going to arrest me or leave me here?"

"What do you think is better for you?"

"I don't think either is better. If you are going to arrest me, please do it now. If not, I would like to be alone."

Doyle had already made up his mind to let the shrinks handle him for the next few days.

*

"Susan, you look unbelievable," Larry told her as she walked into the gated courtyard. The plastic lanterns hung from poles above the guests heads, leading from a pool deck down to the beach. A large side of beef was roasting near the caterers as servers carried silver dishes of crab and shrimp hors d'oeuvres around to the guests. The black tie event was overflowing with people talking and drinking. The light from the pool glowed a soft mint-green blue, which was reflected in the various broaches, rings and other jewelry worn when by guests trying to impress each other. Susan's red-sequined evening gown glittered from the lanterns. The tight material showed off her figure, a point that did not go unnoticed from the looks she received from both the husbands and single men in attendance. Her professionally applied makeup and hair only magnified the natural beauty she had inherited. She had even admitted to herself that she had never in her life looked this good. Susan strolled along next to her husband. She would play her part for a few minutes, and then he would ignore her, like always. She would then be set free to roam around.

Behind them, Wendy made her entrance. Wearing a skin tight white dress, the neckline was covered with blue and silver material that drew attention to the fact that she was not wearing a bra. It looked as if her forty-four D's would pop out at any moment, and, by their reaction so far, not a man at the party would hesitate to lend her a hand if such an event took place. Between the two women stood David. He knew what the men were thinking and he walked around with his head held high. Larry walked near him, trying to get some of the luster to rub off. David saw the looks in their eyes and gave no indication that he was not sleeping with either woman.

After walking around and introducing himself, David took his place with Larry by the bar, and began to unofficially fill him in on the case against the doctor. As the conversation started to flow, Susan signaled to Wendy that they were free to mingle.

Wendy was quickly surrounded by a group of salivating bachelors acting like lapdogs when word passed that she was single. She loved the attention, and knowing that each one could afford the one thousand dollar a plate dinner made the recognition that much better. Of course, not one of them could have told her the color of her eyes.

Susan spotted Sam over in the corner, away from the crowd. During his time on the island he had attended hundreds of fund-raisers, and now they just blended together. He didn't pay, of course, though he could afford to. No, he was there as a courtesy. His paper endorsed only one candidate, and that candidate seemed to always be elected. Sam saw that as a fluke, but politicians are a superstitious bunch when it comes to votes, so Sam always found an invitation in his mailbox.

"We don't like what's going on with the Doc," Larry told David. "He's a friend, and you're a friend, and friends should look after each other."

"I was elected District Attorney on a position against drugs and alcohol abuse. It is my platform. Now, I'm supposed to change it because Whitmore was stupid?" David turned away from Larry and surveyed the guests. Larry stood next to him and smiled.

"Save the speech for the masses. I'm telling you to go easy on the guy. Look around. See all these nice people. They didn't pay for this, I did."

"I don't know anything about that!" David did not like this at all. No one told him how to run his campaign regardless of how much money they invested in him. Larry refilled his glass from a bottle of vodka on the bar next to him. Larry turned to face David, and the smile went away.

"You're playing with the big boys now, David. Don't fuck it up. If you want to play Mr. Small Town District Attorney, then keep doin' what you're doin'. But if you want me to tell these guys where to spend their money, then you pick up your little bat and play ball."

David was about to tell him to go to hell, when Wendy came up to them. She had a large glass in one hand, and she grabbed David's arm with the other.

"I am a little drunk." she said.

"You're a cute little drunk," David replied.

Susan glanced over and saw Wendy hanging on her husband, who seemed to be enjoying it. After a quick goodnight to Sam, she made her way over to David.

"I would like to go home," Susan stated flatly while watching Wendy rub against him.

"Fine. Go. I'm going to stay here." David moved his hand down the curves of the young blonde's body, who smiled up at Susan.

"I'll make sure he gets home," Wendy said with a giggle. Susan had been embarrassed enough for one evening.

"I'm sure you will."

4

***

Monday, September 4

The bay windows in his bedroom allowed the rays of the sun coming up over the Atlantic to filter in through the blinds. Menceti never woke before 8:00 am., so he was not a cheerful man when the phone rang. He picked it up on the third ring. "What?!"

"They grabbed another one, Frank."

"Where the hell are you?!"

"Can we meet you for lunch at Tre's?"

"I'll be there," Frank said and placed the phone back on the receiver. He flipped onto his back, placing his hands behind his head, and tried to wake up. Closing his eyes he concentrated on how to best remedy the situation of which he had just been notified. This was the third time this month; he could not afford the pattern that was starting to emerge. As his mind considered the alternatives, Menceti felt Tanya's fingernails as she reached over and began playing with the hairs on his chest. He grabbed her hand hard and removed it.

"Not now," he told her. "Go play with the dog or something."

*

Susan woke up early and went down to the kitchen. She opened the freezer and pulled out a large bag of frozen blueberry waffles. She broke two waffles from the others and replaced the bag next to the ice tray. She placed them into the toaster oven and went into the den. She flipped on the television and tuned it to The Weather Channel, then picked up the phone and dialed. After two rings, a voice picked up.

"Hello."

"Jeff ?"

"Who's this?"

"Susan. Susan Ranson."

"Hey, what's up?"

At least he remembers me, Susan thought. "What are you doing today ?" She asked.

"No plans, why?"

So far, so good. "I was thinking I could come over and talk with you, do a little interviewing or something?" There was a moments of silence before he answered. *Maybe this wasnt a good idea,* she wondered.

"Sure, bring your suit, we'll take the boat out."

"Great, I'll see you in about an hour then."

"See you then." She hung up. Susan went over to the counter and took the waffles from the toaster. She was sitting down to eat when David walked in from outside. He was wearing the same clothes as the night before. Susan heard two honks, and looking through the window above the sink, she saw Wendy's car. David looked at Susan.

"It's not what you think," he said. His wife's eyes told him she knew otherwise.

*

Even though Bender had suggested it, Laura did not move into his office. She respected him too much, regardless of how his house was kept. She was sitting at her desk reviewing the information that Doyle had faxed her. She had called him earlier and offered to use the FBI's Automated Fingerprint Identification System or AFIS computer to find the owner of the partial prints found on Cathy Whitmore's body. The AFIS department up at Langley, Virginia, had told her that it would be a few hours before they could work in her request, but she should hear back in a day or two. She had just walked into her office after getting a drink of water when the phone rang.

"Special Agent Wilson," she answered.

"Miss Wilson, this is Mike Sebastian, DEA, Ft. Myers. Liz Hobbs thought we should touch base. I understand you're the new AIC down there."

"Yeah, well temporarily. Until John gets back."

"How is the old fart?"

"He's okay. But he won't be doing much housework for a while."

"That geezer hasn't done housework in his life!" The two laughed. That was true.

"What can I do for you, Mr. Sebastian?"

"Call me Mike. I could come down there or you could fly here, whatever. I just want to compare notes, and make sure we don't step on each other's toes, again."

"That sounds like a plan," Laura said as she doodled on the paper desk calendar. "Hey Mike, how far are you from Sanibel Island?"

"We're close by; it's right off the coast. About fifteen minutes from here."

Great, Laura thought, "Listen, how about I come there? I need to speak to someone who is up on Sanibel anyway."

"Sanibel. The bureau must pay a lot more than my outfit," Mike kidded.

"I wish. It's professional, trust me."

"Call me back with the particulars and I'll have someone meet you at the airport," he told her, "I look forward to working with you."

"Me, too. What's your number up there?"

The DEA agent gave her his phone and beeper numbers, and exchanged some more pleasantries before she hung up the phone. She picked it back up and called her boss's old friend to let him know she was coming.

*

David called Wendy from his office and asked her to meet him for lunch. She said breakfast would be better, since she hadn't eaten since last night. They compromised, and she joined him at a small outdoor cafe downtown.

It was a new place, part of the revitalization of the historic buildings of Ft. Myers. It was close to the old courthouse, in a mall that was converted from a theater built at the turn of the century. It was becoming a hangout for the attorneys that worked in the county seat.

Wendy sat across from David inside the small restaurant. It was much too hot outside to occupy the white wrought iron chairs out front. She was swirling her straw around inside the cup of iced cappuccino while he watched. She seductively wrapped her lips around the straw, then bit the top. David's reaction brought out a giggle from her lipstick-coated smile.

"I guess you know that we, Susan and I, don't get along well," he told, her trying to be serious.

"I kinda got that feeling last night when I felt your hands under my dress."

"I'm sorry about that; I was a little drunk."

Wendy felt insulted, "I hope you're not sorry, and I sure hope it wasn't because you were drunk."

That was what David was waiting for. "I'm glad to hear you say that."

Wendy slurped the bottom of her glass with the straw. "After the election, Susan and I are splitting, and I will probably be moving up to Washington, at least half the year."

"So that was not a one night stand?"

"Unless you say so," David said. He wasn't going to leave Susan, but it was nice having something on the side, especially now.

So Susan was full of shit, Wendy thought, *this guy's a big baby. He just needed someone who wanted to be his wife, not his boss.*

"I would love to be your 'other woman.'"

"I just need you to understand, we need to be discreet about it."

"Like last night?" She giggled. David grabbed her arm and pulled her so she was leaning across the table, close to him.

"No! I mean like starting now we can't act like a couple; no one can know about it!" He squeezed her arm. "The people who back me, financially, for the election want a loving husband and wife. Do you understand?"

"Sure, Baby." He released her arm and she rubbed it to start the circulation. "Does that mean I should stop the feature about you?"

David sat back and thought about it. He looked around and watched his colleagues as they undressed Wendy in their heads. Some gave him approving smiles or nods. But this meeting would not be mentioned by them, everyone had their own little secrets.

"No, keep writing. I'll tell Susan and the others that I told you I'd be available 24 hours a day."

"Personally, I think she already knows."

"She's not as smart as she appears," David said. "She told me to get someone else to cover my campaign."

*

Doyle was on the phone with Laura when his pager went off. He gave the FBI agent his home number and copied the time of her flight onto the back of a business card in his walletbefore hanging up. He then phoned the duty officer who transferred him to the Chief of Police. The Chief told Doyle he had just received a disturbing call from Dr. Ramirez. It seemed that Whitmore's sister-in-law had taken custody of the old man and was intending to fly them both back to Canada. Luckily she was stopped at the front desk, tickets in hand. One of the nurses had become suspicious when the old man asked if it would be cold on the plane.

"Why wasn't he arrested? How could this happen, Doyle?"

"Ramirez asked that I wait a few days."

"Since when did you start taking orders from doctors? You're a cop."The Chief replied.

"He said it would upset Whitmore."

"Everyone gets upset when they are arrested, Doyle."

Doyle defended himself. "You didn't see the guy, he wasn't normal." The detective went on to explain his visit with Whitmore.

"Okay, next time call me or something."

"Is he in custody now?"

"Yeah, the county is watching him."

"What about the sister-in-law?"

"We can't charge her with anything; the man was not in custody."

*

Susan walked down the wood planking stopping at the second to last berth at the Lost Cove Marina. He was holding a Margarita in his hand when she saw him. He stood up and waved her on board. She tossed a red canvas gym bag to him, which he caught. Her white cotton skirt caught one of the stanchions when she hopped on board, tearing it down the side and causing her to spill her purse on the deck. Jeff jumped up and ran over to her, picking up the contents while she struggled to free herself and her clothing.

"Rule number one," Jeff said, looking up at her, "Don't wear skirts on boats."

Susan picked up the gym bag containing her tape recorder, some paper, and her swimsuit.

"If you want to go change, I'll cast us off." Susan just nodded and headed below.

The cabin of the boat was much larger than it looked from the outside. The forty-four foot all wood cabin cruiser had been built in 1956 but was in perfect shape. It had two berths, the forward one equipped with a king sized bed. The main room was decorated with hand carved mahogany. Brass railings and etched glass windows were but two of the custom touches. The galley had all the modern conveniences, but they were well integrated by the skillful design of the renovations, as were the sliding glass doors leading aft from the main cabin. The craft was a floating work of art, and she could only estimate what it would cost to build such a vessel today.

Susan pulled two swimsuits from her bag. The first was a black one piece. She had been wearing it the past two years. High cut, but not too revealing. It was the only one that David allowed her to wear in public, and even that was only after she stopped speaking to him for a week.

She also had with her a yellow French-cut bikini. She only wore it when she went to tanning booths during the winter. She took it out and tried it on. Susan studied the reflection in the mirror. She still thought she looked heavy, but what the hell, no one would see her except Jeff. Susan just knew that he would not say anything mean, even if he thought so. She was kind of excited about going out on the boat, and knowing that David would not be around made the temptation too hard to resist.

*

After saying good-bye to Wendy, David made his way back to his office. In the lobby, Shirley saw him as he waited for the elevator.

"David! Wait up!" she yelled, her voice echoing off the marble granite walls and floor. The DA waited patiently for his assistant. They elevator doors opened as she reached him, and they both stepped inside. "Here," she said, catching her breath, "Look at this!" She handed him a green file. Inside were charts and graphs with explanations that he did not understand.

"What am I looking at?" he asked.

Shirley scooted next to him and pointed to the   paragraph titled "Conclusion". "Don't you see?" she asked.

"No," he said after reading the words for the third time, What am I looking at?"

"This is the lab report on the perspiration samples. It clearly states that there were two types of secretions on the sheets. The first was the victim's. That's a match; we expected that, so it's no big deal. But look at the second sample. The secretor status is nil; the person is a non-secretor!" David had no clue as to what she was talking about, and the look on his face betrayed that.

"That means we've really narrowed the field!"

"What the hell are you talking about, Shirley? Is this like DNA or something? I thought that takes weeks to get back."

"Yeah, DNA samples do. But secretor samples don't, we don't need to ship that out. We do the tests right here!" David was still puzzled as the doors to the elevator opened. The two stepped out and walked to his office. Shirley tried to explain along the way.

"A secretor status measures, well not measures, but shows, blood type, a.k.a. DNA, in the peripheral secretions from the body."

"What's a peripheral secretion?" David asked as he grabbed his mail from his secretary.

"Peripheral secretions are sweat, semen, stuff like that," Shirley answered. "The point is that eighty-five percent of human beings are secretors."

David waited for her to continue, but she didn't say anything, just followed him into his office and stood there. David sat behind his desk. "Well, what do you think?" Shirley asked.

"About what?" David was confused. "I have no idea why you are telling me this other than the fact that I will not be getting DNA evidence now, right?"

"Don't you see?" Shirley asked. "All we need to do is find out whether the husband is a secretor. The odds of that are very low; only fifteen percent of the population. It will back us up!If he is a match, it will convince any jury he's guilty!"

Or innocent, David thought; that's all he needed. "Great, leave me the report, and I'll look it over. How reliable is this stuff."

"Very reliable, very reliable," she said.

"Good, thanks a lot," he said, opened up his day planner, and picked up the phone. "Is there anything else?"

"You know about the doctor, don't you?" Shirley asked. David hung up the phone.

"What about him?"

"He tried to leave the country last night." David slammed the planner shut.

"What! Why wasn't I told about it?!" David demanded, coming around from the desk. Shirley stepped back out to where Donna was sitting, "How? When?" David screamed.

"Detective Doyle called earlier and explained it to me," Shirley said. David looked over at his secretary. "Donna, did you know about this?!"

"Yes, sir," Donna said, unshaken. She was accustomed to her boss's temper. "I put a message on your desk about it. That detective wants you to call him." David turned and stormed back into his office and slammed the door. Shirley retreated to her own office, as Donna heard David screaming for her to get Doyle on the phone.

*

"Wow!" Jeff exclaimed. Susan covered herself with her hands. She hadn't counted on that reaction. Jeff was sitting at the controls on the flybridge when she had climbed up the ladder to stand next to him.

"Please don't. I feel fat." She was embarrassed and thought that he was making fun at her expense.

"Fat would be the one word I would not have thought of using to describe you in that suit," he told her honestly. Now Susan was really embarrassed. Jeff thought she looked great and could hardly take his eyes off her. She told him she had bought it a while back but was too shy to wear it at the beach.

"Why don't you go lie out on the deck while I work our way over to Upper Captiva? Then, if you want, we can stop at the joint where Buffett wrote 'Cheeseburger in Paradise'."

"You don't mind?"

"Hell no. I have to sail this pig, so get comfortable. Lay down, get naked if you want to!"

"I feel like I am," she said.

"Believe me, I know what a naked woman looks like and you ain't naked."

"Front or back?" she asked.

"You ain't naked in the front or back. Well maybe the back." He looked down at the small thin band of yellow.

"Please knock it off. I feel ridiculous as it is!" She really did not mind the attention, but this was not the impression she wanted to give. "I meant the front or back deck?"

"Forward or aft," he corrected.

"Forward or aft what?"

"The forward is the front part of the boat, the aft is the back," he explained.

"Oh." Susan said. "So which one?"

"Forward. That way I can look down and stare at you," he teased.

"Aft it is," she said.

She climbed down the stainless steel ladder and laid her towel on the padded couch built into the aftwell. His back was to her, so she laid on her stomach and untied the bikini top. She stared at his tan shoulders and wondered what it would be like. She looked at the ring on her finger and reminded herself she was married. Not that it had stopped David. She closed her eyes and drifted off to sleep.

*

Susan bolted straight up when she felt the ice cold water hit her back. She saw Jeff sitting across from her, holding a water pistol. She had been asleep and was slightly dizzy from the mix of sun and waking up so quickly. It took a few seconds before she realized her top was still on her towel. Quickly grabbing it, she tried to cover herself, but the small piece of cloth only drew more attention to her predicament. Her face was red with embarrassment. She looked over at Jeff whose grin was followed with an approving nod when she dropped the bikini top onto the towel. Susan wanted to be mad, but couldn't. The saying about dreaming aboard boats had proved to be true, and he had satisfied her once already. Jeff did not back away when she went to him. This time it would not be a dream.

*

"I don't know what to say, Mr. Menceti," Alvin stated as he paced back and forth.

"Where did our security break down? Is there a leak that we don't know about?" Menceti asked his lieutenant calmly. Frank then turned to James and Tre who were sitting along the pool quietly, trying not to be the subject of the big man's wrath. But the tone of their boss's voice frightened the three men. The first two times this happened Frank went on a rampage, but he had not even raised his voice at them today. Not once.

"From what I understand, it was just a quirk. A coincidence. Some military helicopter just happened to fly over them, that's all," Alvin said. Frank looked over at Alvin, then leaned back into the white wood framed chair, put his hands on the matching round picnic table in front of him, and let out a deep breath. The sun shone on his face, and the banker loosened his tie and unbuttoned his sportcoat. For the first time, the three underlings noticed their boss was sweating. James quickly went over and raised the large flowered umbrella that stuck up through the middle of the table.

"They were just in the wrong place at the wrong time, Mr. M.," James commented and looked at his two colleagues, who both shrugged their shoulders. Their boss looked up at James, then pushed himself up from the chair, brushing away James' attempts to help.

"A quirk? A coincidence? Is that what you are telling me?" Frank stood up and walked to the other side of the pool. He had a business to run and a bank to manage, and these three Irish or English or French or whatever the hell they were had brought him nothing but bad news and costly mistakes.

"Three shipments in less than a week and it's just coincidence?" James and Alvin were speechless. They needed answers and had none. Tre spoke up, "It's like that saying."

"What the fuck are you talking about, shit for brains?" Menceti asked him.

"Bad things come in threes," Tre repeated.

"Bad things come in threes?" Frank mimicked him, then looked at Alvin and James who turned away. They were just glad that Tre was the center of attention.

"Bad things come in threes?" Their boss asked louder. Tre started to answer, but Menceti turned around, pulled out a 9mm semi automatic from inside his sportcoat, and pulled the trigger five times. Tre fell back. He hadn't felt the last two slugs. Frank turned to James and Alvin. "Damn right bad things come in threes. Now there are only two of you, so no more excuses."

*

The sun was setting on the horizon as Susan and Jeff sat and sipped at the pink frozen drinks.

"I could get used to this," she told him as she wrapped his bare arms around her. She leaned back and rested her head on his chest, closing her eyes.

"So how did you and numbnuts meet?" he asked her. She explained.

"It doesn't sound as bad as I thought."

"It gets better," Susan said. She explained it was when David's parents were killed that the problem began. At first, David was withdrawn and barely talked to her. He threw himself into his work and started to get a reputation as a very tough lawyer. Publicly, they were the perfect couple, but privately, Susan was having second thoughts about the marriage. They had engaged in a very active sex life prior to the accident, but since his parents' death, things had changed. David started to drink and would only touch her if he was drunk. Then the violence started. He would get angry whenever she would mention sex. At first it was just verbal assaults, but then it had turned physical. He would slap her and call her a slut, then leave. He accused her of sleeping around, and of not really loving him, but trapping him into proposing because of his family's wealth. After a few months, she couldn't take it and asked for a divorce. David begged her not to go, promising he would seek help. He went to a counselor with her in Miami. David said he didn't want to go to one locally because he didn't want the newspapers to find out. Susan moved into her own room, and her sex life ended. They gradually stopped going to counseling.

After six months, Susan never mentioned divorce. In 1983, David ran for District Attorney, running on a "get tough with drugs and alcohol" campaign. Using his brother and parents as examples, but not mentioning his own problems, he won. The relationship that looked so loving and together to the public, was hollow and empty in private. The two lived as strangers in the large house. Susan thanked God every night that David was sterile, and no children had to live through this.

"For a long time I have not felt like a woman," Susan told him. "I guess that's why your art appeals to me. It's as if all the anger and loneliness that I feel is on that canvas."

"I guess I should be flattered, but I wish you hated my paintings," Jeff said as he caressed her shoulder.

"Why?" she turned to him.

"Because then you would never be able to relate to the pain in them. You'd be happy," Jeff explained, "You should be happy."

"But even last night," the tears started down her cheek, "I knew I looked good, I mean really good. But no one would talk to me except Sam."

"I talk to you," Jeff said and hugged her.

"I know. You're different; you're not afraid of him."

*

"Your client tried to flee the country," Shirley Lambton, Assistant District Attorney, said.

"My client didn't know up from down. He just did as he was told by an overzealous relative," Elliot Pinder argued as he wiped the dust off his three hundred dollar loafers. He was the best money could buy, and Whitmore had money. With no children or other family, except his sister-in-law, the doctor could afford the best. After all, what good was a beautiful home and fancy cars if you were in prison?

"His wife had a serious drug problem."

"He was trying to help her through it!"

"He was the one who caused it!" Shirley kicked the chair next to her across the room. Pinder looked over at David.

"Stop the theatrics, will you, Mr. Ranson? I'm not impressed." David told Shirley to get the chair and sit down. Obviously Elliot Pinder was not to be intimidated. Whitmore showed no reaction to any of the events in the room. He had been sitting quietly to the right of his lawyer. His hands were folded on the conference table, his eyes burning into the prosecutor.

"I know for a fact that he was illegally treating his wife for an addiction, a job he is not trained for, or licensed to do," David spoke succinctly.

"And I have a motion to suppress the fact that she had a drug problem and the fact that there were marriage problems," Pinder countered.

"Based on what?" the Assistant D.A. asked.

"Based on the fact that the only way the police knew any of that was because my client had confided with his lawyer, Mr. David Ranson, who he believed was advising him on a confidential matter."

"That's a bunch of B.S.," David interjected.

"My client believed that you, Mr. Ranson, were offering legal advice. Therefore, he expected that anything he told you would be privileged information."

"Privileged my ass!" Shirley said.

"Mr. Ranson had acted on my client's behalf before; why not now?" Elliot Pinder relaxed and laid his hands on his lap.

He was good, very good. The prosecutors looked at each other. Yes, David had acted on Whitmore's behalf before, and the case could be argued.

"I was acting as a prosecutor when he told me. I was questioning him on an investigation that I was involved with," David said without emotion.

"Why would a prosecutor be questioning someone who wasn't a suspect in a crime? Or did someone just forget to read him his rights before you walked in, David? You can't have it both ways. Either wrongful imprisonment or my client 'rides the friendly skies' this afternoon."

David was watching his ride to a Congressional seat disappear right before his eyes. "I'm also asking to suppress that so-called confession he made because my client was denied proper counsel."

"He can say what he wants, but it's not true," David tried to sound convincing but knew he didn't. "The police already suspected the problem and would have found out about it on their own. Reasonable Conclusion, counselor. Cathy got the drugs from her husband; the records were meticulously kept by Whitmore. You'll lose on that one."

The look on Pinder's face alerted the District Attorney. Whitmore hadn't told his lawyer about the records, and Elliot Pinder did not like to be the one kept in the dark. The defense attorney asked for some time alone with his client. David was feeling better. He was back in control. The two prosecutors left the small conference room in the county jail. David sent Shirley to get some Cokes, even offering one to the doctor and to Pinder, both of whom refused. After a few minutes the prosecutors were invited back inside.

Elliot Pinder closed his briefcase and set it beside his chair. His client settled back into his trance-like stare at David, who hardly noticed it now.

"Okay," Elliot offered, "False prescriptions, five years probation, no prison time."

"No time, no deal," David had gained some confidence in the hall. That and the fact that a deal would not give him the boost he needed for the campaign.

"David, he operates the only free clinic on the island. Have some heart."

"I have a very strong case."

"Okay," said the defense. "He'll turn over his medical license."

"He's going to lose it anyway."

"Dammit, consider his age! Any time is a death sentence!"

"I represent the people, and the people want someone to pay for this crime!" David said smugly.

"You're using this for politics. Even if you get a conviction, it won't hold on appeal. You know it, and I know it," Pinder wasn't lying, and they all knew it.

"I'm sorry," David said.

"A jury will free him. We both know that; save the old guy the trouble. How about man two, assisted suicide? Look at the guy; he's not Dr. Kovorkian!"

David sat across from him and shook his head, "Was there anything else?"

"What else do you want?" Pinder was exasperated, "Did you just come down to hear me talk?"

David gathered his notes and stood up. Shirley followed her boss's lead.

"All I want is your client behind bars. I'll see you in court, Elliot."

"This is not like you, David," Pinder yelled as the two prosecutors walked out the door.

"This is exactly like me, Elliot!" David answered from the hall, his words echoing off the concrete and cinder block walls and out the exit. David tingled with excitement on his way home as he watched the burning reds and oranges of the dusk sky. He loved a good court battle, especially one before an election!

*

The glowing horizon was also visible from the Gecko as it sailed through Red Fish pass on its way home. Jeff was sitting on the bridge; Susan was by his side. They followed the other day-trippers down Pine Island Sound past Buck Key.

It had been a smoldering hot day, and even though the sun was no longer visible, the humidity still made it feel like it was eighty degrees. The breeze had helped when they were in the Gulf, but the mangroves surrounding the channel contained the heat. The lights of houses near St. James City were visible to their left, near the reflective red and green markers that led the way to Tarpon Bay and the marina. Susan was excited when she saw them. The dolphins were playing about five yards away from the Gecko. Jeff throttled down until they stopped moving and released the anchor. He went down the ladder and disappeared into the boat. Susan was leaning over the side, watching the mammals, getting as close as she could. Jeff returned with a bucket full of bait fish.

"Do you want to feed them?" he asked her.

"At least someone will get some dinner," Susan teased.

"I wanted to go eat on Captiva. You jumped me, remember?" They threw some bait fish near the dolphins, who came over to the boat immediately. The creatures squeaked and whistled and generally clowned around until they were convinced the humans had nothing more to offer them. The phone inside the cabin rang as they watched the animals swim back out to the channel. He went inside and answered it, while she used the head, as he called it. He was up on the bridge when she came out; the cellular phone sat dormant on the shelf behind him.

"I thought you used a radio on a boat?" She asked.

"Sometimes, but the phone is easier. The radio is for longer ranges."

"Who calls you out here?"

"My agent mostly. He said someone wants to buy one of my paintings. They will be waiting for us on the dock when we get back."

"I was hoping we could do something tonight," she said, disappointed

"I'm sorry, but I need to speak to Luis. We could go out tomorrow if you like."

"I never even interviewed you. All we talked about was me, " Susan sighed.

"That's okay, we have plenty of time. Besides, your stories are probably more interesting than mine," Jeff said as he maneuvered the boat around large black lumps floating in the water. He pointed to one, "Manatees."

Susan went down to take a look, leaning over to touch one while they slowly moved alongside.

"You know, I've lived here almost ten years, and this is the first time I ever saw a dolphin or a manatee up close. Thanks, it was really sweet of you."

"Anytime."

She leaned over and kissed him on the cheek. They turned into the marina entrance, passing the rows of private yachts and smaller boats that were tied up.

"David makes enough money; you should get a boat, even if it's just a small one."

"We, I mean David, does have one, over there," Susan pointed it out. It was a twenty-nine foot Sea Ray, white, with a red trimmed hull. It was dwarfed by the sleek forty-five foot Cigarette boat in the slip beside it. "But I don't know how to drive it."

"I can teach you if you want," Jeff offered.

"Thanks, but I'd rather just let someone else do it. I don't even know the language." She paused, and then added, "Most of the time, because of our problems, only he uses it, and then only as a way to get out of the house."

She looked at the boat with disdain as they came closer to its berth, "I really think that he comes out here at night with other women. He claims that he and Larry go night fishing or scuba diving but I suspect he's lying; I just don't have the guts to come out here at night and check on him."

"Probably, he doesn't seem to have changed much since we were kids," Jeff said. Susan was surprised. It was the first time she had heard him say anything about his childhood. But she didn't want to upset him like that time in the restaurant.

"Have you ever caught him?" Jeff asked.

"No, I can't prove that he's cheating. I just know it. Call it woman's intuition." She paused, "But if I could, I'd leave him and sue his ass for every dime in the divorce!"

"Why don't you ask to go diving with them? He couldn't say no," Jeff asked.

"I'm not certified, and I hate fishing."

The fueling station and dockhouse came into view behind some of the larger sailboats. Jeff expertly docked the boat alongside the fuel pump. He filled both tanks of the boat and swiped his card in the machine.

"It's just like a gas station," Susan observed.

"I suppose."

"Oh yeah, you don't own a car, you rent them," she teased.

"For the amount of driving I do, there is no reason for me to buy one," Jeff stated as he started for his private slip. Across the marina, Susan could see the parking lot. Luis and another man were standing there, looking over at them. Susan waved, but neither man waved back.

"Not very friendly are they?" she commented.

Jeff looked up and over at the men, then back to the job at hand of bringing the Gecko into the narrow confines of the slip. He barely touched the old tires that hung over the side to act as cushioning between the boat and dock.

"Your agent looks kind of scary," Susan said, "Especially with that scar on his forehead. Yuck."

"Yeah, he's not a handsome man."

"No, he's not." Susan turned and went inside the cabin. She threw on a skirt and sheer top over the swimsuit, then grabbed her bags.

Back on deck, the two men had walked down to the slip and helped Jeff tie off the lines. Susan kissed the artist and stepped onto the wooden planking. He told her he would call her soon. She strutted past the agent and his friend. She had not felt like this for a long time, she felt like a woman. Luis and Andre watched her go by, then walked up onto the boat.

"Who was that?" Luis asked, stroking the small mustache above his lip.

"The flavor of the month?" Andre asked with a chuckle.

"Something like that." Jeff did not like the comments, but knew they would continue if he showed his annoyance to the two men. The three of them watched Susan as she disappeared down the dock.

"You have good taste, my friend," Luis commented, trying to get a reaction.

"What did you need that was so important that I have to let that," he gestured toward Susan, "go home alone?"

"We have other things to do than to look for some slut to play with," Andre said.

"She's a reporter that is writing about me," Jeff said as Luis opened the door to the cabin.

"Yeah, whatever. We need to talk about the Virgin Islands." The three men walked inside the cabin.

"I heard you got some FBI agent whacked; good job, guys. How'd your boss feel about that?" Jeff could see it was a sore point. *Good*, he thought. Luis sat on the sofa and poured himself a drink. Andre went to the refrigerator and began making a sandwich. "Make yourselves at home," Jeff said sarcastically. Luis bent down and opened the black leather briefcase he had with him.

"This guy who is a banker friend of yours. What's his name..."

"Menceti," Andre yelled from the galley.

"Yeah, Menceti. He is someone we need to get in bed with."

"Francis Menceti is not a real nice guy. Are you sure?" Jeff asked.

"He's a fucking sleazeball, and yeah, we're sure," Andre said as he bit into the large Italian roll filled with cold cuts. Luis laid a pile of photographs on the table. Some showed just Menceti, others had Menceti with people whom Jeff did not recognize, and some even had James, Tre, and Alvin in them.

"Recognize these guys?" Luis said, pointing to a grainy, black and white photo of Alvin.

"Yeah. One of Frank's goons; I think his name is Allen, or Alvin. Something with an "A." Some piece of shit; I've met him a few times," Jeff answered.

"Good. Set up a meeting," Luis said as he sipped the large glass of sweet tea. He never drank alcohol.

"No problem; when?"

"As soon as possible," Andre answered.

"Whatever you say," Jeff rose from the sofa and went to the counter near Andre.

"Hey, asshole," Luis said,"Don't fuck this up." The look on Jeff's face was one of innocence, and he pretended to be deeply hurt.

"Knock it off, Strata," Andre ordered. "If it goes well, you may not have to run any more operations with us."

"You mean *for* you,"Jeff said, "And I'll believe that when I see it."

The two visitors stood up and gathered the materials from the table. Andre grabbed a Coke from the refrigerator, and the two walked out onto the aft deck. It was already growing dark outside. No one else was around, the only sounds were the wildlife that surrounded the marina.

"Oh, and Jeff," Andre added. "I wouldn't be letting any writer talk to me if I were in your position. People end up dead that way." Jeff escorted them off his boat without comment. They would get theirs, he reminded himself, it was just a matter of time.

He waited until the headlights were out of view, then flipped on the television and picked up the phone.

*

The Doyle family held hands and bowed their heads while giving thanks for the food in front of them. When they were done with the blessing, Brian scooped up some mashed potatoes and plopped them onto Jenny's plate.

"I don't want any more, Daddy," the seven year old with pink ribbons in her hair whined.

"It's not that much; you can eat it," her mother told her.

Brian watched his daughter pout and slam her fork down on the glass table.

"That's enough," he told her. The tears started running down her cheek, but the looks on her parents' faces told the little girl she'd better do as they said. But she was young.

"I don't like potatoes, Momma," she tried once more.

"If you don't eat them, you don't get any dessert."

As if on cue, Sarah stood up from the table and walked over to the oven to check on the peach and apple cobblers that were baking.

"Me and Momma made apple cobbler for dinner, Daddy. We used a cookbook and everything."

"That's great, honey; I can't wait to try it."

"You have to eat the apple cause that's the one I made." She put a spoonful of potatoes in her mouth. He was still amazed at how she could be crying one second and laughing the next.

"Why don't you tell your dad what we did at work today?" Sarah said as she sat back down and fixed her plate.

She was the curator for the shell museum on the island. She often brought her daughter to work with her, especially during the summer. Jenny told her dad about the hard day looking at giant spiders.

"Spider crabs, not spiders," her mother corrected.

"Momma's boss said I was very smart," Jenny bragged to her father.

"I always knew you were, and I'll bet you can't wait to start first grade," Doyle told her. Her placement scores were high, but Doyle was not sure he could afford to send Jenny to the private Baptist school Sarah had picked out.

"The only one is in Ft. Myers, and that is a long drive," Brian pointed out.

"But her friends from church are there," Sarah argued.

"I know; I have to think about it," he said. "The island's school is top of the line, even if it is public. Just think about it."

The two sat in silence and watched as Jenny made a disgusting pile of potatoes, meatloaf, and lima beans in the middle of her plate. Suddenly aware of her audience, she covered the food with ketchup and scooped it up into her mouth. She smiled for her fans.

"Maybe you could take a day off. Come with me and Jenny to the beach."

"Honey, do you realize what it's like to be the only full time homicide detective on this island? I head a division that has never solved the only case of murder this community ever had!" Doyle looked at his wife. "And now we have a second one."

"I just thought we could spend some time together now that you caught the man." She looked down at her plate and continued eating.

"I'm sorry. 1 have a feeling this case isn't as cut and dried as it appears. I promise I'll take the first day off that I can." Sarah did not look up.

"Daddy?"

"What, honey?"

"Have you ever shot someone?" Doyle looked at his wife, who seemed just as surprised at the question.

"No, sweetie. Why?"

"Then why do you have a gun?" Doyle saw that she really wanted to know. He did not know what to say. He had never used it, never even pulled it out, except in yearly qualifications. He also had never felt threatened. He did not want to scare his daughter by explaining that it was to shoot other people in case they shot at him.

"His boss told him he has to, because all the other policeman do," Sarah said. The simple explanation satisfied the little girl, and soon she was telling her dad about all the neat things she had found on the beach that day.

Later, sitting in his chair, Brian wondered if he could shoot another human being. He knew he had the skills to do it, but could he actually pull the trigger? He hoped he wouldn't ever find out.

*

Susan pulled in the drive around seven o'clock. David was coming down the stairs and saw his wife open the kitchen door. Dressed in a suit and tie, he was fiddling with the cufflinks on his shirt when she walked in the house. He asked her where she had been.

"Out."

"I know you were out. I want to know where?"

"I was working, interviewing Jeff Strata. I think you know him."

Susan placed a bag from the Dairy Queen on the table. It was the only fast food restaurant on the island. She reached in and pulled out some burgers and fries and set them on two plates..

"What the hell is that?" David asked.

Susan stood at the counter and cocked her head to one side; but did not turn around. "Dinner," she said. She waited for her husband to make some smart-ass comment about how lazy she was or how bad a wife she was or something else just as stupid.

"I'm having dinner at the University Club with the Governor."

"The governor of what?" Susan asked and bit into a burger.

"Of Florida."

"I'm happy for you," she said. "Do you want ketchup for your fries?"

"Yeah, he wants to meet me tonight."

Susan almost spit out her food, "Tonight? Oh great! What time?"

"About twenty minutes," David replied as he grabbed his shoes and sat down to put them on.

"How am I supposed to be ready in twenty minutes?"

"You're not. I'm taking Wendy."

"The Wendy that works with me?!" She should have expected he'd take her out to dinner.

"It's a political thing." David got up and pushed on her chair when he passed by looking for his car keys. "She's taking some photo's."

"I take it you won't be home early," Susan said.

"You told me to get someone else to cover my campaign, so I did. That's all. You can believe what you want."

"I suppose that's where you stayed the other night too.!"

"We talked for a few hours; nothing happened," he lied to his wife. "You don't hear me bitching about you fucking Jeff."

"I'm not even going to acknowledge that statement!" She went into the den and flipped on the television. At least she'd have a peaceful night at home. David ran around getting ready and annoying his wife whenever possible. When he was ready he came back in the den.

"Don't you look just spiffy?" Susan commented.

He adjusted his tie in the mirror next to the door, "I'll pass your regards to Governor Snelling. Oh, by the way, someone named Chris White called about an hour ago. He said there was a crash or something, and you should call him before seven. His number is out near the phone." David quickly stepped out the door. Susan looked up at the clock. It was seven fifteen. That son of a bitch.

She picked up the phone. *Why did she feel guilty about Jeff when she knew he did not give a damn about sleeping with Wendy* she wondered as she listened to Chris' phone ring. He picked up on the ninth ring.

"You just caught me," Chris told her, "I'm on my way to Naples Airport to catch a helicopter, do you want to come along? I'll pick you up in front of Kmart in San Carlos Park."

The television reporter quickly told Susan about the accident. It was some sixteen-year-old kid who had just received his private pilot's license in the Everglades. He had flown his family to Marathon Key for dinner and had not returned. The search went out and a Civil Air Patrol pilot had spotted the wreckage. The first

rescuers on the scene did not find anyone alive; the single-engine PA128 Piper
Warrior had landed upside down in four feet of mud and water. They were still trying
to remove the bodies. The TV station was chartering a helicopter to go out there. The
Bell 209 sat four, but Chris said the only people going were a cameraman, the pilot
and himself.

"We have an open seat, and I thought of you."

"I would love to hitch a ride. I'll leave right now!"

*

Wendy looked stunning in the new dress David had paid for. After tearing the
white number when he pulled it off her the other night, replacing it was the least he
could do. Wendy looked painted into this one, too, which suited David fine. Her
cleavage was shown off by the low neckline, and the circular cuts up the side gave the
impression that she was wearing nothing underneath. The gown was also white, as were
the five inch heels she wore with it. In fact, almost every piece of clothing the girl
owned was white. She believed it went better with her blond hair.

They pulled up to the University Club; the top of the convertible German
sports car was up so as not to ruin her hair. Susan hadn't warranted that much
consideration in years, and the thought put David in a good mood. He waited as the
valet opened his door and slipped the kid a twenty.

"Keep an eye on it, would you?"

He watched as the kid ran around and helped Wendy out of the vehicle. The valet
could not keep his eyes off of her. David walked over and took her hand. He knew that
the teenager was envious. Of his car or of Wendy, he wasn't sure.

*

The pilot was waiting by his weather-beaten chopper when Chris and Susan
pulled into the General Aviation parking lot. The flaking yellow paint was spotted
with gray primer, and the machine looked like it should be up on blocks in someone's
backyard and not flying high above the ground. The pilot walked over and introduced
himself as Jim. He saw the worry in all three faces.

"Don't worry," he assured them. "She flies a lot better than she looks."

"I hope so," Chris said. Susan sat up front, while the two TV newsmen sat in
the back seat. The videographer wanted to be behind the pilot so that they would both
be able to see the crash site at the same time and have the same view. They took off
after receiving clearance and headed to the Everglades.

*

The District Attorney and his mistress were escorted to Governor Snelling's
table. Wendy was awed by the elegance of the room. The ceilings must have been over
twenty feet high, with five giant crystal chandeliers evenly distributed around the
room. The carpet was deep and blood red. Waiters and busboys stood along the
sculptured walls of the private club, waiting to be called. They all wore uniforms,

the busboy's vests were white, while the waiter's wore green. The smell of cigars was rampant. The anti-smoking laws were not enforced here. Separated from the rest were three tables, each recessed into the side walls. A hollow oak partition could be pulled from the wall to close off the three areas forming small meeting or dining rooms. Presently, two of the tables were unoccupied. At the third, directly opposite the entrance to the room, Snelling sat talking with Francis Menceti. Scott Zoe was going over the next week's agenda when he looked up and saw David coming toward them.

"Here he comes, Governor." The Governor looked up and straight at Wendy.

"Damn, Scott. Look at that. Too bad I'm married." *Like that ever stopped you before*, Zoe thought.

"He's married also, sir."

The Governor stood up when they arrived and shook David's hand. He kissed Wendy's.

"You have a lovely wife, David," Snelling said.

"Wendy's not my wife, Governor."

"I'm sorry, I was under the impression you were married." He looked at his chief of staff.

"I am, sir. She's at home."

You two will get right along, Zoe thought.

"Wendy Richardson. I'm a photographer with the local paper, Governor."

"She's following my campaign," David said with a wink..

"You don't have to explain to me, my boy." Wendy blushed, and David could not keep from grinning.

"I'd like you to meet Mr. Francis Menceti, David."

"It's Frank," he said as he reached across and shook hands, "And I hope you won't be taking many pictures tonight, Miss Richardson."

"This is strictly background, Mr. Menceti," Wendy said.

"Frank, Darling'," Snelling said. "Call him Frank."

"Yes, I mean Frank," Wendy repeated.

"I believe you know Scott Zoe, my chief of staff," the governor said.

"We've talked on the phone," David said, shaking Zoe's hand, "But we've never met."

They all waited for Wendy to be seated before they sat down. The waiter came over right away and took their orders. After ordering, Wendy said she needed to go to the ladies room. She excused herself, and left the four men.

"David, I used to have my own *personal photographer*, too. Of course I was much younger then," Snelling said.

"And we didn't bring the bimbos out in public," Zoe added. The Governor nodded in agreement.

"A mistake of inexperience," Snelling said. They all laughed. It was just part of the benefit package of being in politics, they told him. David was reassured that they all could care less about his indiscretions, but he would learn about the proper place and time. When Wendy returned they switched the conversation to politics. They wanted his position on various topics and they gave him what they believed to be the party platform.

"It all boils down to votes," the Governor told him.

Zoe continued, "The whole matter rests with the public's perception of trust. Whoever they trust the most will get the vote."

"But what about people like you, Frank?" David asked. "You spend an awful lot of money on candidates."

"I don't trust any of you; you're all a bunch of crooks!" Frank said, and started laughing. The others joined him and raised their glasses in a toast. David and Wendy laughed too, but neither seemed to get the joke. After a few minutes, after the laughter had died down, David addressed Snelling.

"What I mean, Governor, is what happens when you give money to someone and they are running against what your interests are?" The smiles left all three men's faces.

"This is not small town politics, David. You say what you need to say to get that seat."

"That's right," Frank interjected, "I don't give a flying fuck what you say to get there, as long as you remember your promises to me when you're there." Frank's voice was getting loud, and Scott asked them to tone it down. The room was not very full, but the other diners were looking over.

"What about the voters when I go for reelection?"

"David, David, David. The voters have a short memory; you just repeat the same thing. Trust me, it has worked for a long, long time," Snelling replied.

The waiter came over carrying a phone. He asked for Mr. Menceti, and Frank picked it up and walked over to the corner near the bathroom.

He returned and laid the phone on the tablecloth. It was quickly retrieved by the waiter. Frank did not sit down.

"Is there something wrong?" Snelling asked.

"Something came up, Peter; I need to leave right away." Menceti turned to David and offered his hand, "I'm sorry about this, but business is business."

"I understand completely. It was a pleasure meeting you," David shook his hand.

Frank was halfway across the floor when he turned around and went back to the table. He reached into his pocket.

"Mr. Ranson, I forgot to give you this." He handed David an envelope, "Remember what we talked about tonight." Francis Menceti, then turned and left the club.

*

"I can't see anything!" the helicopter pilot said to himself. The others heard him over the headset. The man sounded worried, and that had the expected effect on his passengers.

"What about all those things?" Susan asked him, pointing to the dials and indicators, trying to help.

"I'm not really equipped for instrument flying," he said. "I didn't realize how dark it was going to be out here."

Susan had noticed where some of the indicators had been removed from the control panel before they took off, but she had trusted the pilot's judgment. Now she wasn't so sure.

"I'm going to turn on the spotlight and try to follow the road."

Susan looked outside. There was no moon, and it was pitch black outside. Since they had overflown Everglades City ten minutes ago, she had not been able to find the horizon. They tried to follow the road below, but she could not see it. She saw only the occasional headlights of someone driving down it. She wished she were one of them at this moment. The helicopter was oscillating; her ears told her that. She looked at an instrument. A little red line on it did not seem right. She then looked over at the pilot. He was sweating, even with the helicopter's air-conditioning blowing full blast. It was evident that their pilot was out of his element.

"Are you all right?" she asked him. He did not answer, but concentrated on flying. She looked into the back seat and saw the others' concerned faces.

"Hey, Jim? Maybe we should just go back?" Chris said over the headset.

"I got paid to take you," the pilot replied. "I can't really afford to cancel; I've already spent a couple hundred bucks on fuel. This ain't American Airlines."

"You'll get paid; just take us back," Chris said.

"I just hope we make it," the videographer said to no one in particular. "There's already been one crash tonight."

*

"There they are."

"I see them, the girl in the white number." The agent's camera auto-winder continued clicking away, taking photos through the zoom lens. His partner aimed a video recorder towards the handsome couple.

David stood outside the club waiting for his car to be brought around. He looked at the check again. Five thousand dollars, and he had only just met the man. Frank Menceti was someone he definitely wanted to stay in touch with.

The valet helped Wendy into the car, then ran around to the driver's side. David gave him another twenty, then pulled out onto College Avenue, spinning the super-wide Goodyear Eagles. They came to the traffic light at US 41. The light was red, and David stopped. Wendy reached over and rubbed his leg.

"What do you want to do now?" David asked her.

She answered by rubbing somewhere else.

*

Susan walked into the general aviation terminal with Chris. The cameraman had gone to get the truck, so they were left watching the Beta-cam and other gear. The small lounge was still open, and the two friends went in to have a drink and wait. The room was dark. The flame from small candles flickered inside colored glass on the tables. The bartender stood behind the empty bar, rinsing beer mugs in the soapy blue water that filled the sink. The two of them walked over to the bar, and Chris laid down a ten spot on the bar.

"A club soda for me and..." He hesitated.

"A drink. I don't care what kind after that." Susan answered.

"And a beer for the lady, please." She sat up on the stool next to his.

"I'll bet that you look great in yellow," the familiar, but slightly slurred voice asked.

*

The black sports car sped past the gates leading into the marina. The parking lot was empty except for the ten or so cars owned by the rental agency. No lights glowed in any offices located in the marina complex. David pulled up to the curb closest to the pier and stopped.

"You can't park here," Wendy told him while pulling the dress back down to her thighs.

"Why not?"

"That's why," she said, pointing to a white sign that read NO PARKING VIOLATORS WILL BE TOWED. David pulled the key out of the ignition and set the parking brake.

"Honey, I'm the District Attorney; they won't tow me."

"It's not my car," Wendy said as she stepped out and followed him towards the water.

*

Laura and Rick were sleeping when the call came in. Rick's hand fumbled around the night table next to his head trying to find the phone in the dark.

"Hello?" he said without opening his eyes.

"Laura Wilson, please," the man's voice asked. Rick rolled over and tapped Laura on the shoulder with the cordless phone.

"It's for you." She grunted a few times, but did not move. He reached over and turned on the lamp. He sat up in the bed and placed the receiver next to her ear.

"Who is it, Rick?" she asked him, unaware the phone was so close to her mouth.

"Agent Oslo," the voice in the phone answered. "He's on the move and coming here, ma'am."

Rick got out of bed and went to the bathroom. Laura opened her eyes and sat up. She picked up the phone. "Who is coming where?" Laura asked.

"Menceti is flying here right now. His jet just left Ft. Myers for Naples, and then it's coming to Key West International."

"Why are you telling me now; can't this wait until morning?" She asked as Rick came back to bed. He flipped off his light, and she flipped on hers and sat up against the headboard.

"You're the AIC. You are supposed to be notified when he's in our area, at least that's what John had us do." This was news to her.

"I wasn't working on this, so I don't know what to tell you," Laura said. "I guess I should be called. Thanks."

"Are you meeting us, or do you want us to come get you?" Laura looked at the clock: 1:39 a.m.. No wonder Bender never had time to unpack those boxes.

"I'll meet you, I guess. Did John come out in the middle of the night?" She knew the answer to that before she asked. "I'm on my way."

Laura stretched her arms and flipped her feet out onto the floor. She went into the bathroom and saw she was a mess. She thanked God she had straight hair. Even though it was past her shoulders, it did not take long to fix. She grabbed her glasses from the shelf above the sink. Laura thought about putting in her contacts but decided it wasn't worth the effort. She was going to a surveillance operation in the middle of the night. She would probably end up in a field somewhere watching a plane land; it really did not matter what she looked like.

*

"I thought I recognized that voice," Susan said as Jeff approached.

"What the hell are you doing here?" He walked over and kissed her on the cheek. Chris moved over, leaving a stool empty between himself and Susan.

"No, thanks," Jeff appreciated the gesture.

"You're not staying? Please sit," Susan said.

"I can't; I'm with some friends," He turned and the two reporters saw Luis and an older man in the booth.

"Isn't that Frank Menceti?" Chris asked.

"Yes, it is," Jeff looked at the television reporter. "I don't think we've met. Jeff Strata, and you are?"

"Chris White. I'm a friend of Susan's. I've seen your work, I think. You're that artist?"

"That's me," Jeff said; he was drunk.

"Chris and I went to college together," Susan added.

"Did you now? Just a bunch of college chums having a drink at..." Jeff looked at his watch, then at Susan, "Two o'clock in the morning."

"We just came off a helicopter," Chris tried to explain. "We were going out to cover a plane crash but couldn't find it."

"Do you want me to help you look, I could ask around," Jeff said. He was very drunk.

"No," Chris said, "I can find it myself. You, you go back, and have a good time."

"Okay," Jeff said and sat down next to Susan. The cameraman came into the bar looking for them. He told Chris that the truck was out front and loaded. They asked Susan if she was coming with them, but Jeff insisted she stay and fly down to the Keys with him and the others.

"The bars are open until four, and then we can fly back," Jeff told her.

"But my car is in San Carlos Park."

"I'll take you to it when we get back."

Susan did not take long to make up her mind. David was out with that slut, so why shouldn't she have some fun, too.

"Okay, I'll stay," she said, and joined the men at the table.

*

"I can't believe she never comes out here," Wendy said. David was laying beside her stroking her long hair with one hand and reaching between her legs with his other. They lay on top of the blankets; the boat's generator was off, and the air-conditioning was not working. David wasn't on the boat enough to warrant running electricity to it.

This was not a new experience for him, and it reminded him of when he was young and he would bring that woman into the small sailboat his dad had bought him. It had only a cuddy cabin, but she didn't care. She was escaping her husband, and he was just a kid. But that was along time ago. Of course, now Susan believed he came and did work there. If she only knew. Now no one would know.

*

They heard the two Pratt and Whitney jet engines outside and walked to the doors. The white corporate jet was taxiing from the runway, and soon Susan would be on her way to Key West and Margaritaville. The group, now even more drunk than before, started singing Jimmy Buffett's "Why Don't We Get Drunk and Screw" as the plane pulled up outside the double glass doors of the terminal.

"Frank," Jeff said, "I see they sent the little one. What's wrong?"

"That stupid little shit of a dog took a dump in the other one, and I can't get the stench out!" Menceti snarled.

The hatch on the side of the Lear 35 opened, and the pilot lowered the small stair. He then hopped out and greeted each passenger, helping them into the plane one by one. He pointed out the wet bar and the snacks.

"Help yourself," the pilot told them.

It took only about five minutes before they pulled out onto the runway. The engine roared, and Jeff yelled as they did a power take off and zoomed up into the night sky.

"Can we see Miami?" Susan asked.

"Hey, Richie?" Menceti yelled.

"Yes, sir?" the pilot answered over the intercom.

"The little lady wants to see Miami."

"We will have to climb to a higher altitude."

"Well god dammit, climb then!"

"I'll have to ask for clearance, Mr. Menceti," the pilot responded. Frank Menceti leaned forward toward Susan. "Watch this," he said to her and winked his eye.

"Whose plane is this?" Frank yelled at Richie.

"Yours, sir."

"Damn right it's mine. Do you want to keep flying it?"

"Yes, sir."

"Then climb."

The jet pulled up till the nose pointed sixty degrees up from the horizon. In the back, the G-force flattened everyone into their seats, and Jeff let out a loud "Yahoo" as they soared up into the night sky. The powerful dash-two engines pushed the plane higher and higher until finally leveling off at close to fifty thousand feet. They were ten miles high when Susan looked out the small oval window of the plane. Far off to the left, the lights of Florida's most famous city were visible.

"That's so pretty," Susan said. The darkness of the Everglades and Gulf of Mexico surrounded the light, making it seem even brighter.

After checking with Frank, the pilots dove the plane toward the little island that was the southernmost tip of the United States. Twenty minutes later they were on the ground. The co-pilot put the red plastic covers over the engine intakes while Richie gave the fuel order to the ground crew that met the plane. They gave Frank their skypage number and asked him to beep them when the group was ready to go home then headed to the Ramada near the airport to catch some sleep. A white limousine pulled up between the Cessna 172 and the GKB Learjet.

"Old Town," Frank told the driver.

*

Laura was watching, along with her team, when the Learjet touched down. They took photographs of the passengers as they exited the plane.

"Who's the girl?" Laura asked while looking through the night vision lenses.

"She's new," Oslo replied.

"Make sure you get some good head shots," she instructed him. Another member of the team was wearing a headset connected to a Motorola radio.

"They're going to Old Town," he said to the team.

"Let's go," Oslo said, packing the gear into the two black Ford Explorers. Only one had U.S. Government plates on the bumper.

"So brief me on this guy." Laura asked Oslo. He pulled out a briefcase and handed her a blue file. They were in the truck with regular Florida tags.

"The big guy is Francis Menceti. He's the CEO of GKB bank and sits on a lot of other boards of other companies. Big Frank is under investigation for money laundering, racketeering, bribery, you name it."

"Why haven't I heard about it?" Laura asked, scanning the file.

"Look at the pictures. See anyone you know?"

She pulled out a pile of surveillance photos. The grainy image told her that they were taken with a telephoto lens from long range. Most were black and white night shots. She flipped through them, looking at the faces of the subjects. Then she saw it and understood. The two photographs were stapled together.

The stretch limo headed East from the airport down Berth Street. The Explorer that Special Agents Dwayne Oslo and Laura Wilson occupied pulled out and followed at a safe distance.

The other truck couldn't be used because of the white federal government license plates, so it headed across the grass to the helipad where the dark blue Jet Ranger was waiting.

Oslo followed Frank and the others along Roosevelt Boulevard until it hit Duval and turned left. The helo was in the air and contacted Laura by radio. She instructed them to take over surveillance of the subjects. After confirming the agents in the air had spotted the car, the black truck pulled to the side and parked.

The limo stopped across from the Kress Building on the corner of Duval and Fleming and let out its passengers. Because they were so close, Oslo and the AIC got out and ran down the street, hoping to catch them on foot. The two agents spotted the four drunks and slowed to a walk. They could hear the helicopter above them but could not see it. Laura turned down the volume on her radio and stuck it in her purse while she ran. Oslo was out of breath and slowing, but Laura's athletic and toned body did not let her down.

They were close to the group when Luis turned around and saw the two agents. He did not know who they were, but instinct told him they were following him and the others. He thought he heard a radio but was not certain.

Laura saw the man turn around and look at them. She grabbed Oslo's arm and rested her head against his shoulder.

"Don't get excited," she said quietly. "We just look less conspicuous this way."

Oslo looked down at her. She was very pretty, even without makeup. He thought, *there could be worse duties in the FBI.* Laura held her breath as the man stared. Finally he turned around and rejoined the others.

Christmas lights were strung everywhere, giving the small town the festive flavor it was known for. Because the Key was only four miles wide and one mile across, there was little chance of Laura losing sight of Frank and his friends. Even so, she had posted three more agents at Roosevelt and US 1, just in case they tried to drive off the island.

They entered Sloppy Joe's Bar, Hemingway's famed hangout, around a quarter till three and watched the suspect and his friends grab a large table near the stage. The band was still playing, entertaining the crowd, which was surprisingly large for this time of night.

It was clear to the agents, as well as the waitress, who was bankrolling the floating party. The money must really be flowing, Laura thought, because the waitress stood right by Frank from the time he sat down.

The one armed bass player amazed most of the crowd but was being insulted by a table full of young college kids near the stage. The musician did not back down, and soon one of the troublemakers was standing up at the stage trying to show his beer-muscles and wanting a fight.

Frank told the kid to sit down, drawing the attention of the young guy and his friends. A large guy from the college table walked over to Frank.

Laura and Oslo spotted the shiny black handle of the forty-five caliber automatic at the same time, but neither agent had a weapon. Oslo informed Laura that he knew Frank had a permit for a concealed weapon but had never noticed him carrying before. Laura did not like the fact that the two of them were watching this and would be unable to do anything if shooting started.

The kid started toward Menceti's table, but, luckily, was intercepted by three very muscular gentlemen. Wearing matching red shirts with the word SECURITY emblazoned on back, they peacefully removed the troublemaker and his buddies from the club. The crowd, including Frank, broke out in applause for the three men. Laura told Oslo she was going outside. She walked out and turned to the side of the building. When she was out of sight of the door, she called in two other agents and told them to come and relieve her and Oslo.

"Make sure you bring your weapons the suspect is armed."

*

The Jeep Cherokee pulled up to the black sports car. Inside, Sanibel Police Officer Brent Kohler called in the tag number on his radio. He was new to the night shift. When his wife had started attending classes at Edison Community College full time he asked to be rescheduled to nights so they would not have to put their two year old in day care. He had noticed the Porsche parked here a couple of times over the last week. Brent was tired and decided enough was enough. He verified the car was not stolen with the dispatcher, and grabbed his pen. After writing out the ticket, he slid it under the windshield of the car. Next time, he decided he would not be so nice.

*

"Last call," the bartender yelled as he picked up the empty shooters in front of Susan and the four men. He then went and turned all the lights on in the room, subtly hinting it was time for all of them to go home. She had stopped drinking when they left Margaritaville and was almost sober.

"One more, bartender," Frank asked the man behind the thirty inches of mahogany.

"No can do, Bud. It was four o'clock when I gave you the last round." Frank looked at Jeff who shrugged his shoulders and then held his hand up to his ear as a reminder for the big man.

"Okay, okay," Frank said. "Can I use your phone ?"

"Local?"

"What the fuck difference does it make! Give me the damn phone. It's a one-eight-hundred number, I have to page our pilots to meet us at the plane!"

The bartender laid the phone next to Frank and dialed the numbers for him. After leaving a message, the group left the bar and headed to the car. The driver had kept up with them and was waiting outside. The five tired party-goers slid quietly into the backseat. The driver closed the door behind them and then took his seat behind the wheel.

"Where to?" he asked.

"The airport," Jeff replied wearily.

The driver of the rented limo clicked twice on the walkie talkie under his coat and pulled out onto the empty street.

"They're moving!" the FBI agent in the aqua KeyCab called over his radio. The taxi pulled out of the cross street and tailed the limo back to the waiting aircraft. *It had been a very long, boring night* the agent thought.

The flashing red beacon and white anti collision lights directed the driver to the plane. Richie was outside waiting to greet his passengers and boss, while his cohort was inside the cockpit finishing the preflight checklist.

Jeff looked over at Luis, who was almost asleep in the car. Next to him, Frank sat looking out the window. This is the *longest* he has ever been quiet, the artist thought to himself. Jeff and Susan sat across from the two. Susan was gently stroking Jeff's right arm. He turned and softly kissed the top of her head, bringing a tired smile to her face. The tired crew stumbled into the plane and sank into the deep, soft, leather seats inside. Richie closed the hatch and went into the cockpit. He dimmed the lighting in the cabin and pulled the curtain behind him to stop the cockpit noise from escaping into the cabin. They were number one for takeoff, so Richie rolled right from the taxiway to the runway without stopping. Quickly, the five million dollar aircraft was nothing more than a faint light in the dark sky.

*

A couple of blocks away Laura dragged herself up the steps and into the Victorian-style house on Francis Street. She had filled out the reports and waited until the subject was on his way off the island before heading back to the rented home.

Due to their jobs, she and Rick moved around too much for it to make sense to buy one. The owners of this house had inherited it from their parents, but, because they lived in Hawaii, they rented it out. Most of the neighborhood was built at the turn of the century but held its age well, unlike the condo she had in Pensacola. It had been less than five years old, and the plumbing needed replacing when she moved out. That was where she met Rick.

He had been the subject of an investigation. A young sailor had died while in training. The kid had graduated from Aircrew Candidate School and was in training to be a Navy rescue swimmer. Rick was an enlisted staff instructor at the school and was involved when the student died while completing one of the exercises. She was assigned to investigate him, but ended up helping to clear his name. She left the Naval Investigative Service soon after and was accepted into the FBI. Because they were both federal service positions, she was able to keep the seniority she had built up in the INS. Rick had stayed in the Navy when they offered him a slot in the Limited

Duty Officer program.

Laura walked through the door and smelled bacon frying. It was five in the morning and Rick was already cooking breakfast. She followed her nose to the kitchen.

"What the hell are you wearing?" she asked, starting to laugh.

"What? This is what I always wear under my flightsuit," he replied in all seriousness.

Her husband had on blue baseball cap that said DET 5 on it in yellow, a red Polo knit shirt with three buttons and a collar, yellow jogging shorts with the word NAVY in blue on the buttocks, black socks and Laura's dark brown, furry moose slippers.

"I know those slippers aren't regulation."

"Just sit down and eat, okay?"

*

The flight home had taken only nineteen minutes, but the sun was peeking out from the horizon as they started their descent into Naples. The bright yellow rays of morning lit up the inside of the aircraft and upset the sleep of all but Luis on the plane.

"We should be in Naples in about five minutes, folks," Richie said over speakers hidden in the cabin.

"How long have you known David?" Susan asked Jeff quietly. The artist rubbed his eyes and stretched in the confined quarters of the Lear.

"He and I attended the same school on the island. That was when it went from eighth to twelfth grade. He was a senior when I started. He also kept a boat down at the dock, and I would see him a lot."

"What is all the animosity about?"

"It's a long story. It's just... I'd rather not try to describe it. It's a guy thing."

Susan did not ask what a guy thing was. It was obvious neither he nor David was going to let anyone else know what caused the feud. And, at that moment, Susan really did not care that much.

The moon was still visible in the morning sky when the plane touched down in Naples. Frank was waking up as they taxied over to the terminal.

"Did you have a good time, little lady?"

"Yes, thank you for letting me come along," Susan replied honestly. Menceti leaned back in his seat, then reached over and slapped Luis on the leg, waking him and startling him at the same time.

"I guess I will call you later?" Jeff asked.

"I don't have to go home yet," she told him.

"We have business to talk over," Luis said.

"How will I get home?" Susan asked Jeff. "My car is up in Ft. Myers."

"Don't worry about it," Menceti answered. He walked up to the cockpit and leaned over Richie's shoulder.

"I would like to bring a photographer out to your boat today or tomorrow," She told Jeff.

"That's fine."

Frank returned to his seat. "It's all set; Richie will take you to your car."

"Thank you again; you are a sweetie." Menceti just nodded. *I'll have to find this one after Jeff is done with her*, he thought.

"Jeff tells me you're writing about him?" Luis asked, finally alert.

"A book on our friend here?" Menceti said, interested for a change..

"No, just an article," Susan replied, "A feature for the paper I work for."

"You should write a book," Jeff teased.

"Yeah, right! Do you know how much a book costs?"

"You should do a book," Menceti said, his mind spinning at the opportunity, "I'll finance it."

Susan looked at Jeff, who just shrugged. He knew that there was some kind of spin on this. She then looked back at Frank. "You're kidding, right?"

"I don't kid about money. We could publish it here, then ship it to bookstores around the globe!"

Books, Jeff thought, *with the center hollowed out and filled with white powder*. Frank asked Luis to hand him a black case from under the seat. He placed it on his lap and opened it. "How much would you need?"

"This is crazy," she said, "I've never written a book. I would need an editor to go over it, this is nuts You'd be wasting your money."

"Okay," he started to close the briefcase.

"Wait! You're serious."

"Yes. Aren't you?" Frank looked at her. This was amusing him, but he also seemed quite serious.

"I don't know the costs off the top of my head," Susan said. "A typical first run would be five thousand books."

He signed a blank check and handed it to Jeff. "Let me know how much, to keep my books straight." Susan's face lit up.

"I guess I'll do a book," she said. She leaned over and kissed Frank on the cheek.

"Just make sure I get the first copy." What the hell did he care, it was just one more place to hide money. This was unbelievable to Susan, and she couldn't thank Jeff or Menceti enough. After pulling up to the terminal, the men got out, leaving Susan inside the plane alone.

They landed at Page Field precisely four minutes and forty-five seconds after leaving Naples. After taxiing to the small terminal, the two pilots turned in an order for fuel, and shut down the aircraft. Susan went inside the building, and waited for Richie to drive her to the car.

5

***

Tuesday, September 5

"Everything's set," Luis said as he walked Frank back to the plane.

"If there are changes, contact Jeffrey. I'm looking forward to doing business with you and your associates."

"Have a good trip."

Frank shook hands and stepped onto the plane. The pilot glanced at Luis, then closed the hatch. The agent walked back to the car where Jeff was waiting.

"Still a little hungover are we?"

"Just shut up," Luis told him quietly.

"You can drop me off at my boat."

"I don't think so, we have to go see one of my friends first," Luis said.

*

The heat and humidity had already taken hold outside when Susan woke up later that afternoon. She showered, then went downstairs. After having breakfast, she collected clothes out of the hamper in her bathroom. Susan then went into David's room to get his laundry. She saw right away that David had not come home. She called her husband's office to confront him, but Donna told her he was at the courthouse. She asked if Susan wanted to leave a message. "No," she replied. She would call back later.

It was almost two o'clock by the time she left her driveway on her way to the View's offices. She wanted to straighten things out with Wendy. She wasn't jealous; this was not David's first affair. But this was the first one that wasn't some nameless, faceless perfume on his shirt. Not only did Susan know the identity of the woman, she spent almost all her time away from David with her. She was not only mad at her husband, who she was sure went after Wendy for that reason, but she was also ticked off at Wendy. The idea just upset her that the girl would go behind her back like this. Susan had taken the job to spend time away from David, but now it would be as if he were always with her. She had no idea what Wendy would tell him about what she said, who she talked to. She was being strangled and needed some air.

The thoughts swam around in her head as she parked outside the small building where the Sanibel View was located. She saw Wendy's car in the lot and hoped that she would find Sam before she saw Wendy. She went inside, walking straight through the newsroom to the back wall where the owner-editor's office was. She didn't knock, but walked right in. Sam was sitting in his chair, talking on the phone. He had his feet up on his desk, and he was flipping a yellow pencil in his hand. Across from his desk, closest to Susan, sat Wendy. Sam motioned for Susan to sit in the black leather chair next to Wendy, while he continued talking. Susan shook her head "No," and mouthed the words "I'll come back later." But Sam, more animated this time, pointed at the chair. He covered the mouthpiece of the phone and whispered, "Sit down!" Susan looked at Wendy, then sat in the chair. Neither said a word, nor looked at each other, as Sam finished the call. After hanging up the phone, Sam turned his attention to the two women in front of him.

"All right," he asked. "What's going on here?" The two answers came simultaneously: "I can't work with her!" "She's having sex with my husband!"

Sam held up his hands. "Wait," he said. "One at a time." He pointed at Wendy. "You first."

"Susan has been getting on my back because I'm doing that feature on her husband. She keeps doing things just to annoy me and thinks that I'm her personal photographer. Like I need to listen to her as if she's my boss or something! I'm sick of it!"

"Sam! I want to..." Susan started to say, but Sam cut her off. "You'll get your turn; let me address Miss Richardson's concerns first."

"Thank you," Wendy said.

"Well, first off, it doesn't matter how Susan feels about you doing a feature on her husband. He's news, and she turned it down when I offered it to her. Second, while it is true that she is not your boss, she is, usually, the lead reporter and the writer of the story, so if she thinks she needs you somewhere, she probably does. Give her some credit, Wendy, you are both professionals. Now, about annoying you, give me an example."

"This is bullshit!" Susan said under her breath before Wendy could say anything. Wendy jumped up and pointed at her, "See! That kind of stuff! She just says stuff to piss me off all the time!"

"Sit down!" Sam said. Wendy slowly took her seat. Sam turned to Susan, "Care to explain yourself, Mrs. Ranson?"

"She's not doing a story, she's just doing my husband!"

"That's a mighty strong accusation. Miss Richardson?"

"I am not, I have to spend time with him for the story, that's all," Wendy replied.

"So," Sam said, "If I were to take you off the story, you would have no reason to go near David Ranson. Is that what you're telling me?"

"No. He and I have become friends," she told him, then turned to Susan. "Just friends!"

"I see," Sam said thoughtfully, "Susan, what about the other issues Wendy brought up, or is there something else you wanted to say?"

Susan sat looking right at her boss, "No," she said calmly, "My only problem is that she's screwing my husband." Wendy huffed and squirmed in her seat, shaking her head.

"Can you prove this?"

"No." Susan answered. "It's just..Dammit I know she is."

"Well, until you can prove it, then the only thing that currently I need to be concerned with is whether you two can work together."

"I can't spend all my time with that little slut..." Susan said.

"Let's keep this civil," Sam told them. Wendy crossed her arms and tapped her foot on the floor impatiently as Susan continued, "I don't know what she'll go and tell my husband. We have enough problems as it is!"

"What do you think," Wendy said. "I'm some kind of spy or something? That I report back to David everything you do? Sorry, honey, I have a life!"

Sam saw that this was going nowhere, and he had, frankly, learned more than he cared to. He felt like a father hearing his daughters talk about their first sexual experience, and it made him very uncomfortable. But, realistically, he knew there was little he could do about it.

"It's a shame that you two are acting like this," Sam said. "The only photographer I have available is Wendy. You two are my A team. You don't have to like each other. But you will have to work together! Now get out of my office! I have better things to do, and so do both of you." The two women stood, and Wendy followed Susan out the door and into the newsroom.

"In all my life I've never met anyone as ungrateful as you!" Wendy said. "The way you treat David! I've seen you! It's the same way you're treating me! Gimme, gimme. Always you. Stop everything and help Susan. You're a total bitch."

"You don't know shit about me or my husband, you little tramp! David is an asshole!" Susan could not believe this woman.

"Yeah right! And I'll bet he married *you* for the money, right!"

Susan was pissed. That girl knew absolute zero about any marriage, let alone hers. The only thing Wendy knew about marriage at all was how to break one up.

"You know what?! I hope you get to know my husband; you'll find out what a prick he is! "

"If he's such a prick, why don't you just leave him?"

"I can't. He won't let me."

"That's not what he told me," Wendy replied. So she already talked about this with David. *He probably charmed her the way he charms everyone*, Susan thought.

"You two deserve each other!" Susan said and walked back to her desk.

*

The DEA occupied almost half of the second floor in the old federal building downtown. The gray-columned structure stood in contrast to the brightly-hued buildings of the revitalized downtown Ft. Myers area. Most people walked by oblivious to the fact that it was occupied, let alone the hub for one of the most secretive government agencies in the nation. Contrary to popular belief, the DEA was a very effective tool against the drug trade, at least along the Florida coast. Over the last five years the small windowless office in the corner of the second floor had coordinated raids that had netted over a billion dollars in drugs and over six hundred eighty million dollars in cash. But this was not common knowledge. The busts received no news video or news write-ups, and Special Agent in Charge Sebastian liked it that way. Publicity blew agents' covers and made criminals think about being more cautious. That made his job tougher. And now this had come across his desk. Sebastian did not need another problem with this operation, especially right now. Too many lives were at stake, too many man hours and dollars were sunk into this operation. Sebastian picked up the phone and dialed. The line rang once, then a machine answered, but there was no greeting to listen to. Just a tone.

"It's me; I want to see you, ASAP!" Sebastian said and hung up the phone.

*

David Ranson and Elliot Pinder sat across from Judge Thomas Daniels in his chambers. They quietly waited while the Judge scanned the papers laid in front of him. He had read them three times and was halfway through the fourth when Pinder coughed. Daniels looked up through the bifocals at the defense attorney.

"Do you have to be somewhere, Elliot?"

Pinder was caught off guard, "No, your Honor. I really had something caught in my throat."

"Uh huh." Daniels read the briefs one more time, then shuffled the papers back into a neat stack and closed the file. He looked at the two prominent attorneys and saw the tension in their faces. The judge opened his mouth to speak, but then opened the file and read the top page one more time. He had already memorized each page but enjoyed watching the two hotshots struggle to maintain their self control. The judge and former prosecutor wanted them to know that this would be his courtroom, and he was in charge.

"The client's rights were ignored, Mr. Ranson. Why was he held for so long without Mr. Pinder being notified?"

"Long? Seventy-two hours is not *long*," David answered.

"It's seventy-two hours longer than he should have been!"Pinder quipped.

"What's going on, Mr. Ranson?" Judge Daniels asked.

"We did not suspect Dr. Whitmore at the time. We were concerned with his mental well being, your Honor."

"Bull, David. You knew exactly what you were doing. I expect more from your office when I see that the DA himself is handling the case." The judge closed the file in front of him. "David, I hope you are ruining this man's life with more than just a few unlabeled plastic bottles."

"Your Honor, I have shown sufficient evidence to charge Dr. Whitmore with murder. He had means, he practically poisoned her with that medication, and he confessed!"

"Your Honor," Pinder responded, " My client only told the police he felt responsible for her death; he never said he caused it. You've read it. That's a far way from a confession for murder."

Daniels wrote on the paper in front of him and handed it to the defense attorney, "The motion to suppress the confession is granted, Mr. Pinder."

"Thank you, your honor. Now I would ask for the court to dismiss the case against my client," Elliot handed over a second paper.

"On what grounds?!" David argued.

"On the grounds that without a confession you have no motive, and without a motive you have no case. Your honor will see that my client had nothing to gain, no property, income, or inheritance."

"What about insurance?" the judge asked.

"Fifty thousand dollars. But your honor can see that my client hardly needed it."

"Do you have anything to tell me before I sign this, David? He's got a point," Judge Daniels asked. David knew he needed a motive; they just hadn't come up with one yet. Damn Pinder. Then, suddenly, it came to him. "Jealousy!"

"What!?" Elliot exclaimed. " Jealousy? Over who?"

"The victim was having an affair; we don't know with whom yet. But we have some leads I am unwilling to present at this time, " David said.

"Unable is more like it! Your Honor, this is a stall tactic. Plain and simple. The state's making this up just to hold my client because they have no case and no suspects!"

"David," the judge said, "I'm all ears, and I better hear something I like."

David tried to remember how Shirley explained it in the elevator. "Your Honor, my office has obtained scientific proof that Mrs. Whitmore had been in bed with someone besides her husband. We are looking for this person right now. His body doesn't secrete DNA in his sweat or something. I'm not sure of the scientific language, but needless to say, it proves that she was not always alone in her bed."

"This is nonsense, your Honor," Pinder whined.

"I can have Shirley here in forty minutes with the test results if you want me to, Judge," David added. "look, Your Honor; I don't want to attack the victim here-we all know the press would love this."

"I know you're not shy of the press, Mr. Ranson." Daniels said. "In fact, give my best to your wife for me."

"Yes your honor, but..."

"But I want to see those test results by tomorrow morning."

Pinder shook his head, "I still don't see how this implicates my client!"

"Easy, Elliot," David said. "The defendant found out and he could not stand that she was having an affair, so he killed her. Plain and simple."

Judge Daniels looked over at the defense, "The state has established a motive..." Elliot could not believe what he was hearing, "Calm down, Elliot," the judge said, "I want to see this test that David is talking about, so I am setting aside the motion to dismiss for twenty-four hours."

"Your honor," Pinder argued, "that has nothing to do with the fact that my clients rights were violated. The police conducted an illegal search. The doctor-patient privilege was not only broken, but shredded apart. Your honor, they would never have known about her problem, nor searched the clinics files if David had not been confided in as a friend by my client."

"David?"

"C'mon, Elliot. Inevitable discovery. Nineteen seventy-four *Nex v Williams*. If the police would have discovered..."

"I know the ruling, David," the Judge interjected.

"We would have found out eventually. The pills could be traced; her husband is a doctor for God's sake. The state's not stupid, your honor. We would have looked."

"I believe the prosecution has made their point. The evidence stays. Motion to suppress is denied. Sorry, Elliot."

*

"What do you think?" Zoe asked his boss over lunch.

"I like the guy. He's going to need a mentor to show him how to play the game."

"And that would be you?"

"Who better?"

The two men sat alone at the table, out of earshot of other diners at Adams Mark V. It had quickly become a favorite of Snelling's since taking office three years before. The five star restaurant had traditionally been the dining place of all chief executives of Florida. The dining room was richly decorated, and the quiet atmosphere and expensive cuisine ensured that the governor's meal would not be interrupted. Scott Zoe took a sip of his ice water.

"Governor, I want to speak to you about Menceti."

Snelling raised his hand to stop him. Zoe waited for him to finish chewing the veal cutlet and drink a sip of wine before speaking.

"I know what you're going to say, but I'm not going to hang him out to dry. He helped get me into politics, he practically raised all the money that got me the Governor's office." Snelling laid his napkin down over the food. The waiter came and took the plate away.

"Sir, I've heard some things."

"Just be quiet for a moment, Scott, and let me finish. "

Zoe sat back and let out a sigh. He was frustrated. Snelling spoke to him like a parent to a child. "I know you don't like him, but he is important to me, and in effect to you. No one in this country makes a million dollars by being a nice guy. Sure, he's stepped on some toes, and he has enemies. But he's an O.K. guy. I wish you could see that."

"I'm just trying to look out for you, sir," Zoe replied sternly.

"I know, but this isn't a major concern."

6

***

Thursday, September 7

"Is that unanimous, Mr. Foreman?"

"It is," the spokesman for the grand jury answered..

Judge Daniels looked down at the prosecution and defense teams standing at the tables in front of him. "Very well. The jury finds that the state has sufficient evidence and has met the burden necessary to hold the defendant over for trial." David smiled as he looked over at Pinder and the defendant. Dr. Whitmore looked back with eyes that caused that smile to disappear from the District Attorney's face. Lisa McCay sat behind her brother-in-law. "I give notice that I want both sides to be ready for opening argument within ninety days, is that a problem gentlemen."

"No, your honor," they answered in unison.

"Good. Now, what about bond, Mr. Pinder?"

"We are asking that Dr. Whitmore be granted a low bond or on his own recognizance."

"Mr. Ranson?"

"The state asks that the defendant not be granted bond. We remind the court that he is charged with a capital offense and has sufficient financial means to be considered a high flight risk."

"Your Honor," Pinder interjected. "Where would my client go? His only family is the community; he has no children, no wife."

"Exactly!" David argued. "He has nothing holding him here!"

Pinder cut him off, "He runs the only free clinic on the island, your Honor!" The judge watched the sparring match in his courtroom and realized he was losing control, "Knock it off, both of you."

"But, your Honor! The defendant tried to flee the country."

"Let's not get dramatic, David," Pinder said."We are only talking Canada- not

Eastern Europe!"

"Mr. Pinder," the Judge replied."Unless something has changed that I am not aware of, Canada is still another country. The state has a point."

Daniels slammed his gavel down on the desk. "One more word and you are both in contempt; now be quiet. I feel like I'm at a tennis match." Using the gavel's handle as a pointer, he motioned at the two opposing lawyers. The courtroom was silent. The judge set the gavel on his desk softly. He closed his eyes and massaged his temples with his fingers. He did not speak for several minutes. "Mr. Pinder, it is true, is it not, that your client was caught with a plane ticket trying to fly to Canada? Just answer yes or no only, please."

"Your Hon..," Pinder stopped when the judge looked up. "Yes, your Honor."

"Because I believe that the defendant has both the means and desire to flee, bail is denied."

"Thank you, your honor," David said. Lisa McCay whispered into Elliot Pinder's ear.

"Your honor?"

"What is it, Mr. Pinder? And keep it short."

"The family of my client respectfully requests that he be allowed to attend his wife's funeral." Judge Daniels looked at the defendant, who was staring down at the table in front of him.

"She was the victim of the crime of which he is accused. Let me hear from the family."

Lisa came out from the gallery. "Thank you, your honor. I am Willard's sister-in-law, Lisa McCay."

"You were the one flying the defendant out of this great country of ours, were you not?" the Judge asked. He saw the reaction of the woman, who was clearly uncomfortable at being reminded.

"Yes, sir. I, well, that is," she was tongue tied. Pinder whispered in her ear. She nodded and continued, "Your honor, our family is small and very close. We, um, don't believe that Willard had anything to do with her murder and think it would only be right that he be present at the funeral."

"It's a little odd, don't you think?"

"Your honor, a man is innocent until proven guilty. It would be a grave injustice if, when the trial is over and my brother-in-law is found innocent, your Honor had kept him from paying his last respects to his wife."

"You're not buying this act, are you, Judge?" David interrupted. "She just wants another chance to get him out of the country."

Daniels looked over at the prosecutor. He had warned the District Attorney.

"That's contempt, one hundred dollar fine, Mr. Prosecutor. I warned you. And it comes from your pocket, not your office!" Daniels turned to Elliot, who was clearly expecting the same. "Mr. Pinder, I am going to grant you your request, but with conditions. The defendant will be escorted by a county deputy, and Miss McCay's identification and driver's license will be surrendered to the court while Dr. Whitmore is outside his cell. I also want you to explain the vast extradition agreement and laws that we share with the Canadian government to your client's family. If I end up looking foolish, their next reunion will be right here in my courtroom!"

"Yes, your Honor."

"I will see you in ninety days, gentlemen." Judge Daniels slapped the gavel down, and both sides emptied into the hall. Elliot walked up to David. "It looks like you got yourself a fight," he said.

"Don't worry, Elliot, I'm up for it," David said.

"I'm asking for a gag order. I don't want my client going to jail just so you can live in Washington."

"Go ahead; it won't happen," David said confidently. *It had better not*, he hoped.

*

Laura drove up to the entrance gate of Key West Naval Air Station. After a salute from the security guard, she made her way over to the hangar where Rick worked. After parking, she walked over to a small open door in the cinder block and steel hangar. Above the doorway, DET THREE was painted in blue block letters. Once inside she was confronted by a steep stairwell. Rick's office was up on the second floor (*second deck* she reminded herself). Laura was halfway up when Rick and another officer came walking down. They were both wearing flightsuits. They all stopped on the steps. "Rick!" Laura exclaimed, surprised.

"Hi, sweetheart!" Rick answered and gave her a hug, "I saw you pull up; I figured I'd come down so you wouldn't have to walk." She gave him a quick kiss.

"Hey, Laura," the other Naval officer said.

"Hi. How's Nicole doing, Lenny?" Laura asked him

"Fine; I'll tell her you said hi," the officer said. "Listen, Romeo, I'm heading out to the bird."

"I'll be right there," Rick said.

"Nah, take your time. I'll do the walk around," Lenny said and headed down the steps. "I'll come get you when I need you."

"Thanks." Rick and Laura headed downstairs and outside.

"I thought we were having lunch," Laura said.

"Me too, but something came up. I'm sorry" he apologized.

"So, what's new at the office? And what was that thing the other night?" She told him about Menceti and about the limousine and all the money he spent.

"But it's dirty money," Rick said."It's obvious he's on borrowed time if you are already watching him."

"I know, but at least when I was with the NIS the money wasn't thrown in my face."

"Yeah," her husband answered. "But they still were currupt. They didn't need money, they stole power. That Admiral had private jets, only they had the word NAVY painted on them. And he and the others were worse because they broke the country's trust and the Navy's. Everyone depended on them, not just some dope dealers and bankers. This Menceti guy isn't a threat to our national security."

"I'm not so sure," Laura replied, and told him about the photo. She knew she wasn't supposed to tell anyone who didn't need to know, but this was Rick. He had access to military secrets his whole adult life, and she knew the information was safe with him.

The couple walked over to some picnic benches near a chain link fence. Beyond the fence the grass ended, and the concrete tarmac baked in the sun. Various types of aircraft and helicopters were parked on the ramp. She explained the investigation, the agencies involved, everything.

"It sounds like you have your hands full," he said.

"Yeah, and on top of all that, John wants me to help some friend of his who's a cop up near Fort Myers," she sounded exhausted.

"Can't you say no?"

"No, not really. I talked to him, and he thinks maybe someone's trying to frame the guy, or cover it up. I don't know" She placed her head against his shoulder. "I don't need all this at once, Rick. It's just overwhelming."

"Don't let it get to you, sweetheart. If it gets to be too much just walk away and take a break. Maybe we can go back up to Panama City for a weekend or something."

"We can't," she sighed. "You fly every weekend."

"Not every weekend."

"Yes. You do. Every weekend," she said, wrapping her arms around him. "But that's okay, at least you're mine all week and not on some aircraft carrier in the Arctic Ocean somewhere." He hugged her tight, and she giggled and hugged back. He could always put her in a good mood. They sat holding each other for a while until Rick saw his pilot walking over. Rick waved to him. "I'll be over in a minute," he yelled. "I guess we're starting our preflight."

"Which one is yours?" Laura asked.

"See that one with the lights blinking?" Rick pointed to a gray helicopter with the number five painted on the door. There were small fiberglass blades and receivers poking out along its aluminum skin. "That's my new toy. I'm the project manager."

" What are all those things sticking out of it ?"

"Those are antennas...antennae? Whatever the plural word for antenna is, that's what they are. She is a gorgeous bird, isn't she?" He beamed with pride. Laura didn't think it was all that exciting, but who was she to ruin Rick's fun. "1 guess I'll let you go. When will you be home?"

"I have no idea, when we are done testing."

"I guess I'll be eating alone," she said and kissed him on the cheek. "Have a good flight. I love you."

"I love you," he said and ran into the hangar.

*

Wendy and Susan were driving west on Periwinkle Way. The two hour long chastising by Sam had not solved their disputes but made it clear that they would have to work together. He said they were a team, and if one quit or was fired due to their problems, the other would be out the door five minutes later. They had not spoken a word since leaving the office for the marina.

"If I'm doing this for you, you need to do something for me," Wendy said.

"What?"

"I need photos of David from when he was younger. I was going to ask him, but since we are out and together..."

"Fine. We can stop at the house after we're done at the boat. You can have every picture of him in the house for all I care, right down to his high school yearbook if you want it." Susan would be happy if they were out of there. *The only one who will miss looking at them is David.*

*

The District Attorney came into the office and stopped at Donna's desk. She was typing away on the word processor, wearing headphones and transcribing the notes he had left on her desk. He tapped her on the shoulder, and she stopped.

"How'd it go?" She could see he was in a good mood.

"Ninety days and we go back in!"

"Good for you!"

"Any messages?" David asked.

"They're on your desk. Your wife called but didn't leave a message."

"Did she say what she wanted?"

"She asked if you were here. I told her you were in court." Susan must have enjoyed that one, he thought, knowing that she had to have guessed where he spent the night. That reminded him of the slip of paper in his pocket. He pulled it out and handed Donna the ticket from the previous night.

"Call Sanibel, and get this taken care of."

*

The clerk knocked on the glass window of the door. After turning down the volume of the portable compact disc player, Laura waved her into John Bender's office. After the other night's operation, the temporary AIC decided she had better familiarize herself with all of the ongoing investigations that the office was involved in. The clerk stepped around the twenty or so different stacks of folders that were piled on the floor. Laura was sitting on the carpet, her back against the wall, leafing through one of them, but put it down when the clerk handed her the white envelope.

"Sorry to bother you, Laura. It's your plane tickets and travel voucher. You leave tomorrow morning at ten a.m. Remember to keep your receipts for your travel claim. Any questions or changes let me know, okay?"

Laura looked at the paperwork inside.

"What about a rental car?" Laura asked.

"Let me see." She handed the packet back to the clerk, who followed the fine print with her index finger.

"Okay, right here." She pointed it out to her supervisor, "You are authorized up to twenty-five dollars a day for car rental. So I guess you can get one, if you want." The girl gave Laura back the tickets and tiptoed back around the files trying not to step on any of them. "I'll be right out here if you need anything."

"Thanks; can you close the door?"

Laura reached over and soon John, Paul, George and Ringo were rockin' away inside the small office.

*

Jeff was hosing off the bow of his boat when he saw Susan's car pull into the parking lot. A few other cars were parked at the marina, most owned by amateur fishermen who would be coming in soon, before the afternoon thundershower. The dark clouds were already forming over the horizon and would soon be drifting towards shore for the daily drenching. That was one of the downfalls to living in the tropics, but the rain usually only came during the summer, and then only in the late afternoon. By seven o'clock the sky would be blue again.

Susan parked in the regulation space and the girls walked out to the slip that the Gecko occupied.

"Hey, stranger!"

"Don't you own a shirt?" Susan asked the bare-chested sailor. He was wearing faded cutoffs, and his old brown leather sandals.

"It's going to rain soon," he pointed to the foreboding sky over the water. "So what's the point."

Jeff invited the girls on board. He turned off the hose and greeted them as they stepped on the slippery deck. Susan told him that they wanted to photograph the boat.

"That's why I'm cleaning it."

Wendy took out her camera and changed lenses, then loaded it with film.

"Do you want him in the photos?" she asked Susan.

"Not like that. Just shoot the boat."

"In that case you guys need to get off or go inside."

"I could go inside and get off?" Jeff said and smiled, but Wendy did not enjoy the pun.

"Do you want me to do this or not?" she asked. He put down the hose and put away the bucket and rags.

"Okay, I'm going," he said and went inside the cabin followed by Susan. The air-conditioning felt good, and she plopped down on the couch, leaned back, and closed her eyes. Jeff was in the galley and pouring them each a glass of sweet tea. He came back into the main cabin and sat down next to Susan. He placed the glass against her neck. "That feels good; just hold it there," she said.

"What a bitch!" he said quietly.

Susan sat up, " Who me?"

"No, the one outside."

"You don't know the half of it," Susan said. "I understand now why she gets along so good with David."

Susan told Jeff about David and Wendy as they watched her through the lace curtains in the small cabin. She was setting up for a shot, and Susan giggled as Jeff made rude gestures to the oblivious photographer. The white fabric made it easy to see out, but the light color reflected the sunlight, and, with the tinted glass, the oval potholes acted like two- way mirrors. After a minute or two they were both in hysterics.

Wendy heard the loud laughter coming from inside but paid little attention. She had been jealous of Susan when she first met Jeff, but David had fixed that. The blonde turned and looked at David's boat three rows over and thought about the other night. She lifted her camera and took a photo of their secret meeting place.

Susan was holding her stomach. It hurt from laughing so much. Jeff leaned over and kissed her. She let him for a moment, then pushed away. "I can't do that; what if she sees us?"

"Who cares?"

"She'll tell David. She might even take a picture, and I can't deny that. Then when we ask for the divorce, I'll be at fault and left out in the cold."

Jeff removed his arm from around her. "I'm sorry."

"I mean, I like it, just not with her around. You understand, don't you?"

"Yeah. I just wanted to kiss you, that's all. I won't get the chance for a couple of days."

She sat back. "Why?"

"I need to go to the Virgin Islands. It was planned before I met you."

"When?"

"I'm leaving today as a matter of fact. In a couple hours, after the rain."

"Can I come with you?" she asked, the sadness in her voice apparent.

"I'm sorry. I would love to, but I can't; it's business."

"I don't care," she told him.

"But my agent would, I'm afraid. Besides, I won't be coming back here right away. I'm stopping off in the Keys on the way home. I could fly you down to meet me there if you want."

"This isn't over me or us or anything is it?"

"No." He looked into her eyes and held the side of her head softly, "Believe me, I don't want this to end. It is just business. The art world is a strange place, and my agent is one of the weirder ones. You met him, you know."

She remembered Luis. He did not say much, and seemed always annoyed when he did speak.

"He's like Wendy, but a guy," Jeff continued, bringing a smile to her saddened face.

"Okay," she replied softly, understanding. He hugged her, then walked over to the galley and refilled his glass. Wendy slid the door open and walked inside. She was soaked with sweat.

"God, it's hot out there," she said and wiped her forehead with a napkin off the table. "I'm done. I shot two rolls. I should have them developed in the next day or two, and you can pick the ones you want."

"Do you want some tea?" Jeff asked.

"Sure," she said as she sat down across from Susan. "It looks like it's going to rain any moment, the sky is really dark."

Jeff handed Wendy the tall plastic glass. She chugged the whole glass and sat it on the table next to her.

"Could I ask a favor?" Jeff looked at the girls. "I need to go get some supplies for the trip. I don't feel like renting a car just to go to the store." Wendy looked at Susan and casually shook her head no.

"Sure," Susan said.

"Susan, we were supposed to go somewhere after this. Remember?"

"It will only take a couple of minutes," Jeff assured her and grabbed a shirt and his wallet. He sat down, took off his sandals, and grabbed a pair of Nike running shoes from under the chair.

"I'll meet you in the car," Wendy said to them as she slid the sliding glass door open. She slammed it shut behind her and they could hear her stomping off the boat. She was pissed and let them know it. Taking advantage of the privacy, Susan asked him about the trip. He told her he'd be back in about a week or ten days.

"Buy me something?"

"Only if you make me this promise?"

"What?"

"I want you to promise that you won't take any more of his abuse and spend as little time as possible with David. And if something happens, you'll contact me immediately. "

"Okay."

"I'll call you when I get to Charlotte Amilie."

"Who's Charlotte Amilie?"

"It's not a who; it's a where. That's a town near the island where I'll be."

A car horn started beeping outside. It was Wendy, waiting for them. Susan kissed him. "I won't be able to kiss you good-bye when we drop you off."

It had started raining by the time they brought Jeff back to his boat. Luis and another man were waiting when they pulled into the marina and had helped unload the supplies, without saying a word to either of the girls. Susan waved good-bye and Jeff watched them drive away until they were out of his sight.

*

"I'm sorry you feel that way, Larry, but that is how I'm handling it! He's already been indicted." David had not expected the backlash.

"I want to get together over dinner or lunch and talk about this. Nobody's happy about this, David," Larry said over the phone.

"When? I'm really backed up for the next couple of days."

"I'm going out of town. I'll be back next week. How about a week from today?"

"Fine."

"We can have dinner at my house; bring Susan."

"I'll see you in a week. Good-bye, Larry." David hung up the phone. *Fuck him,* he thought. David had caught a much larger fish. He reached over and buzzed Donna on the intercom.

"Yes?" her voice hissed through the speaker.

"Get me Scott Zoe with the Governor's office on the phone, please, Donna."

"Right away."

*

The Lexus pulled into the Ranson driveway and parked in its usual space in the carport. The two women got out and quickly ran inside trying not to get wet in the blowing rain. Once inside, Wendy followed Susan upstairs and into David's bedroom.

"He keeps most of the stuff in his closet," Susan said. She pulled down some boxes and opened them, they were filled with mementos of David's youth.

"Here," Susan tossed the stuff onto his unmade bed. "Go through whatever you want, I'm going downstairs and getting something to drink."

"Would you mind if I took this stuff with me back to the office?"

"I don't really care what you do with it."

Susan left the room and headed down into the kitchen, while Wendy stayed up and just searched through boxes and boxes of memoirs. There were photo albums of his family. She found his brother's army uniform and name patch in with his father's and grandfather's military memorabilia. She searched the closet some more and found little league photos and his report card from third grade. She was surrounded by David's things. There was just too much to look through in one afternoon. She grabbed two shoe boxes from the back of the closet that looked like they had not been opened in a very long time. When she pulled off the lids, she found they were full of loose photographs. All the other photos she had seen were in albums or covers, but not these.

"We'd better be getting back!" she heard Susan call from downstairs. She looked at her watch and saw that they had been there for over an hour.

"I'll be right down," she yelled. The photographer gathered up the two shoeboxes and carried them downstairs.

"You don't think he'd mind?"

"Not at all. For you Wendy, anything," Susan said dryly, evoking the expected response from the blonde's middle finger.

*

Luis introduced Special Agent Andre Cortez to Jeff Strata. Jeff just nodded and started to unpack the supplies he had bought. The artist and the DEA informant grabbed the long white slip of paper from the bottom of one of the brown paper bags and handed it to Luis.

"What is this?"

"A receipt. For the food and stuff. You owe me three hundred sixty-two dollars and change."

Luis threw it in the garbage. "The agency isn't paying for your groceries."

"Fine. What are you guys going to eat?"

Luis looked at Jeff and realized he was serious. "I thought you had a shitload of money hidden away, Mr. Artist."

"That doesn't mean I'm buying lunch for the US Government." Jeff picked the crumpled receipt from the trash can. "Three hundred sixty-two dollars, or you two better find some fishing poles."

"Will you take a check?" the agent asked.

"With two forms of ID," answered Jeff sarcastically.

After settling the finances, the three men waited for the rain to die down. Jeff showed Agent Andre Cortez the inner workings of the Gecko, since the DEA agent had never been on a boat bigger than the small flatbottom twelve footer he used for fishing. Luis sat down on the couch and turned on the television.

*

When Susan and Wendy returned to the office, Susan found a note that said Chris White had called. The reporter picked up the phone and dialed the number on the note.

"Action News," the receptionist answered.

"Chris White, please," Susan said.

"One moment."

Susan was transferred to his phone, which rang several times before being picked up. The intern who answered placed her on hold as she ran back to the editing bays to get Chris. The television reporter left the cameraman in the booth, went to his desk, and picked up the phone.

"Susan! Hey, you made it back!"

"Yeah, you should have come with us. We had a great time," she said, "So what's up?"

"You know I called you at work, right?"

"Yeah. that's where I am now. I just got your message."

"Listen, I was hoping you could do me a favor?" he asked.

"Anything. What is it?" Susan owed him, even if they never got to the crash site.

"I'm working on a package, you know, fall sweeps and everything." She knew, and was glad not to have to worry about television ratings. Chris continued, "Anyway I'm looking into the recent killing and how it relates to the investigation of the Blind Pass murder. I mean, they arrested a suspect right away this time, but they still have no one for that woman twenty years ago."

"I thought that was a suicide or accident or something?" Susan asked.

"Well, officially, I think it was just because the locals at the time never solved it and didn't want to scare away the tourists."

"So what can I do to help, Chris? I wasn't even here back then?"

"I need you, and I feel funny asking this," he said. "I need to research the View's records on this. I have copies of the story, but the man who wrote it is really hard to get a hold of."

"Why do you need to talk to him?"

"I want to see his notes, find out his impressions. The stuff he left out of the paper!"

"Who was it?" Susan asked.

"Sam Harden," he replied. "I know you're close with him, and I thought we could see him together. I don't want to go there alone, because he would use the idea, and one of your reporters would do the story."

"And have an exclusive," Susan added.

"This is a good idea, I don't want someone stealing it."

"How do you know I won't steal it?" she teased.

"I know you better than that! Or at least I hope I do," he said, not so sure.

Susan agreed to help him and promised to set up a time for the three of them to meet. He also wanted to know about photographs. The only known in existence belonged to the paper. Susan said he'd have to see a photographer about that. She gave him Wendy's name, but warned him about mentioning this as a favor for her. He understood, but told her he probably wouldn't need them for a while.

*

The rain had finally stopped when Laura walked in the door. Rick was home and had already started cooking dinner when she laid her leather briefcase filled with manila folders on the dining room table. She yelled, "I'm home!" then went upstairs and removed her dripping wet clothes. After jumping in the shower, she dried herself and put on a pleated skirt and cotton top. She saw the umbrella in the corner and wished she had remembered to take it to work with her.

Dinner was on the table when she came down the stairs. Rick was still wearing his flight suit, but it was unzipped, the top half of it was wrapped around his waist with the sleeves tied together in a knot, revealing the gray tank top.

"I thought you were going to throw out that thing," she said half kidding, half seriously.

"Why would I? This is the most comfortable shirt I own."

Laura hated the sleeveless shirts, and he knew it. He had planned to change before she got home. Dinner had just taken a little longer to prepare than he thought. Laura didn't say anything else, but gave him a little grin. He did drive her up a wall sometimes, but he had his good points, and cooking was definitely one of them. He had a three-course meal prepared. Roast turkey, rice, black-eyed peas, homemade slaw, and cornbread muffins. For dessert he had concocted some big chocolate mess with cake, homemade ice-cream, fudge, and chocolate chips. He didn't have a name for it, but it was wonderful. It was a good thing he did not cook every night or she would have weighed two hundred pounds instead of the one hundred twenty that she weighed now.

They ate dessert on the porch, admiring the terrific reds and yellows of the sunset on the horizon. The whitewashed wicker porch swing held both of them, and they sat quietly, savoring the rich, cool taste of the homemade double chocolate ice cream.

When Rick was done, he placed his dish on the wooden deck, leaned back, and spread his arms along the back of the swing. Laura leaned back into his arms, tucking her legs up onto the seat. She placed her head against his chest, and twirled the spoon in the melted ice cream. She had dreamed of times like this when she was a little girl. She took hold of his hand and squeezed softly. It was Laura's way of saying, "I love you." Rick squeezed back and stared out over the water.

"This is nice," he said.

"Yeah, I'm glad we moved into this house; it's so quiet."

He looked out over the trees and saw a helicopter flying in the distance, then let out a small sigh. He didn't want to spoil the moment, but he had to tell her sometime.

"I'm leaving for Roosevelt Roads in the morning."

"Puerto Rico?"

"Yeah. We need to go down there to test some new systems. It's no big deal, just a couple of days."

Laura sat up, finished eating, and handed him her dish, which he laid on top of the other. "I thought you said you wouldn't be going anywhere for at least a few weeks?" she asked, the disappointment was obvious.

"I know I said that. But they have a special range down there that's designed for these kinds of tests." He went to reach for her, but she turned away. He knew it wasn't fair, but what could he do? He belonged to the U.S. Navy, he couldn't say no, he couldn't say anything. Rick placed his hand on her shoulders and silently massaged Laura's neck. He could feel her muscles tighten and could hear her sobbing. It broke his heart. He had been gone five weeks out of the last two months. "Hey, maybe you could come down and meet me there?" She shook her head.

"No, I can't. I have to fly up to Ft. Myers and meet with the DEA," she said without turning around.

"Why?" he asked softly.

"It's because of John being out. I need to coordinate the activities. It's part of being an AIC."

"Like that thing the other night?" Rick wanted to get away from the subject of his leaving.

"Kinda."

Rick stood up and stretched out his hand. She took it and he helped her up off the rocker. She pulled him close, burying her head in his chest. He caressed her cheek, feeling the wetness from where the tears had streamed moments before.

"I love you; you know that?"

"I know. I just miss you," she kissed him lightly on the chest. The sobbing had almost stopped.

"It won't always be like this," he assured her.

"It better not," she said, trying to smile. She lifted her head and looked up into his eyes, he bent down to kiss her lips, but she pulled her head away. "You're not kissing me with that mouth."

"Why, what did I say now?" Rick asked, surprised at her reaction. Laura smiled.

"You have a ring of chocolate and a little mustache; go clean your face!"

Rick looked at her a moment, then pulled her close and kissed her anyway, chocolate and all. She playfully wiggled away. "Oh, yuck!" she exclaimed, "Just for that you can grab those dishes, pretty boy. And there are a whole lot more in the sink to wash."

"Hey, I cooked. You clean; that's the deal."

"That was the deal. Now I need a shower to wipe all this gunk off my face. Maybe if you hurry with the dishes you can join me." He quickly followed her into the house.

*

The Gulf of Mexico silently slid under the Gecko's keel as the craft sailed past the darkened shadow of the Florida Everglades. The warm salt water was seamless and smooth, a "dead calm" the sailors called it. The blood red sky to the west slowly faded into the horizon, and, directly above, the night sky had already taken hold. The stars reflected on the glassy water as Jeff watched from the bridge. It was quiet except for the low hum of the electronics and the distant rumble of the twin diesel engines under his feet. The gentle rocking of the Gecko as it cut through the sea had sucked the energy right out of the two passengers, who were now below in their bunks.

Jeff had checked on them every so often for the last hour, until he was satisfied they were sound asleep. He throttled down and went back to check one final time. After visiting below, he headed back to the bridge, grabbing a slice of cold pizza from the Dominoes box on the table and turning off the television in the main cabin.

Jeff took his seat back at the control console and slowly pushed the throttles back up to an efficient cruising speed. After a quick check of the navigation map, he reached over and turned the volume knob on the radio to low. He picked up the mike, and, after changing the frequency, he pushed the button with his thumb.

"This is the Gecko calling Key West, Gecko calling Key West, any station. Over."

Jeff waited a moment, and, after some static, a voice answered, "Go ahead Gecko, this is Dolphin Bay marina. Over." Jeff reached up and turned the volume until he could barely hear, "Roger, Dolphin Bay, this is the Gecko. I have a change of arrival information, would you please pass a message along to English Harbor, Antigua please. Over."

"Stand by, Gecko. Over." Jeff waited in silence while awaiting the reply. Finally, a different voice came across the airway, "Gecko, Dolphin Bay. State message. Over"

"Roger. Message reads as follows: will not be arriving as planned, stop. Please cancel slip and docking reservations..." Jeff continued with the changes. When he was done, the message was read back for verification, and sent out. After signing off, Jeff pushed the throttles forward, rapidly gaining speed. He did not care if Luis or Andre woke up now.

*

"What the hell? Who was up here?!" David yelled. Susan was downstairs on the couch reading the latest novel from Pat Conroy. She had been waiting for the shit to start since she heard him come in the door.

"What is all this shit doing on my bed?"

"Wendy wanted some of your things for her story." *That should shut him up* Susan thought.

David looked in his closet for the two shoeboxes, which were missing, and he started to sweat. He went through the relics of his past on the bed, throwing things in boxes and trying to figure out what was missing.

Fifteen minutes later David walked into the den. Susan closed the book and grabbed her shoes, ready to keep her promise to Jeff. He would not be hitting her tonight. But when she saw him, she sat back down.

"Who told you she could go through my things?" David asked quietly.

"She told me you said she could. I called your office, but you weren't *available*."

Susan surveyed her husband. He wasn't mad. He looked lost, or scared. At least he wasn't taking it out on her.

"Did you see two shoeboxes? Old, brown, about this big?" David held his hands about a foot apart.

"She took them with her. Wendy said they were filled with photographs."

"They were. Old ones. Ones I didn't want anyone to see!"

David walked out to the kitchen and pulled a bottle of vodka from the cabinet. He poured himself a screwdriver, drank it, and made another. He came into the den and turned on the television. After flipping through the channels, he stopped on the preview channel. When he read what was on, he picked up a pillow and threw it at his wife to get her attention. "Susan, where are all the blank tapes?"

She looked up from her book after pushing the pillow onto the floor, "I don't know. Why?"

"There's a movie on HBO tonight, and I want to tape it."

"I think we have some in the hall closet," she told him. David went out through the kitchen into the unused, but elegantly furnished, dining room. Through a doorway on the other side, there was a small hallway that lead to the wash room. David could not remember the last time he'd been in this part of the house. Along the wall there was a closet door. He opened the door and reached around to turn on the light. The bare bulb clicked on, lighting up the interior of the huge walk in closet.

A few minutes later, Susan heard David walk back into the den. She was busy reading, and did not realize right away that her husband was standing in the middle of the room, holding a large object in front of him, and looking right at her.

"What the hell is this?" David asked. He sounded angry. Susan still did not look up, the book she was reading was infinitely more interesting than arguing with her husband. "What is what?" she answered. David reached over and knocked the book from her hands. She turned to him and saw what had upset him.

"What the hell is this?" he asked, much louder. He was holding the painting that Jeff had given her. Susan had forgotten she had hidden it in the closet. She tried to play down the situation.

"It's a painting," she said.

"I know it's a painting; I'm not an idiot! Where did it come from?"

"It's mine; I bought it a while ago," she said. David knew she was lying.

"Don't bullshit me. This is one of Strata's weirdo psycho pieces of shit, isn't it?

"No," Susan answered. David grabbed her by the hair and dragged her off the couch. Susan was too scared to fight back as he placed the painting right in front of her face. He pointed to a signature on the canvas, "Then what the hell is that!" David asked her.

"I don't know," she said, crying.

"It looks like a fucking signature to me. It reads Jeff Strata, doesn't it?" he asked, and waited for a reply. She just sobbed. "Doesn't it?" David asked again, louder.

"Yes, okay! Yes," She cried. "He gave it to me." David pushed her face until it rubbed the canvas. "Please. Stop. You're hurting me!" she pleaded. David gave a good yank on her hair and pushed her away towards the sofa. She sat on the floor crying and watching her husband.

"Why aren't you with Jeff?" he asked. Susan was too scared to answer. David was pacing back and fourth, out of control. He banged the painting's frame on his knees as he walked. He stopped and looked at his wife. "He killed his mother!"

"What?" Susan asked through the tears. David started pacing again only stopping to direct his words at her. "Jeff Strata. The guy you're fucking! He killed her. Did you know that?"

"What are you talking about?" Susan asked, not believing

"He killed her," David continued. "He got her involved in drugs. He didn't tell you did he?"

"He said he doesn't talk about his family," Susan said.

"Fucking A he doesn't!" David continued, banging the frame harder and harder. "How do you know this?"

"He grew up here. Everyone knew; she was a junkie, and he got her started on the shit. Nineteen seventy-two. Look it up if you don't believe me."

"Why are you saying this?" she sobbed. "Why do you two hate each other?"

David turned to her. "You mean beside the reason he's fucking my wife?!" She looked away.

"I don't want you around him! I don't want his paintings or anything else of his around here! David screamed, and smashed the painting against the floor. Susan ducked as splintered wood flew all around. David grabbed the canvas that was now only connected to a single piece of frame. He went to the kitchen, grabbed a knife from the counter, and sliced the painting. Susan watched, horrified and afraid to move. When he had shredded the canvas, he grabbed his car keys and went out the door. He threw the painting in the garbage, jumped in his car, and took off down the driveway.

Susan sat and cried, still shaking. She was still on the floor an hour later when the phone rang. She reached over to the coffee table and picked up the cordless.

"Hello," she said quietly, still sniffling.

"Susan?" It was a familiar voice.

"Oh, Jeff..." she cried and told him what had happened.

"Susan," Jeff said when she was done, "My mother killed herself. Go read about it. Go look it up. I don't like talking about my family, but go ahead. I want you to find out for yourself."

"I knew you didn't," Susan said, tears still running down her cheek. "I knew you could never do that. I hate him, I really hate him."

"Don't worry," Jeff said. "I'll deal with him when I get back. And I'll work on a new painting just for you, okay?"

"Yes, thank you," she said. He told her he had to leave, but he would call her again. She didn't want to hang up, and they spoke another fifteen minutes until she let him go.

*

It was eight-thirty, and Doyle was putting Jenny to bed when the phone rang. It had been a long day for both him and his young daughter.

After the grand jury hearing, he had left early from work and gone to the causeway with his family. He liked it better than the beach. The small islands that were used to help connect Sanibel to the mainland had real sand, not crushed shells like many of the local beaches. It also had none of the tourist attractions that begged you to spend money like Ft. Myers Beach did. The causeway was clean, had a public restroom facility, and the parking was always free, so it was a natural choice for families.

The detective left his daughter's door ajar and walked out to the living room. His wife was sitting on the loveseat, and he sat down next to her. Sarah handed him the phone, then went back to watching the Boston Pops on PBS.

"This is Brian Doyle."

"Is this Detective Doyle of the Sanibel Police?"

"Who is this?"

Sarah gave her husband a puzzled look and whispered, "Who is it?"

"Yes, sir. My name is Chris White, and I'm a reporter. I'd like to ask you some questions if I may."

Brian cupped his hand over the phone. "A reporter," he told his wife quietly, then spoke into the phone, "With regard to what, Mr. White?"

"The Blind Pass murder, sir. Marjorie Johnson."

He hadn't thought about the case in twenty years, and now he couldn't seem to get away from it. "What do you want to know?" Doyle reluctantly asked the reporter.

"When did you guys stop trying to solve it?"

7

***

Friday, September 8

The Gecko pulled up to the weather-beaten wooden pier, and Luis stepped off onto dry land for the first time in twenty-four hours. Sitting at the bridge, Jeff was so exhausted he had hit the wood pilings hard enough to dislodge one of the rubber tires tied on to them. Luckily, the tires had done their job protecting both the dock and the Gecko from damage. After shutting down the engines and securing the lines, Jeff went inside and told Andre that he was going to sleep.

The three men had been at sea since leaving Tarpon Bay, but because Jeff was the only one on board who knew how to navigate, he had stayed at the controls the whole time. Luis and Andre both had offered to give him a break, but the darkness after Everglades City had nixed that idea. The mangroves along the shore and shallow sand bars made it too risky to allow even seasoned sailors to run the coast at night, let alone two unskilled DEA agents on their first trip. They had made it to Islemorada Key, just below Key Largo. The current had helped them through the Florida Straits, and now they had a clear shot to the Virgin Isles.

Andre wanted to go ashore. He found that his stomach did not enjoy the water. The agent was almost dehydrated from nausea. But Luis was taking no chances. It had taken five years to get this close to Menceti. And this operation was being watched all the way up in Washington. The Agency had never allowed a buy with this much cash, and a lot of people were nervous. But Luis and Sebastian, his supervisor, had argued that this was the only way of getting Menceti himself involved, and pressure had been felt all they way up to the White House regarding the drug trade. The DEA had some evidence linking Menceti to the bombing of a DEA office in South Florida a few years back, and the Agency wanted him in the worst possible way. And since the fiasco that had killed that FBI agent, they knew they needed to grab him before the Bureau did.

There were hundreds of millions of dollars floating out there, and both agencies wanted to make the bust. But Luis was especially nervous since he was the person who signed for the three million in cash. Of course it was all marked money. Seized, ironically, from the very man who they were now after. But, still, three million dollars was three million dollars.

After a long nap Jeff told Luis that he was going up to the marina office. Luis at first said no, but after Jeff explained that he had to pay docking fees and arrange for fuel, the senior agent agreed but sent Andre with him. The two walked over to the office, and Jeff went inside while Andre went in search of something to cure his seasickness. After paying the marina, Jeff called Susan on a pay phone. She was feeling better, David had not come home since taking off the previous evening.

"I got a message, though; David and I are supposed to go have dinner Saturday night with the Kindles," Susan said.

"Who are the Kindles?"

"Larry Kindle and his wife Debbie. They live in that beautiful, gray A-Frame home when you turn into the Sands. The one that sits right on the golf course."

"I'm not real familiar with the Sands," Jeff said. "Why are you going over there?"

"Larry's kind of in charge of financing David's campaign."

"So they aren't friends of yours?" Jeff asked.

"Oh, no," Susan said.

"Fuck David then. Don't go. Let him take that slut instead," Jeff told her. Jeff told Susan that she was going to have to stand up for herself, that he could only take advantage of her if she let him. She promised not to go. Jeff then saw Andre coming back from the small store across the parking lot. "Listen, Susan, honey, I have to go," he said, "I'll call you in a couple days. I love you." The last three words just popped out, surprising both him and Susan. "I love you, too," she answered as she heard the phone click.

Jeff quickly dialed another number. He waited for the line to pick up as he watched Andre gingerly walk across the huge parking lot. The agent did not see him on the phone.

"Hello?" a voice finally said.

"It's me," Jeff said in a hushed voice, "I need a favor..."

*

High above, Laura was on the U.S. Air commuter plane heading north. She sat in the first seat on the left side of the plane. She always sat there; she had the door in front of her, allowing unlimited leg room. And the row on that side was only a single seat wide, allowing her to use her laptop without fighting for elbow space.

She looked out the window after take off and scanned the ground until she saw the Naval Air Station. She searched the sky above it for Rick's helicopter. The one nice thing about her husband being the operations officer was the fact that he made up the flight schedule. When she told him she was leaving at ten, he moved back the departure of his flight so he could see her off. She knew Rick thought it was a small, but romantic gesture, but she teased him that he was just too cheap to pay for long term parking.

She saw what she guessed was his helicopter and watched it until her plane flew into the clouds, Laura grabbed a file from the attaché case, and started reading.

*

After talking with Jeff, Susan called her boss and said she needed to see him. Sam told her he thought it was over Wendy, and the matter was settled. After she convinced him it was unrelated, but without telling him what it was about, he told her he would see her that afternoon. Susan then called Chris and told him that they had a meeting. She dressed and went to the office. Meeting Chris, she escorted him to her cubicle and left him while she went over to the records section. She checked out the microfiche for the weeks following the discovery of Marjorie Johnson's body.

Susan and Chris were sitting at the microfiche reader making copies of the old articles. As they finished with one set, Susan went back over to the records section, and exchanged them. The View also had copies of Ft. Myers and Naples papers, but they all basically repeated the same information. She was on her fourth stack when Sam came out of his office and called for them. Quickly, the two reporters went into his office.

"What can I do for you two?" Sam asked.

Chris recited his idea to Sam. The editor said Chris' assumption was correct. It sounded like a great feature, even if it did upset some of the business people who would rather the incident be forgotten. He said it was almost folklore by now.

"You know, Chris," Sam said. "If it weren't you, I'd probably say no. But I remember how hard you worked when you sat out in my newsroom, and at least you came to me and didn't try to weasel my notes from any of my employees. I respect that."

"But..." Chris said, anticipating.

"But," the old man smiled and nodded. "But, I want Susan to work on this, too. We can work together, and we both benefit. It's the only way."

Chris and Susan agreed. Sam went to a small file cabinet in the corner of his office, and, after unlocking it, opened the bottom drawer. He pulled out some old stencil pad notebooks. The paper was yellowed and brittle with age. A rubber band held them together. When Sam tried to remove it, the band just snapped. Twenty years in storage had taken its elasticity. Sam handed the two his books after they promised to do their best not to damage them.

*

Doyle drove across the causeway and past the tollbooths at Punta Rassa on his way to the lab in Ft. Myers. The detective had received a phone call from the crime lab. The technician told him that some test results needed to be picked up. As he drove, his thoughts wandered back to nineteen seventy-two and Marjorie Thompson.

After talking to the reporter the night before, Doyle could not get the case out of his mind. He remembered the body, all bloated. He still did not know what she would look like alive. She was described as an attractive woman by the few people he interviewed who even remembered her. As he pulled into the lab parking lot in Ft. Myers, he promised himself to have a second look at the file.

Doyle went inside and up to the front desk. After signing in and showing his identification, he walked down to the technician's office. He knocked on the door, and a middle aged woman opened it and invited him in.

"Have a seat," she said. There was no desk in the cramped office. Tables lined the walls. On them sat microscopes, glass slides, and other equipment used for scientific investigation. The room, in fact the whole building, smelled of formaldehyde. On the wall, three white plastic panels were backlit. An x-ray was clipped to the center panel. There were three chairs scattered about the room, though out of the way. Two sets of shelves ran the length of all four walls, stopping only at the doorway. The shelves overflowed with books and magazines of all kinds. There were no windows, and except for the white panels and a small desk lamp, there was no light at all. Doyle grabbed a chair and sat down. The woman introduced herself as Teresa.

"But everyone calls me Terry," she said and sat on the corner of one of the tables. "What can I do for you?" The woman was very friendly.

"I don't know," Doyle said, a little confused. "I talked to someone this morning about some lab tests. Evidently, some of the results have not been picked up yet concerning the Whitmore murder."

"Oh yes," Terry said and jumped down off the table. "That someone would have been me. Now hold on a moment..." She searched over the various tables, finally finding the report she wanted. She handed it over to the detective.

"Here you go," she said. Doyle opened it up and read.

"What is this?" he asked.

"That's the rape kit you ordered. At least the field tech said you did." She took the folder from his hand and scanned it.

"Okay," she explained. "It says here that they found some sperm samples on the vaginal wall, and on the carpet. It looks like they sent some of the sample away for DNA tests, but I'll be honest. I wouldn't get my hopes up. The sample was quite small." She handed the report back to Doyle.

"That's fine," he said. "But why call me? Shouldn't the DA's office get this?"

"I called the prosecutor handling the case two days ago, but he never showed. I just didn't want this to end up lost or forgotten; that's all."

"Thanks," Doyle replied. "I guess I'd better take it then."

"Oh, there was one other thing," Terry said. "You can tell the DA's office that we traced the various hair samples. Besides the gray hairs, we found some others that did not belong to the victim."

"We know about the animal hairs," Doyle said.

"This hair was dark brown, and it wasn't an animal. It was human."

"So?" Doyle asked.

"The old man is gray upstairs; I'm betting he's gray downstairs too."

"Someone else then?"

"Unless there's a new division of the Hair Club for Men."

*

Laura's plane landed at Southwest Florida International Airport two minutes before noon. The small commuter taxied over to the ramp near the west end of the terminal and shut down the engines. As the blades of the twin turboprops stopped spinning, the lone flight attendant opened the door, which allowed the damp, muggy, ninety-degree air to rush inside the cabin, replacing the cool dry air that had been pumped inside the plane since it had departed Key West. The FBI agent was the first to exit the plane, and, in a matter of seconds, Laura was drenched in sweat by the suffocating heat that reflected off the tarmac. She headed toward the open door of the terminal, directed there by the two airline employees who came over to greet the incoming flight. Once inside the terminal, she walked up the carpeted stairwell and into the main terminal. She was coming out of Gate 1A when he saw her.

Ted Cook, DEA, looked at the photograph and up at Laura. Seeing it was the same woman, he went over and introduced himself. After the greeting, he took her down to baggage claim and then out to the white Ford Crown Victoria.

Cook took Laura on a scenic tour of Ft. Myers, pointing out the Red Sox and Twins spring training facilities, the yacht basin, and the Thomas Edison and Henry Ford homes while briefing her on various task forces that the DEA and her office had worked together on. He told her about the young drug dealer who had destroyed the DEA's office near the beach in the late 1980's. It was the first time in the agency's history that one of their offices had been bombed. He explained that the agency took security seriously.

"We found our informant tied to a tree out in Lehigh; that's a town about thirty miles away. He had been left there about a week. Died from multiple fire ant bites. By the time we found him, the little red creatures had eaten most of the flesh from his face."

"It doesn't sound like a fun way to die."

"He was sold out by a deputy from a neighboring county whose sheriff is now serving time for drug smuggling."

Agent Cook let it sink in for a minute as he found a place to park. "Ever since Oklahoma City, finding a place to park seems to have become the most important aspect of my day."

"I'll bet. But I don't see any barriers near any buildings?" Laura noticed.

"That is why we operate the way we do. Secrecy is the only way of life in the DEA."

"I understand, but what about when our agencies are going after the same person or group? It would be beneficial to both of us to share information, don't you think? Look at what happened with my boss. Had we known..."

"I guess there is no easy answer."

Cook led Laura up to the second floor office of the federal building. At the end of the hall, he opened a nondescript wooden door where the FBI agent was met by Mike Sebastian, her counterpart in the DEA.

"Did you like the tour?" Mike asked as he brought her into his office.

"It's very beautiful," she replied.

Cook closed the gray metal door behind them.

The room was darker than the adjoining office. A single fluorescent bulb inside a yellowed plastic cover on the ceiling provided most of the light. There were no windows, though the outline of one was still visible in the plaster wall. Laura assumed by the cracks that they must have been covered over long ago. The scratched, wooden desk in the room was completely covered with files, papers, and books containing countless bits of information that would be worth millions of dollars to various organizations that operated outside the law. Sitting on top of some books near the center of the desk, a small desk lamp was almost as bright as the fluorescent. The large ashtray next to it had spilled over, and the room had a musty odor of cigarettes. It was also quite cold, despite the ninety-degree temperature outside on the street, and Laura found herself rubbing her bare legs to keep warm. She regretted wearing the short skirt without hose.

Sebastian was a large man, but he was not tall. He reminded Laura of John Goodman, the actor, except for the beard. *He would probably make a great Santa Claus,* she thought.

"Did Ted explain that this was a courtesy meeting?"

"Yes, sort of." Agent Cook could see she was cold and handed her his gray sportcoat from the hanger on the back of the door. "Thank you," She said as she covered her legs.

"Sorry about the office, but since we sealed the windows..."

"I'm fine now, thanks."

Sebastian sat in the overstuffed chair behind the desk.

"I want to work together with your office," he stated. "But first let me tell you the agency's policy, then we can talk like regular people."

"That's fine."

"As Ted explained, we are not required to surrender any information. We will cooperate as much as possible, and, of course, an agent's life will never be sacrificed for a bust, not intentionally. If we feel that a law enforcement officer or Justice Department Agent is in grave danger we will help in any way possible. That event in the Virgins was a shame, but the FBI did not notify us about your investigation, and our agents can not recognize the good guys all the time, as I'm sure you are aware."

Laura nodded, "Of course."

"But we can't risk blowing an agent's cover, and risk a leak, just in the name of good feelings between the agencies. There have been too many instances when either an agent or an informant's cover was blown by a law enforcement officer that either was on the take or simply lacked good judgment. That's the official position."

"What about the unofficial? John, agent Bender, said that you two have a pretty good understanding between each other."

Sebastian picked up a rubber band and fiddled with it, stretching it between his fingers.

"That's true. But we have also worked with each other off and on for about fifteen years. You and I have just met."

"I feel like I should be on the defensive here. Should I?" Laura asked.

"No, but it will take some time to build up a trust between us. John and I never let politics enter into our relationship. But you're kind of young, and, like I said, I don't know you."

"I can understand how you feel, but let me assure you, I know what politics can do to an investigation and I am not like that."

"I'm glad to hear it; that's the same thing John said. Now, is there anything I can do for you, bearing in mind what I've just told you."

Laura took out a couple of files and opened them up, showing photographs of various suspects and unknowns. Sebastian named some people, noted others, and gave the FBI agent some new perspectives on some of them.

"How about this one?"

Laura picked a file labeled FALCON. She laid it on the desk in front of Sebastian and opened it up. Inside were various black and white photographs. One showed Menceti, Luis, Jeff, and Susan when they had arrived in the Keys.

Sebastian looked at the photo and told Cook to get the "TUNA" file. He went to the outer office and returned with a thick manila folder. His boss opened it and took out some photographs. They were pictures of Menceti. In some he was alone, and in others he was with groups of people. Though none showed Luis or the others, one showed Wendy and David at the University Club. Sebastian searched through the file and handed some of the papers to Laura.

"No copies, but you can review these."

Laura opened the dossier and scanned the reports.

"Francis Menceti. Goes by the name Frank, Frankie," Sebastian recited the information from memory. "Suspected drug trafficker, money launderer. Linked to seven deaths that we know of, but we can't prove anything yet. Linked to bombings in Florida and even Oklahoma, but nothing solid. Ties to organized crime in Far East, Russia, and the U.S. He's been importing Valium into the US from Hong Kong through the Virgin Isles for at least a year. Oh, and he holds the same position in GKB as our beloved Governor Snelling. Took over after Snelling was elected. He's a pretty slick character, takes few risks..." Sebastian went over all the details..

"He sounds real professional," Laura said after closing the file.

"This is the guy that had your boss shot. The man plays rough."

"Why wasn't something said about this in Miami? We were told the very, very basics. I mean, this man has tried to kill federal agents."

"That's politics. Liz Hobbs wants to make a name for herself, and you can't do that by sharing information."

"Have you even questioned him?" Laura was angry.

"Not yet."

"Why?"

"Hold on just a minute. Your man Jack Sutton held out on us that the Bureau was even interested in this guy. Politics goes both ways." He told her about the disappearance of Tre.

"We don't know as much about it as you think. We suspected him of laundering money for the cartels or the Mafia, but we haven't made the connection yet."

"Well, Frankie is in business for himself. He made some deals with heavies in Hong Kong. The market there has been drying up since the Chinese moved in. They're looking for a market for opium. What better place than the largest drug market in the world?"

"The U.S.? Opium? That has never been a real problem."

"Do you live in a bubble over there? Christ, you can't swing a dead cat without hitting some Japanese or Chinese, Vietnamese or Korean immigrant anywhere in this country. And they bring their culture with them. Call your L.A. office, ask them about Asian gangs, they'll tell you - it's big business. The market is growing. We have seen a 1000 percent increase in the last three years."

Laura sat quietly. Everything Sebastian said was true; she had just not put it together before. Now it was making sense.

"What is Valium used for?"

"Its original use was and still is to relieve stress, give the user a dreamlike sensation. But there are no real medical uses anymore, though it's still prescribed." Cook explained. "Man made drugs work better, cost less, and are not as addictive, but the FDA still allows Valium in limited use."

"Some people may argue that there are much better medications to treat anxiety that are a whole lot safer. Xanox, Xandrid, a hundred others."

"Why is Valium big, then? I would think that people would sell the other stuff." Laura asked.

"Because the prescription pills are expensive and traceable. Valium is not."

"It seems that we should be working together on this," Laura said.

"Are you offering us something?" Sebastian asked.

"I don't want us killing each other or stepping on each other's toes on this thing. But if we agree, we turn everything, and I mean everything, over to each other. No more secrets."

Sebastian sat back and thought quietly. He reasoned he had nothing to lose and thought Laura naive enough that she would believe he turned over everything he had, but he needed to buy some time to clear it through channels. "It sounds fine to me, just give me time to convince my boss. She won't like it, but I think I can get her to agree on it."

"Fine, I'll stop back in the morning, how's that?"

"I'm going out of town tomorrow, but Ted will be here; just work through him, okay?" Sebastian stood and reached out his hand, she took it. "I look forward to working with you, Laura."

As he said the words, she decided that she wouldn't tell him what she knew of the Governor's interest in Frank. There was no reason to. But she would turn over the money laundering and the offshore accounts. She called the rental car agency from downstairs and had them bring the car to her. After receiving directions from the rental agent, she headed out to Sanibel.

About an hour later, Laura arrived at Caribbean Plantation. She drove through the gate and checked in at the office. She signed for the room; there would be hell to pay if she ever had to explain why she stayed at the most expensive resort on the island, but she wanted to work with Doyle. She called him, and they made arrangements to meet at the small yacht club at the tip of Captiva.

He was waiting when she arrived, and, after introductions, Doyle asked if she wanted some lunch. Neither of them had eaten, so they went into the restaurant that overlooked the boats. A waiter handed them their menus and waited. Laura's heart skipped a beat when she saw the prices. *Thank God for expense accounts,* she thought. She ordered a fried chicken salad; he had a hamburger. The waiter took the orders and disappeared from view.

"They serve great food here," Doyle said. He saw her reaction to the price, "I think you'll be quite happy with it. And the service is great."

"For these prices, they should spoon feed it to me."

"They're not that bad," he said, laughing.

"John said you got a good offer when you left us, but I think he understated. The Bureau doesn't pay enough to live like this." Just as she finished speaking, her pager went off.

"I left my phone in the car."

"There's a pay phone outside," Doyle told her.

"I'll be right back," she said and left in search of the phone. The detective wondered what Laura thought of him. It had never been about the money. Doyle had gone through the academy together with Laura's boss, John Bender, in the late 60's. They had been assigned to room together while in training. The two became close friends, and both transferred to the Washington, D.C. office after graduation. For a few years everything was great. The two built up a reputation as a great team, solving a well known armored car robbery and some anti-war bombings. They were moving up quickly, and some higher-ups noticed their success.

When Nixon took office, the new President informed the FBI that he was concerned with the various subcultures and philosophies taking root in America. He had aides prepare a list of enemies, and he ordered their movements and activities monitored. At first, it seemed reasonable. Many of the names were legitimate hate groups or known terrorists. But as more and more people were added, it became clear that the President was using the list to intimidate and harass people for political and even personal reasons. If a college professor or news reporter showed Nixon in a bad light, he made the list. If a movie star or writer said he did not agree with the policies of the President, he made the list. Doyle became disenchanted with the government and with Nixon when he tried to make the FBI his own little Gestapo. When, in 1972, it looked like Nixon was going to be reelected, Special Agent Brian Doyle made his decision. He could no longer work for a paranoid President. Doyle decided he wanted nothing to do with it. The riots were breaking out, and Vietnam was still going on. He was not the only one who had lost faith in the government. It was then that the opportunity to come to Sanibel came, and Doyle took it. Doyle tried to get his partner to come along, but his friend John had declined the offer. After Watergate, the Bureau had regained its stature as the premiere law enforcement agency in the world.

"It's my office," Laura said as she returned to the table. "Good news, maybe. The computer center said they may have a lead on those partial prints you sent me."

"Maybe it's not a dead end after all," he said.

"I told them to FedEx the stuff to me here. I should have it in the morning!"

"I appreciate all the help you and your office have given me."

"I don't have nearly the experience that John has, but if there's anything I can do..." Laura offered. "You were talking about some possible corruption or something?"

"I just want a fresh perspective on this; that's all," Doyle said. "It's just a theory, based on what the defendant said."

"Let me see what you've got."

8

***

Saturday, September 9

The Gecko arrived at the Virgin Islands Saturday evening. Jeff first piloted the boat up the yacht-strewn English Harbor at The Middle Ground, Antigua's star shaped peninsula that separates English Harbor from Flameout Harbor, but there were no slips available.

"I understand; I'll try somewhere else," Jeff said placing the radio mike down."Shit." He turned to the wall chart and, after studying it, changed course and pushed the throttles forward. The twin diesels roared to life as Andre walked into the small pilot bridge from the cabin.

"What gives?"

"They have no slips available; we're going to have to go to Charlotte Amilie," Jeff answered.

"Is it a problem?"

"No, just an inconvenience."

"Why can't we just pull in along a pier or something?"

"Haven't you ever been on a boat before?!"

"No. Okay, Popeye? I've never been on a fucking boat this long before! I hate fucking boats anyway. How long until we get to Chocolate Emily or whatever this place is?"

"Charlotte Amilie," Jeff said slowly, as if speaking to a child. "And we'll be there in a little while. Just go back and relax and get out of my hair, okay?"

Andre opened his mouth to respond but could not think of anything clever to say, so he turned and headed back to the main cabin.

A couple of hours later, after the Gecko tied up to the wooden dock and all electrical cables were connected, and after he paid for the full tank of fuel, Jeff finally stepped off the boat and onto dry land.

"Where do you think you're going?" Luis called after him. Jeff continued walking away, and without turning back he answered, "To have a drink and relax."

"Where?"

Jeff, still without looking back, pointed toward a small wooden shack about a hundred yards past the concrete seawall at the end of the dock.

"Hold up!" Luis yelled as he and Andre scrambled off the boat and ran after him. When Jeff entered the wooden shack, he turned towards the dark hallway and the restrooms. After relieving himself, he stepped over to a pay phone that hung on the wall near the sink, across from the urinals. Jeff dialed the phone, contacting James to set up a time and place to meet. After he hung up the phone, he made another call.

"Hello," a male voice answered.

"It's me," Jeff replied.

"Everything's set."

"Great."

Jeff hung up the receiver and started washing his hands as the door flew open, slamming into the wall with a bang. Luis stepped into the washroom, followed by Andre, who closed the door behind him and stood by it. The two agents were sweating and flustered. Luis quickly walked along the stalls lined against the wall, searching under them for feet or shadows. Jeff did not turn to watch him, but followed the agents reflection in the mirror above the sink. Luis, convinced they were alone, came up to the sink next to Jeff.

"What the fuck was that?!" Luis demanded.

"What?" Jeff replied innocently.

Luis grabbed Jeff's hair and pulled his head back until the artist was off balance. The agent's face was red with anger, and sweat dripped from his forehead. His jaw was clenched shut, and he spit out the words through his teeth, "This fucking game you're playing! Taking off like that! I don't know what you're trying to pull, but don't fuck with me! You got that, dipshit?"

There was no fear in Jeff's eyes, in fact just the opposite. He was extremely amused by Luis's outburst. The agent saw the comical smile on Jeff's face and knew he had lost. Luis jerked his hand forward and released his grip, causing Jeff to hit his face on the mirror. But he would not show pain, instead he started to laugh.

"I just wanted to pee, sir. That's all. Just to pee."

"Uh-huh," Luis said, unconvinced.

"You see, while you two were sleeping I had to stay by the wheel for hours and hours," Jeff turned on the faucet, letting the water flow. "Just me and my bladder, rocking, and rolling. My bladder just filing up more and more with each splash of seawater. I just kept thinking about how full I felt, how much I needed to take a piss, until I thought I would burst." Jeff could see the effect was working, "Rocking and rolling, and rocking and rolling, and I just kept thinking it would be so nice to just use the head, just relieve all that pressure, just like this faucet."

It was too much. Andre went over to the urinal.

"You're such an asshole," Luis said as he too went to relieve himself. Jeff smiled, knowing that when it came to mind games, these two were amateurs. He waited until they were done and sarcastically turned on the faucet and held out a towel for each of them. They took them grudgingly.

"Oh yeah," Jeff said. "We meet Thursday, three thirty in the afternoon, near the marina office."

"When did this happen?" Luis asked

"I called just before you came in."

"Why Thursday? Why not now?"

"Because we were supposed to be at another harbor, I suppose. Plans change." Luis looked unconvinced.

"I don't make the deal," Jeff said. "I'm just passing the message. That's all."

*

At the same time, but on the opposite side of the island, the GKB Gulfstream IV touched down. On board Snelling and Frank Menceti chatted. They headed up to Menceti's villa, a stunning marble structure that overlooked the harbor. Snelling was not even unpacked when the girls arrived. They were locals, between fifteen and seventeen years old.

"Francis, you are truly the best!" Snelling told his friend three hours later around the pool.

"Remember that," he answered. This was not the first time, but at least these girls were willing. Menceti had grown tired of cleaning up after his friend.

On the next hill over, Agent Sabastian watched through the cross hairs.

"Son of a bitch!"

*

The riverfront streets were jammed with bargain hunters who visited the row upon row of shops and attractions. Many featured the sparkling jewels St. Thomas was known for, as well as small trinkets and souvenirs for all the tourists from the many cruise ships lighting up the harbor.

Andre and Jeff traveled around the island on rented scooters, blending in with the other tourists who visited the Caribbean paradise. The visitors flooded the many restaurants and duty free shops that lined the path back to the lighted harbor where both large and small ships were docked.

Inside Jeff's boat, Luis was watching the black travel bag that contained three million dollars in cash. He did not like the fact that Jeff was out roaming the streets, even if he was being watched. Andre was new to the agency, and Jeff was a sly little bastard. The alternative would have been to leave the money with the rookie. But Luis had signed for it, so that wasn't going to happen.

*

Susan stopped at the end of the driveway. She wanted a nap; her eyes were tired from reading for the last five hours. She had found the article on the death of Jeff's mother, and it had been reported just like he said. There was not even an investigation. If the boy had killed his mother, why would he have gone out with his grandfather searching mangroves and barrier islands for three months after her death was ruled a suicide? The case was closed by police; he had nothing to gain by finding the body. He also had nothing to gain by killing the woman; she wasn't even insured.

She reached into the little metal box and grabbed the mail sitting inside. Laying it next to her on the seat she parked her car in the garage.

After going inside, she grabbed a Coke from the fridge, took her shoes off, and sat down in the den. She flipped through a magazine, then put it aside. Most of the mail was bills or other junk that she would give to David. A small card fell out from between the gas bill and an advertisement for an encyclopedia set. She picked it up, and it instantly brought a smile to her face. On one side was an aerial photograph showing a lush green island chain surrounded by the aqua blue water of the Caribbean. She flipped it over and read the note from Jeff saying how much he missed her; and that he would be leaving for Key West Thursday afternoon. He also reminded her of her promise regarding dinner with David. He hoped she had kept it, since she probably would not receive the card until Thursday. Susan had forgotten all about the dinner. She still had not canceled it.

*

"He refused to request one."

"I can't do anything about that, Doyle. If you have a complaint, call the Attorney General in Hollywood. It's out of our hands," the Chief said. The detective went and closed the door, leaving the two men alone.

"Maybe the hair is Ranson's. What if what Whitmore told us is true? That he was having an affair with Cathy? Maybe he did set up this doctor. From what I've seen, I wouldn't put it past the guy."

"Are you now telling me that David Ranson, the District Attorney of Lee County, may have committed a crime he is now prosecuting?" The Chief sat at his desk and looked up at the detective standing if front of him. "That would be something. The news people would have a field day."

"It would explain why he took such an interest in the case," Doyle said. "It would certainly explain why he never bothered to pick up that other report. For all we know, that could be Ranson's sperm they found!"

"So now it's not just his hair but his sperm, too. Do you have a DNA test handy? Maybe you have a witness who watched David Ranson kill Cathy Whitmore," the Chief said. "Maybe the reason he has such an interest is the fact that *it's an election year*! And that's a hell of a lot more plausible! I cannot believe, no, I will not destroy a man's career just because you think he may have done something!"

"We already have," Doyle argued, "Everything we have against the doctor can be explained away just as easily. Wouldn't you like to have some physical evidence that ties someone directly to the crime?"

"I would love that, but I don't think it's going to happen in this case."

"So I should just drop it, even if we might be putting an innocent man in prison," Doyle asked.

The Chief sat back in his chair and chewed on the yellow No.2 pencil as he thought. Doyle stood in front of him quietly. He did not want to destroy an innocent man, either. But which one was innocent?

"Can you get a hair sample from Ranson?" the Chief finally asked.

"What, just go and ask him? I doubt it!" Doyle replied. "If he's innocent, he'll go nuts with this, and if he's guilty, he won't do it, and we've tipped him off."

"Yeah, you're right," the Chief agreed. "We need to think of a way to get a sample, then take it and get it analyzed."

"The report would not be admissible, besides the fact that it's illegal!"

"It's not illegal to have someone's hair sampled without consent, as long as we don't use the sample as evidence against him."

"But we are using it as evidence!"

"No," the Chief spoke slowly, thinking of each word. "We are using all our available means to determine, through reasonable investigative practices, whether or not the suspect of a homicide investigation had motive, means, and opportunity to commit the crime. If we determine that other persons fit the criteria more closely than the initial suspect, then we should focus on the latter person. Technically, the finding will be used in conjunction with Dr. Whitmore, not Ranson."

"We would be walking the line, and I don't want to be alone on this," Doyle said.

"It's the only way we can be sure."

"I know." Doyle replied. He wasn't sure if it was legal or not, but would it be worse to let a guilty man go free?

*

The sun had already set as Jeff and Andre sat in the little seaside restaurant and ordered dinner. Andre was enjoying himself. He was wary of Jeff, but thought that he had everything under control. He wondered what Luis would say when he told him of the motor scooters and shopping. Maybe it was better he didn't say anything, Andre decided. Jeff stood up and said he needed to use the bathroom.

"That's all, right?" Andre asked.

"You can come too if you don't believe me," Jeff replied seemingly hurt at the lack of trust.

"No, go ahead. Hell, I'm not your baby-sitter," Andre told him. Jeff left the young agent alone at the table.

The food was already on the table when Jeff returned. There were piles of it. Lobster, crab, shrimp. Andre had never eaten so good. Jeff sat down.

"Hungry?" Jeff asked as he watched Andre devour a pile of shrimp.

"This stuff is great, and so cheap!"

Jeff had just bitten into a ring of fried calamari when two gorgeous women walked by. They were both wearing sundresses over bikinis. The white fabric was so sheer, it was as if it were nonexistent. The taller one said "hi" as she passed by and sat at the bar.

"Check them out," Andre said.

"Go say "hi"; see if they'll come over," Jeff suggested.

"Oh yeah, right."

"Why not?" Jeff asked as he waved to one. She waved back.

"Okay," Andre whispered, leaning over the table toward Jeff. "Just suppose that they come over. And suppose that they invite us to go party with them, and then later they want to, you know..."

"I know...what?" Jeff was playing with him.

"You know.." Andre spun his fork around, rolled his eyes, danced a little in his chair, "Come back to play spin the pickle or something?"

Jeff looked at the girls, then at Andre, then back to the girls. He seemed a little confused at the point Andre was making. "So they come here and then later they want to..." Jeff hesitated, "...have sex? And there's a problem here?"

"Of course!"

"Listen Andre, I just can't see the down side," Jeff waved again, the girl waved back. Andre grabbed his hand.

"Knock that off; what do you think, that we can just bring them back to the boat - Luis will have a conniption! I've never seen a conniption, but he'll have one; don't you see that?"

Jeff sat quietly for a minute, placing his hand to his chin, then rubbing his cheek while in thought. "Andre, look around." The young agent looked around at the restaurants, buildings, and harbor.

"What do you see all around us?" Jeff said opening his arms wide and looking around and up toward the sky.

"I don't know. What?"

"Look hard."

Andre looked around, and wondered what Jeff was talking about, and what he was supposed to be seeing.

"Hotels, my friend," Jeff finally said. "We are surrounded by hotels. We don't have to go back to the boat; we just rent a room."

Andre shook his head, "Oh, no! What will Luis say? No way!"

"C'mon, live a little. Luis is not your dad!"

"I can't."

"Sure you can."

"No."

"Yes."

"No."

Jeff stood and walked over to the women, continually turning back to see

Andre's eyes pleading to stop. The two women chatted with Jeff a few minutes, then grabbed their glasses and were escorted back to the table where Andre sat. The agent was regretting ever leaving the Gecko. Jeff said he'd be right back, he was getting a second bottle of wine. The two women fawned over Andre, speaking a language he did not understand, or try to. Jeff returned and poured them each a glass. Andre did not notice that the others did not drink.

It did not take long before the drugged alcohol affected the young agent's senses, and with a cue from Jeff, the four left to find a hotel room. They rented two suites, charging both to Andre's credit card. The couples separated. Once inside the hotel room, Andre forgot about his girlfriend back home and started to undress. He passed out before his shirt was unbuttoned.

In the adjoining room, Jeff waited for the knock. He opened the door and pulled the woman inside. He told the two prostitutes that they were to watch the young agent and not let him leave the room until they heard from Jeff. He pulled ten one hundred dollar bills from his pocket and tore them in half. He handed the halves to them and promised the other halves when he returned.

Jeff rushed downstairs and looked at his watch; he was a little late, but nothing a greedy cab driver could not make up.

"Just sit and wait here," Jeff said.

"No problem, sir;" the taxi driver had already made an extra five hundred dollars for a ten dollar ride. He was more than happy to sit and sleep while he waited for the hurried young American to return.

Jeff quickly made his way to the stubby corporate jet. As he ran up, a squat old man smoking a cigar came from the other side of the plane.

"All set," he said as the two shook hands.

"Let's go, we haven't much time," Jeff ordered as he jumped inside the Lear 35. It would take a little over two hours for them to arrive in Ft. Myers.

*

Susan was just about asleep when she heard a car coming up the driveway. The crunch of shells and the sound of the engine caused her to get up and look out the window. Through the blinds she saw David's Porsche pull up in front of the house. She looked over at the clock; he was early. She was hoping to be out of the house by the time he came home; she had promised to meet Chris and research documents for his story. She went to the heavy wood door, and twisted the deadbolt until she heard the reassuring click that told her the lock was in place. She crawled back into bed and relaxed under the satin sheets. Even with air conditioning, it was too hot for the comforter. It wasn't until she heard the slam of the car door that Susan remembered the postcard on the counter. She had left it stacked with the other mail, and now David was sure to find it. She sprang from the bed and out to the stairwell. Rushing down, she was met by David, who was coming through the doorway from outside.

"Oh, you're home," David said, surprised. She had startled him.

"Yeah," she said nervously, "I was about to make dinner."

"What are you making," he said, disinterested. She looked on the counter, beyond David, and saw the card sticking out from the mail stack.

"Chicken...something."

David looked over at her. Her hair was a mess, clothes wrinkled and unkempt. "Chicken what?"

"I don't... I haven't decided yet," Susan said. She continuously shifted her eyes back and fourth between David and the postcard. She tried to be nice, tried to keep the conversation growing so that he would move from between her and the mail.

"David..Honey..Go in the den, I'll make dinner," She said. He looked at her. *Something was wrong here, definitely wrong,* David thought. *Susan is not like this, especially lately.*

"I'm not hungry," he said.

Shit. Susan needed to do something to get him out of her way.

"Go fix yourself a drink, watch TV if you want, I'm not watching anything."

"I don't feel like it," he said and went over to the refrigerator. He passed by her, and she cautiously reached over and grabbed the mail. He had been watching her reflection in the door of the refrigerator and turned when he saw her move.

"What do you have there?" he asked.

"Nothing," she said as she hid the mail behind her back and slowly moved away. David reached his arm out toward her and stepped slowly.

"Give it to me."

"What?" She tensed up, and squeezed the mail tightly, crushing the envelopes, which gave off a crackling sound.

"Whatever you've been hiding," he said and stepped quickly, grabbing her arm. She tried to pull away but his grip was too tight.

"You're hurting my arm!" she screamed.

"What have you got there?" he yelled back.

He spun her around, and she let go of the letters, causing them to fall all over the tile floor. " The mail! Just the mail!" she cried.

He reached down to pick it up, and she grabbed the postcard. He forced it from her hand, tearing off the edge in the process.

"What the fuck is this?" he said as he read it.

"It's mine. It was addressed to me," she said, moving away and rubbing her arm. Tears were streaming down her cheeks.

"It seems you have an admirer," he said as he flipped the card over to look at the picture. "Let me guess; I've met him before?"

"It's mine," she whispered.

He turned to her and reached into his pocket. Pulling out a lighter, David flicked it until a yellow flame danced under the postcard. She watched helplessly as David teasingly dangled the paper over the flame.

"Please, don't," she whispered. David sat with a smile on his face, nodding his head. She wanted to turn away, but she couldn't. He held it closer and closer until the edges started to turn brown, and a little wisp of smoke rose from the glossy picture.

Suddenly, the loud deafening buzzer of the smoke detector sounded. David looked up. Susan rushed him, and snatched the card from his hand. He turned to her and, with the back of his hand, slapped her cheek so hard she fell back. The diamond ring had sliced open the flesh right below her left eye, and red blood ran down her face.

She screamed and ran upstairs. David, after momentarily distracted by the sight of the blood, looked back at the screeching alarm and hit at it until it flew from the ceiling, smashing itself upon the hard ceramic tile of the counter top. He poured a double shot of vodka, drank it, then poured another in the hope of calming his nerves. He could hear his wife's footsteps going between the bathroom and bedroom upstairs.

"God dammit! Of all the nights!" he said out loud to no one. He was due at Larry's for dinner; that's why he came home early. That was why he thought it strange that Susan was cooking. "Shit!" he said, knowing he'd never be able to take her now.

David started up the stairs. He heard the loud click of the deadbolt come from Susan's room. At the top of the stairs, he gently knocked on her door.

"Are you okay?" he asked knowing it sounded more sincere than he felt. He could hear her crying, and knew that if he spoke gently, she would play her part.

"Get away from me, you bastard!" she replied through the door.

"We're supposed to go to Larry's for dinner tonight," he said. He heard her walk to the door, and then the loud click of the bolt unlocking. David stepped back as the door slowly cracked open. Susan's face appeared in the doorway. She had a huge welt on her cheek, and dried blood surrounded a two-inch cut above it. David knew that she could not go with him, even if she wanted to, which she didn't.

"Fuck it. I can't take you like that," David said, "I need to call Wendy." He turned and went downstairs. She waited until his car left the driveway before she let more tears flow.

*

It was dark by the time Jeff arrived in Ft. Myers. After landing, the Lear 35 taxied behind the Follow-me truck to the transient ramp and shut down. Two fuel trucks quickly pulled up next to the plane, and the young drivers jumped out. One ran over to the pilot, while the other pulled the hose to each side of the plane. The pilot told him to top off both tanks and reminded him to fill the wings simultaneously so the jet would not tip over. Jeff climbed out of the plane, carrying a small bag. The pilot had started to cover up the engines, but Jeff stopped him.

"Hey, don't do that," Jeff said, "I won't be long, okay?"

"Hey, whatever you want, my man. I'll just wait here."

"Where's the phone?"

The old man pointed toward the small terminal building several hundred yards away, past a row of single-engine Cessnas. "They have a car, too, that they let you use for free, if you ask em," the old man added. Jeff walked over to the phone, slipped a quarter in the slot, and dialed.

Susan was sitting and sobbing against her door when the phone rang. She didn't want to answer it, but did anyway.

"Hello," she said almost in a whisper, her voice still shaking from crying.

Jeff heard the female voice but wasn't sure he dialed right, "Susan?"

"Jeff?"

"Hey, sweetie, you sound different."

"It's probably the phone lines. You being so far away and all."

"Oh," he said, knowing that wasn't the problem, "Honey, I can't talk long, I was just thinking about you and wanted to say hi."

"Hi," she said, with a small laugh. She needed this, she actually felt a little better hearing his voice. "I got your card; thanks."

"I wish you were here with me."

"So do I," she said and started crying. Jeff heard the change in her voice.

"Are you okay?" he asked, concerned.

"We had an argument."

"You sound like you're crying, David didn't hit you again?" There was a pause, and Jeff heard more sobbing. "Baby?" he asked again.

"Just a little- I'm okay. At least I'm out of that dinner, he took Wendy instead." She sounded tired, worn out.

"Well, that's good, at least you're away from him for a while," he assured her, "Listen, I have to go, but I'll call you later. Are you going to be home?"

"I don't have anyplace else," she said with a sigh.

"You will soon. I promise."

Jeff hung up the phone and walked up the stairs and inside the small terminal at Page Field. As the doors closed behind him, the noise from the airfield was deadened. The woman working behind the counter looked up from a paperback, watched him come in, then turned her attention back to the novel. Jeff stepped up to the desk and waited what he considered an extended length of time before clearing his throat. After three progressively louder attempts, she finally looked from around the edge of the book.

"May I help you?"

"Yeah; I hope so, anyway," Jeff said. "I understand you have a courtesy car here for pilots?"

"Yes, we do," she answered curtly. "Are you a pilot?"

Jeff thought better than be truthful. "I just came off that Lear outside. Could I use that car?"

"We have rentals, you know."

"I know, but we're only going to be here for a few hours."

The woman saw that he was not going to go away. "Fine," she said, "But you need to sign for the keys."

*

Larry closed the door behind him as he followed David into the study, leaving the women in the kitchen. Larry's wife gathered the dishes from the table and dumped them in the sink.

"If I ever had this kind of money, I'd never do the dishes. I'd hire someone to do it," Wendy said.

"Before we had money, I used to say that too. I hired someone to clean the house and keep the grounds clean."

"What happened?"

"I missed it. I sat around doing nothing except watching them. So, one day I decided I was happier when we didn't have servants."

"I wouldn't miss it," Wendy said. "Sometimes I sit and dream about living like you all do. I think it would be heaven."

Larry's wife turned and looked at Wendy. *There is the type of woman of whom every wife is afraid,* she thought.

"You know he's married," Debbie said.

"So what's your point," Wendy replied smiling.

Larry stepped behind the three-foot wide oak bar and poured himself a glass of scotch whiskey. He looked over at David, who was admiring the collection of model cars displayed in a lighted oak case. "You want a drink?"

"No."

"David, it isn't only the doctor, it's the things like tonight. I mean bringing another woman to dinner. And that show with that guy and your wife at the club. People notice this shit."

"Yeah, well, who gives a fuck who I bring to your house, Larry? You? I had an argument with Susan, and she wouldn't come."

"Wouldn't, or couldn't?"

"What's the difference?"

"The difference, David, is that wife abuse is not a generally accepted pastime of elected officials, in case you've been living in a cave for the last twenty years." David became defensive.

"What's that got to do with my campaign?"

Larry came over and sat close to David. He stared him straight in the eyes. "Listen, I know you have a problem, and, frankly, I wouldn't normally give a shit except for the fact that you want to use my money for an election. Then every one of your problems becomes my problem." He relaxed, " I don't want any problems."

"So what are you saying?" David asked. Larry put down his drink, leaned forward and cupped his hands together. "I.. well, all of us... look David, there's no easy way of saying it."

David stood, "You don't have to, Larry. I don't need your damn money. As a matter of fact, I don't want it!" Before Larry could say anything, David was out in the hall. He went into the kitchen and grabbed Wendy's arm, pulling her to her feet.

"Let's go, we are leaving!" he ordered, dragging Wendy to the door and out to the car.

Larry and his wife followed behind. "Wait, David," they shouted, but he paid no attention. He threw Wendy into the passenger seat, and slammed the door behind her. Turning to Larry, David yelled, "I hope you fucking die!" and jumped in his car. The Kindles shook their heads in disgust as they watched him speed out of the driveway and down Periwinkle Way.

"What happened?" Wendy asked.

"They call themselves my friends? They stabbed me in the back--that's what happened. Fuck 'em."

Wendy didn't know what to do, so she sat quietly while they sped along the western beach of the island. David made not a sound.

"Do you want to get a drink or something?" she asked finally.

"No," he said without taking his eyes off the road.

"It might calm you down."

"I said no. I can't go to a bar with you. According to Mr. Kindle, it would be bad. I have something better in mind." They stopped and picked up some beer at a twenty-four hour convenience store. He then drove them to the marina. He stepped out of the car and went around to Wendy's side. He opened her door, but she didn't move.

"I don't know if this is a good idea," Wendy said. She was frightened by David's anger which seemed to have grown.

"I don't care. How's that!?" he said, and pulled her out of the car.

" David! That hurts," she said as he continued to drag her behind. They came to the boat, and he pushed her on board.

"Here!" he said holding out a beer.

"I don't want one!" she told him. He threw the bottle at her, hitting her leg. She let out a scream, and he jumped down and clamped his hand over her mouth.

"Shut up, you bitch. Shut the fuck up!" She started to cry. He grabbed a bottle of beer and opened it. He held it out for her.

"Now drink it!" he said. She was scared, and took it. She drank it. He handed her another and another, until she felt nothing at all. David took out his anger in a sexual frenzy that Wendy neither felt, nor cared about. Then, after he was finished, she passed out. He drank one more beer, then fell asleep beside her.

*

Officer Brent Kohler sat on the hood of the Cherokee and waited for the flatbed tow truck to show. There was no one around, and the only sound was the water splashing against the rows of white fiberglass tied to the dock. Whoever owned the black Porsche had parked illegally one too many times, and the rookie cop was going to teach the guy a lesson.

The yellow, flashing lights of the truck were visible before it turned in to the parking lot. The officer jumped from the hood and waited while the eighteen year old driver pulled up beside him. The officer pointed to the sleek sports car and the long haired kid put the truck in position in front of the car.

He jumped out, and, after handing a clipboard full of paperwork to the officer, the driver went and stood near the back of the truck cab. He reached under the overhang of the ramp and manipulated the three black handles that lowered the flat steel bed down to ground level. The noise from the hydraulic pumps and revving diesel engine disturbed some of the birds that were in the trees above; they took off for a quieter resting place. Kohler sat inside the car and filled in the required forms that would be given to the impound yard over in Fort Myers, saving himself the trip later; he then called in the information over the radio to the dispatcher.

Inside David's boat, the District Attorney was laying on top of his young mistress, neither had on a stitch of clothing. He was almost asleep when he heard a loud grinding from outside the boat. He lifted his head so that he could hear more clearly. It sounded like a garbage truck, but not quite. His stirring woke up Wendy.

"Stop," she said, pushing him away. The alcohol was still affecting her. He grabbed her arms and sat up on the overstuffed padding. "Please stop."

"Shut up for a second," David said. She came to slowly, rubbing her head. She looked over at him, hatred showing through the bloodshot eyes.

"I can't believe you!" she said. "You raped me!"

"Knock it off; I think someone's outside."

Wendy slid away from him and looked for her panties, while David looked out from the cuddy cabin through the small oval window. When he opened the curtains, the yellow emergency lights from the truck reflected on the bulkhead inside the small stateroom.

"They're towing my fucking car!" he screamed excitedly, pushing Wendy out of his way. He found his tan pants on the floor put them on.

"Good," she said.

"Stay here!" he ordered.

Officer Kohler was about to leave when he saw David emerge from the boat wearing only a pair of tan pants. The car was already pulled up onto the tilt bed when David approached the two men.

"What the fuck are you doing?" David screamed. Officer Kohler turned to him.

"Is this your car?"

"You're damn right it is! Get it off this fucking truck!" he yelled.

Both the towing service driver and Kohler could smell the alcohol in and around David.

"Sir, have you been drinking?"

David looked at the young officer and did not recognize him.

"Do you know who I am? I'm David Ranson, the District Attorney! Now get my car down!"

Kohler picked up the clipboard and started writing in it. "Hello, Mr. Ranson. I'm officer Kohler, and that man over there is John." The driver gave a nod, then climbed up into his truck. "Now, then. I'm sorry, but you will have to talk to John's boss about getting your car back."

"I'm not talking to John or his fucking boss," David said, slurring the words in anger. "I'm talking to you. Now, Officer, I am ordering you, give me my fucking car."

"I can't do that, sir." Kohler looked up at John and waved him on. The truck started moving, and David lost it. He was jumping up and down, screaming, "You sorry excuse for a fucking cop! I'll have your badge! You are nothing! I'm the fucking DA!"

Officer Kohler took as much abuse as David could give out and calmly waited for him to finish. He leaned his six foot, five inch, two hundred forty-five pound frame against the Cherokee and crossed his arms, saying nothing. It reminded Kohler of his three years as a U.S. Marine Embassy Guard, when the foreign protesters would stand at the gates for hours screaming. The ranting lasted for ten minutes after the car and driver had disappeared. Finally, David stopped screaming, realizing that the officer was not going to be intimidated. David stopped and took a deep breath. Here it comes, thought Kohler, the deal--making.

"Okay, officer, look. You got me. I admit it. Just give me my ticket, and get my car back here. I'll straighten all this out in the morning."

"You know I can't do that, sir."

The rants and verbal assaults started again but lasted only a few minutes. They ended abruptly when Kohler opened the door to his truck and tried to leave. David panicked and grabbed the officers arm. Kohler easily disengaged David's grip from his shirt and started the truck's engine.

"Okay, okay. Don't give me my car--but don't leave me here!" David pleaded. "C'mon. Do me a favor!" He held on the door frame.

"Sorry. You're a big boy-- the D.A., remember?" Kohler said with a grin.

"Can I have a ride? Just a ride home."

"Do I look like a taxi? You can call home!"

"Why are you being such a hardass?"

Kohler looked at him as if he'd been insulted. "Hardass? Hardass? Sir, I have not arrested you. I believe that is a huge favor. Now the only way I can give you a ride is if I do arrest you. Is that what you want?"

"No. Fuck it. I'll walk," David said, and moved away from the car. Kohler nodded, then waved and pulled out across the parking lot. David walked back toward the boat. He went inside and saw that Wendy had blacked out again. She lay on the thin mattress naked except for one sock, and panties wrapped around one leg. The District Attorney collected his clothes and quietly dressed. He then reached into a cabinet and grabbed a small black pouch. He checked its contents, then climbed up out of the boat and headed home.

David had walked only a mile or so when he suddenly felt a sharp pain in his foot. He reached down and felt something sticking out of the sole of his shoe. He pulled it and felt a burning sensation as the small roofing nail came out. He sat on the ground and took off his shoe. His bleeding foot left a warm sticky goo inside the shoe and on the sock. He put them back on, after making sure that nothing else was in there, and continued walking. Larry's house was not that far away.

\
*

Larry and Debbie went up to the master bedroom to get ready for bed. The room was on the second floor and took up a large portion of the house. There were his and her bathrooms, a Jacuzzi, and a handmade bed that was at least one and a half times as large as a standard king-size. They both disappeared into their respective bathrooms. Larry was still shaving when he heard Debbie turn on the wide screen television.

"Did you know he was having an affair," Debbie asked while laying on the bed.

"David's never said anything," Larry lied as he looked at his face in the mirror, "but I suspected. Why? Who told you?"

"That girl, Wendy."

"She said she and David were.."

"She didn't come right out and say it, but she alluded to it."

Larry came out into the bedroom. Debbie was lying across the bed, wearing a sheer black teddy.

"Do I have anything to worry about? Is there anything you want to tell me?" She asked seductively.

"Hell no, Deb. I forgot other women existed after I saw you," he replied, walking slowly towards her.

"You are so full of shit.." she started to laugh and reached for him. "All men are such lousy liars"

"We are? Maybe I should jump in the shower."

"You don't need a shower."

"If you say so," he reached down and pulled her close. Her nose twitched, and she pushed him back. "On second thought.."

"I told you," Larry went to the bathroom and turned on the water. The steam poured out from the doorway.

"Close the door, you're fogging up the T.V. !" Larry's head stuck out the door. "Honey, do we have any more champagne?"

"I'll go see," she said. Debbie hopped off the bed, went out the bedroom and down the stairs. She headed into the study and over to the bar. As she bent over to look in the cabinet, she felt a sharp prick in her neck. A black gloved hand covered her mouth and lifted her up. She tried to fight, but the drugs soon took effect.

*

Susan heard the door slam and looked at the clock. 4:30 a.m. She heard David as he climbed up the stairs. His steps stopped at her door. She heard him jiggle the handle and remembered that she had unlocked it to show him the cut. She turned to the doorway in time to see the door open and his silhouette come into her room.

"Get out!" she screamed at him.

"I need you, Susan!" he said. "Help me!"

Susan backed away from him as the dark figure loomed at her. "Get away from me, you bastard!"

She pushed further across the bed, until she suddenly fell off the side and onto the floor.

"Susan, help me!" David said. She had her back to the wall, and, as he approached her bed, she put her feet up against the box spring. Using the wall as leverage, she pushed the bed with her legs. The bed frame was on coasters, and David had no warning when the bed came at him in the dark. It hit him below the knee, knocking him backward. He spun as he fell and slammed his head against a night table.

Susan did not hear a sound but was afraid to move. She slowly, quietly worked her way to the door, then to the steps. Once downstairs, she dialed 911 and stayed on the line until she saw Officer Kohler's truck pull in the drive.

*

"I think that's everything," Jeff said. He climbed into the plane and sat in the copilot's seat. The old man had already started the number two engine. As he went down the checklist for the remaining engine, he turned to Jeff.

"I tried to return the keys to that car, but the door was locked so I slid them through the mail chute. I don't know what happened to the girl who works here," Jeff said.

"She's gone. I told her you'd leave the car out front," the pilot said.

"I did; they'll see it. Where's the little guy with the flashlights?" Jeff asked.

"The ground crew? They went home right after they fueled the plane. This airport isn't a controlled field after midnight. There's no one here but us."

"That means there's no one here to see us leave, either."

"You got it, *amigo*. Is the shipment secured?"

Jeff looked back at the five duffle bags containing cash and drugs buckled into the seats. "Yeah, all secure. I'll bet Uncle Sam never thought about this when they were training you to fly?"

"They should have never pulled my wings then," the man replied. "Now, let's get the fuck out of here!" Soon, the Lear was just a speck on the horizon.

9

***

Sunday, September 10

Jeff knocked hard on the hotel door. It was ten-thirty in the morning, and the sun was already shining. One of the girls answered the door wearing nothing but her panties. Jeff pushed open the door and went inside. On the bed, the other girl was still sleeping, as was agent Andre Cortez.

"Any problems?" he asked the older prostitute quietly. She shook her head no. Jeff handed her the money and she gently woke up her friend. The two women quickly dressed and left. Jeff waited a few minutes until he was sure they were gone.

"Let's go! It's time to get up!" Jeff yelled as he pulled Andre off the bed. The agent was very hungover, and it took almost thirty minutes before they left the hotel.

"Where the fuck have you two been?" Luis demanded when Andre and Jeff jumped down onto the deck of the Gheko. The agent was unshaven and still wearing the same clothes as when they left. It was obvious he had not slept.

"Your boy here got a little drunk and disappeared into a hotel. I couldn't just leave him, and we don't have a phone on board, so I couldn't call." Andre was already cowering. He had royally screwed the pooch on this one and knew it. Luis looked at Jeff, but what could he say?

"Get inside!"

Andre quickly walked past Luis into the boat, but Jeff was stopped by the senior agent. Luis slammed Jeff up against the cabin wall, reached up with his right arm, took hold and jacked Jeff up by the neck.

"I don't know how, or why," he whispered. "But I know that this is your fault, and I will find out what you are up to." Luis pushed Jeff in through the door.

*

The hotel phone rang, waking Laura. "Agent Wilson?"

"Yes,"she answered, her eyes still closed.

"This is Detective Doyle. I just received a report from one of our officers, and I thought it might interest you. May I come by and pick you up?" Laura wanted to just roll over and go back to sleep, but this was why she had come here. She sat up. The room was still dark, due to the heavy curtains that filtered out any of the sun's rays. This made it seem much earlier than it was. She lifted her watch from the night stand and looked at it.

"Yeah, sure. Can you give me ten minutes to get ready?"

"No problem."

*

Jeff, Luis, and Andre sat at the white plastic table overlooking the bay watching party boats leave the dock, taking their passengers for a five hour tour around the islands. A ticket booth was near the entrance of the dock, and some tour guides were handing out tickets to the vacationers streaming from the matching tour buses.

"Just a quick hop from one island to the next and customs is bypassed, English ships to American ships, they hardly look," Jeff explained to Andre. "The shit comes in from Hong Kong and then goes to your friends."

"How's it get on the English ships?"

"Don't worry," Luis interrupted, "it gets there. Now the two of you shut up."

A little while later a beat up tan and rust Toyota Land Cruiser parked nearby, and two men stepped out. Alvin and James were both dressed in brightly colored pastel shorts and shirts that advertised the island. They looked more like tourists than the tourists did. Alvin walked over to a food counter near the ticket booth and bought some fried potato wedges, while James went straight to the table.

*

"Officer Kohler is new to the Sanibel Police Force, but he's dedicated," Doyle explained. "He doesn't know his place yet, at least according to some of the local politicians."

"You mean he doesn't fix tickets."

"And then some. He seems to enjoy upsetting our local legislature and community leaders. Lucky for us in this case."

"So where are we going?"

"Lee County Hospital to meet with him."

*

"How much ?" Luis asked.

"Five million. That comes out to one hundred and fifty per vial. It's not negotiable," James said.

"That's too much; I'll take my business elsewhere," Jeff said and looked over at the DEA agent. Luis did not like this at all.

"Excuse us for a moment, mate," the red-haired Irishman replied. He grabbed his partner and walked over to the car. The two were having a very animated discussion when the DEA agent turned to Jeff.

"You're blowing it," he said quietly.

"Don't worry; I know what I'm doing. Stay here." Jeff walked over to the two who quieted down when he got close.

*

Wendy awoke in David's boat. Her head was pounding, and her beeper wasn't helping any. The memories of the previous night were blurred, but David's actions came back as she looked down at her bare leg and saw the bruise that the bottle had left. She touched it and grimaced at the pain. She reached down and pulled on her panties then sat up, swinging her legs slowly until they rested over the edge of the small bunk.. The dizziness and nausea quickly caught up with her, and she swallowed hard, and trying not to vomit.

"David," she called as she tucked her head down, resting it on her hands. She waited for an answer, then called again louder, "David! David, I'm going to be sick!"

She felt the bile forming in her throat. The taste was in her mouth as she bent over, placing her head between her knees. She opened her mouth to yell one last time, but as she did, she felt her stomach tighten. She couldn't stop it. The warm mass of foul liquid and indistinguishable yellow and green chunks spilled from her mouth. Wave upon wave came up, spewing on the deck, the mattress, and her clothes that still lay on the floor. It dripped from her mouth and chin, it went up her nostrils and burned her throat. Although lasting only minutes, it seemed like hours. Finally, there was nothing coming out but a clear liquid that had a rancid taste. But by then Wendy was too weak to care; the cramps in her abdomen from the dry heaves took over. The tears flowed from her eyes; her hands shook. She closed her eyes, then lay back on the sheets and curled up into a ball until the spasms stopped. She wished David was there, yet she was glad he wasn't.

After a while, she felt strong enough to sit up again. The overwhelming stench filled the small cabin. Wendy stood up, though she still felt wobbly, and pulled open the blinds. The sun was shining brightly. She opened the door and stepped out onto the deck. She was half naked, but she needed the air and was not about to put on her vomit stained dress. Once on the deck, she saw a small garden hose wrapped on a stanchion two slips down. Thankfully, there was no one in sight and only a few cars in the parking lot. No doubt fisherman who would be well offshore by this time of the morning. She limped over to the hose, the leg stung when she tried to put weight on it.

Wendy started rinsing off. The water was freezing, but it felt good.

"Hey you! Missy! What are you doing!" The voice startled Wendy. She turned and saw an old bearded man hobbling towards her from the marina office. Wendy thought of running, but he was almost upon her. She covered herself with her hands.

"What are you doing here! This is not a public shower," he yelled. His worn face looked into hers, never wandering, ignoring her nakedness. He stopped about three feet away, out of breath. He grabbed the hose from her hand, and took a sip of the running water.

Wendy backed up slowly, trying to make her way towards the boat. The old man took off the blue stain covered T-shirt and handed it to her. "Put this on, cover yourself," he instructed. She took the shirt and put it on. It smelled bad, but not nearly as bad as her own. "This ain't no damn commune here, young lady," the man said almost as if to himself. "You damn snowbirds come down here every year bringing your vulgar morals and such."

"I'm not from..."Wendy started to say.

"I don't have to put up with it," the old man interrupted, pointing his finger at her. " You keep your clothes on around here--this ain't New York City, or Miami! We have respectable folk here, you understand?"

Wendy waited to make sure he was done speaking this time.

"Well?" he asked.

"Yes, sir. I understand," she replied.

"Well, good then. It don't make no sense to be runnin' around without a stitch of clothing on. Havin' no respect for themselves..." the old man continued to mumble to himself. The man reached into his cutoff black shorts and pulled out an old, half smoked cigar. Wendy stepped away towards the boat as the man lit the cigar and started to smoke. He puffed away silently a few moments.

"Missy, I don't know you. What you doing here anyway?"

Wendy took a deep breath. She explained about her and David. About her affair, and that they had been coming here often. She told him about the previous night, leaving out the sex and anger. She did not remember anything after passing out and assumed that David had woke up earlier and driven home.

The old man listened attentively, asking a few questions here and there, but mainly just letting her speak. He stood and took a few puffs on his cigar when she was done, while he sorted things out in his head.

"You know, that David fellow has been bad news ever since I knowed him, and even before that," he said. "Now, it sounds as if you got what you deserve little lady." Wendy started to speak, but the old man raised up his hand.

"Hush a moment," he said. "It's my turn to speak. I reckon I don't know you from Adam, and even if you are cheatin' a woman out of her husband, which I don't condone, mind you, but even with that no man ought to leave a woman alone out in the middle of nowhere. `Specially an incapacitated woman such as yourself, all naked and unclothed." Wendy stood quietly. The old man was right. *How could I have gotten into this* she wondered. The old man took another long and deliberate puff on his cigar.

"You know, I could have you arrested," he said.

"For what?"

"Don't worry, I ain't gonna," he replied. "But I could for trespassin' and public lewdness. But, there ain't no sense in gettin' you in trouble with the law. But I will be havin' a say with that boyfriend of yours. Now go git dressed, and, when you're ready to leave, come up and I'll get you a cab." The old man headed back to the office as Wendy walked back to the boat.

*

"Look, guys," Jeff said, "we're all friends here, and I'm sure we can work this out. We were only willing to spend three million, but you want five. Why don't we give you the money we have now, as a down payment, and you give me all the vials?" Alvin and James stood across from Luis and Andre. They were staring each other down as if in an old spaghetti western, but this wasn't a movie.

"Now why would we do that?" Alvin asked turning to Jeff.

"Listen, my people had a little problem with the exchange rate, okay? Five million dollars is three million pounds," Jeff explained for the benefit of the two agents. "Call Frank--I'm sure he won't have a problem with this."

"You fucking little wanker! You know we always deal in pounds," Alvin said. "How the fuck can we justify changing that much currency? I ought to just shoot you dead right here!"

Alvin reached into his coat, but Jeff quickly grabbed his arm.

"I wouldn't be doing that if I were you, Alvin," Jeff told him.

"And why the bloody hell not!" Jeff nodded to the two agents who walked away. Jeff lead the two dealers out of earshot of the two agents. He stood with his back to Luis and Andre.

Luis watched Jeff, while reaching into his pocket and pulling out a pack of Marlboros. He offered one to Andre.

"Don't smoke, thanks."

"I need to quit," Luis said, keeping his eyes on the others.

"What do you think he's doing?" Andre asked.

"Probably saying what serious buyers we are, that we're connected, the basic bullshit that all little snitches say to keep us in play."

"Maybe he's selling us out?" Andre said.

"Not a chance, that prick knows it would be a prison sentence," Luis answered. " And that's the best he could hope for. And he'd probably be dead inside anyway. These guys play for keeps."

Jeff held Alvin's arm firmly. He turned to make sure that the agents could not hear him, then looked straight into Alvin's eyes. Jeff's expression told them he was serious.

"Those two gentlemen behind me are DEA agents and they want to bust your asses and Frank's."

Alvin and James watched Luis and Andre standing there smoking a cigarette.

Jeff continued.

"If you give us the drugs now and say that there is a bigger shipment coming in next time, then we can all leave smiling and never see each other again. If you don't follow my instructions then the drugs will be confiscated and you'll have to answer to Frank."

"But so will you, and Frank won't be happy about this," James said.

"Hey," Jeff said. "I just found out who they were, and I have a way of taking care of them. But you guys have to play along."

"What if we just kill all of you and disappear?" Alvin's glare moved away. Jeff followed the short man's eyes until he saw the muzzle of a high powered rifle sticking out from the roof of a building. Jeff just smiled.

"Because there are two helicopters full of agents ready to take you down circling out there." The two smugglers followed Jeff's gaze up into the sky, searching.

"I don't bloody see them," Alvin said

"They're there, believe me," Jeff assured them. They stopped scanning the sky and turned back to Jeff. They wondered why this man would implicate himself, knowing full well this would be the end of his life in this business, and probably the end of his life period. There had to be a good reason, Alvin thought. "Listen to me," Jeff continued. "If we play this my way, we not only keep the shipment, but get three million dollars as a bonus. Those two aren't going to need it where they're going!" That was the clincher. Their expressions told Jeff all he needed to know.

"Okay, Yank. What do you want us to do?" Jeff relaxed, although his outward appearance did not change. The hardest part was over, and he was still alive, at least for the time being. "Okay, this is what I need.."

*

Wendy drove down the Kindle's driveway for the second time in less than twenty-four hours. The yellow tape was becoming an all-too-familiar sight for the news photographer. On the phone Sam had warned her that it was not going to be a pleasing, but she had nothing left to be sick on, so, after a shower and change of clothes, she headed right over.

As she neared the house, a policeman stopped her and checked her credentials. After getting permission from the sergeant, she was shown a place to park and instructed to see the detective in charge before she took any photographs.

"And who would that be, Sergeant?" she asked.

He pointed to man who had just walked out the front door. "That's him, Detective Doyle."

Wendy headed over to Doyle, who was talking with a young woman. But as she crossed the driveway, a black Porsche came speeding down the drive and stopped with a screech of tires. If she had not seen the car, Wendy would not have recognized him. The top of David's head was wrapped completely with white gauze. His left eye was hidden behind a bandage, and his left cheek was swollen. Oblivious to Wendy's presence, David stepped out of the car and walked directly towards Doyle. He was limping, and Wendy saw that his foot was bare, except for an ace bandage. Overall, he looked as if he had been in a bad car accident.

"David!" she yelled to him and ran to catch up. He stopped and turned and seeing her, waited. She wasn't sure if she was mad at him or happy to he was there. The only thing she was sure of was that she wanted an explanation.

"Where the hell were you, and what the hell happened last night?" she asked a little too loudly.

"Keep your voice down!" he said. "I can explain."

Wendy looked at him,"I want to hear this!" David looked around. His appearance was drawing a lot of stares, and he didn't want the attention.

"Not here. Not now," he told her."I'll call you later."

Wendy looked him over, adjusted the gauze over his eye, then took his hand. "Okay, later. You promise?"

David wanted to get away from her as quickly as possible, "Yeah, yeah, I promise. Now let me go!" She released her grip, and he looked around to see if anyone was watching. No one was paying much attention; there was a much more serious situation.

Doyle saw David limping toward him and walked over. Special Agent Laura Wilson followed. David reached out his hand, but Doyle refused to take it. The District Attorney pulled his arm back.

"What gives, detective?" David asked. Doyle glanced at Laura, then back to David.

"You tell me, Mr. Ranson."

David looked confused, "What are you talking about?"

Doyle spread his arms out and looked around, "I mean all this, David. Tell me what happened. I assume you know."

"Know what? I just got here. I just found out." The pain killers from the hospital had kicked in, keeping David relatively calm. He wondered if they were also the cause of his confusion.

"Found out what, David?"

Doyle watched the D.A. for his reaction to the question. David began telling Doyle about the dinner and the nail he stepped on in the driveway, of his wife being hysterical and so on. It was all in the report that Doyle read this morning. But he noticed David was acting different, very much out of character. The last time the detective had even questioned his judgment, David had blown up, yet he was calm today. Doyle had made a mental note of it, to be used later. As he listened to David's explanation, he couldn't help but be impressed by the details. But Officer Kohler was right; David's appearance was consistent with the events that took place here last night. The hospital said they were sure that at least one of his wounds was caused by a metal blade.

"David, let me ask you this," Doyle interrupted. David stopped talking, and the detective continued, "You told an officer last night that you were here alone for dinner; is that correct?"

David thought a moment, "No, that is not correct."

"So the officer lied. He made that up?"

David was starting to get upset, which made the pounding in his head more pronounced, "What are you getting at, Doyle?"

"Why don't you just answer the question, Mr. Ranson?" Laura asked. David turned to her.

"And you are?" he snarled.

Laura calmly took out her identification and showed it to him. "FBI, and I'm assisting Detective Doyle. Do you have a problem with that, Mr. Ranson?"

"What's the FBI doing here? This isn't your jurisdiction," he asked.

"That's none of your concern. Just answer the question," she replied. She had met men like David before and knew how to handle them.

"I'm the prosecution in this county; I don't have to answer any of your Goddamn questions." David replied, with a little more emotion. "I ask the questions. Not you, and not Detective Doyle here, me. And I believe I am done talking to both of you. I'm going in to look at the crime scene." David walked away toward the house. Laura and Doyle watched as he entered the doorway.

"Do you think he had anything to do with this?" Laura asked.

"He either knows something or is the cockiest man I ever met. I don't know which, but I'd love to find out," Doyle replied.

"Isn't it a mistake to let him in the crime scene?"

Doyle shook his head, "No, I think it would be more a mistake if we didn't. You don't know our distinguished District Attorney, David Ranson. If we kept him away, he would scream bloody murder, no pun intended."

"Even if he was part of it?" Laura asked.

"Yeah, I think so," Doyle said. "And what if he isn't responsible? Then What? No, it's better to let him in there."

"But you are going to question him?"

Doyle watched as David stood in the doorway talking to one of the officers. David looked out and saw Doyle watching him. Their eyes met for a moment, then David disappeared inside. "Yeah, I'll talk to him. But I want to check some things out first."

"I think we should go and talk to your Chief," Laura said.

"Why?"

"Because yesterday I saw some photographs that you are not going to believe," Laura told him.

Inside the Kindle's home, David wandered around the crime scene, asking questions to the investigators as they worked collecting evidence. Debbie's body was found upstairs on the bed. She was naked and, from the bruises, probably raped. The medical examiner thought she had died an hour or two after her husband because of the clotting and other conditions of the body. She had a small trace of blood on her neck that matched a hypodermic needle that was found on the bedroom floor. Her teddy had been ripped in half and tied around her wrists, then to the bed. Her eyes seemed to bulge from her skull, and her tongue was nearly bitten in half. A blue cap off a hypodermic needle was also found in the kitchen by the Florida Department of Law Enforcement agents, who at first thought it belonged to either the paramedics or the coroner, but he now believed it to be from the needle in her neck.

Larry Kindle was in much worse condition. His body hung out of the Jacuzzi. His right arm had been almost completely severed with a knife, attached only by some white fatty tissue to the shoulder. His face was unrecognizable due to stab wounds, and both his calves had the tendons cut. He was facing the bed as if watching over his wife. Yet, even as badly mutilated as he was, not any of the individual wounds were fatal. Had it not been for the time of death, the medical examiner would have guessed the killer had made Larry watch Debbie die.

David walked around silently. He showed no emotion, at least none that Officer Kohler could see. Doyle had asked that he shadow the District Attorney but not make it obvious. After the bodies were removed, David went out to his car and left. Kohler followed in his own car. David drove fast, but not excessively so, back to his boat. Kohler did not follow him into the parking lot but pulled ahead and parked on the small shoulder. He walked back and watched as David untied his boat and sailed it out of the marina. The officer went back to his car and went to find a phone to call in.

*

The phone rang in Doyle's office, and his Chief picked up. It was Officer Kohler. He reported what happened, and the Chief told him to take the rest of the day off. After hanging up, he gave the news to Laura and Doyle. Laura went over and closed the door.

"What I am going to tell you is strictly confidential," she said. "I don't even think I'm cleared to tell you this, but after seeing that scene this morning and the way that Ranson is acting, I don't have a choice."

"Okay, we're all ears, and it won't leave this room," the Chief said. Doyle agreed. Laura explained how they had been watching Menceti and outlined as much of the investigation as she had to in order for the two officers to grasp the scope of his crimes.

"The other night, our surveillance teams photographed and videotaped David Ranson meeting Francis Menceti at the University Club in Ft. Myers. We have heard his name mentioned several times recently in wire taps from Menceti to his organization, and we have a copy of a cashier's check for five thousand dollars drawn from GKB to Ranson's personal account."

"Shit," the Chief said.

"Exactly," Laura replied. "This man is bad news, but I didn't know anything about these other events. Not that I would have any reason to."

"Has he done anything illegal?" Doyle asked.

"No, nothing that would show he was violent. The check he accepted is suspicious, but not illegal."

"Could it be a bribe?" the Chief asked.

Laura shook her head, "Why would he? It's not like Menceti is up on charges or even being investigated in Ranson's jurisdiction. He rarely even comes over here. Even GKB doesn't have any contracts or anything going on that he could influence."

"But he will probably be our next congressman," Doyle said.

"You can't get in trouble for bribing someone who wants to be a congressman," the Chief said.

"What about an illegal contribution?" Doyle asked.

"It went to his personal account," Laura answered. *Menceti was slick*, Doyle decided.

"So let's look at what we have," the Chief said. "Let's put everything out on the table."

The three of them outlined anything strange or peculiar about David Ranson's recent behavior. They examined how he acted at the two murder scenes and at the hospital the night before. His recent dinner guests. How he had convinced Doyle that it had to be Doctor Whitmore. How convenient it was that he cut his foot and injured himself in his wife's bedroom the same night that his financial advisor and his wife were brutally murdered. The evidence report that was ignored and the old doctor's theory. In the end the three law enforcement officers could not help but suspect that David Ranson was guilty of something. The Chief told Doyle to go back over Whitmore's house and see what else he could find. He would have someone from the FDLE meet him. Then he was to go to the Kindle's and do the same.

"I want to see his car payments, mortgage, credit cards. I want to know everything-- look at who paid back his student loans. And I think we need to contact the State Attorney General's office," Laura said. "If this involves the governor's office and our surveillance links these guys together, I don't want any tip-offs." The Chief and Doyle agreed.

*

Luis' patience was running out, and he was relieved when Jeff and the others started to walk back to him.

"Everything's cool," Jeff said to the agent. "We have three million now, you'll get the rest with the next shipment." The DEA agent retrieved the silver case from the car. He opened the suitcase, and the two Brits counted the money.

"Just like last time, eh?" he said, reaching out to the American.

"Just like last time," Jeff smiled and shook his hand.

"Where is the product?" Luis asked.

"We will get it tonight," Jeff answered. "Right Alvin?"

"Yeah."

Luis closed the cases after they were done counting, "Then you will get the money tonight."

"Of course, at time of delivery," Alvin agreed. "Jeff knows all the arrangements."They looked over at Luis. "Your associate Mr. Strata said you would be interested in obtaining another shipment?"

Luis turned to Jeff, who nodded. "What have you got?" Luis asked.

*

Rockman authorized the Sanibel Police to start an investigation but asked that it involve as few people as possible, due to Governor Snelling's involvement. The Florida Attorney General told them that he would make arrangements to fly over within the next twenty four hours. He said he would like to meet with both Doyle and the Chief.

"What about Special Agent Wilson?" the Chief asked.

"She's FBI, they have no official reason to be involved in this," Rockman replied. "Other than the fact that the FBI has observed the D.A. meeting with Menceti and the Governor."

"I'd feel a lot more comfortable if she were here; she seems to have a grasp of what's going on. Besides, I trust her judgment." Rockman knew what the officer was insinuating.

"Listen, Chief, I am a member of the cabinet, but the Governor's office and mine are completely separated. This is Florida, remember, and I am elected all by myself. The only people I need to satisfy are the voters."

"I still would feel better if we had someone who isn't on the state payroll involved."

"If that's how you feel, I have no objections," Rockman conceded. It would be better for him also if the FBI helped. Regardless of the state constitution, going after Snelling or David Ranson was going to be difficult.

"You're in," the Chief said as he hung up the phone. Laura smiled, "Now let's hope my boss feels the same way." While waiting for approval from Washington, the Chief and Laura took out all the files on both the Whitmore and Kindle deaths. They started looking through them again for inconsistencies. Doyle, meanwhile, was back at the Whitmores' walking through the crime scene with the FDLE techs. They gathered in the bedroom; the yellow police tape was still visible outside the sliding glass doors. The blue mattress and bedding had been taken to the lab, but the rest of the room looked the same as the last time Doyle had been there. The setting sun cast a yellowish light in the room, highlighting the dust particles that floated in the air. Doyle explained to the three technicians what he wanted them to do.

"I'm sorry to drag you out on a Sunday night like this, but some things have changed like I told your supervisor over the phone. I want you all to do another thorough search, but this time I want it to go out of the bedroom." He heard them groan. "I know, this sucks. But I want to dust everything we can. If you think this is bad, try being in prison for something you didn't do. Any questions?"

"What do you mean everywhere?"

"Exactly what it sounds like, everywhere," Doyle answered. "Okay, people, let's do it!"

*

It was eight o'clock that night when Sam walked out of his office. Locking the door behind him, he saw Chris still reading the old notebooks. The rest of the room was empty, except for Wendy who was over at a layout table sorting through the newly-developed pictures of the Kindle home. Sam walked over to where Chris was sitting. "Exciting reading, huh?"

Chris looked up at him, "Yeah, actually. You take really good notes, I'm impressed."

"Thanks; I'm glad someone appreciates my work," Sam replied.

"Oh, Sam," Wendy said from across the room. "You know we all love you!" She smiled but continued placing and cutting the photographs. Sam adjusted his hat, let out a sigh, and walked towards the door. "Goodnight, kids. Wendy, lock up when you leave."

Chris heard the door close and decided to take a break. He put down the notebook and rubbed his eyes. After stretching out his arms, he rolled his head around listening to the bones crackle in his neck.. He pushed back his chair from the desk and stood up. He saw Wendy and went over to see what she was doing. She heard him walk up, but continued working.

"What have you got there?" he asked.

"Some photographs of today's murder," she said. He reached over to a stack of black and white pictures and looked through them one at a time. "These are pretty good," he said. "You got right in there."

"That's what a zoom lens is for."

"It looks pretty bad in there. It was pretty disgusting, I'll bet." Wendy asked him for one of the photographs he was holding. He handed it to her, and she placed it on the razor cutter.

"Have you ever been to a murder scene?" she asked.

"No."

She turned and looked at him, "Never?"

"Nope, not-a-one."

"That's odd," she said and turned back to her work.

"Not really; there aren't as many as people think. I mean, c'mon, this is Lee County, not Dade County."

"I guess you're right," she agreed. Chris put the photographs down and walked back to the desk. "Time to get back to work," he said and picked up another notebook.

*

David tried sitting up on the seat but fell over, almost landing on the empty bottle of tequila that rolled around on the deck of his boat. His head hit the mangrove bushes as he pulled himself up on the rail. The tide had pushed the little

Sea Ray into the shrub that lined the shore of the small barrier island. He made it over to the console, reached down, and turned the key. The motor cranked on the third try, and he steered away from the shoreline. He had only traveled a few feet when the propeller snagged a section of steel pipe that was sticking up out of the sandy bottom. Instantly two of the three aluminum blades sheered off the prop. The small boat quickly lost its momentum and drifted back towards the mangroves. He looked over the side and saw that the water was shallow, but with his foot still cut up from the other night, he figured it wasn't worth the effort. "Fuck em," he said when he saw he wasn't going anywhere. The tide would lift him off in a couple of hours. He turned off the key, went down into the cabin, and passed out again.

*

"Where are they?" Jeff asked, again. He, Luis, and Andre had been sitting at the small cafe for three hours longer than they planned. They had the two metal cases at their feet. Earlier they had contained the cash, but Luis wasn't the trusting kind, so now the three men were each wearing one million dollars in money belts under their shirts. It was Jeff's idea; in case they had to take off in a hurry, the containers would be a great diversion. It had taken some convincing to let Jeff carry some of it, but most people don't realize how much space a million dollars takes up. The three of them looked like they were wearing bullet-proof vests. *Now that would have been a good idea*, Andre thought.

About every five minutes a waitress would stop at the table and ask if they wanted to order something. Luis kept speaking for them and telling her only water. For close to four hours, the three of them had done nothing but sit there and drink water. Even the conversation had ended after the first fifteen minutes. They had nothing left to say after spending all the whole trip alone together on the boat. Jeff couldn't take it any more and stood up.

"Where do you think you're going?" Luis asked.

"To take a piss! I've been sitting here for hours drinking water," Jeff replied. "My bladder is about to rupture!"

"Sit down," Luis ordered. Jeff looked at him like the guy was crazy.

"No, I gotta piss."

"You're not getting out of my sight with that money around your waist," Luis said. Jeff started jumping up and down. "Fuck it, shoot me." He started taking off his shirt right there in the cafe. Andre jumped up and pulled Jeff's shirt back down to hide the money that was showing.

"What the hell are you doing?" Luis asked. The vein in his forehead started to show, and his face was glowing red, "Sit down and hold it!"

Jeff leaned over, his whole body shaking, "Hey, man, I've gotta piss like a racehorse, okay?! Now if you don't want the money to go, fine, I'll take it off here, but I really need to take a leak!" Luis didn't like it, but now he had to go, too. "We all go," he said. "Together!"

"We can't do that," Jeff said. "What if they come while we're gone?"

"Shit," Luis didn't like it, but he was right. "Okay, you two go; I'll wait here!"

"I don't have to go," Andre said.

"You're fucking goin'," Jeff said as he pulled Andre from the chair. Jeff practically ran into the bathroom. He went up to a urinal and relieved himself. Andre followed and figured he might as well try since he was already there. As the agent stepped up to the urinal next to Jeff, he did not see the door to the stall behind him open. Andre never felt the steel blade as it came up through the back of his neck and severed his spinal cord.

Outside in the cafe, Luis knew something was wrong. He shouldn't have let Jeff out of his sight. The agent felt for the standard issue nine millimeter in his pocket, slid the safety off, and went over to the men's room. He opened the door and looked inside, only to see Jeff's body face down in a puddle of blood on the floor. His shirt had been torn off, and his pants were down around his ankles. He went over to the two stalls and kicked open the doors. Andre was no where to be found. Luis gently nudged Jeff's stomach with his foot, but he saw no movement. "You dumb fucker," Luis yelled. "What the fuck happened?!" But Jeff's body did not move. A trail of bloody footprints and scrapes led to a window on the opposite wall. Luis ran and climbed out the window. He was behind the restaurant in a small alleyway. He saw no one. He ran around and back into the cafe, frantically searching for a familiar or better, a suspicious, face. But he found none.

Luis ran out of the restaurant and into the street. He looked around but didn't even know what he was looking for. Andre just seemed to disappear into thin air, along with two million dollars. Luis had just lost his informant and his partner, and he was just plain pissed off. His left hand was in his pocket, gripping the weapon. He spun around a half dozen times. "Shit!" he yelled and ran to the car.

*

Scott Zoe was helping his son do his algebra homework. Since the divorce, Scott rarely spent any time with him, and it showed in their relationship. Mark lived with his mother most of the time, but she was off in California somewhere with the national party leaders. Politics had brought them together, but it had also ripped them apart. They had spent only five months of their six-year marriage together. Had it not been for Mark, they would not have stayed together that long. He was now fourteen. A very independent fourteen. He rarely even talked to Scott now, preferring his friends at the private academy he had attended since he was ten. But he was still only fourteen, and occasionally he liked to get outside of that structured environment. He would come see his dad, half because he wanted too, half because he knew he should. So when the phone rang, Scott was a little hesitant to answer. But after the third ring he picked up the phone.

"Zoe residence."

"May I speak to Scott, please."

"Speaking."

"Scott, this is Rockman. We have a little problem."

"What is it?" Zoe asked. There was a pause on the line. It had to be serious if Rockman was calling personally.

"I should not even be telling you this, but the shit is coming down, and I think Snelling's going with it." Scott's heart sank as the Attorney General explained what had happened. How that one dinner had dragged him into it. He listened to how the FBI had video tape and photographs. It had taken less than five minutes for Rockman to read the obituary of Zoe's once promising career.

"What should I do?" Scott asked, though he was still numb from the news.

"If you don't want to go down with them, then resign and come talk to me. I can work a deal, Scott." Zoe hung up the phone after telling Rockman he'd consider it and get back to his office in the morning.

10

* * *

Monday, September 11

Luis parked in the lot and headed down the wooden planks to where the Gheko was tied. He had been out searching for Andre all night, without any luck. He was tired and angry and out two million dollars. *Fuck that asshole Strata,* he thought as he stepped up onto the deck, *he deserved what he got.* He went over to the door, which was still locked, and to which he now remembered Jeff had the key. Luis went to the back and pulled at the sliding glass door. It slid open easily. Luis entered and locked the door behind him. The shore power was still connected, and the air conditioner had kept the cabin at a cool seventy degrees. Luis went right down the stairwell and into his cabin to get some clean clothes. Since he did not have the key, and didn't know how to sail, there was little chance that the boat would be leaving anytime soon. He decided to get a shower then call Sebastian for plane tickets. He still hadn't figured a way of reporting the missing cash or Andre's disappearance. Though he knew that Sebastian wouldn't shed a tear for Jeff's death, he dreaded reporting that, too. He had been their one solid contact to Menceti. Now they'd have to start from scratch.

The agent stripped and went into the head. He turned on the shower and stepped inside. The warm, clean water felt great. Luis hadn't noticed the blood that had splattered on his leg while kicking Jeff. It was now caked on, and took some scrubbing before it rinsed away. He had just started shampooing when he felt it. At first he thought it was from the wake of a passing ship, but then the lights blinked and he heard the generators kick in. Someone had disconnected the power and was trying to start the engines. Luis quickly rinsed his face and grabbed a towel. He opened the door to the main cabin passageway and turned to go upstairs. He felt the sting of the gun butt as the world went black..

*

Zoe sat in front of Snelling as the Governor read the piece of paper. He placed it down on the table and looked up at his Chief of Staff. Zoe could not look at his boss, instead he just stared out the window at the Old Capitol building a few hundred feet away.

"Scott, I can't accept this. I won't accept this," Snelling said.

"I have no choice. Neither do you, Governor," Zoe answered.

"Tell me why?"

"It's in the letter, it's all in the letter," he said pointing to the paper on the desk. "I can't take not being with my son. It's bad enough I lost my wife. He and I talked last night for a long time."

"Oh come on. We all make sacrifices, it's part of the job," Snelling was trying to browbeat him into taking back the resignation. But Zoe wouldn't budge. "Fine," the Governor said, "I'll put you on administrative leave. It will give you time to think about it."

"No, Governor, no leaves, no vacation, I just want out," Zoe tried to sound convincing.

"Fine," Snelling said. "Effective immediately. Do you have some replacements in mind? You're leaving me in a very tough spot, you know."

"I drafted a list last night. I'll drop it off by lunch."

Zoe stood up and walked out without another word between them. Snelling called in his secretary and told her to notify the communications office that he would need a press conference for the announcement. He then asked her to notify the Lieutenant Governor, the cabinet, and various staff. He went and sat at his desk as she wrote it all down. She then dropped off phone messages that he would need to personally return and went back out of the office. He asked her to close the door as she left.

Snelling watched all the people walking around out on the capitol grounds, before deciding to get started on his work. He went through the messages tossing some away, placing others on different files on his desk so he would have the information on whatever he was discussing at his fingertips. About two thirds of the way through the pile he found a note that read simply "Call me-immediate-RE: Zoe 853-3791. Snelling buzzed his secretary. She came in and looked at the paper. She told him she hadn't written the message and had no idea how it got there.

The Governor dialed the phone and it was answered after a single ring.

"Hello." It was a woman's voice.

"Who is this?" Snelling asked cautiously.

"This must be Governor Snelling."

"You know who I am, who are you?" the Governor asked.

"That doesn't matter, Governor. We have a mutual business partner who pays me for information. Do you know the man I am talking about?" It had to be Menceti.

"Go on."

"Let's just say that I found out that someone other than the two of us knows what you are up to. And let's just pretend that the person is down in southwest Florida, and about to be indicted. And let's even pretend that your chief of staff found out about it and decided to jump ship before anything happened. Am I making myself clear, Governor?" So Scott was stabbing him in the back.

"I think so, but what do you want from me?" Snelling asked.

"Nothing, I'm just doing our friend a favor, but I could not get a hold of him so I thought I would tell you in case it could be of use. TTFN." The woman hung up the phone then turned back to the computer on the desk. She needed to finish her research paper before heading back over to her internship at the Attorney General's Office. She never realized how much money she could make as a receptionist, if she had, she never would have gone to college.

Snelling thought about this for a minute. He needed to contact Menceti, but if he were under investigation, then he had better not contact him. Shit, he needed Scott now, or maybe Zoe was a part of it. He buzzed his secretary.

"Yes, Governor?"

"Get me Mr. Menceti on the phone, please?"

"Yes, sir."

While waiting for the call to go through, Snelling pulled out a manila envelope from the top drawer of his desk. He reached in and took out a small accountant's notebook. He opened it and checked the pages to be sure they were all there. He then pulled a deposit book from the envelope and checked that. Everything was still intact.

"Mr. Menceti on line one, Governor," his secretary said over the intercom. Snelling picked up the phone, and pushed the little square button.

"Peter?" Menceti said, unsure if anyone was on the line.

"Francis, I had a very strange call this morning I want to ask you about."

"Don't worry, Peter; I've taken care of everything." But Snelling was worried. When Menceti called him by his first name, the Governor knew it was time to start worrying.

"I think we should meet, Francis."

"That would not be a good idea right now," Menceti said. "I have some other business to attend to. Maybe this weekend."

"I really must insist we meet sooner, Francis," Snelling said.

"I told you, Peter, there is nothing to worry about. I will come and see you Saturday."

Menceti hung up. Snelling wanted something done now. But he was also afraid of what Menceti would do. The man was anything but political.

*

The Federal Express driver knocked harder this time, but still no one came to the door. He opened the little black mailbox that hung on the wall next to the door and placed an *Attempt to Deliver* form inside, next to the one he had left the day before.

11

***

Tuesday, September 12

Lance Rockman flew into Fort Myers early Tuesday morning. He was met by Doyle and Laura. They drove straight to the county courthouse where they sat in a meeting room and went over their findings. They had uncovered more incriminating evidence in the last forty-eight hours, but the most incriminating was the fact that David Ranson had not been seen since Sunday morning when he had left on his boat. His car had been impounded already, due to parking tickets, but the police would need a search warrant to go to his house.

Florida's Attorney General looked over the reports and agreed. He told them that the removal of an elected District Attorney had never occurred in Florida to his knowledge. And although it was possible, it was far from guaranteed even if David was found guilty. There had been few provisions in the state constitution for this, so he wanted to move cautiously, but as quickly as possible.

They took their findings to Judge Dempsey. He was a man who not only respected the law, but cherished it. He signed the warrant immediately.

The police arrived at Ranson's house along with a team from the FDLE to serve the warrant. No one answered, so Doyle had Officer Kohler force open the door. Inside the house, the investigators and technicians went into every room. They searched not only through desks and drawers, but emptied the jars in the refrigerator and cupboards, looking for the weapon that killed Larry Kindle.

They found David's financial records. On the desk near them Doyle saw a receipt for two hundred seventy-eight dollars to the video store. This triggered his memory. He had objected when David offered to return the videos found in Cathy Whitmore's bedroom, but the D.A. had overridden him. The detective wanted to know why. Why would a prosecutor return a potential piece of evidence? Doyle sent an officer to the video store to find out.

Susan was busy writing on her computer when Sam came out of his office calling out for her. "Right here, Sam," she said. She had not seen David for the last few days, and the relief from that stress had given her writing renewed life.

"I need to speak with you right now!" Sam said and went back to his desk. Susan quickly finished her thought before saving it. She went over to his office. He told her to come in, have a seat, and shut the door. He offered her some coffee, but she said no. He stood and walked around his desk, finally sitting in the chair next to her.

"What's going on, Sam?" she asked, eyeing him suspiciously.

"I don't want you to get upset," he said, taking her hand. "But I just got off the phone with a police officer friend of mine." *Oh my God*, she thought, *David's back!* She could feel the tension come back into her shoulders. She realized over the last few days that she had lost all feelings for him. She did not care whether he was ever coming home. Sam saw her tense up.

"This is about David, isn't it?" she asked.

"Yes, but it's not what you think."

"He's back, isn't he?"

Sam saw the anguish in her face. He shook his head no. "I don't know how else to tell you, but the police are at your house right now with a search warrant."

"Oh, my God," Susan screamed and tried to get up. Sam held her down; she fought him, but the old man was a lot stronger.

"Let me go, Sam! Let me go!"

"Hold it!" he said, trying to calm her down. Outside in the newsroom, her screaming had drawn the other reporter's attention, and one of the women opened the door to Sam's office. Inside she saw Sam trying to keep Susan in the chair. "What's going on in here?" the woman demanded to know.

"Help me calm her down!" Sam said. The woman came in and assisted her boss. "Settle down, Susan! If you go over there like this they'll put you in jail!"

"Don't you know what they're doing to my house? My house!" she said, and started to cry. The fight left her, and she broke down in the chair. The other reporter handed her a tissue. She looked over at Sam, who motioned for her to leave. Reluctantly, she stepped out of the office, disappearing behind the office staff that had gathered at the door. Sam told them to get back to work, then closed the door. Susan was just sitting there, mumbling about how the police were going through her food, and her clothes, and her closets. Sam tried to comfort her, but they both knew how a house looked after a search like this.

"Why, Sam?" Susan looked up at him through tear swollen eyes.

"I don't know, honey, I don't know," he said softly. He had asked his source at the police the same thing, but had gotten no response. But the old man had his suspicions.

"What are they looking for? If they'd asked I could have found it for them," she sobbed. But they both knew the police did not work that way. Sam offered to drive her home after she regained her composure, but she said no. He told her to forget about work for a while, take some time off until this all blew over. She quietly left his office. She drew stares as she gathered her things, not even bothering to turn off her computer. Sam walked her to her car, making sure she was okay. She gave him a hug. He shut the driver's door behind her, and she gave him a wave as she pulled out onto Periwinkle Way.

*

"See, there it is," the teenager said as he pointed to the boat. The Cape Coral police officer looked over at his partner. They had responded to the report of a boat caught in one of the barrier islands at the mouth of the Coloosahatchee River. The small cuddy cabin was sitting in some mangrove trees, almost completely on its side. The area where it sat was well outside any channels, so it was not a navigation hazard. But the aft end was below the surface of the water, and the rest would probably follow when the tide came in a few hours from now.

"Have you gone over to it?" the officer asked. The teenager and his friends said they hadn't. As soon as they saw it they called it in, one explained, because it wasn't there earlier. One of his friends thought it might be abandoned, and if so, what were the chances of the group keeping it? Not very good, the officer told them. Someone had to own it. The two police officers notified the Florida Marine Patrol, then told the teenagers not to leave. The officer climbed back on board his Jet Ski and followed his partner over to the twenty-two foot Sea Ray. They climbed aboard the boat.

"Hello? Anyone on board? This is the police," they yelled. The boat was a mess; the fiberglass had been cracked by the mangrove stumps. The deck was covered with a few inches of water, and sand had piled up in the lowest corner. The seat cushions were missing, as was the lid to the engine compartment. Inside, the officers could see the engine was submerged in salt water. They worked their way up towards the small door of the cuddy cabin, and the officer saw that the keys were still in the ignition. His partner opened the cuddy door, which had been jammed shut by mangrove branches, and heard a low moan. Inside they found David lying on a cushion in an inch of water. The officer pulled out his radio and called for assistance.

*

Scott Zoe, former Chief of Staff, opened the glass door and stepped outside into the sunshine. He headed across the concrete walkway that separated the Old Capitol from the nondescript high-rise that now housed the government for the State of Florida. It was lunch time, and there were many people outside enjoying the cloudless day in Tallahassee. He had turned in his list of replacements just a few minutes before. He felt mixed emotions about whom he should recommend. At first he listed men who he either suspected were on the take, or who he felt should not be in service to the government. He figured that their careers would get sunk with the investigation. But then his loyalty to the Governor kicked in, so he added some men who were very good, and very honest. He would allow Snelling to pick which way he wanted to go.

But as of now, Scott felt mighty refreshed. He knew the feeling would not last forever, or even the rest of the day after it sank in that he was no longer employed. But for this moment it felt good. He had decided that his resignation was enough; he would not be calling Rockman back. He knew what Snelling did, but the man was his friend as well as his boss. They had known each other a very long time, and Zoe did not want to lose his friendship. That was why he gave the Governor the excuse that he did. No one would ever need to know that it was to save his own hide. And after a few years, when Mark was in college, Zoe could come back to politics, no questions asked.

Across the street, two men sat on the steps of the Barnett Bank building. They watched Zoe as he walked across the plaza then up on the sidewalk along Monroe Avenue. They were both in their early twenties, white, and over six feet tall. They both wore sunglasses, shorts, and running shoes. One had on a T-shirt that read *Florida State University*. The other had a tank top with the Greek letters of one of FSU's fraternities emblazoned on the front and had a red cloth backpack. They looked like any of the thousands of students that lived in the area.

The two men waited for Scott to walk by, ran across the crosswalk, and followed behind. They walked past the various stores and restaurants that lined the city's main thoroughfare, turning down College Avenue. Scott had noticed the two men, but was not suspicious in any way. The street led right into the heart of FSU, and Scott looked down the sidewalk at the rows of frat houses that ended at the university. He crossed over to the right side of the street and ducked inside Goodies Eatery. The small sandwich shop was crowded by lawyers and government employees that worked downtown. Most wore suits, even though it was over ninety degrees outside. The employees, by contrast, were local college students who wore the latest MTV fashions and tried to study between orders. The little shop only sat about thirty people, so most of the customers ate their lunch standing in small groups of three and four. Scott heard parts of conversations as he waited at the counter. The group of three older men in the corner near the restroom discussed some legislation that they were lobbying for. They recognized Zoe and invited him to join them, but he declined.

"May I help you?" the girl asked at the counter when it was his turn.

"I'd like a meatball and cheese sub, please," he said.

"It's going to be a few minutes; is that okay," the girl asked. She waited for him to complain about the wait and give her some lecture as to how important he was, why he needed it right now, and did not have all day. Out of habit, Scott almost did just that. But then it hit him that he had nowhere to be; so he just smiled and told her that would be fine.

The girl was pleasantly surprised and smiled back, "I'll bring it out to you if you want to take a seat." She put a rush on his order.

Outside, the two men had watched Zoe cross the street and go inside the small restaurant. They continued walking, then ducked into a coffee shop. They took a seat at a table near the large window that faced the street.

*

Susan could not believe the condition of the house when she arrived. They had torn everything apart. She asked how long they would be there, but no one could give her an answer. One of the investigators commented that it would be at least another day. The house was just too large. When she asked what they were looking for, an officer directed her to Doyle. He showed her the warrant, but explained only that the search was in regard to a current investigation. She was escorted up to her bedroom by Laura and Doyle, who allowed her to pack a suitcase with some clothes.

"Must you?" Susan asked Doyle. He was listing every item as she packed it.

"Yes ma'am. I'm sorry."

"I'll bet you are," she remarked. After grabbing the necessities from her bathroom, she zipped the suitcase. "I'm done," she told them and walked down the stairs and out to her car. Laura and Doyle followed.

"We may need to talk to you," Laura said handing Susan her card. "Where can we get a hold of you if we need to?"

Susan gave her a dirty look, then said, "Why do you need to talk with me? You have my house and my husband." She started the car.

"Still, we may need to speak with you," Doyle said.

"Well it's going to have to be long distance," Susan answered. "Because I plan to get as far away from here as possible." Doyle knelt down, leaned on the door and looked inside the window at her. He carefully placed his fingers over the crack so that she would not put the glass up. "Speaking of going away, you don't know where your husband would be, do you?" He spoke the words slowly, intentionally. The insinuation was clear, and that angered Susan.

"If you think, for one minute, that I would have anything to do with that bastard, you're crazy!" she told him in no uncertain terms. "If you want to know where my dear husband is, go ask Miss Wendy Richardson. She's fucking him, not me!" Susan pushed the button and tried to put the window up, but Doyle held it.

"Where can we find Miss Richardson?" he asked.

"Try the Sanibel View. She works there!" she said. The detective let go of the window and stepped back from the car. Susan put it in gear and quickly drove away. Laura and Doyle looked over at each other.

"I think there's someone who we need to talk to!" the FBI agent said.

*

After finishing his lunch, Scott Zoe went outside and across the street to a pay phone. The two men watched as he dialed, talked for a moment, and hung up. When the former Chief of Staff started to walk away, the two observers left a twenty on the table to cover the two cups of coffee and quickly exited out the door. When they saw Scott walk to the garage, the two men turned, ran back around the corner and jumped into the black Mustang convertible. They squealed the tires as they backed out into traffic, almost sideswiping a city bus. They went north on Monroe then turned down Call Street just as Zoe was pulling from the parking garage. They were going too fast and had to zip around in front of him.

"Shit, now what?!"

"Just calm down," the driver said and adjusted the rear view mirror as they stopped at a red light.

Zoe had watched the Mustang go around him, but paid little attention. He drove down towards the university following the black convertible. On either side huge fraternity and sorority houses of all shapes and colors lined the street. Inside the Mustang, the driver watched as Zoe's turn signal come on, then watched as his quarry turned down a side street and disappeared from view. He punched the gas, speeding up the hill towards the front gate of the university. Upon reaching the gate, the Mustangs tires squealed as the driver ran the stop sign and turned left, hoping to cut off his subject. They drove two blocks when Zoe's car went through the intersection ahead of them. The two men turned right, pulling behind Zoe's car down the one way street. The Mustang's passenger reached into his backpack and pulled out the cellular phone.

Scott Zoe drove down toward Florida High. He turned right into the bus lane and followed the horseshoe-shaped drive to the front of the school. Mark was waiting outside with some friends. The younger Zoe opened the passenger door and jumped inside.

"Thanks, Dad!" Mark said and threw his books into the back seat.

"I see you got my message," his father said.

"So do you have something planned" his son asked, "or were you just bored with your first day off?"

"Both, actually," Zoe said. The former Chief of Staff saw the smile in his child's face and thought giving up his post had not been such a bad idea after all. He pulled out of the driveway and back onto Pensacola Avenue. He glanced up into his rearview mirror and saw a black Mustang convertible behind him. The windows of the car were tinted, and the roof was up. It looked familiar, and he was wondering where he had seen it before when it suddenly sped up and pulled next to him. Thinking it was someone he knew, Zoe pushed the button on the arm rest, causing his window to go down. At the same time the window of the Mustang went down. Scott saw the metal barrel and immediately hit the breaks as the man in the Mustang pulled the trigger of the MAC 10. White flashes erupted from inside the black car, leaving a row of jagged holes along the front driver's side fender of Zoe's car.

Zoe's engine blew as a bullet entered a valve cover and bent a rod. The sedan spun out of control and smashed through the chain-link fence onto the football field. A phys-ed class and their teachers watched in horror as the car slammed into the bleachers. The Mustang sped away up the street , its occupants sure that they had accomplished their task.

*

The four of them sat in Sam's office. Wendy declined a lawyer, but had insisted Sam be present during the questioning. Doyle and Laura had agreed but made it known it was only as a courtesy. They informed her of Susan's accusations and told her that she was not a suspect. Doyle read Wendy her rights, but she waived them saying she had nothing to hide.

"So, what happened after dinner the other night?" Laura asked.

"Nothing," Wendy replied after looking over at Sam. "David dropped me off at home, then he left."

"You didn't stay with him anywhere? A hotel, your place?" Doyle asked.

"No," Wendy said angrily, "he just dropped me off at home. That was it."

Doyle wrote some notes on his pad while Laura watched Susan nervously shift back and fourth in her seat. "So, you were not having an affair with Mr. Ranson?"

Wendy looked indignant. "No, I was not! Who told you that?!"

"Mrs. Ranson," Laura replied.

"Well, she's lying!" Wendy was not about to say anything, especially after lying to Sam the other night. She was trapped. She hoped David would understand. Doyle wrote more notes on the pad, then flipped it over. "I have your address as nineteen Southeast Eighth Lane in Cape Coral; is that correct, Miss Richardson?"

"Yes."

"Well, then," he said standing up. "I have no more questions, but keep yourself available." Wendy nodded. The detectives thanked Sam and walked out to the parking lot. They stopped at the car.

"I don't believe her," Laura said.

"I've been lied to so many times the last few days, I don't even believe myself," Doyle said, smiling.

"I'd like to go talk to the toll booth operator. He should remember a black Porsche coming through the other night, don't you think?"

Doyle shook his head, "On this island, no way. This is Sanibel. A car that costs less than fifty thousand dollars, now that they'd remember."

*

"Is he physically able?" the judge asked.

"The doctor said he was severely dehydrated, but we can get enough blood for the test without endangering his condition," Rockman said.

"What about the semen?"

"We'll have to wait a day or two, your honor. But I'd like to get the warrant signed now so we can go ahead when the doctor gives us the green light."

The judge read the request again, then signed his name at the bottom. He handed back the paper and walked the Attorney General out. He did not like having

Rockman come to his home, but it was better than driving all the way downtown. "It's getting a little cooler out," the old man said as they stepped onto the porch of the large Victorian home. It bordered on a private country club of which the judge was a member.

"At least the humidity has gone down," Rockman agreed. He walked down the steps and across the spacious lawn to his car. In the distance he could see a lone golfer trying to beat the sunset.

Rockman called the hospital and had Doyle paged to tell him they had the warrant. He also asked that Laura contact the Federal Elections Commission and ask that they contact him as soon as possible.

*

"I heard Susan took off," Chris said, trying to make conversation.

"Yeah. No one knows where she went, except probably Sam," Wendy replied. They were alone. It was a little after six o'clock, and almost everyone had gone for the day; those that hadn't were out eating dinner with Sam. He had announced that he was treating the news Staff to drinks and a buffet at the Dockside lounge. But Chris wasn't on Staff anymore, and Wendy knew she'd feel awkward.

Chris sat at Susan's desk as he read through Sam's notes. Wendy walked over to a large table in the center of the newsroom. She dumped two boxes of photographs on the table and started sifting through them. Chris walked over and picked one up. It looked old, it even had a white border along the edge. "What's this stuff?"

"It's David's."

"David who?" he asked, putting one photo down and picking up another.

"David Ranson, I was doing a story on his life. It was about his campaign for Congress."

"Pretty incredible, huh? I guess you can still do a story, it'll just have a different ending."

"Yeah, I guess," she said, her voiced trailing off. They sat in silence for a while as he looked through all the images. Wendy would occasionally look off into space, trying to keep the tears away.

"I thought you were helping Susan?"

"Not really, she was helping me."

"With what?"

"I was looking at how much our police force has improved since the Blind Pass thing back in the seventies."

"Oh," Wendy said as she recalled the police questioning her. She started dividing the photographs, trying to put them in some sort of order. He was right, she still had a story to do. Chris helped stack the pictures. It wasn't easy, since they were various sizes. Under a small pile, Chris found a roll of film, still undeveloped.

"Where should I put this?" he asked, holding it up. Wendy took it from his hand and examined it closely.

"It looks pretty old, early eighties," she said.

"I wonder what's on it."

"There's only one way to find out."

Inside the darkroom, Chris watched as Wendy expertly went through the process of developing the film. He leaned over and sniffed at one of the chemical baths, it was nauseating. Wendy laughed. *It feels good to laugh,* she thought. After a few minutes images started to appear. Most of them were of a man and a woman. They were dressed like flower children, and both Wendy and Chris knew right away that the film was at least twenty years old. After studying the images they realized the man was a young David Ranson. He was probably in his late teens or early twenties. But they had no idea who the woman was.

All the photographs looked like they had been shot on the same day. They were taken at the Lost Cove Marina. All the photographs were of either David or the woman. All except one- a photograph of David and a young black man that showed the two pointing at the sign. It was obvious that the other man had taken the rest of the pictures. The photos of David and this mysterious woman left no doubt that two were more than friends. Most showed them holding each other or kissing. A few of them had been taken inside a boat, probably by David, and showed the woman in various stages of undress.

"This is probably why he never got them developed," Wendy said, "He probably didn't want to answer questions about the last few photos."

"What does he care?" Chris asked.

"Twenty years ago, this could have been considered pornography. He could have been arrested if he had tried to get them developed. It would have been scandalous."

"She looks older than David. I wonder who she is?"

"There's one way to find out," Wendy replied and opened the door to the news room.

*

Sebastian sat staring at his phone in the dimly lit office. It was eight o'clock and still no word. He had received the message from Luis hours before after two days of nothing. His senior field agent had radioed the Coast Guard earlier that morning, saying only to contact Sebastian and tell him the boat would be arriving in Miami in four days and that Jeff was not with him, but had "Gone on to Vancouver" and Andre had " flown to Dover". The code would tell Sebastian that Jeff was dead and Andre missing. Luis usually did not go in for the codeword messages, and this made Sebastian nervous. He knew that anyone could have heard the conversation; that the Gheko's radio was far from a secure line of communication, but if the deal had gone sour Luis could have- should have- contacted the U.S. officials on the island and spoke with his boss directly. What good does it do to tell Sebastian now?

On board the Gheko, Luis was not thinking of Sebastian's reaction. He was just praying that he'd be around to hear it. The DEA agent was sitting outside on the aft deck. The sun was setting in the west, and all there was nothing but blue water for as far as his eyes could see. Luis's face was badly sunburned, as was the rest of his body. He was naked. The nylon rope had rubbed through the skin around his wrists and ankles. Every now and again a small wave would splash on the deck, allowing the salt water into the open flesh He would try to scream as it burned, but his parched throat would not let out any sounds. His eyes were swollen, his lips cracked from the heat of the sun. But as the night started to fall, the cool ocean breeze caused the man's teeth to chatter.

Alvin looked down at him and laughed to himself, for it had been so easy. He took the leather strap and snapped it down across the agent's stomach. There were so many welts already that he couldn't even tell where it hit. Luis twisted and turned, but he couldn't get free. They had stopped asking him anything after he had made the radio message. He knew they were just slowly killing him. The beatings went on through the night. Around two a.m. James came out and took over. But the agent no longer felt any pain. He just laid there as the strap hit him again and again. After about fifteen minutes, James reached down and untied the ropes.

"What are you doing?" Alvin asked.

"It's just not fun anymore," James replied as he dragged Luis to the back of the boat. "Give me a hand." Alvin knelt down and picked up the agent's legs, while James held his arms. With one hard swing they threw him off the back of the boat, then watched his body disappear into the dark water.

12

***

Friday, September 15

"We have a match!" Doyle said and hung up the phone. "The lab just verified that not only was David a non-secretor, but his fingerprints were found all over the Whitmore house. Not just in the bedroom. I'm talking bathroom, kitchen, and hallway." Rockman looked over at Laura.

"Add that to the blood samples," Laura said. "And I think we have a winner even without a weapon."

"Pick him up!" Rockman said.

*

David sat on the adjustable bed wearing a short yellow hospital gown that had an open slit up the back. In the corner of the room, a television stared down, its screen dark. David was getting his blood pressure checked by a very plump, very serious-looking nurse when the two law enforcement officers walked in. David saw them enter, then looked away. Laura asked the nurse to leave. She unwrapped the black band from David's arm, made a notation on her chart, then left without a word. Doyle pulled out his handcuffs.

"David Ranson, you are under arrest for the murder of Cathy Whitmore, Larry Kindle, and Debbie Kindle. Please turn around!" Doyle reached out for David's arm, but he pulled away. Doyle spun the District Attorney, pushing him face down on the bed.

"What the hell are you doing!" David screamed as he tried to free his arms. "I'm in the fucking hospital!"

"What's going on in here ?!" a doctor said as he ran into the room. He had heard the screaming down the hall. As he entered, he saw the two men struggling on the bed. The doctor went over to pull Doyle off, but was stopped by Laura. She held up her identification.

"FBI. This man is under arrest," she said. The surgeon was angry. The screaming drew a crowd in the hall of both patients and staff.

"This is a hospital, the man is obviously sick!"

"You tell 'em, Doc!" David yelled.

Doyle produced a paper from his pocket as he held David down on the bed, "Release form, Doc. Signed, sealed, and delivered ten minutes ago!" The doctor grabbed the document and read it. It said that David Ranson was free to leave, and the document had been signed by his doctor. The man handed the form back.

"Fine, but could you keep it down?!" he said. "We still have other patients."

"No problem, doctor," Doyle said. "I think we are about ready to go!" He backed off the bed, leaned down and grabbed the handcuffs that bound David's hands behind his back. He pulled the District Attorney up off the bed by the cuffs, as David used his fingers to try and hold the hospital gown closed.
But he could only reach on side of it, and from the back his body was visible.

"Dammit, Doyle! At least let me put some clothes on!" he yelled.

"Don't worry; Agent Wilson will bring your things," the detective answered and pushed David out into the hall. Laura stayed in the room, and packed the D.A.'s belongings.

"Come on, let me have some dignity! Have some compassion!" David cried as they arrived at the elevator. It seemed as if every person on the floor was staring at him.

"Yeah, just like you showed old Doc Whitmore, right?" Doyle said, remembering. He read him his rights as they rode down to the parking garage.

In the conference room of the county courthouse three hours later, David sat dressed in the standard prison jumpsuit. He no longer looked like the powerful district attorney; in fact, he didn't even look that powerful a man. The stress of the last few days had hollowed out his face more than anyone would have thought, and it almost made him look weak. Next to him sat Matt Ginsberg, his attorney. Ginsberg was not the best attorney in the area, but he was the best that would represent David Ranson. Most of the members of the Lee County Bar Association wanted little to do with the case, and that was due not to financial but personal reasons. They all had faced the District Attorney in court, and most had at least a few clients found guilty after David prosecuted the case. So they were waiting for David to fall, so they could get their clients retried. If a lawyer represented the DA now, there might be a conflict of interest ruling later. So that left Ginsberg. Matt Ginsberg was in it for the money. The money and free publicity that the story would generate, and he was willing to sacrifice a few former clients to move up into the top echelon of well-known lawyers.

Across from them sat Rockman and Laura. Doyle was standing behind, along the wall. Rockman now looked like the former police officer and Dade County District

Attorney that he was.

"I thought standard procedure in a case like this was to ask the Governor to select a special prosecutor from another county?" Ginsberg said to no one in particular.

"I felt this would be the only way to ensure that the state's case would not be tainted," Rockman replied. "Further, I intend for this to be seen by other officials as an example of how harshly my office will deal with those officials that break the public trust."

"Uh huh," Ginsberg grunted opening his briefcase.

Doyle watched with interest. His job was basically over, and he did not even need to be there, but he felt betrayed by David. The man had led him on a wild goose chase with all the theories and innuendoes. David had played the detective for a fool, and Doyle resented it. He had never taken any of his work personally until this case.

"I want to protest the fact that my client was not allowed to dress before that man arrested him," Ginsberg said, looking over at Doyle.

Doyle quickly moved over and put his face in David's. "Yeah, and I'd like to protest the fact that the victims aren't breathing anymore, Counselor," the detective said angrily. Laura tugged at his arm, and pulled Doyle back away. This outburst was not like him, but twenty years of frustration over unsolved murder cases was taking its toll.

"Detective Doyle broke no laws or regulations," Rockman said. "No rights were violated. Now can we get to the charges?" He read off the charges: three counts murder in the first degree, conspiracy to commit murder, breaking and entering, and some minor related charges. David just shook his head and looked down at the ground laughing.

"And those are just the state's charges, not federal," Rockman said when he was done. "Mr. Ranson, is there something funny here?"

David looked up at him. He jumped up out of his seat, banged his handcuffed hands on the table, and became serious, "No, there's not. As a matter of fact this is all some sick fucking joke!" The deputy in the room grabbed him and forced him back down in the chair.

"Settle down, David," Ginsberg said and turned to Laura. "And what does the government have against Mr. Ranson, Agent Wilson?"

"We plan on charging your client with tax evasion and accepting illegal political contributions."

"I see," the defense attorney said. None of this was a surprise, he already had the proper documentation in front of him, search warrants, arrest warrants, lab reports. "As you can see, we would like to get this over with as quickly as possible."

"I noticed the preferential treatment," Laura said. "A first appearance this afternoon, Counselor. How many of your client's friends in this building slept here last night and still haven't seen a judge?"

"First off, my client has no friends in this building," Ginsberg said. "And second, my client has a right to be heard within twenty-four hours of his arrest. You wouldn't deny him his rights under the law, would you agent Wilson?"

Laura decided she did not like this guy at all. The defense attorney opened his briefcase and pulled out some papers and a yellow legal pad.

"I'm going to ask for a dismissal, Lance, the evidence is weak."

"Every defense attorney asks for a dismissal and thinks the evidence is weak," Rockman said. "Now can we can go on with this seriously. We have three dead bodies, and I can prove your client is to blame."

"You want somebody to blame?" David asked. "Go look at that fucking psycho Jeff Strata. Who the hell knows what goes through his head." The name was meaningless to the prosecution; Rockman did not remember hearing it before.

"Why don't we just concentrate on you for a moment, okay, David?" Laura said.

"What's the matter, honey? Not getting enough at home?" he replied.

"Shut up, David!" Ginsberg told him.

"Why should I? Because this bastard wants to use me to win his next election," David looked over at the Attorney General. "Or do you just get your rocks off harassing those of us who work for a living, Lance?"

"Does your client want to hear what evidence we have against him?" Rockman asked.

"I'd love to hear this!" David said.

They showed him the lab reports. The medical test results that showed he was not a secretor. Like the Doc, he was part of the fifteen percent. They showed the fingerprints, with photographs of the interior of Whitmore's house. There were markings on the photos that corresponded with each fingerprint. They gave him a copy of the receipt for the X-rated videos and a test that showed the blood on the front step of Larry Kindle's house matched his own.

"I stopped and tried to get a ride home; I cut my foot!" David said

"How convenient," Rockman said "And then you just happened to fall and hit your head later when you attacked your wife!"

"I didn't attack her."

Rockman handed a hospital report that stated he attacked her, it was signed by Susan. Then he presented the report from Officer Kohler regarding both the argument at the Marina, with no mention of any injuries, and of his arrival at David's home right after the time of the killing.

"Okay, I'll admit it looks bad," David said, against Ginsberg's advice. "But I haven't killed anyone! I swear to God I haven't! Why don't you people believe me?"

"Do you remember Scott Zoe, Mr. Ranson?" Laura asked. "Someone tried to kill him and his son last night after he decided to testify against you and some of your friends. Are you sure you were on that boat all night?"

"You can't be seriously considering..."

"You've already been placed at the murder scenes of three people." Rockman replied. "What's two more?"

"I don't even know what you're talking about!" David said. His attorney did not like the way this was turning.

"This is turning into a witch hunt. The next thing you'll be blaming him for is the Lindbergh kidnapping!" Ginsberg stood up and packed the documents in his briefcase. "Let's go, David. I think this meeting is over."

*

It was three-thirty when David was called in front of the judge. Standing there, he smiled as he saw the honorable Judge Randolf Dean presiding. David was a good friend of Judge Dean. But, more importantly, he knew that Dean was a card-carrying defender of individual rights. So much so that David had lambasted the judge's sentencing record in the paper as so liberal it was practically non-existent.

After the charges were read to the court, David entered a plea of "Not Guilty."

"What are your views towards bond, Mr. Rockman?" the judge asked.

"Your honor," Rockman replied. "The state argues that the defendant is a danger to society, and due to the uniqueness of the case, as well as the defendant's position in the prosecutor's office, we request that no bond be issued. We ask that the court look at the violent nature of the crimes Mr. Ranson is charged with."

"Mr. Ginsberg?"

"The defense would like to point out that Mr. Ranson is a respected member of the bar as well as the community, he is not a danger to anyone, and he has no criminal record. Further, there are no witnesses, no murder weapon, and the case is circumstantial at best. The prosecution is fishing, your honor."

"Your honor, this is a capitol offense," Rockman added.

"Mr. Rockman," Judge Dean said. "As someone who has known David for a long time I find it hard to keep him under lock and key. I understand that you, sir, are not from this area, and may not understand fully the defendant's ties. I respect Mr. Ranson's reputation, and I do not believe that he is a danger to the public."

"Your honor!" Rockman tried to interrupt, but backed off as the judge continued to speak. "But the charge is murder, and three people are dead. So I will grant bond in the amount of five hundred thousand dollars."

"That's a little excessive," Ginsberg was cut off.

"Make that all cash, Mr. Ranson," the judge said and banged his gavel down. "Next!"

*

Susan saw the small red light flashing when she entered her hotel room. She picked up the phone and called the front desk.

"This is Susan Ranson, I have a message?"

"Yes ma'am. A gentleman called and left a phone number." She wrote the number down and hung up. Then she dialed the number. It was a pager. She punched in her phone and room number, then waited. A minute later the phone rang.

"Jeff?" she said

"Susan?" he said, sounding unsure.

"Yeah, it's me. You got my message!"

"How did you know what marina I was coming into?"

"I didn't!"

"What did you do?" He asked. "Leave a message at every marina in the phone book?"

"Yes," she said, "And even some that weren't listed. I needed to see you!"

He hesitated before answering, "Let me clean up the boat."

"No! Now!"

"Okay," he said, and told her how to get to the marina. After he hung up, Jeff went below deck and locked the cabin doors. Then he grabbed a mop.

*

"Hey, Doc! It's time to go home," the deputy said, and unlocked the cell door. The heavy steel bars slid open quietly. Whitmore sat on the soiled blue and white striped mattress and said not a word as the deputy placed the doctor's clothing next to him. The old man stood and removed the gray jumpsuit. He lifted the hanger holding the clothes he had been wearing the day of his arrest. They had been cleaned, and he carefully tore open the clear plastic bag from the hanger and removed his shirt, then pants.

After dressing, he was handcuffed and lead out to a hallway, then to a window with a small counter in front. He was handed back his personal items. After checking the contents, he signed an inventory sheet that stated everything he had with him at his arrest was returned to him. He then followed the deputy down the hall toward the lobby. They stopped at the secure door leading to the outside and freedom. "Don't you want to know why you're getting out of here, Doc?" the deputy asked.

The old man just looked straight ahead at the door; his eyes revealed no emotion, no wonder, nothing. The deputy reached down to unlock the handcuffs from around his wrist. "In case you were wondering," the deputy said. "They arrested the district attorney, Ranson. Seems he was boffin' your wife, Doc. Now what do you think about that?"

Whitmore didn't say or do anything. He just watched the deputy turn the key and remove the restraints.

*

Wendy saw the old whitewashed wooden sign and turned left down the dirt covered road. The canopy of leaves from overhanging trees blotted out the sunshine as they made their way toward the lake. It took a few minutes for the boathouse to become visible through the thick vegetation, but finally an old tin Quonset hut appeared.

An AM radio hung from the half open battered metal door. Muddy Waters' *My Home on the Delta* was playing through the static. The blues legend's guitar resonated off the cabin and across the lake, and the two reporters walked up to the old man. He was sanding the wooden hull of a small boat that had been overturned and now rested on a pair of rotten, paint-splattered planks. The man's skin was a black as the oil they pumped from the Gulf, his beard as gray as an oyster's shell. He was wearing faded blue denim overalls, but they did not hide his powerful body. Wendy saw his face as he turned to see who was interrupting his afternoon and recognized it from the photo in her pocket. Though he was much older, she was sure it was the same man. He put down the sanding pad and wiped his hands on a rag he kept in his back pocket as his two visitors approached.

"What can I do for you folks?" the old man asked as they stepped up to the boat.

"My name's Wendy, Mr. Booker, and this is Chris," she answered. "We would like to ask you some questions if you have some time?"

"What kind of questions?" he asked, trying to figure out who these two people were and how they knew who he was.

"Well," Chris said. "We'd like to ask you about David Ranson. We understand that you knew him."

Booker didn't recognize the name. "No," he said. "I can't seem to place the name. What did this fella do?" Chris and Wendy both hesitated at the answer. It was clear from the way Chris talked on the drive up that he thought David had a lot to do with the recent deaths. But Wendy had defended him and still could not bring herself around to believe it.

"We don't really know," Wendy said.

"Are you people police officers?" the old man asked. "'Cause I don't know no David Ranson."

"No sir," Chris interrupted. "We're reporters. We are doing a story on Mr. Ranson, and we came across this." Wendy pulled the picture out and handed it to Booker, who took a long look at it. "Well if this Ranson didn't do anything, then why are you askin' questions about him?" he asked without taking his eyes away from the photograph.

"He's also a candidate for Congress," Wendy said.

"That so?" he said, as he recognized the image.

"That is you, isn't it?" Chris asked. Booker took a last glance, then returned the picture.

"Yes, that's me," he replied, dumbstruck. He walked around the small shack, followed by the other two. Once around the side, the lake was clearly visible. It was surrounded by greenery. Spanish moss hung down from the many trees lining the banks. These were not the familiar palm variety found on Sanibel, they were too far north for that. These were large oaks and pine. The only palm trees in this part of Florida were planted by landscaping companies. The water stopped about twenty feet from where they stood. The edge of the lake was hidden by the cattails and elephant grasses that grew up through the shallow water. The buzzing of insects increased, and a small cloud of gnats whisked by Wendy, who swatted at them. Booker unstacked some folding chairs, and the three of them sat down around a rusty card table, the top of which was covered with a vinyl floral print. A large chunk of the covering was torn away, leaving yellow foam padding sticking out from underneath. A pitcher of ice water sat on the table, and the old man offered them each a drink. There was only one glass in sight, so both reporters declined.

Booker poured himself a tall cold one, and the ice clanked as it fell into the glass.

"So, do you remember?"

"Oh yeah," he said, watching a dragonfly hop from plant to plant. "That boy was trouble, I remember that." The two reporters took out a small tape recorder and laid it on the table. The old man told them of his memories.

"I remember the day that picture was taken. It was easy enough to remember, I suppose, when you see what happened after that." He took a sip of water. "I was minding the marina, like I had done every day for ten years or so when I saw his boat come in."

"David's?" Wendy asked.

Booker ignored the question. "That Ranson boy was at the helm and had a problem pulling it up to the slip. I yelled and asked if he needed help. He threw the rope over, and I pulled him in. I had just finished securing the line when the boy comes over and puts his arm around me. I was so surprised I just stood there as the young lady came out from the cabin and took our picture; that was the one you showed me." He stopped talking and sipped some more water. It dawned on Chris that the man was done.

"Who was the woman?" Wendy asked.

"You said that there was something after the picture was taken?" he asked.

"Oh, yes," the old man continued. "It was later that day. By then it wasn't quite dark, yet not light out. The sky was red that night; it turned the water red with its reflection. It had rained earlier, and the humidity forgot to leave after the rain died. I was inside going over the day's receipts when the boy came up--I heard him come up. Actually, I heard his bike clanking over the boards like a train going over tracks. I remember watching him from the office window as he went down to the boat, and I remember seein' his momma come out from inside. She was all drugged up with that absent stare in her eyes. She hadn't always been like that. Then that Ranson boy, the one you were asking about, he walked up right behind her. He stepped off the boat, then past the boy as if he weren't even there. Strange, too, cause normally he'd say somthin'. But not that day. He just walked by. I turned my head so that he wouldn't see me when he went past the window. Anyway, the girl, she just stood on the boat lookin' past the boy, the building, everything, into the parking lot. I heard some yelling, so I ran into the back storeroom and looked outside. There, in the middle of the lot I saw Ranson. And he was standing next to the drivers window of the girl's husband's car. I watched as that Ranson kid swung his fist into the car window and hit that other feller so hard his head snapped back. Well, there was some more yellin' and screamin' after that, until the car just drove off in a hurry. The Ranson boy walked back to the boat, past the boy who was now crying. He grabbed the girl by the hair and pulled her into the boat. She was just hollerin as loud as could be."

"Did you call the police?" Wendy asked. Booker turned and looked at her seriously.

"Ma'am, do you see this?" he asked, tugging at his skin. "This is South Florida, and back then a man who looked like me didn't get involved in a dispute between a white man and his woman." He stared at her, waiting to see his words register on her face.

"So then what happened?" Chris asked impatiently.

Booker took a mouthful of water, then continued, "After 'bout an hour, that troublemaker came out by himself, got in his car and left."

"And the woman?"

"I waited until I was sure David wasn't coming back, then I went out to the boat. Her boy saw me comin' and went inside first. I called to see if she was all right. But then I heard the boy scream and went in to look for myself. She was beat pretty bad."

Chris looked at Wendy, who was upset as she heard the old man describe how the woman looked. "So, what? You just left her there?" Wendy asked.

"Oh, no," he said. "She was in bad shape, real bad. I put her in my car and took her and the boy to the hospital."

"But I thought you didn't want to get involved?"

"I didn't, but I couldn't just let her sit there hurtin'. No, I let her and the boy off at the front door of the hospital," Booker replied.

"What about the father?" Chris asked.

"I never saw him again."

"And the woman?"

"Well now," Booker said. "That's where this got real bad. After I dropped her off, the boy took her inside, but she wouldn't let a doctor treat her, so they called the boy's grandpappy and he came and picked them up. Then, just a few days later, she and her son were out crabbin' on the grandpappy's boat when she supposedly fell off and drowned. The boy said she'd done it on purpose, but I guess only Jesus knows for sure."

"What was her name?!" Wendy asked. Booker tried to think of it.

"I don't recall," he said, disappointed with the effects of getting old.

"Do you remember the boy's name?" Wendy asked him.

"It's been twenty years," he said, then paused, trying to remember. "It was Justin...or Jeremy..." The old man looked confused.

"Johnny?" Chris said.

"Jeffrey?"

The old man looked up at Wendy and smiled a toothless grin, "What you said.

That was it, Jeffrey. Jeffrey Stratan." He slapped his thigh with his hand and laughed, relieved that his mind wasn't all mush.

"How about Jeffrey Strata?" Chris said.

"Okay! Strata! Strata, whatever you want!" Booker said happily.

*

Matt Ginsberg had little problem getting the cash for David. All the DA needed to do was put up his mortgage. After that it was just half an hour's worth of paperwork. The defense attorney brought his client some clean clothes. All he had with him when he was brought into custody were the clothes he was found in and that stupid little hospital gown. After taking a shower and changing into the custom-tailored Italian suit, David called all the television stations and newspapers and informed them that he would be having a news conference in -- he checked his watch -- thirty minutes. The timing of his release was perfect. It was almost five o'clock. He would be broadcast live just in time to catch the voters at home eating dinner.

"I think you're making a mistake with this news conference, David," Ginsberg said.

"What the hell do you know about politics?" David replied, adjusting his tie.

"Nothing. But I know about law, and any statements you say..."

"Yeah, yeah, yeah," David said, admiring his reflection in the mirror of the men's room. "It can all be held against me. I know that; I'm not an idiot. I'm going out there to tell the voters I'm innocent and that I am still the best man for Congress! That this is some kind of political bullshit to keep me out of office!"

Ginsberg sighed, "Maybe you should tell them you're guilty instead. They all think Washington is full of crooks anyway. Tell them you'll fit right in."

Outside on the courthouse steps, all the local television stations focused their cameras on the makeshift podium. The local radio stations were there too. All the microphones resembled a bouquet as the technicians did sound checks. The newspapers were there also, except for the Sanibel View, which David had conveniently forgotten to notify. He was not about to reward Wendy for not providing him an alibi.

By 5:45 p.m. a crowd of onlookers had gathered around the press to see what was so newsworthy. David peeked out like a bride looking in the church on her wedding day and decided to wait another fifteen minutes. A sense of the dramatic always made for better news coverage. A block away an old man walked into a pawn shop and placed fifty dollars on the glass counter.

*

Susan sat in the waterside lounge looking over at Jeff as soft music played in the background. They sat at a table drinking frozen strawberry daiquiris and looking out over the water at the sun as it sank in the distance. He told her he had spent enough time on the boat and insisted they go out to eat. They did not have reservations at the small Italian restaurant, but the wait was not long. It was only September; tourist season had not started yet.   Jeff told her about the Virgin Islands and gave her some small souvenirs he had bought for her. She told him of the tragic death of Larry Kindle and his wife. The man in the booth behind them heard her talking about David's arrest.

"Are you talking about that District Attorney up in Ft. Myers?" the man asked leaning over the back of the booth.

"Yes," Susan said. "Why?"

"Because he's going to be on TV in a minute, " The man pointed to the television above the bar. Susan had not realized that Key West was less than a hundred miles due south of Naples, so of course the local television signal reached them. Susan and Jeff stood up from their table and walked over to watch. They asked the bartender to turn up the sound, but he said he couldn't because the people in the restaurant would complain. They saw David walk out to the podium accompanied by Ginsberg. He was smiling as he started to address the crowd.

Suddenly everyone started to run as David fell to the ground. The camera swung around to show people ducking and diving away. The lack of sound made the images bolder, as the cameraman showed an old man holding a gun out in front of him. He was running up the steps to where David lay. Ginsberg was nowhere to be found. The gunman pointed the small automatic down at David and fired repeatedly at point blank range. The camera continued to roll as the gunman, who Susan now recognized as Doc Whitmore, placed the gun to his own mouth and pulled the trigger. The picture went to black.

Susan was in shock. She sat with her jaw wide open staring at the blackened television screen, as did everyone else in the room except Jeff. He reached over and touched her on the shoulder. She jumped, then turned to him. She said nothing as she looked at him, the television, and then Jeff again. He watched her eyes as they glossed over and swelled up with tears.

"Are those tears of sadness or of joy?" he asked. She said nothing. He helped her out of the chair, paid the check, and left.

*

Chris watched the sun go down as the two reporters sped past the rural scenery of central Florida, on their way home. They didn't talk much as they watched the large horse ranches and small exit ramp towns rush by at seventy miles an hour. Wendy finally mentioned that they should call the police, but Chris wanted to wait until they got back; he wanted to be the one who broke the story. Not that there was much of a story other than the one connecting Jeff Strata to the alleged murderer. But Wendy hoped that it would at least raise doubts about David's involvement. She still believed in him.

"I think we should at least tell Susan," Chris said.

"Why?" Wendy snapped.

"Mainly because she is probably with that Jeff guy, or is on her way to see him," he replied, trying not to start an argument. He thought it was something they should do. He was still friends with her.

"How?" Wendy asked. "We don't even know where she is."

The phone rang in the View's newsroom. Scarlet Jones, the social reporter and a local debutante, was at her desk finishing up the weekly gossip report. Expecting a call from her husband, she pressed the flashing button and picked it up.

"Scarlet Jones speaking," she said seductively.

"I'm not your husband, Scarlet," Wendy said, unamused. "Put Sam on."

"He's not here," Scarlet snapped. "He left a few hours ago. What do you want?"

"I need the phone number to wherever Susan Ranson is staying. I'm sure that Sam has it," Wendy told her. "It's probably on his desk somewhere on a post it note or something."

"I really don't have the time for this..." Scarlet said before being interrupted.

"Cut the crap, and just get me the number!"

Scarlet went into Sam's office to look. A few minutes later she came out holding a bright pink piece of paper. Susan's name was on it, as was a phone number. She gave the number to Wendy, then hung up. She started back to Sam's office when the phone rang again.

"Now what!" she yelled into the phone.

"Scarlet?" It was her husband. She placed the note on her desk and sat down to talk. She picked up her purse and pulled out a pack of cigarettes, took one out and lit it. The movement of her purse blew the bright pink paper face down on the floor near the trash can.

Wendy phoned Susan's hotel. She left a message at the front desk and asked for the fax number. They found a twenty-four hour copy center near the University of Florida campus in Gainesville and faxed down their notes and a copy of the photograph of David and Jeff's mother.

*

Governor Peter Snelling was sitting at home trying to think of a way out of the mess he was in. He had relied so heavily on Zoe for the past few years. Now, when he needed him most, the man had left him. *And* lied to him, the governor reminded himself. That was what angered Snelling the most. If the man had wanted to quit, fine. But he didn't have to lie. *Menceti will have to handle it now*, the governor thought. Frank would probably try to reason with Zoe. If that didn't work, he'd try buying him back, and finally, he'd try to scare him as a last resort. That was when the phone rang. Thinking it was Menceti, he answered it himself.

"You son of a bitch!"

It wasn't Menceti; it was Zoe. "Scott, calm down," Snelling said.

"The hell I will!" Zoe yelled into the phone. "Who do you think you are?!"

"Hold on. What are you talking about?!" the governor asked. The anger flowed through Zoe's voice.

"You know damn right well what I'm talking about! You and that psychopath Menceti tried to kill me and my son!"

Snelling could not believe what he was hearing. That idiot, Menceti. "Now Scott, hold on. Please! I knew nothing."

"No, Governor, it's you that had better hold on!" Zoe said and hung up the phone. Snelling quickly called Menceti, but there was no answer at any of his phones. He dialed Frank's beeper and left his home phone and the numbers 9-1-1.

13
***
Saturday, September 16

Jeff lightly brushed Susan's hair from her face as she slept. The gentle roll of the water under the keel, along with some sleeping pills, had helped; she had finally nodded off a little after two a.m. But he had stayed up all night, sitting next to her on the small recliner inside his cabin. Susan had stirred a little at first, but for the last two hours she had lain still.

After he was convinced she would not wake for a while, Jeff got dressed and searched in her purse for her car keys. He wrote a note, telling Susan where he went in case she did wake up. He then walked out on the deck, hopped over the side onto the dock, went to the gold Lexus, and drove off to the northwest side of Key West.

It took only a few minutes to get to the Days Inn. Susan had rented a room the day before, but she had not been back since seeing the video of David's news conference on CNN.

The bars had been closed for a little over an hour, and all but the most diehard fisherman were still asleep as Jeff walked into the hotel's lobby. The night manager was a young guy in his twenties sitting at a small desk along the wall a few feet behind a large counter top that separated the office from the reception area. From the man's haircut and generally clean appearance, Jeff figured he was one of the sailors stationed down the street at the Navy annex. As Jeff approached the counter, the manager put down the book he was reading, and walked over.

"Can I help you?" he asked, looking surprised that anyone was awake at that hour.

"Yeah, I'd like to check out of room two-nineteen," Jeff answered and placed the key on the counter. The manager picked it up and stood in front of a computer, punching some of the keys. When the screen came up, the kid looked around the computer at Jeff. "Your name's not Susan."

"No, she's my girlfriend." The receptionist shrugged, then asked if he just wanted the credit card billed or to pay cash. Jeff told him the credit card would be fine, after all, he was sure that David would not mind now. A printer below the counter started spitting out a receipt. The night manager reached down and ripped it off, handing it to Jeff, who started to walk away.

"Wait a minute, I have something else for her!" The kid said, disappearing into a doorway in the back. He came out carrying a small stack of papers. "A fax came in for her last night It's a dollar a page."

Jeff walked out to the car, reading the message from Wendy informing Susan that there was a lot more to David and Jeff's relationship than either had let on. Jeff found a phone and called Menceti at home.

"Frank, it's Jeff Strata."

Menceti screamed a row of obscenities at him for waking him up. When he was done, Jeff told him that some reporter was trying to connect him to David Ranson's murder.

"You've never even met the man, they'll be no heat."

"Yeah, well I was kinda having it on with Susan Ranson."

"Who the hell is Susan Ranson?" Frank asked.

"His wife," Jeff answered and explained. Another barrage of four letter words about being stupid lasted for close to five minutes. Frank asked what he needed, and Jeff said he had to use the jet for a few hours.

"When?" Menceti asked.

"Now, Frank! I can be waiting at the airport in five minutes."

"Fine," he said. "I'll have the jet there as soon as I hang up. It'll probably take about thirty minutes."

"Thanks."

"Well don't thank me yet," Frank said. "When you get done up there I want you to take care of the Ranson woman."

"What?! Why?"

"Because she can connect us; because she was the D.A.'s wife," Frank was annoyed at having been questioned. "Because I don't know what her game is, and because I fucking said so, that's why!"

"I just don't think..."

"Your not thinking got us in this mess! I don't give a rat's ass what you think. I just want it done. Get rid of her. Now where are those other two idiots? I haven't heard from them since you left the Virgins."

"I don't know, Frank," Jeff said. "They left yesterday morning when we pulled in; I thought they'd be with you."

"Those two morons; they're probably down at some titty bar givin' some dumb bitch all my money! If you hear from them, you tell them to call me; you got it?"

"Yeah," Jeff said, then hung up the phone. *Neither Alvin nor James would be seeing Frank anytime soon unless they had been real good swimmers,* Jeff thought as he drove to the airport.

*

Wendy drove over the causeway and onto Sanibel. Beside her, Chris was sitting with his head against the window, half asleep. The sun had yet to make an appearance in the sky behind them, and the three quarter moon was still visible over the horizon. Along the water the boat ramps were busy as sportsmen launched their boats hoping to get an early start on the weekend. The two reporters had not gone home after leaving Booker's. They had stopped for dinner at a 24 hour Denny's near Gainsville, and they transcribed the taped interview while they ate. It was close to eleven o'clock when they started back. After driving for over five hours down Interstate 75, they had stopped again for breakfast. Wendy wanted to be at the marina as soon as it opened.

They pulled into the parking lot and parked near the office. Wendy walked over, but the door was locked, and the CLOSED sign still hung in the window. She went back to the car, where Chris was now sleeping in the passenger seat. After two hours of watching various fisherman and families back up to the water and slide their boats in, a pick-up truck headed over toward her and parked. Inside, the manager of the marina stepped out. He looked over at Wendy. If he remembered her from the other morning, he did not show it. *At least this time I'm wearing clothes,* she thought as she followed him over to the office. He unlocked the door and walked in, ducking under the counter top before popping up on the other side.

The old cracker paid no attention to her as he got the small bait and tackle area set up for the days business. He disappeared into the back office, then emerged chewing on a toothpick and carrying the cash register drawer. After setting it in place he finally asked her what she wanted. She told him that she was a reporter, and showed him her press pass. He did not seem too impressed, so she explained that they were doing a story on David, and that they had come from talking with Booker.

"Old Booker," the man said. "How is the old fart? I didn't know he was still alive."

"He's fine," Wendy replied. "As a matter of fact he's why we're here. He said you would have some records and that we might be able to have a look at them."

"What kind of records?" he asked suspiciously.

"Oh, really only David Ranson's," she replied. The old man looked at her as the toothpick in his mouth drooped toward the ground.

"Why should I let you look at those records?" he asked. "They are, um, confidential."

Wendy saw that she wasn't going to get them easily. Then she remembered the other day. "You don't remember me, do you?" she asked.

He looked close, then suddenly it all came back."You're that woman from the boat, the naked one!"

"Yes," Wendy answered. "Remember what you told me that day?"

The fire went out of the old man's face, and the toothpick drooped. "No."

"You told me that the man who left me was married, that he was treating me badly; don't you remember? You told me to get rid of him!"

"I did?"

"Yes, you did."

The marina manager eyed her for a moment, the pulled the toothpick from his mouth. "What's that got to do with giving you a look at that file?" he asked.

"Everything," she lied. "I need to prove to his wife that the boat is still here. I told her that I was meeting him at the boat, but he told her that he sold the thing a long time ago."

"Why don't you just bring her down here, so she can see for herself?" he asked.

"Because he moved it, silly," she said and pointed to the empty space where David's boat had been. He looked at the space, then at Wendy, then back at the space. "Okay, he said. I'll let you have it, but I need it back by noon."

She followed him back, and he searched through some file drawers and storage boxes. After finding it, he handed it to her. "Oh, do you have any other logbooks that might show who came and went, or anything like that?"

"We have something like that, to write down accidents and stuff."

"Is this stuff like what happened the other day when I was here?" The way she said it made the old man blush. He didn't like being embarrassed.

"Yeah, that kind of stuff," he said. "What do you want them for?"

"Just to show his wife, to show her I was here."

"I'm really not supposed to let you have these," he paused, then saw her disappointment. "But I guess it won't hurt. What ones do you need?"

"Just the current year," she replied. He reached into a second drawer, where she saw a whole stack of books with the spines facing up. They were in order by year. "Oh, and nineteen seventy-two, also." The old man pulled out the two green hardcover notebooks. "Thanks."

"You can't tell anyone," he said as the door banged shut behind her.

She ran to the car and slammed the door as she got behind the wheel. The sound woke Chris, and he looked around as they pulled out of the parking lot. "Where are we?" he asked. Wendy laid the file on his lap.

*

On the east side of the state, two federal agents were standing near a chain link fence topped with barbed wire. Deep reds and yellows accented the horizon, but it was still dark in the shadows where they sat watching the gloss white jet as it was pulled from the hanger. The lineman driving the tow tractor was on the payroll and notified the feds whenever this particular plane was to be readied for flight.

He had phoned the duty officer at the Miami office, and within fifteen minutes Special Agent Chris Murry and his new partner were watching through the telephoto lens, hoping to see something that would make the early wake up worth it. The pilot pulled up in a Ford Explorer, parking it inside the storage hanger before he went about his preflight. He was in his early fifties and overweight; Murry had seen him before. The pilot was very meticulous in his inspection of the plane, a carryover of his years in the military flying high performance fighters. He crawled up on the wing and looked inside the engine nacelles, and even used a flashlight to search the concrete around the sleek corporate jet for FOD, small bits of anything that could be sucked up by and wreck the two turbines. After checking the exterior of the plane, he unlocked the hatch and went inside. Murry saw the cabin windows light up as the aircraft came to life. The strobe lights came on, then were turned off. After finishing the rest of the checklist, the pilot stepped out of the plane and waited for two fuel trucks to come over. It didn't take long before the two white tank trucks drove up, effectively, though not intentionally, blocking the agent's view of the aircraft's door.

"Shit, I can't see anything," Murry said.

"Neither can I."

They needed a better angle. Agent Murry zipped shut a large black bag after loading it with the video camera and blank tapes while his partner lifted the camera and tripod. They had not moved ten feet when the fuel trucks moved away, and the jet engines started. The hatch was closed, and the plane quickly began taxiing to the runway.

"Did you see anyone get on?"

"No."

"Oh, shit," Murry said, upset at himself for blowing the surveillance. "Let's hope he's empty and going to pick someone up!" The two loaded the car and headed to the tower to find out the planes flight plan.

*

Laura was wakened by the phone ringing. She reached over and answered. It was the front desk of the resort. They apologized for waking her, but the woman said a "Mr. Sebastian" had called several times.

"Thank you," Laura said. "Did he leave a number where I can reach him?"

"He's on the line now, ma'am; that's why I woke you. He said it was urgent."

Laura asked that she put the call through. She rubbed her eyes, sat up, and put on her glasses. Reaching over to the night stand, she turned on the light as Sebastian came on the line.

"Good morning," he said. "I've been trying to reach you for over an hour.

I guess your beeper isn't working."

"It should be," she said. "Hold on a minute." She climbed out of the king size bed and went over to the small two cushion sofa. Her pager was sitting on the blouse she had worn the day before. She picked it up, then quickly dropped it as the vibrations startled her. She pressed the little red button on the side realizing what she had done. She opened the briefcase that was on the table, pulled out the fingerprint report from the lab, then went back to the phone.

"Are you still there?" she asked.

"Yes, I'm here," he said. "Now, what was so important that it couldn't wait until Monday?"

"I received a report from the lab in Langley on a set of prints, and I need your help."

"Why do you need my help?" he asked. "We don't even process prints; we use the bureau's lab."

"I know, and I guess that's the problem," Laura said. "Who's number three two seven seven one?"

The line went quiet while she waited for a response. She could hear what sounded like a metal file cabinet opening and closing before Sebastian picked the phone back up.

"What is file three two seven seven one?" she repeated.

"I have better things to do than look up file numbers for you," he said. "I'm missing two agents and someone leaked it to the press this morning."

"Yeah and I have bodies piling up all around me, Mr. Sebastian. And one of the many unexplained things I have found is a fingerprint lifted off one of the bodies that pops up with your agency's number on it. Now who is this guy?"

Sebastian opened the file. It had Jeff Strata's name on the inside. "This is a non-secure line," he said, "I am going to have to terminate this call."

"Don't you hang up on me!" Laura warned him.

"Look, lady, I may get a man killed if I give you this information; he's a long time snitch."

*

The car was parked in front of the 7-11 convenience store. Wendy and Chris were eating breakfast burritos and coffee while reading through the logbooks. "Wow, I can't believe this stuff. That old man is really bored. He writes down everything."

"Like what?" Wendy asked as she read through the book labeled *1972*.

"Well, like I didn't know you had a mole on your left breast?"

"Give me that!" she exclaimed, laughing but embarrassed. They both spilled their coffee as she wrestled the book from him. "Okay, okay. I give," he said finally.

Chris opened David's records. "I still don't understand why you want this," he said and closed the folder. "Big deal, so he had a boat at the same marina for a long time. What's that have to do with anything?"

"Are there any notes by that Booker guy in there?" Wendy asked.

Chris opened up the file and flipped through the pages. He stopped and read some handwriting at the bottom of the page labeled *SEPTEMBER 1972*. "Yeah, here's something," he said, then read the notation aloud to Wendy. "It says, '*9/23. Caused problem with daughter of slip #23, Strata family. David started fight with her husband in P. Lot. Called and informed David's father that we may cancel lease if problem keeps up. Gerald Ranson said he'd talk to his son.- Booker.*"

"Is there anything else after that?"

Chris turned the page. "Here's another one. It's about a week later, the . It reads, '*9/27. Ranson boy informed me that he would not be around for a while; he was leaving for college. Verified with Mr. Ranson, asked to keep an eye boat- Booker.*' I wonder if that was around the same time that Jeff's mother drowned?" Chris checked his notes from the visit with Booker. "Oh shit! That wasn't close to the same day," he told Wendy. "It was the same day! That's too much of a coincidence. There's something more going on here."

"Damn," she said when she saw the entry in the logbook.

"What?"

She closed it and held the book up to her chest, where she squeezed it with both hands. "I thought there might be something that I could use to show David was innocent. But I guess he and Cathy Whitmore spent some time together on his boat. It's all in here." Her voice cracked as she read, "July eighteenth, this year, David is with that Cathy woman again, this is the third night this week. Every woman David brought here was wearing a gold band on her finger."

"We need to show that to the police," Chris said as he watched a tear run down her cheek.

"I know."

"Listen," Chris said. "Maybe they were just friends. It doesn't say they did anything; I mean there was nothing out in the open, right?" But Wendy knew. She knew what he had done with her, and there was no reason to think that Cathy had not done just the same. He saw the solemn look on her face. "You know, maybe it's a different David and Cathy?" he said trying to cheer her up. "It doesn't say David Ranson, eleven one-oh-one Periwinkle does it?"

Wendy looked over, "David doesn't live at eleven- *one*-oh-one, he lives at eleven-*seven*-zero-one Periwinkle."

"No," Chris said. "According to this, he lives at eleven-*one*-zero-one." He held up the file and written on it was the address Chris said: *11101 Periwinkle Way.*

"I'm sure that he lives at eleven-*seven*-oh-one."

"Maybe it *is* someone else," she said hopefully.

"Let's go find out!"

They drove down Periwinkle, and saw that the Ranson house was indeed 11701. They continued on down the road to see if there even was a 11101 Periwinkle Way. At first, all the homes sat way back from the roadway and were all large beautiful structures. Chris guessed, correctly, that they were individually designed; no two were alike. As the addresses fell into the two hundreds, and then the one hundreds, the houses became older and smaller. No longer were they surrounded by the million-dollar hide-a-ways of the rich and famous. The houses now resembled a typical middle class neighborhood. They were two or three bedrooms, mostly ranch style homes with smaller yards. Most were concrete block construction, with the occasional Cape Cod or split level wood frame thrown in by the builders to break up the routine.

"Okay, slow down," Chris said and counted down the house numbers. "Eleven-fourteen, eleven-twelve, eleven-oh-eight, wait a minute."

She stopped the car. "Where is it? Did we pass it?"

He turned and looked back. There was a large patch of tall grass between 1112 and 1108. The field was about a quarter of an acre in size and was relatively square. Through the grass, a canal was visible.

"It must be that empty lot," he said and stepped out of the car. Wendy put the gearshift in park, but left the car running as she followed him. Chris was walking toward the center of the property when he tripped over a small pile of bricks and fell to his knees. The grass was overgrown between six and seven inches high, and unkempt. Chris felt around and noticed that the thick weeds hid not only bricks, but what looked to be part of an old concrete slab.

"Are you okay?" she yelled after watching him fall.

"Be careful," he told Wendy. "It looks like a construction area around here." He stood up and held a brick in the air to show her.

As he dropped the brick, a woman wearing a thick terry cloth robe came out of the house directly across the street. She went to the bottom of her driveway and picked up the morning paper. It was then that she saw Wendy's car sitting in the street. It took another second until she saw the two reporters in the field.

"What are you two doing over there?" she asked, walking over.

"Good morning," Chris yelled as he leaned on Wendy's shoulder and limped back to the side of the road.

"We were looking for a house," Wendy said. The woman looked relieved.

"Well that sure is a nice lot," she said. "I'm sure all the others on the block would be glad to see you build."

"I'm sorry, we don't want to buy a house, we were actually looking for a house," Chris said and gave her the address. She looked at his face.

"You're a reporter, aren't you?" she asked, smiling. "I thought I recognized your face."

"The address, ma'am?" he asked. "Do you know where it is?"

The woman spread her arms, turning her attention give to the property,

"This is it," she said. "You found the right place."

"But there's nothing here," Wendy mumbled.

"Oh, it was knocked down years ago," she said. "That was where Marjorie Johnson lived. The house was vacant for a while; the woman who owned it was from Chicago or somewhere north and couldn't find anyone to rent it. After a while, the teenagers would go in there and spray paint things and do drugs and other things that I don't want to even think about."

"What happened to the house?"

"The traffic was getting bad from all the curiosity seekers. The house was in real bad shape anyway, so the city condemned it and tore it down. It was just as well, it was full of rats."

"So they just knocked it down, huh?" Chris said. "And Miss Johnson herself lived here?"

"Up until the night she died, I suppose."

The three were staring at the place where the house had been. Chris and Wendy were both imagining what the house would have looked like. Chris could even see Marjorie as she sat out next to the water, dressed in flower-printed polyester slacks and a tube top. But when he imagined her turning around to look at him, all he could see was the swollen, water-logged face from the photograph in Sam's file. The leaves sticking out of her cracked, partially open mouth. The eyes hanging by the muscle tissue. It made him squirm.

"Would you like to come in for some coffee?" the woman asked.

"No, thank you though. We need to get rolling," Wendy said. "The news never stops."

The two walked back to the car; Wendy looked at her watch. It was only six o'clock, but the temperature was already over eighty degrees, and the humidity was well above ninety percent.

The air conditioning felt good as Chris opened the door to the car. Wendy helped him get in, his knee was really hurting, and he let out a moan as he slid into the passenger seat. After he was inside, she closed his door and then jumped in behind the wheel. "Where to?" she asked. Chris did not answer, but sat there trying to put everything together in some logical order.

"Hey, Socrates. Where do you want to go next?" she said loud enough to interrupt his thoughts.

"Oh, I don't care. I could use a shower," he answered.

"Sounds like a plan." Soon they were heading off the island.

"That doesn't seem odd to you?" Chris asked thirty minutes later, amazed that Wendy just refused to accept his explanation. She leaned out the window, dropping four quarters into the yellow basket. The light turned green, and a gate lifted to allow them through the toll and onto the bridge that crossed the river. They were leaving Fort Myers and entering Cape Coral.

"No," she answered. "It doesn't. So what, big deal? He left for college in

September. I still don't know what that has to do with Jeff's mother killing herself."

"But most colleges start in August."

"When my family moved to Florida, it was the middle of October. I was in high school, I just transferred into a new school."

"Did you go to college?"

"Just the community college here," she answered

"I don't know about community college, but universities aren't like that," Chris argued. "You don't just transfer in during the middle of a semester."

"Maybe his college did," she said. She hated being reminded that she had never finished her degree.

"Okay fine, say that you're right," he rolled his eyes. "Let's pretend that they did let him in late. Explain the address mix up on the files?"

"I can't," she said.

"Right,"Chris said. She was finally taking the blinders down around David Ranson. "No one could explain that! Not logically!"

"So what's your point?" she asked. Chris held the file up in his hands and shifted in his seat until he was facing Wendy.

"Say you're a young kid, twelve maybe thirteen years old. You're hanging out at a marina, having a good time fishing and all. Now you never see your dad. He works on a shrimp boat or something, so you are only close to your mother."

"Okay."

"Okay, so your mom starts hanging around with some young guy who's rich and all. He's not much older than you are, but your mom really likes him. As a matter of fact, she starts spending all her time with him whenever your dad's away.

"Go on," she said.

"Well anyway, you're old enough to know what the birds and the bees are and about drugs, and you start wondering why your mom seems all out of it when she's with this guy. But you're her only son, and you don't want to get your mom mad, so you just keep your mouth shut," he paused there, and lowered his voice a little for effect. "But then, one day, you see that guy hit your mom, I mean beat the hell out of her. Then when your dad comes over, the guy beats him up and makes him so mad that he leaves you forever. How do you think you'd react?" Wendy thought about it.

"I know what you're doing, okay," she said.

"Well, what would you do," Chris asked again.

"I would probably cry," she answered.

"Okay, but besides that?"

"I'm just a kid; what else can I do?" Chris held up the file from the marina.

"You're not just a kid; you're a thirteen-year old boy," Chris explained, "You're probably as tall as you're going to get, or close to it. Most thirteen-year old boys I know are larger and stronger than many women in their thirties."

"So?" Wendy said as she turned and drove down the street toward her apartment.

"So," Chris continued. "You go into the office where your friend, the old manager, works. You wait until he is either outside working or with someone, and you sneak a peek at the file of the guy who beat up your mom."

"Why would I look at his file?" Wendy asked, "I'm thirteen. What do I care?"

"Because it has the guy's *address* on it," he replied. "Maybe you want some revenge?"

"Whoa, wait a minute," Susan said as she parked the car in front of her apartment. "Are you saying that Jeff, as a thirteen year old boy, went to Marjorie Johnson's house by mistake because he was pissed off at David?"

"Why not?"

"Then why kill her?" Wendy asked. "She looks nothing like David. Besides, he would have had to know that David didn't live there. Christ, the kid was a millionaire?"

"Yeah, Wendy. That makes sense to us; we're adults," Chris argued as they got out and walked up the stairs to her apartment. "But we are talking about a kid. His body is grown, but he still thinks like a child. This is someone who thinks a hundred dollars is a lot of money!"

"Hey, to some of us adults, it still is a lot of money," Wendy said.

"You know what I mean," Chris said. "And as far as whether David looked like that dead woman, who knows? In the dark, under a blanket? She was probably the about same size..."

"But still, he's thirteen years old. You don't think of killing anyone at that age."

"Where have you been?" he said and chuckled. "It happens all the time!"

"It's a stupid theory," she told him and opened the door to her apartment.

*

Susan woke and called out for Jeff. When he didn't answer, she slowly climbed out of bed. She rubbed her temples with her fingers trying to get rid of the headache the pills had given her. After using the bathroom, she scrubbed her teeth and swallowed two aspirin. She walked down the narrow passageway and up the steps to the main cabin.

"Jeff?" she yelled again. She looked out on the deck, then out to the office. She noticed her car was gone and figured he probably went out somewhere. She knew how much of an emotional wreck she had been the night before. She had bawled like a baby after watching David get shot. She didn't know why. Maybe there was a small part of her that still loved him. But for whatever reason, it was over now. She felt much better, though she was a long way from feeling good. *How is someone supposed to act when your husband dies before you get a chance to divorce him for beating you up?* she kept asking herself.

She went over to the phone to do what she always did when she was lost and confused. She called Sam. While waiting for Sam to pick up, Susan saw the note Jeff had left her on the table. *Well at least that was one less hassle,* she thought, even if she didn't use the room. She pulled the phone a few inches away from her ear, so she wouldn't have to listen to the prerecorded advertisement for the Sanibel View. The jingle was annoying enough the first time, but after the fifth, it was downright cruel to make her wait on hold. She was about to hang up when she heard Sam answer.

"Hey, stranger," she said. "Long time, no hear."

"It seems a lot longer than a few days, doesn't it?" Sam said, happy to hear the familiar voice." How are you doing?"

"Fine, if I hadn't been on hold so long," she said, trying to sound upbeat.

"Well, we've been busy, but not in a way that I would like."

"I know the feeling," she told him, no longer trying to disguise the emotions in her voice.

"Where are you?"

"In Key West," she said. "I needed a little vacation."

"You take all the time you need."

They talked for close to half an hour about everything but David or his death. He tried to make her feel better by sticking in as many tasteless jokes as he could remember. She had always teased him because he never remembered the punch lines.

"Well, listen, honey," he said. " I need to go back to work, okay?"

"Yeah," she said sadly. "Thanks for everything Sam."

"That's what I'm here for," he told her. "Oh, what should I tell anyone who is looking for you? Is there a phone number or something?"

"No, not really. Just tell them I'm in Key West, out on a boat, and that I'll be back in a few weeks."

"Okay, that's what I'll tell them. You take care now," he said, and she heard him hang up.

*

After leaving Miami and picking up Jeff in Key West, the GKB jet landed at Page field, in Ft. Myers. It taxied up to the small terminal run by Anderson Aviation. Jeff unbuckled from the seat to the right of the pilot and told him to refuel. They'd be going right back to Key West in about an hour, maybe less.

Jeff went inside the terminal and up to the desk. The same girl as before was working, talking to a pair of gruff gray-haired men wearing old army bomber jackets, who were trying to rent a plane for the day. As the two read through the logbooks of the various planes, arguing over which was in better mechanical condition, she saw Jeff walk up and smiled, recognizing him.

"I need to help this gentleman," she said to the retired military pilots.

"Just give me a call when you decide what plane you want, okay?" Both men said sure, go ahead, and continued arguing with each other. She went over to Jeff, who noticed she was much more pleasant than the last time they spoke.

"Thanks, you saved me," she said. "Those two come in every weekend, and it's the same routine, over and over. Sometimes they don't even rent a plane at all."

"Maybe they just like to argue with each other," Jeff said watching the two men.

"I just wish they'd do it somewhere else," she said, then turned her full attention to him, "So what can I do for you today?"

"I'd like to borrow that car again if it's possible?" he had put his most boyish charm into the question.

She leaned on the counter, "I think we can do that, since you did return it last time." She reached into the cash drawer under the counter and took out the key, which she held out to him. As he went to grab it she pulled it away teasingly, "I need it back before close this time."

"Not more than an hour," he promised.

"Okay," she handed him the keys. "You realize if you're late, I get to keep that jet of yours."

"You can have it now if you want," he said joking. She yelled to the offices in the back, "Jimmy, I quit! This guy just gave me his Learjet!"

"Okay," a voice said from beyond the doorway. "Just lock up as you leave."

The girl turned back to Jeff, "I'll see you in an hour."

"Do you have a phone book?" Jeff asked as a second thought.

"White or yellow pages?"

"Yellow."

She handed him the phone book and placed her business phone on the counter for him to use. She was called back to settle the argument at the other end of the counter. Jeff looked up the Sanibel View, and called saying he was supposed to get in touch with someone named Wendy.

"Wendy Richardson?" the receptionist asked.

"She's blonde and *well proportioned*," Jeff said.

"That must be Wendy Richardson."

"Is there a way to get in touch with her?"

She looked at her watch. It was only 9:15 a.m. "It's her day off. She's probably at home; it's way too early for her to be awake. If you leave your name and number, I'll put a message on her desk."

Jeff thought a moment. "No, don't worry about it," he told her, "I'm a friend of a friend, and I was supposed to help her move something. I have a pickup truck, and I just drove in from Naples, but I lost her address."

"I'm sorry, but I can't give out addresses."

"No, that's cool. I'll just go home and go back to bed. I don't even know her anyway," Jeff sounded very convincing, even to himself. The receptionist was new, though, and didn't want Wendy to be upset with her. Maybe they did give out home addresses; she didn't know for sure what the policy was.

"I'll give you the address, but you didn't get it from me, okay?"

"Hey, thanks," Jeff said grabbing a pen. "At least she won't be bitching at me!"

*

"I'll wash that mole if you need help," Chris yelled from the living room.

"Me and my mole are just fine, thank you," she answered. "Just be quiet and watch television or something." He reached over and picked up the phone as he flipped through the television channels. He stopped on some kind of beach workout program. It had girls, sand, and weight lifting; he was happy.

The receptionist at the station answered, then transferred him to the news desk. Theory or not, he was going to follow up on this Jeffrey Strata person.

"Yeah, Bob, this is Chris," he said when the assignment editor picked up the call. "I know it's my day off, but I need someone with a camera to meet with me."

"No one's around, man, they're all out," Bob said.

"What do you mean no one's around? It's the weekend; you guys don't do shit on the weekends," Chris said. It was the truth. They reporters almost had to make up hard news on Saturdays. That was the breaks of working in a vacation resort during the off season. "Come on, Bob!"

"No way, Chris. Everybody's out covering the shooting."

"What shooting?" Chris said, his journalistic juices flowing. A reporter's nightmare: there was a big story, and he wasn't in on it.

"David Ranson," Bob said. "Where the hell have you been, in a cave?"

The assignment editor gave Chris a quick rundown of David's murder by the doctor. Chris told him the information he and Wendy had might provide a link between Jeff Strata and the killings. The assignment editor told him to hold on. The editor went and grabbed Chuck Allen, the weekend anchorman, and Chris gave him a quick synopsis of his theory, and what he found out. Chuck told Bob to send over someone with a video camera, even if it were the sports guy.

"I'll be here waiting," Chris said, and, after asking Wendy for the address and phone number, he hung up. Wendy came out of her bedroom after changing into clean clothes. Her hair was still wet from the shower as she threw a towel at the television reporter.

"You will not believe this..." he told her everything, and she sat down as the knot in her stomach twisted with each word. When he was done telling what he knew, they turned on CNN's Headline News. After watching the video, which was shown in graphic detail following a disclaimer, the young photographer ran to the bathroom and threw up. Chris ran in after her and wiped her mouth with a rag as she cried.

"Just leave me alone, please," she said. Chris watched her for a moment then walked out of the bathroom. Wendy sat on the floor, near the toilet until her stomach settled down. After brushing her teeth, she rinsed with mouthwash to get rid of the taste that still lingered. She came of the bathroom to the kitchen where Chris was sitting. He had poured her some orange juice, which sat on the table next to a plate of toast. She sat down and nibbled at the toast, hoping it would not come back up, and told Chris to go get a shower. She said she was going to get a newspaper so she could read about what happened because there was no way she could watch any more television reports. Chris asked her not to lock the door on her way out, in case the cameraman showed up while he was in the bathroom. After she left, he came out and turned the sound of the television up, so he could hear over the water.

Jeff drove into the parking lot and watched Wendy get into her car and leave. He casually strolled up to her apartment checked the door handle. It was unlocked. He went inside the apartment. Once in, he heard the shower; though it took him a second to figure out what the sound was. The television was tuned to the local morning news. Jeff was not prepared to find someone in the apartment; he had hoped to surprise Wendy. He took the fax she had sent to Susan out of his pocket and read it once again.

All the other times, he had planned his movements and watched the house. David had been so predictable. Except when he had shown up in the middle of the night at the Kindle's with his foot bleeding. But even then, there was no one around, and it had all worked out for the best. But Jeff had had no time to figure this out, and he started to chew on his finger while deciding whether to come back later. He did not know the decision was about to be made for him.

During a commercial break, a news brief appeared on the television. It was Chuck Allen reporting that the station had just received information that connected Jeff Strata to the killings.

"Our own Chris White will be bringing that report live at noon," Chuck read the tease to the camera. "Only on Eyewitness News at Noon."

Suddenly, to Jeff's surprise, Chris came running out from the bathroom screaming at the television, "What the hell I told those guys not to..." He stopped when he saw Jeff standing there. Jeff hesitated until he saw the recognition in Chris' face.

"Hey, you're Jeff Strata," the reporter said.

Jeff leapt over the small coffee table that separated them and attacked. He wrestled Chris to the floor, pulled out a knife, and placed it to his throat.

"Where did that bitch go?!" The knife was pushing so hard against his throat that the reporter could not breathe.

"Wendy... she," he gagged. "Went to the office."

"How long?!" Jeff asked pressing the knife harder, drawing blood.

"Um- about an hour," Chris answered, as tears from choking ran from his eyes.

"Wrong! I just called there!" Jeff was turning red, his lip was turned up, and the straining muscles on his face gave him the look of a madman. He was using all the power he had, but unconsciously. The anger was real, and it was dangerous. The cold brutal eyes of a killer looked into Chris's face, "I'll bet she is coming right back, isn't she?!"

Chris closed his eyes as he felt the blood trickle down his throat. He couldn't swallow, and Jeff's knee was now digging into his gut.

"Isn't she!" Jeff repeated.

Chris nodded.

*

Zoe called Snelling from Rockman's office. Three FDLE and two FBI agents were in the room monitoring the call. They had received permission for the tap late last night, thanks in no small part to the Federal Elections Commission. After being told of the call by his secretary, Snelling asked her to put it through.

"Scott?" Snelling asked calmly, "Where are you?"

"I'm somewhere safe, with my son," Zoe replied. He saw the okay sign from the agents, indicating the recording was working.

"I didn't know, Scott, honest," Snelling said sincerely.

"That doesn't matter now, Governor."

"Scott, I can't apologize enough."

"No," Zoe said, "you can't."

"I'd like to make it up to you somehow," Snelling said.

"I don't know how you could," Zoe said. Now for the kicker, "Governor, you know the manila envelope in your desk?"

Snelling was confused and nervous. Of course he knew about the envelope. He just didn't know anyone else did. What was Zoe trying to pull? A threat? Did he want money? Was it a bluff? "I have a lot of envelopes in my desk, Scott. You of all people know that. You'll have to be more specific."

"I think you know the one, Governor," Zoe said. "It has an accounting book inside where you record all the payoffs from Menceti as well as some of your other friends. Records that I made copies of. Is that specific enough for you, Governor?"

Snelling didn't know what to say or do. "What do you want?" he blurted out.

"What was that, Governor? I didn't hear you," Zoe said, more for his own benefit than the recorder's.

"I asked what do you want?!" Snelling said into the phone, trying to hold his anger. " Money?! You ungrateful son of a bitch! Money, is that it, is that what this is all about?!"

"I don't know, Governor, what are you offering?" Zoe said. Everyone around him was smiling. They had him. Snelling was trying to think of some amount that would buy him Scott's silence when the secretary buzzed him. The Governor smacked down the button, "Dammit! I'm on the phone!" He snapped.

"I'm sorry sir, Mr. Menceti is on line two, and he said it was urgent."

"Shit," Snelling said. He hit the button for line one, "Hold on, Scott, I have to take this other call! Don't hang up!"

Snelling pushed in the button and heard Menceti's voice on the line, "Peter whatever you do, don't talk to Zoe if he calls!"

"Why not?!"

"Because he turned himself into Rockman, and they may try to set you up, you dumb shit!" Menceti snapped. Snelling reached over and hung up the phone. Now only a single light was blinking. Line one. Zoe. The Governor reached over and pushed it down.

"Governor?" Zoe asked, his voice echoing over the speaker-phone. Snelling sat there, silent. Zoe repeated himself to make sure Snelling was still on the line, "Governor? Are you there?"

"May you rot in hell, Scott," he growled as the connection cut off.

*

Wendy read the story concerning David's death. Almost every paper had it one the front of page one. Even USA Today showed a color picture of the moment right before with Whitmore holding out the gun, pointing it at David while he stood at the podium on the steps. The tears were gone, but the shock was just setting in as she opened her door and walked inside. She didn't notice that the coffee table had been moved or the small red stains on the rug in front of the television set. After reading the article, she put down the paper and stared at a commercial on TV

She could hear the shower running and walked down the hall. She had been gone a little over half an hour, and she couldn't believe that Chris was taking so long.

"What the hell?" she said. His clothes were piled on the floor in front of the door, which was slightly ajar. "What are you doing in there?" she yelled into the bathroom. She waited, but did not hear a reply. "I said what's taking you so long, come on!" Still nothing. Wendy thought he was trying some juvenile way of getting her to join him. "I'm not coming in there, Chris," she said. But she only heard the running water. She began to wonder if he was in there, so she cautiously pushed open the door.

"Chris?" she called out. "Okay, Chris, this isn't funny. If you don't answer me, I'm throwing all of your clothes outside in the street." She walked in a little further. "Chris if you're in here, I am going to be so pissed!"

She took a few more steps, until she stood right in front of the shower curtain. She saw a naked back through it, "You son of a bitch!" she said angrily,

"I knew this was just some stupid way of..." The shower curtain ripped aside, and Jeff sprang out with the knife and grabbed her around the throat. Inside the tub, Chris's body lay bleeding.

Jeff pushed her back, almost lifting Wendy off the floor. She tried to push his hands away, but his fingers were holding so tight her skin was squeezing out from between them. He was not wearing any clothes as he brought her into the kitchen. She tried to kick him as he forced her down onto a chair. But he swiped at her leg with a knife, deeply slicing her knee with the stainless steel blade. She tried to scream, but his grip around her throat would not allow her larynx enough air. She felt the life slip away as the shortage of oxygen made her feel dizzy.

Wendy became hysterical at the thought of dying and frantically grabbed at his hand around her neck. He saw that she was about to pass out and released his grip slightly. Her body relaxed and she started to hiccup as the air flowed back inside her body. He knew he only had a few seconds before she became aware of what was going on. He reached up and tore the small set of curtains from the kitchen window. He used the thin material to tie her arms behind her back and to the chair. She was coming to as he ripped off her pantyhose and used them to tie her legs. She choked and gagged for a few minutes, and he waited for her to get fully conscious. When she did, Wendy started to cry, but no sound came out. Across from her, Jeff stood watching her. When he saw her eyes look at him, he spoke. His voice was calm and deliberate.

"I need to know what you told the police?" he asked. She just whimpered and started to cry. This was not the man she knew. This person was evil. He looked over at the clock on the wall; he didn't have time for this. He placed the knife on the small kitchen table. He went over to her and pulled her head back by her hair until their faces were less than an inch apart. She could feel his warm breath on her face, and tried to turn away, but he yanked her head back into place until all they saw were each others eyes.

"Now, I will only ask you one more time darling. What did you tell the police about me and David?"

"Nothing," she said.

"Liar!" Jeff yelled. Wendy sat still and quiet, afraid to move. She thought back to Chris's theory. Why didn't she believe him? Why didn't they tell the police? Jeff let her go, then went and picked up the knife. He used the tip to clean his fingernails.

"You see, lying just doesn't help your situation."

"I'll tell you anything I know. Just don't kill me!" she said.

"Oh, I'm not going to kill you," he said in an almost friendly way. "That is unless you want me too. Do you want me to kill you?" She shook her head no.

"Well then, just tell me what I want to know, and you'll be fine."

"Please don't rape me," she murmured, staring at him.

"Rape? Rape? I never raped anyone in my whole life." He sounded offended, but not angry. But then he saw the way she was watching him. He looked down at himself and seemingly realized for the first time that he was naked. "I'm sorry. Does my body offend you?"

She just sat not making a sound, frozen by fear of saying the wrong thing, of making him angry, of dying or worse.

"No?" he asked and waited for an answer, but the woman said nothing. "Would you feel more comfortable if I put something on?"

Wendy nodded slowly when she saw he wanted an answer. "You probably wouldn't have said that a month ago when we first met," he said, "but, that's all right. I'm not offended. I'm secure with my body. I'll be right back." He went down the hall to the bathroom. He did not leave sight of Wendy, except for a second or two while he pulled a towel off the rack above Chris's dead body after turning off the shower. Jeff wrapped the towel around himself, then went back to the kitchen.

"Better?" he asked. She nodded. "Good," he said. "Now I don't assault a woman unless she really wants it, like that doctor's wife, or that Kindle woman. I mean, after a little juice, you can see it in their eyes. David taught me that. You remember David, don't you?"

She didn't move a muscle. "I'll bet you do. No, I did not come for that, Miss Richardson. Although I'll bet it would be fun."

He walked closer to her and bent down beside her. He spoke into her ear. "I just need some information," he said, emphasizing the words. Then he stood back up in front of her. "That you and your big-mouthed, big shot news reporter boyfriend there have. I don't think he'll be doing any more live reports, how about you?"

"I'll tell you whatever you want," she said almost in a whisper. "Please don't kill me."

After Jeff was convinced that they had not contacted the police, he placed Wendy's body in her bed, along with Chris. Jeff then jumped in the shower and washed the blood from his body before putting back on his clothes, which he had neatly folded and placed on a shelf in the hall closet to keep from getting soiled. He took a last look at the apartment and saw the bloody drag marks leading to the bedroom. *Needles are so much cleaner*, he thought and walked out to the car.

*

The detective cringed as Laura sped north on U.S. 41, zigzagging in and out of lanes, almost hitting a stalled car near the intersection at College Parkway. They passed by the endless restaurants and retail stores that lined the main route through FT. Myers, then turned right after the blue sign with a silhouette of an airplane. They quickly drove past row upon row of small single engine air planes that were lined up behind the chain link fence that surrounded Page Field. Eventually, the two reached a gate. The sign read *Anderson Air General Aviation Terminal* . A painted black arrow pointed the way. Laura followed the signs until she pulled up to the mirrored glass building. They parked right in the loading zone out front, then walked inside. The small terminal was empty except for the lone receptionist sitting behind the semi-circular counter.

Laura and Doyle pulled out their identification and showed it to the woman.

"Have you seen this guy?" Laura asked, and handed over a photograph. The surveillance photo was in black and white, and it was obviously taken at night. It showed Frank Menceti and Jeff Strata. It looked like they were talking, and were unaware of being photographed.

"Which one?" the receptionist asked.

"This one," Doyle said, pointing at Menceti. The woman looked hard, then shook her head.

"I'm sorry, I haven't seen either of them," she said, "but I just punched in a few minutes ago. Were they supposed to be here?"

"Yeah," Laura said, "their jet supposedly landed about an hour ago." Murry had called and given her the information after talking to the FAA. The local air traffic controller said that they had closed their flight plan from Page Field.

"Was there someone here before you? You said you just punched in," Doyle asked.

"Yeah, Nancy. She goes to breakfast around nine-thirty," the woman answered. "She should be back in about thirty minutes or so."

"Is there anyone who might have been here this morning?" Laura asked.

"One of the ground crew would have been here." Laura told her they would like to question them, and the receptionist radioed for them to come to the office. "They'll be right out there," she said, pointing to a pair of tinted glass doors leading out to the concrete tarmac. Laura and the detective walked out the door, as a badly beaten golf cart drove over to them from one of the hangars. On the cart, three teenage guys were riding, all dressed in blue shorts and white shirts. Behind them, on the tarmac, sat the GKB jet. The pilot was signing the fuel receipt and talking to the driver of one of the fuel trucks. Doyle went over to the cart, and showed them the photo. Laura started walking toward the plane.

"Oh yeah, he's here," the scruffiest of the three said. "He's with that guy over there," the lineman pointed to the GKB pilot. Doyle held the photo up closer, "You're sure it's him?"

"No doubt in my mind," the kid said, "but I never saw this old guy before."

Doyle showed them the photo again, "Which guy are you saying you saw get off the plane?"

"Him," the lineman said, pointing at the picture of Jeff.

"Drive me over to that woman," Doyle told them, hopping on the cart.

"Sure," the driver said and headed over to catch up with Laura. The FBI agent was almost to the jet. The pilot noticed her out of the corner of his eye and didn't think much of it. But then he saw Doyle on the cart, pointing in his direction. Very few people wore suits on Saturdays in South Florida, and the pilot didn't like to associate with any of them.

"Excuse me," Laura said drawing his attention. The pilot saw her reach into her purse, and pull out some kind of ID. He quickly turned and walked away from the plane. Laura started following him, when the man broke into a run. He was heading toward a hangar close by when Laura yelled for him to stop. Doyle saw what was happening and ordered the driver of the cart to cut the guy off. The two other ground crew jumped off the cart to give it more speed, and they caught up with the pilot a few yards away from the hangar door. Doyle jumped off and grabbed him, swinging him over to the cart. The guy was too out of breath to give much resistance. Laura caught up as Doyle put handcuffs on him.

"Just like Cops!" the driver of the cart said referring to the television show of the same name, "Who's got a videocam!"

"Hey where were you going?" Doyle asked the pilot.

"No where."

"Then why were you running?" Laura asked.

"Agent Wilson, I don't think this gentleman is going to answer our questions."

"I don't know nothing, I want a lawyer if I'm under arrest."

Laura, the pilot, and Doyle sat up on the cart as the lineman drove them back to the terminal. As the cart pulled up, an Airport Security truck drove over to them. Inside, a young guy in his early twenties looked out from the four wheel drive truck. He was wearing an earring and wrap around sunglasses, and a cigarette hung from the corner of his mouth. He explained that an aircraft mechanic had seen them and called because he didn't know what was going on. Doyle held up his badge.

"Sanibel Homicide," he said.

"You're a little out of your jurisdiction, aren't you, detective?" the security officer said while still sitting in his truck. He was obviously intent on giving them a hard time. Doyle figured the guy was just upset that they he wasn't in on the bust.

"Well I'm not," Laura said. The officer examined the federal agent's identification, then handed it back.

"Now what brings the Feds to our part of town?" he said, smiling. "It must be that District Attorney blowin' his damn head off."

"If you want to make yourself useful, how about calling for a local who does have jurisdiction to come and take this gentleman into custody?" Laura said, none too pleasantly. The officer picked up the radio and called the county sheriff's office.

"If you are going to arrest me, at least let me close up that jet," the pilot said. "I'm responsible for it."

Doyle asked one of the linemen, who said he could get a mechanic to go do it. Then the detective sat down on the golf cart next to the pilot.

"We may not even have to arrest you," Doyle said, "If you tell us who was on that plane of yours when you landed this morning." The man looked up at the detective, then turned around so that his hands were facing him.

"Shit, that's all you want?" he said. "First take these cuffs off. My hands are turning blue."

Doyle removed the cuffs, and the pilot started massaging his wrists. "Jeff Strata, that's who."

"Not Menceti?" Laura asked. The man's face twisted up as if they had just insulted him. "Hell no. He's got his own pilots. I'm strictly low level stuff."

Laura's beeper went off. She excused herself and went inside. The number on her beeper didn't jump from her memory, but she knew that if they beeped her this early on a Saturday, it was probably important. She asked to use the phone. It was Sam Harden informing her that Susan had just called, and she knew about David's death.

"She saw it on television, of all places," Sam said.

"How did she take it?" Laura asked. "Is she all right?"

"She said she was, but I think she's still upset over it."

"I'd like to speak with her," Laura asked.

Sam told her Susan was in the Keys and that she would be back in a few weeks. That didn't seem to please the FBI agent. Laura asked for a phone number or some other way to get in touch with Mrs. Ranson.

"I have no number," he said. "She's off with that Jeff character." Suddenly Sam was barraged with questions: Where was she staying? The exact time of the last contact with her? Where were they going and when?

"Hold on!" Sam yelled into the phone. "I don't know anything except what I told you."

"Mr. Harden," Laura said, "I'm going to have someone come and ask you all this again. I know you think you told me everything, but there may be some detail that you can't remember right now, okay?"

"I'm worried about her too. I think it's a waste of time," he told her. "But if it's about Susan's safety, I have no objections."

"Also," she said, "If you hear from Susan again, tell her to go to the police. If not the police then somewhere, anywhere away from that man."

*

The green and white patrol car of the Lee County Sheriff's Department followed behind Jeff as he turned right toward the airport. The killer watched the officer in the rear view mirror, then glanced down at the speedometer in front of him. He was not about to get caught because of some stupid traffic violation, especially now that he had seen the story on television. Wendy had not told him much; he should have asked that reporter he found first, but that was in the past. Right now, he had to concentrate on getting back to the plane. The two cars snaked their way along the road bordering the airfield. Jeff kept waiting for the deputy to turn off, but he just sat behind him playing follow the leader. *Was he tailing him, did they already know what he did?* The thoughts raced through his mind as he came upon the entrance gate.

The deputy turned on his signal first, and Jeff, who was becoming paranoid, continued past the parking lot. He grinned as he watched the deputy turn out from behind him. But the suspicions did not leave him, and he turned up the next entrance, where the Lear was visible. Right away he knew something was wrong when he saw a man he didn't know putting the red engine covers on the plane. Jeff hit the gas and headed to south on U.S. 41 to his alternate transportation.

*

"I'm sorry it took so long, we didn't know it was related. Can we help?" the Cape Coral police officer told Doyle over the phone. The bodies of Wendy and Chris had been discovered by the sports cameraman that Chris's assignment editor had sent over. Jeff had forgotten to lock the door, so the man had walked in just a few minutes after the murders had taken place. The blood had not even dried when the police arrived. But Cape Coral had not put the connection of the deaths together until they found out what the interview was about. It was only by chance that the investigating officer in the Cape called Doyle's Chief. The officer had found the logbooks and file and thought there might have been a break-in or something at the marina. But after a short conversation, the Chief thought that Doyle would want to know about the deaths and told the Cape Coral officer that he should contact the detective. And that had taken another forty minutes.

"No, thanks. It's not your fault," Doyle told him. He hung up the phone and looked at his watch. They had been waiting two hours for Jeff to come back to the plane. The deputy had taken the pilot to the county lockup. There was no reason why Jeff hadn't shown up yet, unless he knew they were looking for him. He went outside to a small plastic picnic table where Laura was sitting. A brightly colored beach umbrella over the table provided some shade. A couple of hundred yards away, a small piper was starting its engine, but other than that, the only noise was the sound of the breeze hitting the umbrella. Laura sat drinking a Coke. She was sweating, it was hot out. Doyle had taken off the jacket of his suit and undone the top button of his shirt underneath the tie.

"Listen to this," Doyle said. "They just found that Richardson woman, dead, along with some reporter. Supposedly, they found something that linked Jeff Strata to the killing."

"Strata, Jeff Strata. I know I've heard that name before. Wasn't this the same guy that Ranson told us to look at when we arrested him?" Laura asked.

"Yeah, now that you mention it," Doyle said.

Laura looked up at the detective, raising her hand to shade her eyes, "He's pretty popular for being dead."

"I don't think he's going to show," Doyle said, sitting down. "He'd have been here by now."

"Where would he go?"

"I can only think of one place if I were him," Doyle said.

"Let's give Sebastian a call," Laura replied. "But first, we need to notify the airports, at least give them his name and description."

"You're the Fed, you call Sebastian. I'll call my boss and the airports."

*

Jeff turned into the strip mall across from the Office Max supply outlet in Naples and used the pay phone. He called Gulf Air and asked for reservations for the next flight to Key West.

"That leaves in about forty minutes," the clerk said.

"I'll be there!" he said and hung up. Fifteen minutes later, he pulled into the Naples Airport parking lot. He ran inside. The terminal was not very large. It was carpeted and relatively new. It was designed like a circus tent; the inside was circular and open. Along the edges the various airlines had rented spaces. The only scheduled aircraft that flew in were small commuter types that seated twenty or so passengers. It was not crowded; there were only a few passengers milling about. He stopped running once inside but walked quickly past American, Continental, and the other major carriers and commuters until he saw the small Gulf Air counter.

"I'm not too late for Key West am I?" he said to the clerk.

"No, it's a little delayed due to bad weather," she told him.

"How much of a delay?"

"About ten minutes," she replied. "Due to some rain squalls in the Gulf. Typical summer weather in Florida. What's your name?"

"Alvarez, Luis Alvarez," Jeff said. The clerk punched the name into her computer. She asked for any baggage while the printer spit out his boarding pass. She prepared his ticket and handed it to him. "Here you go," she said, "I'll call you when we're ready to board."

Jeff went over to the lounge and sat down after buying a Coke from the snack bar. He was finally relaxed when two Naples Police officers walked over to the various airline counters. They stopped at each one, said something to the agent behind the counter, then moved on until they had spoken with all of them. They then went and sat in the middle of the small terminal and stood watch.

Over the loud speaker, he heard a female voice paging "Mr. Luis Alvarez" to come to the Gulf Air terminal. She had to repeat it a couple of times before he remembered it was him. He nervously walked over to the counter, where the clerk was waiting for him.

"I was paged," he said keeping an eye on the two officers. One of them had taken notice of him and watched Jeff go up to the counter.

"Yes, sir," she said. "I'm sorry, but I need to see some identification."

"Is this is in relation to the alert you just received?"

"How do you know about that?" she asked, surprised. He handed over Luis's DEA identification. Jeff's photo had replaced the original. It wasn't perfect, but unless the person looking at it knew what the real one was like, they would never know the difference. He was betting the clerk did not know. He was right.

"I'm sorry," she said handing it back to him. "We had to ask."

"That's why we send out bulletins," Jeff said. "What did they tell you, so I have the latest information?"

She said the police told her they were just looking for a man, but no photograph was available yet. Jeff told her to keep up the good work and that she should notify one of the police officers if she saw anyone who fit the description. Minutes later he was sitting on the plane waiting for clearance to take off.

*

"Jeff Strata is dead, killed in the Virgin Islands," Sebastian said.

"Now his ghost is apparently flying around in private jets," Laura replied. "Look, Mike, I have an eyewitness that places Jeff here! Today! Several eyewitnesses in fact."

"I have a report, the last report from one of my best agents," Sebastian pleaded. "He was also the man who has handled Jeff since the beginning saying that Strata is dead. The guy saw it with his own eyes."

"All I can say is that he's mistaken."

"The man's a professional, Laura."

"I don't doubt his abilities, But could you call and verify? Because I got people dying all around me, and this man's name keeps popping up."

"I'd like to, but I haven't heard from Alvarez in a couple of days. I don't know where he is."

"Well, try, please, Mike."

Sebastian was caught in a situation already. He was already getting pressure from both above and below. Especially since the U.S. Treasury was out three million dollars. Maybe it was Strata. "Fine, Laura, I'll fax his file to you."

The FBI agent gave Sebastian Anderson Aviation's fax number. Twenty minutes later, the photograph was faxed to her office and every other law enforcement agent from Orlando to Key West, along with the description of the car he had borrowed.

*

Back at the Naples airport, the two officers started making the rounds again after receiving the radio call. They worked their way up to the Gulf Air desk. They asked the girl if she had received the updated bulletin; she said not yet. They asked to see the passenger list for any flights that went to Key West that day. She handed it to them.

"No, not on it," the officer said. "Ma'am was there anyone who resembled the description you received?"

"Just Mr. Alvarez, but he was one of you guys!"

The officers looked confused. "A police officer?"

"I guess," she answered. "He was a Federal Agent. I think it was the DEA."

They showed her the new bulletin with Jeff's photo. "Yeah that's him."

They contacted the FBI, who contacted Laura. She called Sebastian.

"What was the name of your agent that was missing?"

"Andre Gomez," Sebastian said.

"Not him, the one who called in the report on Jeff?"

"Luis Alvarez. Why? What's going on?"

"He's not missing anymore," Laura said. "He just hopped a plane to Key West. and he looks remarkably like Jeffrey Strata!"

"Oh, shit!" Laura heard him say as an officer handed her a message. They found Anderson Aviation's car in the Naples airport parking lot.

"When does the plane land?" Sebastian asked. "I'll have ten agents meet that son of a bitch!"

"Too late," Laura said. "It landed eight minutes ago!"

The senior DEA agent punched down hard on his desk, then regained his self control. There had to be something they could do. *Wait a minute.* "Laura!"

"What?"

"What day is it? It's Saturday, right?"

"Yeah, why?"

"Where are you?"

"Page Field," she said.

"Wait for me there, I'll get us a helicopter! We're going to find that son of a bitch!" Sebastian hung up the phone, then called the National Guard commander in Tampa.

*

As soon as Jeff had arrived in Key West International he had quickly walked out to the parking lot. As fast as possible he had found Susan's Lexus, paid the parking attendant, and headed to the Marina. The wind was gusting; the temperature had dropped at least twenty degrees when he arrived near the boat. He saw the leaves on the trees had all turned up towards the sky ready for the refreshing water droplets that would soon fall from the ever-darkening sky. He went into the marina office and waited to pay his bill. The manager, wearing a shirt with the name "Joey" embroidered on it, saw him walk in.

"I'll be with you in a minute, Jeff," he said, then continued to argue with the owner of one of the larger yachts because the man's boat did not fit into the slip he had reserved. Jeff stood by impatiently, but there was nothing he could do without causing a scene, so he just leaned against the wall of the small office.

"Hey, Jeff," the manager asked, "Would you watch the phones, I need to straighten this out I'll be right back."

Jeff huffed, "Yeah, fine. But I need to shove off before this rain gets here." The manager followed the other man outside and down towards the water.

*

Sebastian called Laura and told her that a helicopter would be flying them to the Keys and should be there anytime. He also told her that he faxed out a photo of Jeff's boat to her office with a note asking them to start calling all the marinas, and getting locals to help if they needed the manpower.

"Tell them there is a woman on board," Laura said.

"Who?"

"Susan Ranson, David Ranson's wife."

"Are you shitting me? Is she involved?!" Sebastian asked.

"We don't know. I doubt it," Laura replied. "But I don't want anyone assuming anything. We've already done that enough with this thing!"

"We should have them check both Jeff Strata's and Susan Ranson's credit cards," Doyle added.

"Yeah, good point," Laura said."And add David's, too!"

*

Jeff was standing against the wall when the phone rang. He looked around for his friend to come back, but he was down near a hundred-foot yacht arguing. Jeff reached over and picked up the phone.

"Marina office," he said.

"This is Officer Nelson, down at Key West P.D. We are looking for a boat named the Gheko. It's an old, white, twin-deck cruiser, about forty, forty-five feet. Do you know if it's used your facilities in the last two days?"

"Hold on," Jeff said, "let me look." After he laid the telephone receiver on the desktop, Jeff opened some file drawers and banged the stapler on the counter so the officer on the line could hear it. Then he picked up the phone. "No, I'm sorry. I don't have any record of it. What is it, a smuggler or something"

"No," the officer said. "Some guy just looking for his girlfriend's parents."

Jeff laughed. *Oh yeah, that's believable.* He decided to have a little fun. "Isn't that a waste of my taxes, officer? What's your badge number, I want to know who this kid is that gets to..." The phone clicked as the rookie police officer hung up. He only had about a thousand more places to call.

"Who was that?" his friend asked, coming back inside.

"A bunch of kids," Jeff said. "They called like five times since you were out there."

"What did they want?"

"Nothing, just swearing and blowing whistles, shit like that," Jeff said. The man reached over and unplugged the phone from the wall.

"The hell with them, I just won't answer it," the man said. "The afternoon rain's comin' anyway."

"I know," Jeff said and paid for the slip rental and fuel from the day he arrived. "I'm trying to beat it out of here."

The man gave him the receipt, and Jeff went down to the Gheko. He undid the lines after starting the engines and headed out into the channel through the small bay.

*

"Joint Task Force Four's liaison offered to ask the Coast Guard to look for the boat," Sebastian told Laura as they waited for their ride south. The helicopter was less than a minute out, and they could see the small dot growing larger in the sky.

"How about Customs? "Laura asked.

"The customs people have both P-3's and Citation jets."

"Do you think they'd help?" Doyle asked.   "After all this guy is beating them, too."

"Yeah, but this guy is smart," Sebastian did not sound confident. "I mean, really smart."

"Smarter than you?" Doyle said.

"Oh, yeah. He's been hauling drugs his whole life. He knows every trick there is." The three of them could clearly see the helicopter now.

*

One quarter mile away from the marina, the roar of diesel engines came to life, as Jeff pushed the throttles forward. The bow started to rise out of the water as the boats speed increased. Inside, below decks, Susan lay sleeping. The aspirin had gotten rid of her headache, but the fatigue from going to bed late and waking up early had caught up with her.

The rolling thunder echoed off the waterfront condos and into Jeff Strata's ears. He looked at the horizon and saw the black skies. Lightning was visible, touching down onto the waves or hitting the metal buoy that floated in the Gulf. The air temperature had continued to drop as they headed farther and farther out to sea. Jeff inhaled deeply. The water gave off the distinctive smell of rain as the Gulf turned from light green to dark blue.

*

Specialist 4 Mark McGuire slid the door back and stood on the edge watching the earth seemingly rise to meet him. He stepped out to the ground the moment the olive drab helicopter touched down. What had started as a typical weekend training flight had suddenly become very interesting. The three impatient passengers started running up to the helicopter but halted at the raised hand of the crew Chief. He motioned for them to back away, and pointed to the fuel truck heading across the tarmac toward them. The crewman pulled the quick release cap from the fuel cell as the white truck came to a stop just out of reach of the spinning blades of the helo. The driver jumped out, ran to the back of the vehicle, and pulled out a length of thin cables. He connected them to a steel rod in the concrete and to the helicopter. After grounding the Huey to the truck and the pavement, the driver pulled a large black rubber hose to the crewman, who helped him connect it to the UH-1B. Over the incredible noise McGuire exchanged hand signals with the driver, informing each other of their intentions. The crewman then grabbed a rucksack from inside the door and sprinted to the waiting passengers who were covering their ears with their hands. He handed each a small blue box that contained yellow foam hearing protectors. He showed them how to put them in their ears. He then pulled three strange looking devices that resembled two halves of an orange connected by a metal strip from a big box and gave one to each passenger.

"Mickey Mouse ears" he screamed as he handed one to each of them. "They will protect your hearing." Doyle started to take the yellow foamies out of his ears but was stopped by the airman. "No, you wear both at the same time!"

"We are in a hurry!" the DEA agent shouted, pointing to his watch. The crewman nodded.

"We barely made it down here. You wouldn't want us to run out over the Gulf, would you?" McGuire asked as he put on his best public relations smile. Civilians.

The fuel truck driver unhooked the hose and the ground cable, wrapping them as quickly as he could. He then ran back to the crewman, he raised his hand, and held up three fingers.

"I only gave you three hundred gallons. I have a LifeFlight helo on its way, it gets priority." The driver pointed to the white, orange and blue Aerospecial 350 helicopter heading across the field toward them. "I'll come back to you!" The crew Chief shook his head and grabbed his pen, "No time! We'll go with that!" McGuire signed the fuel receipt and led the three quickly into the helicopter, which then lifted off. Laura watched the Medivac land on the painted circle they had just occupied while they climbed out towards Key West.

*

Inside the Gheko, Susan was awakened by the vibrations of the powerful Detroit V-10's positioned under the stateroom. She felt the waves slapping the bow of the craft that indicated that she and the boat were underway. She quickly dressed and went topside to find out what was happening. She looked up in the pilot house but saw no one. What she did see were waves crashing over the bow, and, looking behind her, she could make out the entrance to the marina, though it was fading in the mist of the heavy downpour of rain. She was scared; she had never been out on the water when it was raining, much less during a storm.

Seeing no one inside, she realized that the boat was being controlled from the fly bridge. She grabbed a windbreaker and slid open the aft glass door. She went out and climbed the ladder to the fly bridge where she saw Jeff at the wheel. He was drenched. The rain was coming down heavily, and the rocking of the boat was exaggerated because of their height above the water.

"Where are we going?" she yelled to him.

"Go back inside!" he said and pointed down at the ladder.

"Here!" She took off her jacket. After wrapping it around him, she kissed his cheek and climbed back down.

*

Even wearing both sets of hearing protection, it was still noisy. And bumpy. And windy, and grimy, and hot. It was all these, plus a hundred other things that made Laura feel sick. She wondered how Rick did this every day. Not only did he fly like this, but the career Navy man seemed to enjoyed it. Her husband was a strange guy.

They knew they had little chance of catching Jeff at the airport or even the marina. The UH-1B flew little faster than a small Cessna. But they did not need a runway to land, and the plan was to fly around the island and find the boat. Hopefully, it would be found by the FBI and local police that were already in Key West.

Once identified, the helo would head to its location and wait for Jeff to show up. It was an optimistic plan at best. They had no clue as to where the boat was tied up. The only person with that information was Jeff, and they didn't expect much help from him. There were over 40 marinas on Key West alone, and dozens, if not hundreds, of privately owned and rented slips. The odds did not look good. They also had a warrant in their possession for Susan Ranson. No one on board the helicopter believed that she was in on it, but they were tired of surprises. Besides, if she wasn't in on it, at least she would stay alive if the authorities picked her up.

*

The Gheko was rocking violently as Susan searched through the drawers in her cabin for her clothes. She was soaking wet and wanted to change so she wouldn't drip all over the rug. Her suitcase lay empty in the corner. Finding nothing in any of the drawers she walked down the passageway. The other cabin doors were locked, so she went back to the galley and grabbed the spare key from its hook. Jeff had shown her where it was when they were back at Sanibel, just in case.

She went down below deck and opened up the door closest to the cabin she was using. When she opened the thick wood door, she immediately saw the large red stain on the carpet. There were flies all around on the walls. A wooden chair sat in the corner, with a dark substance coating the seat. The back of the chair had deep gouges in it, as did the ends of the wooden arms, where a persons fingertips would be. Beside the stain on the floor, Susan saw a small white object. She reached down and picked it up. It looked like a tooth, at least part of one. It fell from her hand as she drew back after realizing what it was. She wiped her hands on her pants, but the moisture from the rain caused the dry blood to liquefy, leaving red streaks across her thighs.

She also saw a black leather bag next to the stained rug. She went over and cautiously unzipped it, scared to guess at what she would find. Inside she saw only one thing. Stacks and stacks of hundred dollar bills. They too had red stains. Blood stains. Susan quickly left the room and shut the door behind her. She hurried back to the kitchen; she was scared and confused. She wasn't prepared for this, and her thoughts kept racing back to that tooth just sitting on the carpet. She started to panic. What did she know about Jeff anyway? Where did all that money come from? Why was there blood on it? She started searching for something to protect herself with, as her mind imagined what went on in the room.

She searched the drawers but found nothing except plastic forks and spoons. She pulled out another drawer as the craft was hit broadside by a massive wave. She fell to the floor. The drawer emptied on top of her. Susan tried to stand up, when she felt a stinging in her hand. She looked down to see a hypodermic needle sticking in her palm. Close to it, a white cardboard box was open, half filled with needles, the rest scattered on the carpeted floor. They all had blue caps.

*

The Florida National Guard pilot did not like what he saw or heard. He turned to Sebastian, who leaned up to hear him.

"We can't make Key West, I'm diverting to Marathon! The weather is bad. They reported a micro burst a few minutes ago.

"What's that?"

"Wind shear! This bird ain't all weather capable! I can't go in there, too dangerous. I'm sorry." And he was sorry, but he would be even more sorry if they were dead, hit by winds that blew straight down at over one hundred miles an hour. Wind shear could push a jumbo jet into the ground; it would have no trouble with a Huey. Sebastian informed Laura and Doyle about the problem. Laura leaned forward and asked the pilot if he could contact NAS Key West. He nodded his head and started turning the dials on his radio.

*

Laura's husband was sitting in the operations office when the phone rang. The petty officer that worked for him was down buying them popcorn in the coffee mess at the end of the hall, so the Lieutenant answered it himself.

"Detachment Two Operations, Lieutenant Cox, this is a non-secure line."

"This is the Master Chief Regis, sir. I need you down here in Maintenance Control right away, sir! Your wife is on the radio! "

"On what radio?" Rick asked.

"She's calling from a helicopter, she wants to speak with you!" Regis said. "And she said you'd better damn well hurry, sir. Her words not mine!" *What the hell was going on, what was his wife doing on the radio?* Rick thought as he took off through the door.

Rick was out of breath when ran into the maintenance office, where all work stopped the moment he opened the door. The Master Chief Regis did not like people using the squadron frequency for personal messages, and the look he gave Rick showed it. He handed the mike to the Lieutenant, holding on to it just long enough to show his disapproval. Although Rick was an officer and outranked him, it wasn't smart to anger a Master Chief with twenty-six years in the Navy..

"She is November Golf 664," Regis told him. Rick picked up the gray microphone and depressed the button on its base.

"November Golf 664, this is Toad base."

"Golf 664, stand by," the National Guard pilot answered.

McGuire had already pulled the headset and mike from the storage bag velcroed to the bulkhead of the chopper. He connected a cable to the jack on the wall and ran it to the connector on the headset. Laura took off the Mickey Mouse ears and replaced them with the headset. McGuire showed her how to work the microphone. She depressed the red button attached to the cord and spoke.

"Rick, it's me." Her voice crackled over the airway and exited the speaker. He took a deep breath and depressed the mike.

"Laura?" He was surprised, but quickly regained his composure, "Use call signs. November Golf 664, copy?"

"I don't have time," Laura said. "I need you to get a helicopter up to meet us at the airport in Marathon Key. We will be there in fifteen minutes, okay?"

"This is interesting," Regis quietly commented to the petty officer next to him.

"I can't do that. I don't have the authority to do that." Rick would be hearing about this one. The faces in the maintenance office told him that.

"Find someone who does," she continued. "Contact special agent Nina Sanchez, FBI in Miami at... do you have a pen?" The petty officers next to him each held out a pen.

"Go ahead."

*

Jeff was a natural sailor. His grandfather had told him so when Jeff was five, and he had not lied. He had been using every bit of knowledge and experience he had to keep the Gheko under control since leaving the safety of the harbor. The waves that broke over the bow had ripped away some stanchions that now dangled from the line they were supposed to hold up. But the worst was over for the time being. He could see the rain showers all around him, but he had found a spot where the storm had let up. Even though the waves were still a problem, he could relax a bit now that the raindrops were not stinging his face. He estimated the Gheko was about fifteen nautical miles south of Key West when the sun broke through off the port side. No one would catch them now.

*

"Admiral, I know that's what the Coast Guard is for, but they don't have the assets here, and we do!" Rick's Commanding Officer argued. The buck had been passed up the chain of command to the four-star flag officer on the other end of the line, and he did not want to make the decision either.

" I wish I could help, Commander, but the military is strictly forbidden to intercede. We are not a law enforcement agency!" The Admiral said. "Tell them to use a local police helicopter if the Coast Guard can't send one."

"Sir, we have some violent storms in the area right now. The only all-weather helo within a hundred miles is ours." But the Admiral just repeated his answer.

"Tell him about the woman on board," Rick said.

"Here," his commander handed Rick the phone. "You tell him."

Rick didn't want to take it, but his CO gave him no choice. "Admiral, this is Lieutenant Rick Cox, sir. I may have a way out of this."

"I'm listening, Lieutenant."

"Sir," Rick explained. "A woman is on the boat, and we have reason to believe that she is being held against her will or is unable to leave."

"Even if she is, that's still kidnapping," the flag officer said.

"It could also be considered a SAR operation, Admiral."

"That's twisting it just a little, isn't it?"

"Yes sir, a whole bunch, actually, sir." Cox said. "But at least she'd be out of danger. Of course, we would not have jurisdiction to arrest the owner of the boat."

Safe in his office at the Pentagon, the veteran naval officer wanted to know why this happened on his duty day. Such a snafu. The Admiral wondered whether the writers of the constitution ever thought up this scenario. But he thought Jeff was correct, they could call it a Search and Rescue operation, though it would be real close to the line.

"Give me your CO, Lieutenant," the Admiral ordered. Rick handed the phone back, "Yes, Admiral?"

"I'll give you authorization to search for the boat, but that's all until I contact you again. I repeat, do not have any of your people try to board the vessel until you here from me, understood?"

"Yes sir," the commander said, and hung up the phone.

"You can search, but don't make any attempt to go aboard," he repeated

218 BLIND PASS - Sean Michael Dever

to Cox. "Do you understand?"

"Yes, sir!" Rick said and went down to the coffee mess to tell his crew. Rick would follow the Admiral's order. He would not go aboard. But that didn't mean the FBI couldn't. Or even the DEA.

Master Chief Regis had already told his men to preflight the ESH-60 for SAR, just in case. They had thrown in some blankets and extra medical kits. They pulled some extra life rafts from another helicopter and threw them in, too.

The engines were up to speed when Rick and the two pilots ran out to Toad Five. They jumped on board, and the pilot engaged the rotor which began to turn the blades. Slowly at first, then at an ever- increasing rate, until they formed enough lift to raise the huge aircraft off the ground. Once in the air, Rick opened the large canvas bag next to him and started undressing.

*

"Summer in Florida," Jeff said out loud, to no one. He normally cursed the afternoon thunderstorms, but not today. They were very violent and built quickly. But they had allowed for his escape. It was two in the afternoon, and he estimated the large, anvil-shaped clouds had already risen up to thirty thousand feet. The only way they could find him now was with an airplane, and he could just hide under a cloud when they came by. But even if a plane found him, and the chances were almost nil, what could they do, wave their wings? Helicopters or a Coast Guard cutter, they were what worried him. But no one would come out in this soup in a helo, and he could keep pace with most of the Coast Guard cutter s stationed in the area. The twin diesels that the DEA had paid for made sure of that.

He could see some other squalls around him, but he knew that by seven o'clock that evening, he would be watching the sun set. No one saw him leave, but even if they did, he couldn't be followed. This was the open sea. They would never find him, just some wreckage of this old boat, while he would be standing on the beach in the Virgin Islands.

It did not matter now. Jeff Strata was gone. The passport in the bag in the cabin said he was Ernie Lanklin from Sydney, Australia. According to the ship's log, he had reported on board the small English freighter "Lady Salsteder" two days ago as a cook's assistant.

He looked at his watch then at the horizon. It was threatening; they would be hitting another gale soon. It was either now or wait until seven o'clock. He wanted to enjoy the sunset, so he tied off the rudder, set the throttles, and turned towards the ladder.

*

Toad Five gently settled onto the main and only runway at Marathon Key Airport. It taxied over to the small, white concrete block building that served as the terminal. The rain pelted the gray metal skin of the ESH-60G. The bird waited for the white Dodge pick up truck with a sign reading "Follow Me."

Once there, the one of a kind helicopter was directed to stop near the now quiet UH-1B. The side door opened, and Cox jumped out to the tarmac and looked around. He looked like some kind of alien from outer space, wearing his black, standard Navy issue neoprene wet suit and large, white flight helmet with tinted visor. He flipped the visor up and scanned the area around the smaller National Guard helicopter. He didn't see his wife with the other two men standing inside the glass door of the general aviation office, which was in the opposite direction

But Laura saw her husband standing out in the pouring rain. Even looking as he did, she could tell it was Rick.

"Let's go!" she yelled. The door flew open as Doyle and Sebastian followed her out into the downpour, still wearing their ear protection. Although the spinning rotor was well above them, all three ducked as they followed Rick into the helo. When they were all seated and strapped in, Rick tapped the two pilots on the shoulder and the machine quickly took to the air. Rick smiled to Laura as he shook his head in disbelief.

"You made it," she said and blew him a kiss.

"This is a SAR mission! First one we've ever been on where we rescue the victims *before* they call for help!" he said.

"Is that what they came up with?" she asked back over the noise of the engines. He nodded.

"The weather's pretty bad," Sebastian said nervously. "Is it okay to be flying in this?"

"This is its element," Rick said, lovingly tapping the bulkhead. "This helicopter is designed for bad weather." The reassurance didn't seem to quench the DEA agent's fears.

"How will we find this guy in the rain?" Doyle asked. Rick pointed to the small electronic bay along the forward wall, "I-R. Infer-red. Global Positioning System, Nightsong System, we have it all. It locks onto a target using heat, not sight. It's connected to the flight controls and auto-hover."

Doyle's expression showed he did not understand what Rick was talking about, so the naval officer just gave him a big grin, "You'll see!"

*

The Gulfstream landed at Ft Lauderdale executive airport. Menceti was waiting after being flown to the airport by helicopter. The hundred-grand he spent on that desk jockey at the police dispatch room had paid off. Thank God the fed had asked for Metro Dade's help. Frank had headed to the roof, and his secretary had been able to stall them long enough to get on board the waiting helicopter. He was sure that the FBI was sitting in his office right then, waiting for him to return from a meeting, or late lunch or whatever his secretary had thought up to tell them. He looked down as he flew over the city on the way to Ft. Lauderdale Executive Airport and his waiting Gulfstream jet. He knew that after the day was over, he would never see Miami again. But there was one last thing. He took out his cellular phone and dialed.

*

Snelling sat at his desk. He had just hung up on Frank, who had called from the helicopter. The only hope he had of getting out of the mess his life had become in the last seventy two hours was with Menceti's influence. Snelling knew that he would not be re-elected, he had hoped that they might let him finish out his term, but now just he prayed that he would not be put in jail. He could not handle jail time, but his prayers would not be answered.

"Sir, Lorraine in the communications office said that her phones have been ringing nonstop for twenty minutes. She needs to talk to you!"

"Tell her to wait!" he said. *So, this is how it will end.*

*

Toad Five landed in a hastily formed landing zone in a supermarket parking lot on Key West. Sebastian jumped out to meet with both the DEA and FBI teams and run the search from the ground. As soon as he was clear, the Navy helicopter again took to the air to start a search over the water. Sebastian climbed into a waiting car to check out the marinas that Jeff had used in the past. Other agents were already talking to the Days Inn staff and anywhere else Susan had used a credit card.

Sebastian drove with two agents to a small marina on the east side of the island, near the airport. Jeff used to rent a slip, but not for over a month now. The harbor master for the small basin told them to check down along Sunset Pier. He said he had given Jeff the names of some marinas and slips for rent near there.

Four FBI agents met Sebastian at the entrance to the pier. They worked through the crowd checking the boats that were tied up alongside the seawall, but the daily sunset celebration was in full swing and the agents were soon separated. The rain had stopped, and the sun was visible near the crimson glowing thunderheads offshore. Hundreds of merchants and sidewalk performers lined the sea wall, while thousands of tourists took in the strange acts along the water. Above it all, speakers blared out Jimi Hendrix's *All Along the Watchtower*, while escape artists, magicians and T-shirt vendors hawked their wares, trying to relieve the tourists of their money. Sebastian tried to ignore it all, even the man with trained housecats that jumped through hoops. When they gathered at the other end of the pier, all the agents had come up empty. Sebastian thought it was hopeless. He had missed something; if only Luis was there, he would know where to look. Then it hit him. He told the agents to get a hold of the Miami office and find out the last place Luis' credit cards had been used to buy gas.

"Look at marinas," Sebastian said. "It would be diesel fuel!"

Miami quickly called back and gave them the name of a marina only a few blocks from where they were sitting. "Leave it to Jeff to be such a cheap bastard. The fuel was bought just this morning!"

Sebastian quickly interviewed Joey, the manager of the marina. He told the agent that Jeff had been in a rush and pulled out over an hour before. When asked why he didn't report it, he explained that Jeff had been watching the phones, and about the prank calls.

The information was radioed to the various agencies that were searching the Gulf of Mexico for the Gecko. The Coast Guard had committed two Falcon jets and a C-130 Hercules then placed two SH-53 Sea Stallion helicopters on standby until the weather improved. Customs had ordered a P-3 Orion into the area, but it had yet to arrive from its base in Corpus Christi, Texas. The Coast Guard coordinated the search, breaking it down in a circular pattern with the marina in the center. The two Falcon jets went to the farthest area. The weather was better out there, and the two jets could work together to cover the area. The Hercules was given the area of most probability between ten and thirty miles off shore because it was a wide area, and the plane had the most range. The Navy ESH-60 was to stay inside of ten miles and check the various inlets, cays, and islands while working its way west. All were to stay in constant contact with the C-130 in case the ship was found

Fifteen hundred feet above the Gulf, and two miles to the west of the marina, Toad Five started the second leg of the search grid. The sea state was heavy, and visibility was down to less than a mile. In the back of the helo, Rick sat at a console looking up at the small television screen. The screen was duplicated in the cockpit for the pilots to see.

Rick was using a joystick to control the IRDS The six to ten foot waves had all but rendered the radar useless. They had found two small boats so far, but neither had been the Gheko. As Rick searched with the IRDS, the other four pairs of eyes on board scanned the horizon. The weather was getting worse, and everyone on board felt it. The winds from the afternoon storms were still coming inland, causing the helo to drop and buck like a bronco.

"I thought you said this was safe!" Doyle yelled.

"It is!" Rick said, clearly enjoying the ride more than the others. "It's better than an E ticket at Disneyland!"

*

Frank Menceti, meanwhile, was sitting inside his jet waiting for the co-pilot, who was inside the terminal checking the weather and filing for the international flight. A white airport truck drove up and parked at a nearby hangar, out of sight of Menceti. Inside, Murry and two other federal agents read the tail numbers of the Gulfstream and matched them to the information on the freshly-signed warrant. The strobe lights of the plane were on, so they knew someone was inside. That someone had to be Menceti. The three FBI agents scurried out of the van. Murry directed one to the bed of the truck, where he lifted up a set of yellow wooden chocks. The three men then headed to the plane. The jet wash blew through their hair, and they put their hands up over their ears to shut out the engine noise. As Murry and his partner climbed up the ladder to the door of the plane, the other, younger, agent carrying the chocks crouched under the wing and scurried over to the main landing gear. He shoved the oversized wooden blocks against the tires of the aircraft, then ran over to the others.

*

"Mr. Rockman's office is on the phone," Snelling's secretary told him for the second time.

"Tell him I went out for lunch, and I'll be back in an hour."

The Governor walked out of his office, ignoring the messages that were scattered all over his desk. He walked down the quiet carpeted hallway of the Capitol, ignoring the greetings from the visitors and staff members that met him in the hallway. Snelling took the elevator to the garage and went over to his car, passing the empty space where Scott Zoe used to park on his way. Being Saturday, the garage was fairly empty, and no one saw him as he retrieved a small black case from the trunk. He went back into the elevator, exited at the lobby, and walked outside to the small grassy park in front of the Florida House of Representatives. He stopped at his favorite vendor, Jimmy, and grabbed a hot dog. Standing silently, he half listened as Jimmy talked about the Seminoles and FSU's chances for a national championship. Florida's Governor did not taste the hot peppers or mustard or notice the ketchup that dripped onto his tie.

The Governor of the State of Florida, the Honorable Peter Snelling envied the anonymous little hot dog vendor. He could do anything: cheat on his wife, gamble, take money from unscrupulous people, and who would care? Maybe some close friends or family members, but certainly not the press. Snelling wished he could trade places. After finishing his lunch, Snelling headed to the building directly in front of the white high rise where the government was now located. The Old Capitol was a museum now, but for a long time it had housed the working office of his predecessors. The building was restored inside and out to its turn of the century condition. A few visitors frequented the building, but not many. They were almost all school students, which meant that the place was almost desolate on weekends. Guards, mostly retirees from various police forces in the state, watched over the contents and rooms inside.

Unlike the twenty-eight floor capitol center behind it, the historic building did not yet have high security metal detectors or other safety devices. The only security it had was an alarm system to prevent break-ins at night. So when Snelling entered carrying the small case, the guard on duty had little reason for concern

*

Richie, GKB's senior pilot, was busy going down the preflight checklist when he heard the pounding on the door. He depressed the button on the control yoke and spoke into the mike attached to his headset.

"Mr. Menceti, would you mind opening the door so I don't have to restart my checklist? Thanks."

"What the hell do I pay you for," Frank mumbled as he went over to unlock the hatch. He believed it would be the co-pilot, but just as he the door cracked open, Menceti got a long enough glimpse to see the suitcoats and badges of Murry and the other Federal agents. Menceti quickly slammed the door shut. Murry pushed against the hatch, but the agent's lack of balance allowed Frank get the hatch locked. "Federal Agents, we have a warrant!" Murry yelled, but there was no use.

"Damn!" his partner said, kicking the door. The co-pilot had been walking out and was oblivious to the commotion until he came around the side of the plane.

"Freeze!" Murry said, drawing his gun. The co-pilot did not try to run, instead he just placed his briefcase on the ground and raised his hands above his head. Murry's partner ran down the steps and over to him kicking the briefcase away. "Hey, take it easy!" the co-pilot yelled. "It's just clearances in there!"

"I'll give you a clearance," the agent said and pulled him off the ground, marching him up the stairs to where Murry was standing. "Open the door!" Murry commanded.

"I can't," the co-pilot said.

"You mean you won't!"

"No," the co-pilot reached over to the handle and tried to turn it, "I mean I can't! My key is inside, and this is locked!"

*

"Why don't you put on some dry clothes?" Jeff asked when he saw Susan standing in the galley, dripping wet.

"I can't find them."

"They're hanging up in my closet," he said. "Did you look there?"

"Jeff, why are we out in this?" she asked. He saw for the first time she was upset.

"We had to leave in a hurry, I'm sorry," he said and purposely strode past her to the control console and the bridge just forward of the main cabin.

"I want to know why."

"We had a problem," he answered while switching channels on the radio. "Someone was looking for me."

"Who?"

"That's none of your concern; you just sit back and enjoy the ride."

"Is it the police?" she asked. He stopped what he was doing, turned and looked at her.

"No, it is not the police. Why would the police come after me?"

"So someone's coming after us?" she asked, her voice was growing louder, and she sounded concerned.

"No, that's not what I meant," Jeff said and went back to the radio. It crackled and came to life.

"Does this have something to do with that room?" she asked, fearful now.

"What room?"

"The room where I found this," she said and took the tooth chip from her pocket. He turned and saw what she was holding. He slowly walked over to her. She backed away in fear.

"What do you have there?" he said still moving toward her. He was looking at her, not the tooth. She tripped over a small table, backing away until he had her up against the wall. He reached over, took the tooth from her hand, and examined it.

"What is it?" he asked her.

"You know what it is," she replied, her voice cracking as she trembled, afraid.

"Why don't you tell me?" he said.

"It's a, ah, tooth. A human tooth, I think," she said.

"Now what would a human tooth be doing on my boat?" he said and walked back to the control console, chuckling. Susan had not moved from the wall of the cabin, but stayed still, perfectly still. The look in Jeff's eyes was the same from that first meeting when she asked about his parents. It was cold and evil, and it frightened her they way he could change so quickly from one extreme to the other. She stood silently and watched him as he pulled down the radio microphone from above.

"Any station, any station, I am looking for the United States Coast Guard Over, US Coast Guard please come in, over"

"This is the U.S. Coast Guard; please identify, over."

"Coast Guard, please contact the FBI and notify them that Frank Menceti, that's M-E-N-C-E-T-I is probably heading towards St. Croix aboard a Gulfstream Four, most likely out of Ft. Lauderdale. Tail Number is November Golf Kilo Bravo Two, say again November Golf Kilo Bravo Two, over"

"Standby over, over," there was a pause as the radio operator wrote down the information. "Copy message; please identify yourself. Over."

"Negative. Out" Jeff said and turned off the radio. "All done," he said to himself. There was no turning back now.

"Why did you just do that? Why would the FBI want Frank?"

"Look, Susan, don't you worry about it, all right!" He was becoming agitated at all the questions.

Susan was scared, but she was also putting together what was happening. The needles, the money, the blood. It came to her all too late. She had been so stupid, so naive. She knew nothing of this man, and the rumors were starting to make sense. "Listen," she said, "I just want to go back. Let's just turn around and go back, okay, honey?" She was too scared to sound sincere, and Jeff knew it. He sat up in the captain's chair behind the console and stared out the window over the bow.

"We can't go back," he said.

"Sure we can," she said.

"No," he said. "I'm sure we can't, okay? Frank wants me to kill you, Susan. And I just don't want to do that." She fell back against the wooden bulkhead at the words "kill you." She thought she was going to faint, and steadied herself against a small bookcase. Her mind went back to the cabin, the blood.

"Why does he want you to kill me?" she asked slowly, not really wanting to know the answer. She tasted the bile in her throat and felt a pain in her stomach as she waited for an answer. Jeff sat up at the other end, shaking his head and mumbling to himself until she couldn't take it any longer.

"Why does he want to kill me!" she screamed. His head swiveled around, and that look was back on Jeff's face.

"Because he thinks you know too much!" he said.

"About what?" She cried, "I just found that tooth and blood. Is it over drugs, or the money?"

"Yeah!" Jeff said, "I would say it's the money and the drugs!"

"Oh my God," she crouched down and began to cry, really cry. She was becoming hysterical. He told her over and over that he wasn't going to hurt her, but she just grew more out of control every time he said it. He banged his fist on the wall next to him and kicked at the floor.

"Shut up!" he said. "Be quiet! Stop crying! Nothing's going to happen to you!" But she just kept crying. Jeff started to wonder whether Frank was right. But he just wouldn't be able to, he loved her. He made her smile, except with the damn tears! He couldn't live like this. Her emotions were grinding on his nerves. He would tell her everything; that was the only way. If she still wanted to be with him, fine. If not, then he would just have to live with himself. "Susan, shut up! I need to tell you something!"

*

Inside the Gulfstream, Frank watched out the side double pane windows as the agent dragged the other pilot up the stairs. He heard them banging outside and knew it would just be a matter of time until they forced their way in. He rushed up to the cockpit and told Richie to get them the hell out of there. "Now!" The pilot had no idea what was going on. He thought the banging was from luggage or something. "I said now!" Frank repeated.

"I don't have my co-pilot," he said. Frank sat down and strapped in the right seat, "You do now!"

"You don't know how to fly!?" Richie said.

"Look, I don't care if you make God your co-pilot, just get us out of here!"

"We don't have clearance!" Richie said. Frank pointed to the window

"The FBI is at the fucking door! That's your clearance!"

"What the hell do they want?!" Richie asked, still not grasping what was happening. Frank grabbed him by the sleeve and drew him close.

"You and I, mister, have been laundering money. And both our asses are in jail if you don't get us out of here!" Finally the gravity of the situation hit the pilot. Richie rapidly started flipping switches, while reciting the checklist to himself. Both engines started to whine, as they came to life.

*

Outside, Murry was prying at the door with a crowbar when he heard the power surge of electricity from the plane's generator. The co-pilot saw the compressor blades in the left engine start to spin and heard the increasing whine of the engines. Inside the cockpit, Richie pulled up on a red painted lever, then released it. Frank pushed the twin throttles forward before Richie could stop him.

"The brake!" the copilot yelled and jumped off the ladder, down to the tarmac. The large jet lurched forward, but only for an inch until the tires slammed into the chocks. Murry told the others to get down off the ladder as it moved with the aircraft. The agent grabbed hold of the small railing and continued to work at the door release. The pitch of the twin turbojets screamed even louder as inside Frank fought off the pilot and pushed the engines to red line.

The jet started to vibrate violently as Frank pushed and pulled on the throttles, trying to get the plane to jump over the large wooden chocks. Murry realized he wasn't going to get in, he had trouble standing up. He ran down the stairs and away toward the back of the plane to where the others were standing.

Inside the right engine, a flawed compressor blade began to develop a hairline crack. The vibration and jarring of the airplane caused the stress to travel down the blade, which was revolving at thousands of revolutions per second. The crack expanded and grew with each revolution.

*

The guard smiled at the Governor when he entered the historic building. Snelling could not remember the last time he had gone through the doors and marveled at how beautifully decorated and furnished the Old Capitol building was. He walked over to his left, and momentarily stopped at the red velvet covered ropes that blocked the hallway from visitors. The security guard watched as the Governor stepped over the barricade and headed down the hall.

"That's a restricted area!" he yelled, and went over to the Governor, who had stopped and turned around. The guard was just a few feet away when a wave of recognition came over his face.

"Governor, I'm sorry. I didn't know it was you."

"I just have some thinking to do," Snelling replied. "Is that okay?"

"Yes sir, take as long as you like."

*

The pilot watched the pressure drop on the number two engine. He reached over to shut it down but was pushed away by Frank. He started to yell at his boss when the red light flashed on the control panel and a loud alarm screamed. Richie turned to the control panel.

Outside the aircraft, the loud metallic clanking drew the attention of everyone within earshot. Suddenly a loud flash, heat, and flame burst from the right side of the sleek aircraft, lifting the whole plane off the ground for a moment. Once in the air, the plane was freed from the restraint of the chocks on the tires. The thrust from the remaining engine spun the plane to the right, the jet blast blowing back the co-pilot and federal agents as they dove to the ground. Pieces of shrapnel flew everywhere, and one of the tires on the main mounts blew apart when a red hot chunk of aluminum flew into it.

Inside the plane, Frank's body was limp in the seat, though his hands still gripped the throttles on the console. He had turned to the window in time to see the knifelike pieces of compressor blade fly at him. His head and body had been punctured over seventy times as molten metal had slipped through the thin skin of the plane. Somehow, Richie was still alive and conscious. But his neck had been broken when the plane spun around. He watched through the windscreen as the engine pushed what was left of the once beautiful jet forward across the parking ramp toward a fuel truck that had been deserted by its driver only seconds earlier. He could not move any part of his body, could not get to Frank's hands or the throttle. He said a prayer as the multi-million dollar jet slammed into the yellow tanker and exploded into a single massive fireball that rose higher than the control tower.

*

The gunshot rang out loud and clear. The security guard at the Old Capitol building ran to the sound, almost tripping over the rope barricade. He drew his gun and ran inside the historic room to his left. After entering, he just stood and looked down at the floor. Snelling was lying in a pool of blood. Gray matter was visible along the ceder wall, and the guard thanked the Lord above that the man had at least landed face down. He took the radio from the belt on his waist. Within minutes the police had sealed the building.

*

The Coast Guard command center phone rang. The message from the Key West station regarding Frank was quickly passed up the chain of command and out to the FBI's Miami office. The receptionist took the message to the field office, who in turn contacted Sabastion.

"Where did this come from?" the DEA agent asked.

"It was picked up in Miami, Ft. Myers, Tampa, all over the damn place. We're trying to triangulate the signals now. We should have an area for you in a few minutes."

"Did anyone check it out?" The duty officer described the scene at the airport. "Well, that's one less bad guy."

*

"But I wasn't going to take you from this world, Susan. I could never leave you." Jeff told her about faking his death and about the murder of Luis and Andre. He sat up there steering the Gheko, describing the scenes as if he were telling her about his latest fishing expedition.

Jeff told her how he had killed James and Alvin, and that the tooth was probably Alvin's though it might have been James', he wasn't sure. It took all of about twenty minutes for him to finish all the grisly details. Now she just sat there; a catatonic look was on her face. The tears were gone, the emotion was gone. This was too much to comprehend. She sat on the floor, her back against the wall. Jeff loved her, she had no doubts about that. And Jeff was also a psychopath. There was no doubt about that either. She knew he would never let her go, or turn back. She believed he was going to kill her. Letting him talk might give her time to think of a way out.

"Is that all? Are they the only people you slaughtered?" she asked, *like it makes a difference.*

"I said they were the people I killed, not slaughtered," Jeff said matter-of-factly. "I've slaughtered various others."

"What's the difference?" she asked. There was no more emotion in her voice; she was numb.

"The people I slaughtered wanted to die, begged to die," he said, turning to face her. "I did them a favor. Just like that doctor in Michigan. I relieved them of their pain." She needed to know if he believed it. Even from across the room, his expression told her he did. Jeff Strata was a sociopath, lacking any conscience, any sense of right or wrong.

"Who were they?" she said. "Some junkies all strung out?"

"No! They were not junkies!" the temper was back.

"I'm sorry, I didn't mean that," she said. "Who were they then?"

"Just people. People with problems," Jeff replied.

"How did you know they had problems; did they tell you? Did they come to you?" she asked, trying to keep him talking. She still did not see anything that she could use to protect herself. It was if he had taken anything off the boat that could be used as a weapon, but she kept scanning the room.

"In a way, yes," he answered, "through David." Susan listened, but did not think about the answer. She had studied people like Jeff in a college psych class.

He was dangerous because he was obviously impervious to feeling any sense of remorse. Another characteristic she remembered was that sociopathic people tend to get angry quickly, and so the last thing she wanted to do was argue with him. It was better to just let him talk, while she made her way to one of the small bar stools in the galley behind his seat.

"David who?" she asked, "David from the Bible?" She started inching along the floor to the small bar, toward the stool with the metal legs.

"No, your David."

"My David?" She answered not thinking about anything except getting to the galley. "Who's my David?"

"David Ranson," Jeff said. "Your former husband." Susan stopped in her tracks when she heard his answer.

"David?" she asked, knowing that as bad as her husband was, he was not like Jeff.

"Oh, yes! He certainly did!" Jeff replied. "He killed them. He just left it to me do the physical part. But they were all ready to die when I got them."

"No, he didn't."

"You are wrong, my dear Susan," Jeff said with a sadistic chuckle. "David killed them just like he killed my mother."

"Your mother drowned," Susan said, confused. "She killed herself. You told me yourself."

"No! David killed her--he and those drugs! He made her do it, he made her want to be a whore and a liar!" Jeff yelled.

"Who else wanted to die, Jeff?" she asked, but he just turned around and ignored her. "Who else?!"

Nothing.

"Who else!" she screamed.

"That doctor's wife. Yeah, oh yeah!" He looked over at Susan, who was pale with disbelief. "You didn't know about that did you? No. David was fucking her and giving her drugs just like he did my mother."

"So you killed her?"

"No, he killed her!" Jeff said. "Just like that Larry Kindle and his wife. He even begged me to help her first, but I explained that that's not how David wanted me to do things."

"But those people didn't do anything to you!" she cried. Fear had replaced the numbness again. She knew she needed to get away from him, but there was nowhere for her to go. He was insane.

"But it's not about me. It's not about what I want," Jeff said. "It's about what they want."

"Why would David tell you to hurt those people?" she sobbed and placed her head in her hands; she couldn't listen to him anymore. She did not want nor expect an answer. But she got one anyway.

"Because he cares about them," Jeff explained. "He wants them to feel good, get away from their earthly troubles. That's why he gives them drugs, to free their souls. You see, that was why the first to go was his parents." Susan looked up, her mouth open. David's parents had been killed years ago.

"David put me up to it, a snip of a cable here," Jeff held up his fingers as if they were scissors. "A twist of the wrench there. It was just bad luck that the other man was coming down the road when the steering box came loose. But David saved him, too, I suppose. He was an alcoholic."

Susan did not, could not believe what she was hearing. Was this a delusion, or did her husband really hire Jeff to kill his own parents?

"Why did David tell you to *help* his parents?" she asked.

"He cared about them a great deal."

"That's all? He just cared about them?" Susan asked. "He didn't pay you or anything?"

"What do you think I am, an assassin or something from a spy novel?" Jeff said angrily. "I would not kill for money!"

"I'm sorry! I didn't mean to imply you would!" she said trying to calm him down. He relaxed back into his chair. Susan was trying not to provoke him, but she desperately wanted to understand him. By understanding him, she thought she might stay alive long enough to get away from him. "If you hurt, I mean, helped his parents only because he cared for them, then why didn't you hurt me?"

"David never cared for you," he stated matter-of-factly. "When David came back to me, he was already showing other women how to get away. But not you. No he never cared; that's why I took you in." Had Jeff been watching them all those years? Susan knew that he was crazy, but she somehow believed him about the other women. She had never even suspected. Jeff saw the troubled look on her face.

"Don't worry about the others," he said. "They are all together now. David made them to be like my momma, and they wanted me to kill them. They wanted to die, just like my momma."

"David would not have wanted that to happen," Susan said. Even if he had cheated.

"Why do you defend him so?" Jeff's voice was rising again, but Susan did not heed the warning. "You told me you hated him?!"

"I did!" she said. "But not enough to see him dead." She was close enough to reach out and grab the stool's leg with her hand when he spun around on the chair and faced her. Fire was in his eyes, which made her even more frightened.

"But he hit you; he cheated on you!" Jeff declared in anger. "No, you hated him! Or you loved him and lied to me! Which is it!" he demanded.

Susan slowly pulled herself up on the stool and smiled as she wrapped her fingers around the metal leg. "How can I love someone like David? I love you!" It took a moment or two before she watched the strain in his face slowly go away. He calmed down, and the tension seemed to leave his body as he believed the act. She continued to soothe him until he turned around so that his back was to her. Her hand was shaking, and she was afraid he would hear her heart pounding as he leaned his head back into her breast, and stared out the windshield at the rough water. Slowly, gradually, Susan removed her hand from his head, though she let him rest against her. Susan reached down with her hand and started to lift the stool into the air. It wasn't heavy, but she hoped it was solid enough to do the job.

"I'm not like David," Jeff said softly. "I would never leave you."

Susan gripped the stool with her other hand, "I know you'd never leave me, Jeff." She raised the stool up to swing it and hit Jeff across the back of the head

"Not like that blond woman tried to do to David," Jeff said. "But she's with him now."

"Wendy?" she asked, still gripping the stool. What had he done to her?

Jeff replied, "She didn't want to die at first, but then she begged me, too; I saw it in her eyes."

"When?"

"This morning, While you were asleep, I flew up and helped her. She was already with another man," he said. "We met him once, at the airport."

"Chris?!" Her anger mixed with fear and astonishment and disbelief. In one smooth move she lifted the stool and hit him with all her might. There was a loud, booming *crack!* as the wooden seat connected with the bone of his skull, throwing him from his chair. But his arm had caught in the wheel, and he spun it as he fell. The boat's rudder cut sharply to port, then back to starboard as his hand fell out of the wheel, knocking charts and books off the shelves. Susan covered her head with her hands as they fell down on her.

*

"He just went in there?"

"You didn't check the bag?" the state trooper asked.

"Where were you?" the guard asked defensively. Dressed in a suit and tie instead of the usual tan uniform and smokie hat, the trooper was one of the personal bodyguards responsible for Snelling's safety. *But how do you protect a man from himself* he wondered. He looked back at the security guard, who was now answering the questions of another state trooper, and knew it was not this man's fault. He would not, could not question or search the Governor. At least without good cause, and there was no way to know what he was going to do. Yet the bodyguard also knew that the man would be blamed along with the rest of them for not being able to read minds. The trooper turned and walked outside; there was nothing left for him to protect.

*

Dazed, and head pounding, Susan tried to lift herself off the ground, but her arms felt too weak. She rubbed her head, feeling something wet and sticky above her eye. She pressed her temple, and a sharp pain shot through her skull and down to her stomach. Feeling lightheaded and nauseated, she slowly turned her head to the right. On the floor beside her, Jeff was coughing and wheezing. He lay unconscious, and Susan realized that the stool had hit its mark. Blood was coming from his ears. After a few minutes, Susan tried to move again, this time she succeeded in sitting up. She could feel the Gheko spinning and looked out the windows. The rain had started coming down again. She watched the wheel turn back and forth as the water hit the rudder of the boat. She saw a wave hit the side, and it knocked her down again.

*

The crew of the Coast Guard C-130 Hercules spotted a small white cabin cruiser about twelve miles southwest of Key West. It reported its position and went down lower to take a look. The winds and rain were much worse on the deck as the plane flew only a couple of hundred feet above the whitecaps. They passed on the starboard side, the forward observer snapping photographs while the two aft observers agreed that this was Jeff's boat. But they also saw that it was floundering in the heavy seas After notifying the coordinator that they had a positive identification of the boat, they reported that there were no signs of life on board. The coordinating officer instructed the Hercules pilot to contact Toad Five and gave the boat's position.

"Okay, Coast Guard, I have it," Rick said and entered the coordinates into the global positioning system.

"You'd better hurry! The waves are beating the hell out of them!"

*

Susan finished tying Jeff to the wooden rails near the bar. She thought she heard a plane, but could not make her way to the aft glass doors, due to the battering of waves the Gheko was taking. She had no idea how to control the craft, and the woman was scared. She would need Jeff to make it back, but she feared waking him. He was a murderer and a drug dealer, regardless of why he did it. She sat down trembling and frozen. She was alone in the middle of the sea, and she couldn't even find a life jacket. All her hope was gone.

Then Susan saw it, or thought she did, through the mist and rain. A huge white, four-engine aircraft with an orange stripe came out of the gray horizon and flew alongside, then disappeared back into the clouds. She wondered if she had imagined it because the plane had only been there for an instant.

"We'll continue to monitor the craft, but I don't think anyone is on board," the pilot told his crew.

The Hercules came down toward the starboard side as a wave smashed into the Gheko spinning it around until only the aft end of the boat was visible to the pilot. He watched as a cushion and what looked like a cooler were washed overboard. Other debris was floating nearby. As the huge aircraft passed directly over the boat, something flew out through the large glass doors of the cabin, shattering them.

"Shit, what the hell was that!!" the pilot exclaimed as they barely cleared the flymast of the small cabin cruiser. He banked the plane as hard as he could and dove for the deck, a loud high pitched horn sounding, from the confused radar altimeter telling him that the landing gear was not down. The co-pilot silenced the alarm, placed his hands on the controls to back up the aircraft commander, and watched the surface of the Gulf to ensure they did not fly into it. As the big plane turned 360 degrees, the forward observer scanned the boat with his binoculars. He reported that a woman, at least it looked like a woman, was on the deck waving her arms. As they got closer, he could see that she was covered with something.

"Flight, I see a lone figure, female, on aft deck!"

The pilot called Toad Five and reported what they saw, updating the boat's position. Rick informed them they were less than five minutes away. The crew of the Navy helicopter had still not received authorization for any rescue attempt, but now there was a life at stake. This was real, and Rick knew that he would go in without permission if he had to.

Rick worked the joystick until the cursor on the screen bracketed the Gheko. He locked on the GPS and IRDS camera initiating the Nightsong System. The helicopter's spotlight was slaved to the camera. The pilot notified him that they had a good image on their screen. Rick stood up and went over to the black canvas bag. He pulled out his swim fins, snorkel and mask. He put his survival vest on over the wetsuit. It held flares, a knife, a strobe light, and medical supplies. He didn't know what he would find if he went on board. He then went over and instructed Laura and Doyle on operating the winch above the door.

"My life will depend on it, so if you have any questions, ask now!"

They went over it one more time.

Jeff had awakened and laughed to himself when he saw how Susan had restrained him. He gave one good yank, and the thirty-year old wood gave way, breaking at the base. He had meant to replace the rails; they were old and rotten inside, but he was glad he hadn't had the time. He quickly untied himself. He saw the smashed glass doors and knew that Susan was out on the deck somewhere.

But his boat, his home, was in real trouble, so he went to the bridge and grabbed the wheel.. He attempted to steer the ship, but then the engines had cut out, as had the sumps. He ran down below deck and saw the water that was rushing in. The keel had split. This in itself was bad, but as it split, it had ruptured the fuel tank, which was now a mix of salt water and diesel fuel.

All his skills as a sailor could not save his one and only possession. He went out the forward cabin door onto the deck and grabbed the one life jacket attached to the outer bulkhead. Then he went back inside and made his way to the aft deck, where he could see Susan. She was outside on her knees, waving her arms.

The Hercules pilot saw the man run out and grab the woman. The man on the boat looked up as the aircraft passed overhead, then pulled her back inside the cabin, disappearing from view. "Toad Five, Coast Guard-there's definitely something happening here!"

Susan screamed and kicked hysterically as Jeff carried her inside. "Don't kill me!" she cried when he pushed her down onto the sofa, now wet from the rain and salt water coming into the cabin. She saw he was holding a life jacket.

"I know you didn't mean to hurt me," Jeff said calmly, "that you are just scared. That's okay!"

"Please don't kill me," she whimpered.

"I'm not," he said, "this is for you, Susan, take it." He held out the life jacket, but she did not move. He stepped closer, and she covered her head with her arms. He took hold of her right arm.

"Please don't kill me," she cried, and tried to pull away. But he overpowered her. He took her arm and forced it in through the life jacket; he grabbed the left one, but she didn't fight. After placing the float on her, he buckled the front. She sat and sobbed and watched him

"Why? What are you doing?"

"I'm giving you life."

"You're a murderer," she said, quietly. When he was done, he tried to hug her, but she curled up onto the couch. She was still in the fetal position when a wave crashed down on the side of the boat, almost causing it to capsize.

"I'm not a murderer," Jeff said, "they killed my mother."

"No one killed anyone but you!"

"If I were a killer, I would have killed you."

Toad Five had a lock on the Gheko and approached from the side. Rick slid open the door and reached out, gripping the cable. After he hooked it on to the D ring of his vest, he reviewed one more time how to operate the winch. He then gave Laura his headset, so she could talk with the pilot and hung out the side of the door. The rain hit his face, and Rick pulled his mask down. The wind buffeted the helo as they flew overtop the Gecko. Looking down, Rick could see the glass from the shattered door lying on the deck. He could also see the diesel fuel that surrounded the boat. The craft was low in the water, and Rick knew there wasn't much time. Disobeying a direct order from a four-star Admiral, the

Navy Lieutenant stepped out of the helicopter and hung in mid air.

"What about Marjorie Johnson, what did she do?" Susan yelled. Jeff turned away. The water was now inside the cabin, but he did not seem to notice as he paced in front of her. He hid his head in his hands. When he looked up, Susan was not sure if it was the rain or tears that ran down his cheek.

"I went to the wrong house," he screamed.

"What do you mean the wrong house?"

"David raped my mother! He raped her and beat her, and no one did anything. I tried to tell the police, the doctors, but no one did anything." He fell to his knees and cried, "He gave her drugs, and my father wanted nothing to do with her. And no one would listen to a twelve-year old boy!"

Susan was scared. He was changing, his anger was working its way into his face, as he clenched his fist tighter. He saw he was frightening her and turned away.

Rick was lowered down to the deck. He looked inside the cabin and saw Jeff on his knees; his head was down resting on the waterlogged carpet. Across from him, Susan was sitting on the couch wearing the orange life vest. She was staring down at Jeff. Rick reached down and picked up a piece of broken plastic floating at his feet. He threw it at Susan, hitting her. She looked up and looked around until she saw the Lieutenant. He was waving his arms and she nodded. She cautiously slid down the couch to the door as Jeff kneeled on the deck crying. When she was close to the opening, she stood up and started to run out into Rick's waiting arms. Just then Jeff saw her, and he jumped up and over, tackling Susan. "Let me go," she screamed as Jeff held her down. Rick struggled with the D ring, trying to unclip himself so he could help her.

"I'm a dead man," Jeff screamed, "I wanted to be with you, live with you, sail away, the two of us!" The two of them lay on the deck, struggling. Susan managed to free her body from him, but Jeff held onto her legs. Using his arms, he started pulling her back into the cabin.

"Let me go!" she said kicking him, trying to crawl toward Rick. "You killed my husband, you killed my friends..."

"I did that for both of us! We can be together forever!" Jeff said and pulled her back.

Susan was clawing at the deck, trying not to get dragged back inside, when the craft shook and buckled as the Gheko's keel snapped in half. The bow of the boat dipped below the surface as the hull filled with seawater. The angle caused Susan to start sliding toward Jeff. Grabbing at the deck, she picked up one of the shards of glass and rolled onto her back. She sat up as she slid, her arms stretched out. Jeff thought she was coming back to him, so he released his grip and put out his arms to catch her. She wrapped her fist around the glass and drove it into his eye as another breaker smashed into the Gheko. She was thrown against the cabin. The wave knocked Jeff inside, and he rolled and slid almost into the galley. The wave had caused Rick to be lifted back into the air, and he was helplessly dangling off the side of the boat when Susan saw him.

Up in the helo, Laura saw what was happening and informed the pilots. They moved a little to the right and placed Rick back down on the deck of the Gecko near Susan.

Rick helped her up into his arms and gave a thumbs up. Doyle pushed the button on the winch, but nothing happened. He looked down in time to see another large wave hit the Gheko. The water cascaded over Rick and the girl. Both Laura and Doyle felt Toad Five drop as the weight of the wave pulled them toward the rough seas below. Rick felt the wave try to rip Susan from his arms, but he did not let go.

Rick looked up to see what was taking so long. While all their attention was drawn to the winch, Jeff emerged from the froth of the wave. He had crawled out of the main cabin. He held onto a railing, and reached into a wooden storage boxes on the deck. He searched around, and his hand came up holding a flare gun. He stumbled toward Rick and Susan as they dangled just above the deck. Laura looked down out of the helicopter and saw Jeff pointing the gun at them.

"Get them up, get them up!" Laura cried.

"I'm trying!" the pilot responded, "that wave disengaged the auto-hover."

Jeff raised the flare gun, aimed it at Susan, but did not fire. He just stood there.

Up in the helo, Doyle pulled out his gun. "Shoot him!" Laura said as she mashed the buttons on the winch. Doyle aimed and fired. The deck in front of Jeff jumped as the bullets missed its mark. Jeff looked up at the detective, and for a brief second, his eyes locked with Doyle's. Susan saw this and started yelling, "Don't shoot, Don't shoot!"

But her voice was lost over the howl of the rotor wash. Doyle shot again, but missed. This time Jeff raised the flare gun and aimed it at the Navy helicopter. As he did, Rick reached into his survival vest and removed a little round tube the size of a pencil. He spun around on the cable and pointed it at Jeff. Rick pulled back his thumb and released the small metal pin. A puff of smoke rose from the tube, and Jeff's eyes broke away from Doyle and went down to his chest. He looked then looked over to Rick and Susan. As the cable spun them around Susan saw that Jeff was looking down at a phosphorous flare burning brightly in his chest. She watched his eyes roll back in his head as his body went limp and fell to the deck.

Susan felt the cable as it started to hoist them up into the waiting helicopter, but she could not take her eyes off Jeff's body as the flare continued to burn. She felt the waiting hands of Laura and Doyle pull her into the aircraft, but she continued to watch as the Gheko broke up under the pounding waves. The others joined her. They watched as Jeff sank along with his boat, until all that was visible was the faint orange glow of the flare under the water.

A New Beginning

* **

One year later...

The Fourteenth Annual Sanibel Jazz Festival was just as large as in previous years. Newly elected Governor Lance Rockman was the distinguished guest. After his role in uncovering Snelling's corruption was made public, Rockman had easily won office.

The Lee County District Attorney was also at the festival, enjoying some barbequed chicken wings with some friends. Shirley Lambton was gearing up for her campaign to win the special election in November.

Susan Ranson was in her tent when Doyle walked by with his family. The recently retired police detective had just returned from a vacation in Key West, accommodations compliments of Rick and Laura. He stopped at the tent and said hello to Susan, then introduced his wife and daughter. Susan no longer worked at the paper. She was a successful author. The biography of Jeff Strata had been in the top ten non-fiction best-seller list for over twenty weeks. Jeff's art was also selling, at prices too high for Doyle to think about. Susan was hard at work on her second book. It was another biography, about the unexplained death of a woman whose body was found long ago, in a remote inlet known as Blind Pass.

THE END

*Sean Michael Dever writes The Movie Buff, a weekly
entertainment opinion column. He has worked in feature
films, television, radio, and the music industry. After leaving the US Navy,
where he flew as an aircrewman, he attended and graduated
from Florida State University. He currently
lives in Southwest Florida.*

Look for Rick Cox and Laura Wilson to return in
So Others May Live *Fall 1998*
Dishonorable Men *Summer 1999*

A young sailor is dead.
U.S. Navy Airman Robert Lee Jr. stopped breathing at the hands
of his instructor during an exercise at the navy's elite Rescue
Swimmer School in Florida. Was it a training accident or
murder?. Did his instructor, Petty Officer First Class Rick Cox
push too hard or was it something else that started a decade
earlier in a lake near Naples, Florida.
A highly decorated but extremely intense man, Cox becomes the
main focus of veteran Naval Investigative Service Special Agent
Jack Litton and newcomer Laura Wilson.
But when the accident inquiry begins to look like a political
witch-hunt, will Special Agent Wilson sit by as her boss ignores
the facts and uses a personal vendetta to give the brass and the
victim's family what they want? Or will she jeopardize her career
to gain the trust of a man she believes is innocent, but refuses to
rely on anyone but himself?
***
Find out the story of Rick Cox and Agent Laura Wilson before
BLIND PASS...

Coming September 1998
ISBN 0-9658180-2-0

To order additional copies of Blind Pass, or to find out about any of Sean Michael Dever's other books, complete the information below.

Ship to: (please print)
Name _____
Address _____
City, State, Zip_____
Day Phone (optional)_____

_____ copies of Blind Pass @ $8.95 each $_____
Postage and Handling @ $1.50/book $_____
Florida Residents add 6% sales tax $_____
Total Amount enclosed $_____
_____ place x if you want more information about Sean Michael Dever's other books.

Make checks payable to :   Blind Pass
                          Duchess Publications, P.O.Box 150053
                          Cape Coral, Florida 33915-0053

To order additional copies of Blind Pass, or to find out about any of Sean Michael Dever's other books, complete the information below.

Ship to: (please print)
Name _____
Address _____
City, State, Zip_____
Day Phone (optional)_____

_____ copies of Blind Pass @ $8.95 each $_____
Postage and Handling @ $1.50/book $_____
Florida Residents add 6% sales tax $_____
Total Amount enclosed $_____
_____ place x if you want more information about Sean Michael Dever's other books.

Make checks payable to :   Blind Pass
                          Duchess Publications, P.O.Box 150053
                          Cape Coral, Florida 33915-0053
Retailer's orders please contact for special pricing.

More information may be obtained by visiting us at duchpub @ aol.com